AF600192

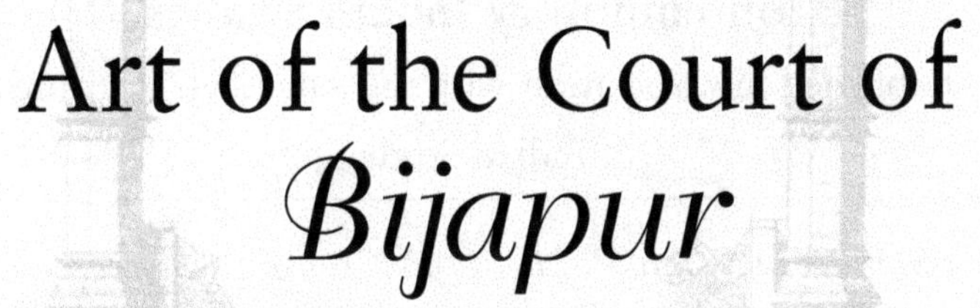

Art of the Court of *Bijapur*

Contemporary Indian Studies

Published in association with the American Institute of Indian Studies

---

Susan S. Wadley, Chair, Publications Committee/general editor

Books in this series are recipients of the
Edward Cameron Dimock Jr. Prize in the Indian Humanities
and the
Joseph W. Elder Prize in the Indian Social Sciences
awarded by the American Institute of Indian Studies and are published with the Institute's generous support.

A list of titles in this series appears at the back of the book.

Art of the Court of *Bijapur*

DEBORAH HUTTON

INDIANA UNIVERSITY PRESS
Bloomington & Indianapolis

Publication of this book has been aided by a grant from the Millard Meiss Publication Fund of the College Art Association.

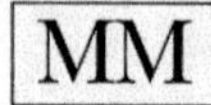

This book is a publication of

Indiana University Press
601 North Morton Street
Bloomington, IN 47404-3797 USA

http://iupress.indiana.edu
Telephone orders 800-842-6796
Fax orders 812-855-7931
Orders by e-mail iuporder@indiana.edu

The paper used in this publication meets the minimum requirements of American National Standard for Information Sciences—Permanence of Paper for Printed Library Materials, ANSI Z39.48-1984.

Manufactured in the United States of America

Library of Congress Cataloging-in-Publication Data

Hutton, Deborah S.
Art of the court of Bijapur / Deborah Hutton.
p. cm. — (Contemporary Indian studies)
Includes bibliographical references and index.
ISBN 0-253-34784-X (cloth)
1. Art, Indic—India—Bijapur (Karnataka)
2. Art, Islamic—India—Bijapur (Karnataka)
3. Art and society—India—Bijapur (Karnataka)
I. Title. II. Series.
N7308.B55H88 2006
709.54'87—dc22

2006004183

1 2 3 4 5 11 10 09 08 07 06

To David

CONTENTS

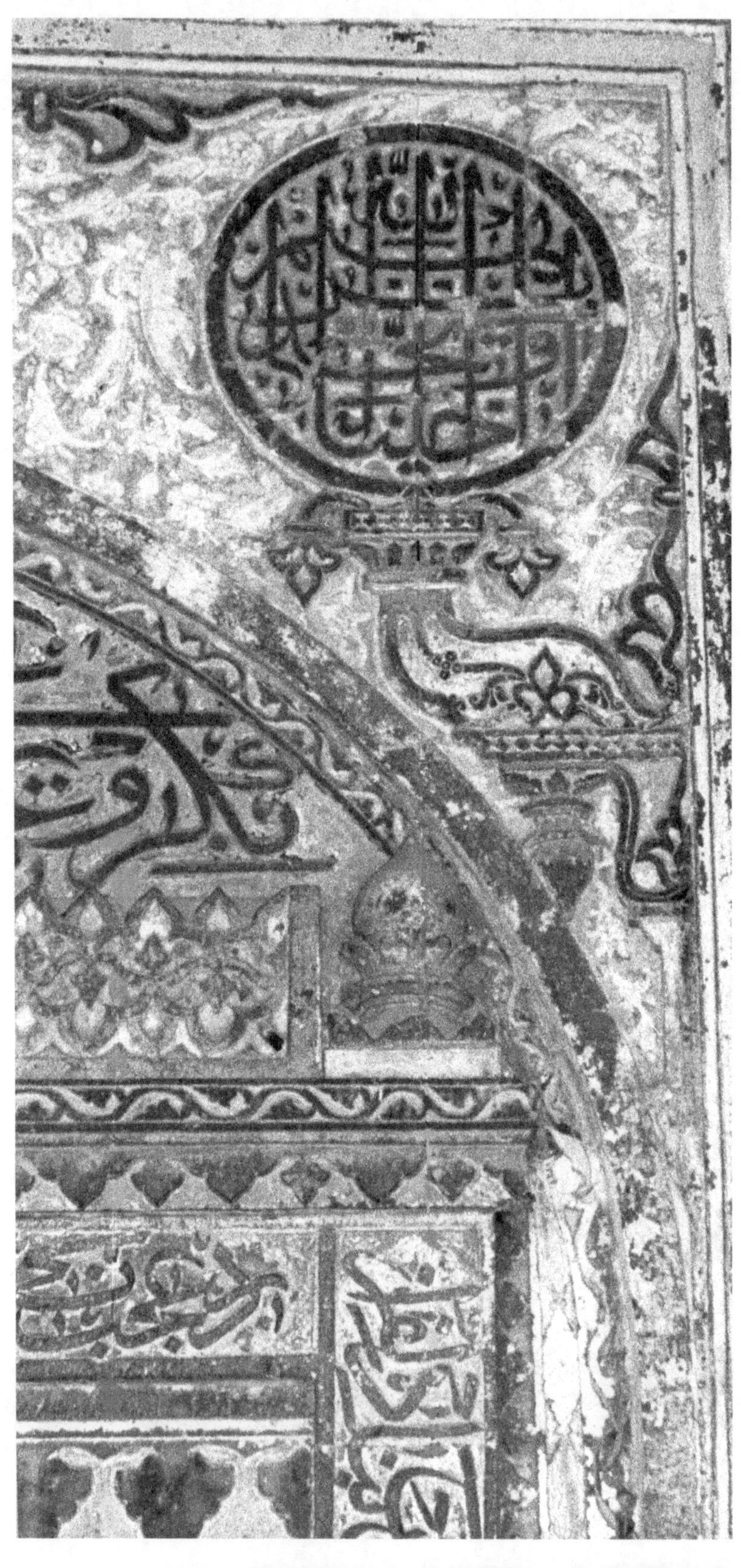

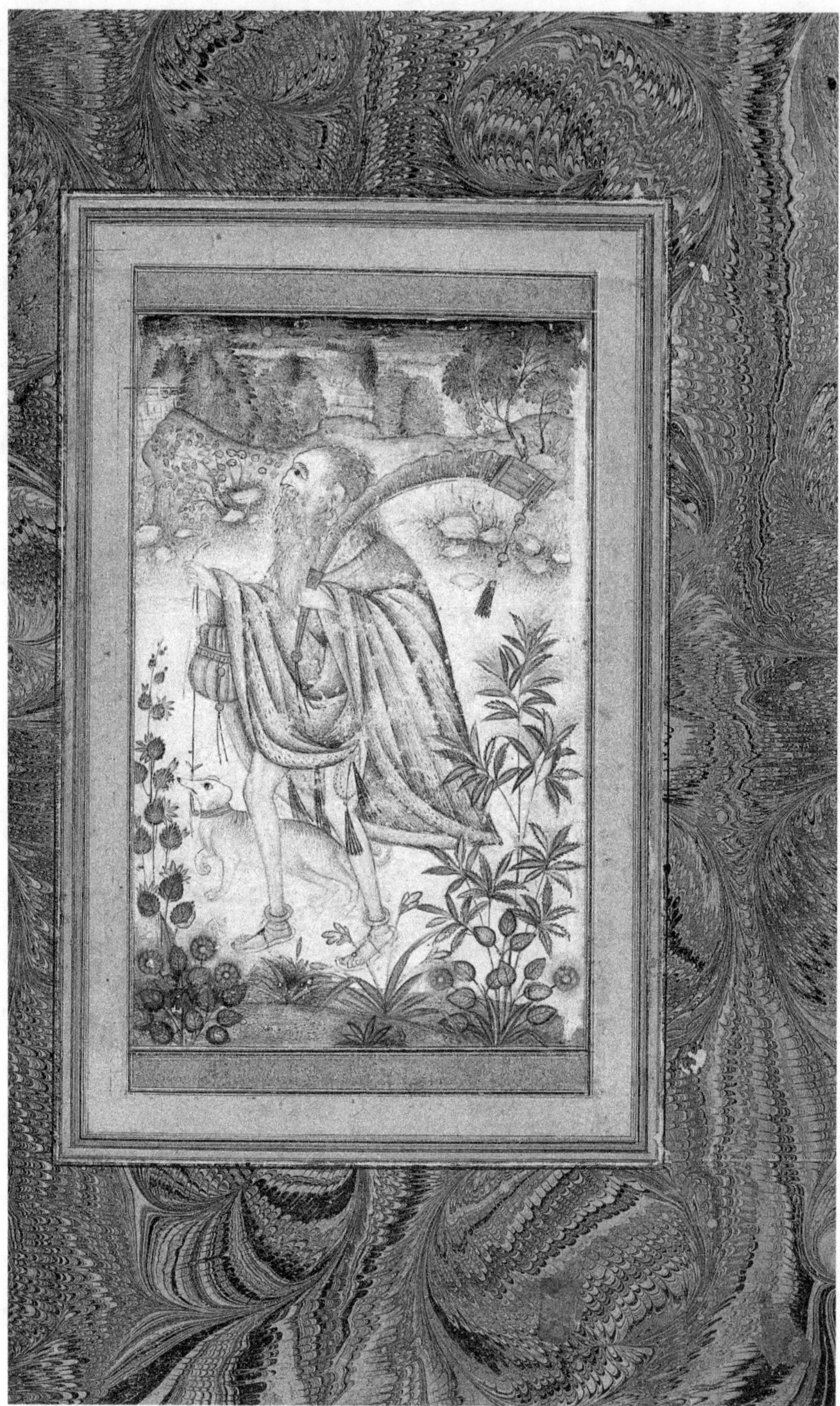

Illustrations

Color Plates

Figures

Acknowledgments

Through the years, many individuals and institutions, more than I can possibly list here, have assisted in the development of this project. Without their support, this book would not have happened, and so I offer my sincere thanks to everyone who lent help, whether financial backing, intellectual insight, time, or encouragement.

The American Institute for Indian Studies provided not one but two crucial avenues of support. A fellowship from AIIS allowed me to carry out research in India during 1997 and 1998. The AIIS Edward Cameron Dimock Jr. Prize in the Indian Humanities for an unpublished book manuscript, which this work was awarded in 2004, provided both the opportunity and supplemental funds for the book to be published by Indiana University Press. I also would like to thank the College Art Association Millard Meiss Publication Fund, whose generous grant allowed for the inclusion of so many images vital to the success of this book. The University of Minnesota Graduate School provided financial support as well.

My research in Hyderabad was made both productive and pleasant because of the expertise and hospitality so generously shared by Jagdish Mittal, Sadiq Naqvi, and Dr. Khan and the rest of the staff at the Salar Jung Museum. Various staff members at the Chester Beatty Library, the British Library, the British Museum, the Metropolitan Museum of Art, the Sackler Museum at Harvard University, and the Boston Museum of Fine Arts kindly assisted first with my archival research and then again when I was gathering images for my book. Mike Seigel in the Department of Geography at Rutgers University made the wonderful maps that help illuminate my study, and the Asia Society allowed me to reuse portions of my article "Carved in Stone: The Codification of a Visual Identity for the Indo-Islamic Sultanate of Bijapur" from volume 55 of *Archives of Asian Art*.

I owe much, much gratitude to Catherine Asher, who continues to provide me with a wonderful academic role model. I also would like to thank Frederick Asher, John Archer, Iraj Bashiri, and Ann Waltner for fostering my intellectual growth. Various colleagues have given generously of their time to read over parts or all of the manuscript at various stages of the process. Heartfelt appreciation goes out to Rebecca Brown, Rebecca Tucker, Pika Ghosh, and Sharon Littlefield, as well as the two anonymous AIIS reviewers. All offered valuable insights and suggestions for improving my text, which have made the book much better than it would have been otherwise. At Skidmore College, Terri Brandt and Elisa Travisiono provided indispensable administrative assistance while preparing the manuscript for the AIIS competition deadline. Thank you for your time and sense of humor! I offer deep gratitude to Rebecca Tolen, my editor at Indiana University Press, for patiently guiding me through the publishing process and helping to improve my writing along the way. Elaine Otto, copyeditor extraordinaire, further improved the text. I am indebted to her as well as the design staff at Indiana University Press, who elegantly arranged the parts into a whole.

Of course, none of this would have been possible or worthwhile without the support of my family and friends. Most especially, I offer my thanks to David Rubin, upon whose unfailing good humor, patience, and love I continually rely.

Art of the Court of *Bijapur*

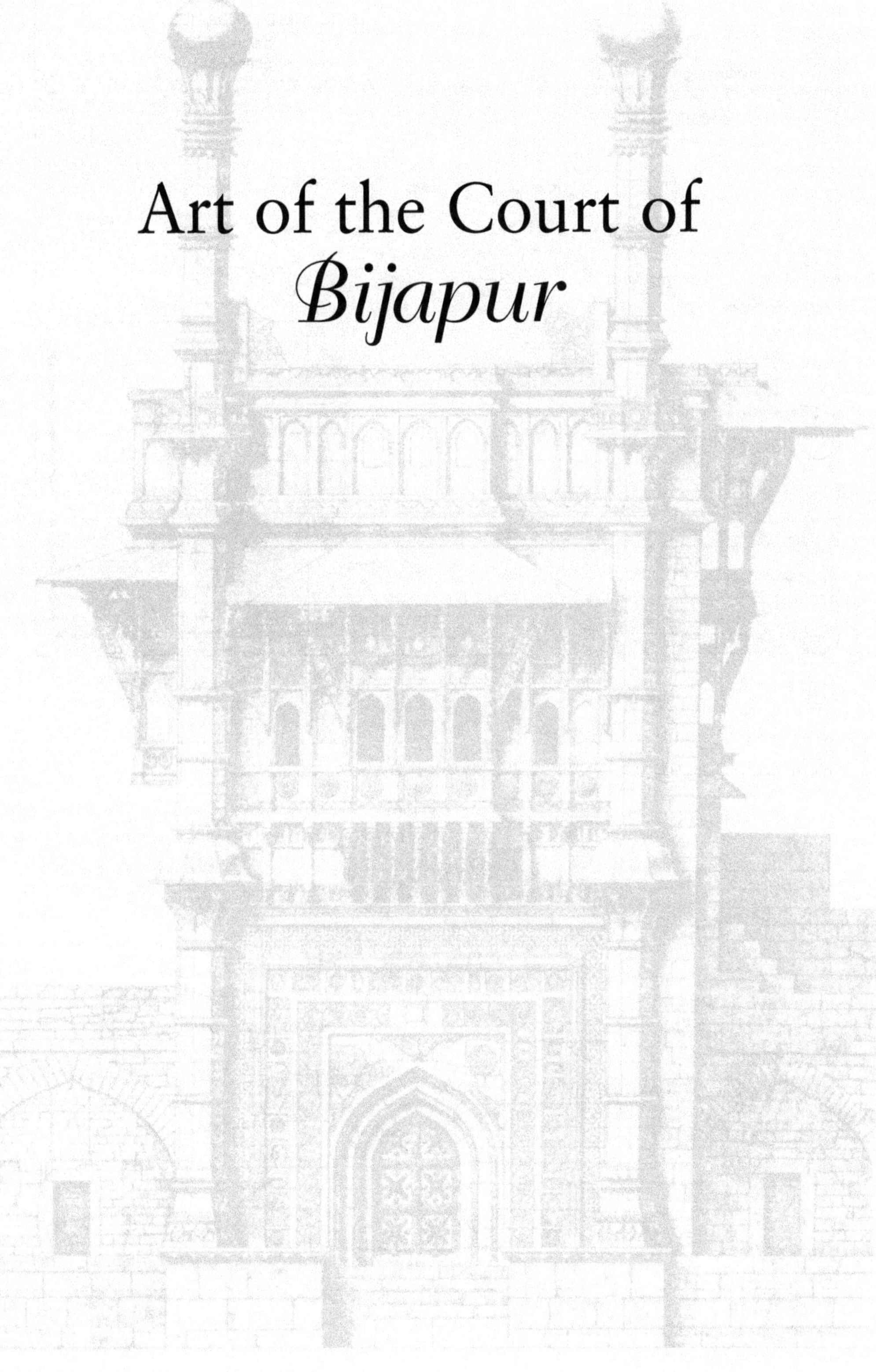

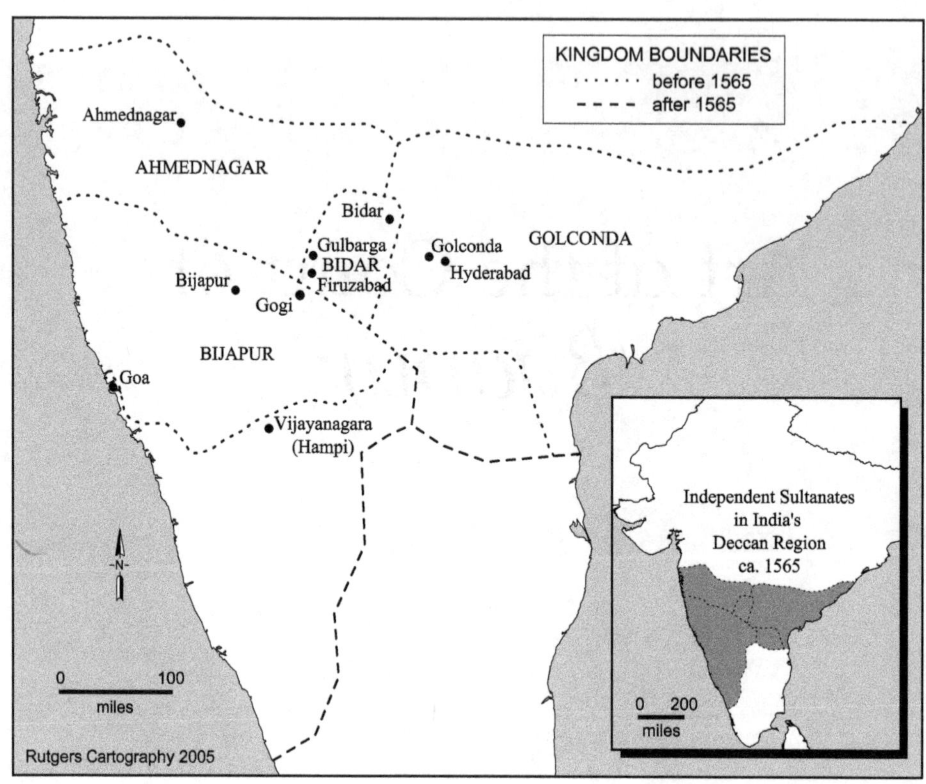

Map 1. The Deccan, showing approximate pre- and post-1565 boundaries of the kingdoms.

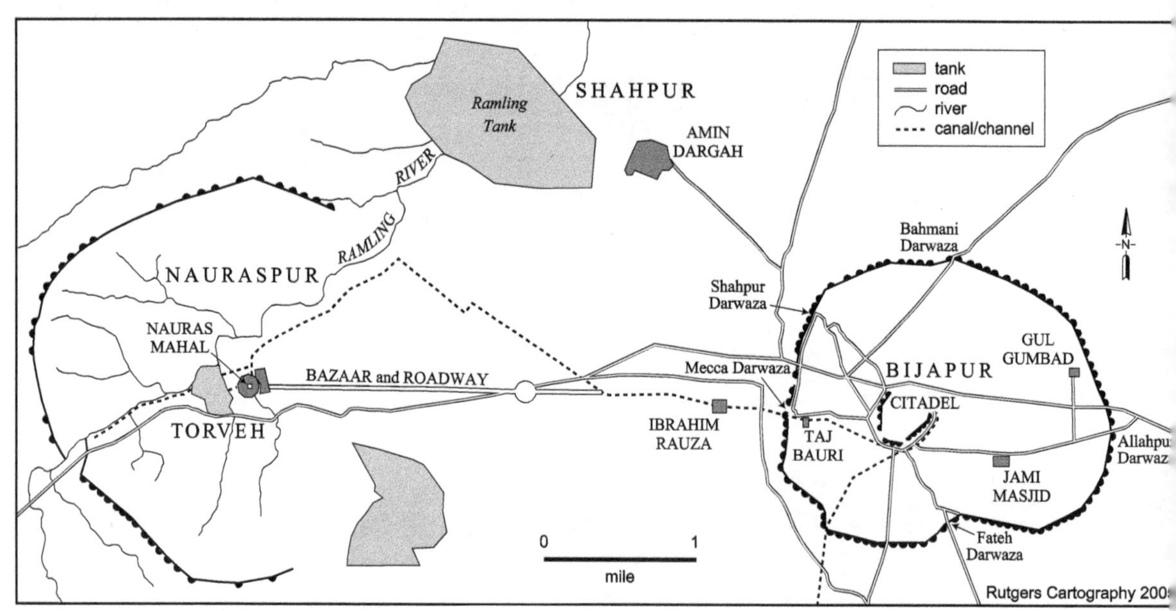

Map 2. The environs of Bijapur, Shahpur, and Nauraspur.

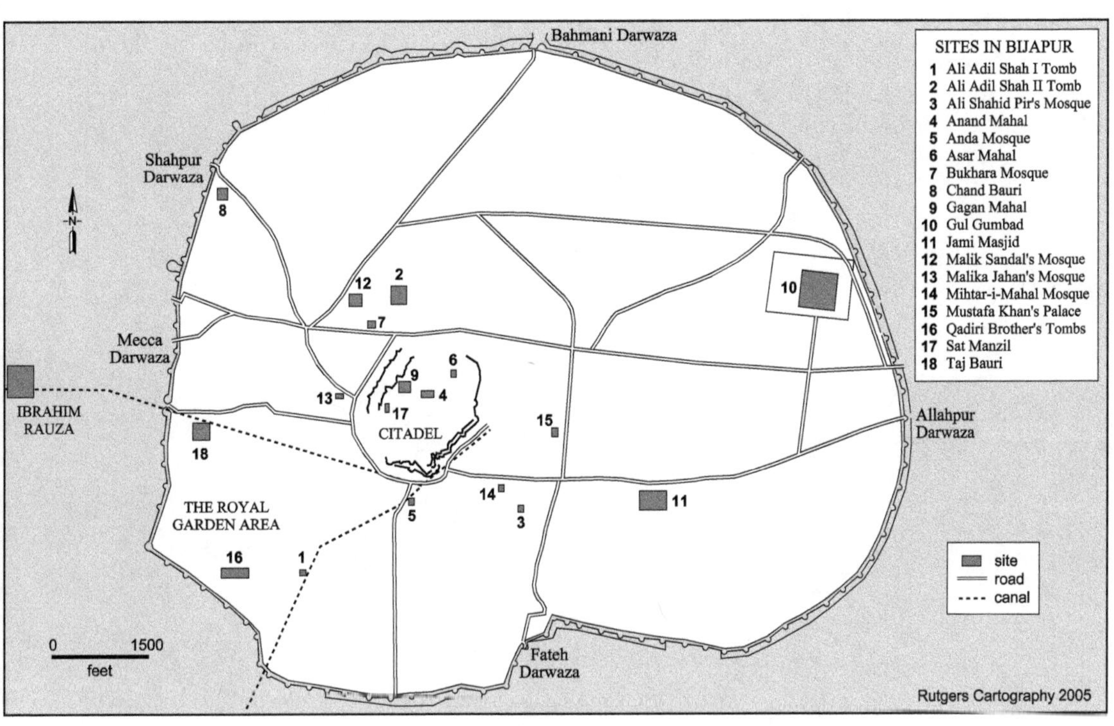

Map 3. Bijapur.

1
Introduction

If they made the Elixir of Mirth and Pleasure,
They would make it from the Holy Dust of Bijapur.

Muhammad Zuhur bin Zuhuri composed these lines[1] while court poet to Bijapur, an Indo-Islamic kingdom that flourished during the sixteenth and seventeenth centuries under the rule of the Adil Shah dynasty (1490–1686). As a court poet, Zuhuri's job was not to record events or people as they actually were but rather to create panegyric verse, works devoted to exalting the kingdom, its capital, court, and leaders through elegant description and potent metaphors. In both purpose and character, Zuhuri's verse parallels much of Bijapur's elite visual arts, from single-page manuscript paintings to royal tomb complexes, created during Adil Shahi rule. Like Zuhuri, the makers of Bijapur's courtly art used metaphor and embellishment to convey meaning and endow prestige. They shaped an image for Bijapur based on poetic ideals rather than everyday realities, holy dust rather than prosaic dirt. The surviving artworks from the sixteenth and seventeenth centuries present Bijapur as an ideal place filled with earthly delights and mystical import. Like dust, a material made of many particles whose specific combination bespeaks its locale, the art also incorporates varied elements to create a distinct mixture, one that speaks to the diverse ethnic, religious, and linguistic environment of Bijapur. Employing the lenses of courtly identity and intercultural exchange, this book traces the development of Bijapuri art between the mid-sixteenth and mid-seventeenth centuries, when both kingdom and art reached their pinnacle.

Located in the southwest section of the Deccan, the plateau that connects the northern and southern portions of the Indian subcontinent, Adil

Shahi Bijapur was one of five sultanates (kingdoms governed by Muslim sultans) formed from the breakup of the earlier Indo-Islamic Bahmani dynasty, which had controlled the region since 1345. Bijapur and its neighbor to the east, the Qutb Shahi kingdom of Golconda, eventually emerged as the largest, longest lasting, and most powerful of the Bahmani splinter states. The Adil Shahi kingdom, founded in 1490 by Yusuf Adil Khan, a provincial Bahmani leader, reached its height during the reigns of Ali I (r. 1558–80), Ibrahim II (r. 1580–1627), and Muhammad (r. 1627–56) Adil Shah. The sultanate's capital was the city of Bijapur, situated on flat basalt terrain in what is today the northern portion of Karnataka state. During the Adil Shahi period, the capital was home to the sultan and royal family as well as most of the nobles, military leaders, and high-ranking administrators who together formed Bijapur's court. Artisans, musicians, and others who, although not high-ranking, worked for the court and so contributed to the courtly environment, lived there as well. The city dominated political, economic, cultural, and artistic life to the extent that the entire Adil Shahi kingdom, like its neighboring Deccani kingdoms, is commonly referred to by the name of its capital (in this case, Bijapur).

This study focuses on painting and architecture made for the Adil Shahi court, by which I mean not only the Adil Shah royal family but also those high-ranking courtiers whose fortunes were largely tied to the dynasty and who were important patrons of art. The surviving courtly art includes illustrated manuscripts, single-page album paintings, city walls, royal palaces, mosques, and tombs. The most prized works date to the first half of the seventeenth century. For example, the well-known Ibrahim Rauza (pl. 25), a royal tomb complex datable to 1626–33 and deemed "the Taj Mahal of the South" by early British scholars as well as modern travel guide writers, marks the epitome of Bijapur's recognized architectural style. The complex features bulbous domes with lotus petal bases, slim decorative minarets, broad cornices topped with finials, intricate brackets, and an abundance of calligraphic inscriptions, all carved from stone (figs. 4.1–4.5). The various architectural elements come together to create a monument that is at once holy and worldly, grand and intimate. One can trace the elements of this exuberant architectural style to a variety of sources, including local religious architecture serving both Hindu and Muslim communities. The artisans and patron used them, however, to create a unique monument, one that served to tie the Adil Shahi royal family directly to their capital city of Bijapur and to create a visual legacy for both city and dynasty.

Likewise, the artist of the well-known seventeenth-century painting of a *yogini,* a female Hindu ascetic, now housed in the Chester Beatty Library, Dublin (and thus commonly referred to as "the Chester Beatty yogini"), drew on numerous traditions to produce the distinct image. The painting (pl. 16), one of the most celebrated Bijapuri works, depicts a young woman dressed as an ascetic yet curiously bedecked in jewels. She holds a myna bird that turns its head to gaze at her, while on either side of the pair bloom large pink flowers. The juxtaposition of the peculiar and beautiful recalls Zuhuri's "elixir of mirth and pleasure." These feelings are augmented by the painting's colors—bright pinks, oranges, and thickly applied gold set against various shades of green and brown—and its style, which features lyrical lines and the exaggeration of select elements (the elongation of the yogini's face, for example). The Chester Beatty yogini, like the Ibrahim Rauza, is a prized example of the elegance, sophistication, and multiculturalism that marks the fully developed style of art at the court of Bijapur.

The makeup of Bijapur's court was diverse and constantly shifting. The Adil Shahi kings were Indian Muslims, originally of Central Asian origin, who at certain points in their history affiliated with Shia Islam and at other times with Sunni Islam. The nobility included local Indians, both Hindus and Muslims, as well as émigrés from Iran or parts of Central Asia and Habshis, East Africans, most likely from Ethiopia or Somalia. The courtiers frequently moved from one Deccan kingdom to the next in search of better positions. Although little documentation regarding artists survives, it is likely that they too traveled from court to court in search of patronage and came from diverse backgrounds, both Indian and Iranian. The various Bahmani splinter states, of which Bijapur was a part, acted in many respects like siblings, alternatively banding together and fighting one another. The sultanates' shared Bahmani heritage linked them together, but the competitive political atmospheres within and among the courts pushed the kingdoms apart, fostering a sense of instability. Over time Bijapur and Golconda emerged as the strongest of these Deccani kingdoms, and as Bijapur's standing grew, more courtiers and presumably more artists emigrated there.

By the early seventeenth century, when Bijapur was at its height politically as well as culturally, kingdoms ruled by Muslim sultans had been a major part of India's political landscape for over four hundred years (and the religion of Islam had been present on the subcontinent for nearly nine hundred years). The Deccan plateau, more specifically, had been governed by one sultanate or another for three hundred years. Thus Islamic culture was not new to India, nor was the practice of cultural interaction. For example, Hindawi, an early form of Urdu that combined elements of Persian and local Indian languages, was already being employed in North Indian literature by the fourteenth century. The growth of the vernacular language was closely intertwined with that of Sufism, Islamic mysticism, which as it spread throughout South Asia incorporated many Hindu elements and local traditions into its practices.[2] By the time of Bijapur's artistic heyday in the sixteenth and seventeenth centuries, Indo-Persian cultural exchange and Hindu-Muslim religious interaction were well established in South Asia. Yet such interaction was constantly shifting and developing, responding to local cultural and political contexts and incorporating new influences. For example, Dakhni or Deccani Urdu, a variation of north Indian Hindawi incorporating words and imagery from local Deccan and South Indian languages such as Marathi, Kannada, and Telugu, flourished during the Deccan sultanate period. Frequently employed in original works of poetry, whether courtly or Sufic or both (as was often the case), Deccani Urdu was one of Bijapur's main languages and a crucial source of local cultural expression.

The other primary language at the Adil Shahi court was Persian, used in dynastic histories and for most official state documents. This usage connected Bijapur to the larger Persian-speaking world, which during the early modern era included two powerful empires, the Safavids in Iran (1502–1736) and the Mughals in North India (1526–1858). In addition to sharing many Persianate social structures, cultural traditions, and artistic practices, Bijapur and its neighboring Deccan states actively fostered political and commercial ties with the two empires. Typically, however, the Deccan sultanates favored the Safavids as a way of distinguishing and buttressing themselves from the Mughals who were pushing farther and farther southward (and who ultimately would bring an end to the independent Deccan kingdoms). Thus Bijapuri art can be positioned within several contexts: the greater Persianate world of the early modern period, the larger history of Islamic India with its tradition of intercultural exchange, the post-Bahmani Deccan, and the immediate Adil Shahi courtly environment.

Despite its multifaceted visual history, the art of Bijapur has been vastly understudied. Investigating Bijapur's artistic development expands our conceptualization of Indo-Persian art and, by extension, broadens the definitions of both Islamic and South Asian art. Scholarly publications, museum exhibitions, and tourist itineraries regarding Islamic art in South Asia overwhelmingly focus on north India and the lavish art of the Mughal dynasty. Therefore, in popular parlance, Mughal artworks, such as the famed Taj Mahal, have come to represent the shape of Indo-Islamic art. But the Mughals were only one—albeit the biggest and wealthiest one—of many Islamic kingdoms and princely states that existed in South Asia between the twelfth and twentieth centuries. The sundry visual remains of these various dynasties remind us that Islamic art of South Asia took not just one form but a range of forms, for Islamic and Indic cultures have never been monolithic, unchanging entities.

For example, one art historian has described the Chester Beatty yogini as the ultimate synthesis of artistic traditions, combining Persian and Indian, as well as European and Chinese, visual elements in this single remarkable painting.[3] While this account is apt, it could also be applied to many sixteenth- and seventeenth-century Mughal paintings that fuse a variety of traditions. Yet the Chester Beatty yogini and other Bijapuri paintings from the same period are markedly different than Mughal paintings, which tend to emphasize action, history, and portraiture in a way that Bijapuri paintings do not, reminding us that art is more than just the sum of its parts. People (including patrons, artists, and viewers), historical circumstances, cultural developments, political motivations, and local constructions of identity all shape the forms art takes at specific times and places. Moreover, the ways in which cultures in this fertile area have interacted over the centuries have taken various shapes, often ones that resist our modern notions of religion, state, and identity. In fact, based on such vicissitude and permeability, one may fruitfully debate the merits of considering "Indo-Islamic art" as a distinct, clearly definable category within the larger field of South Asian art. At a time when popular western media see Islamic culture as something that clashes with other civilizations more often than not and when the Indian media are recording the unfortunately real communal clashes happening on the subcontinent, reconsidering our definitions of Islamic and Indic cultures is an important endeavor.

Bijapuri courtly art illustrates the ways in which the visual arts were intertwined with identity construction in the early modern period. The "politics of identity" is a common phrase in postmodern parlance, but if the post-Enlightenment aspects of the concept, such as the emphasis on individualism over collectivity, are separated out, it is also an idea well suited to the exploration of artistic development in earlier periods. Layers of identity, whether religious, linguistic, or familial, shaped people's lives and the art they produced. Moreover, the surviving artworks provide valuable insights, sometimes the best clues we have, into these multiple layers of identity. This is because art often serves to make visible, to put into concrete form, ideas and beliefs that otherwise have no physical shape. Courtly art seems particularly appropriate for study from the perspective of identity formation, as so much of elite art was tied to political concerns, class constructions, and economic standing, which relied on a rich visual environment for their potency. Bijapur's courtly art expressed power in such ways, but it also reinforced beliefs connected to religious mysticism and created unique multivalent metaphors drawn from poetry, music, and a variety of visual traditions. Thus Bijapuri art provides an encompassing model of courtly art as operating in the realms of political, economic, and religious power while forming the identity not of an individual but of the entire kingdom.

While the sultanate of Bijapur lasted from 1490 until 1686, several dramatic political events combined with significant artistic developments focus this study on the years between 1565 and 1635. In 1565 during the reign of Ali Adil Shah I, Bijapur, as part of a grand military alliance, defeated the large and wealthy kingdom of Vijayanagara to the south. This victory greatly increased the wealth, size, and standing of Bijapur, which managed to obtain the best and biggest portion of the victory spoils, including land containing diamond mines and fertile black soil. Only after 1565 did the city of Bijapur truly begin to develop architecturally, and the earliest surviving illustrated manuscripts are datable to approximately 1570. Seventy years later, the sultanate suffered a change in fortune. In 1635, the Mughal Empire, which had been pushing southward and threatening the Deccan kingdoms for some time, forced Muhammad Adil Shah, Ali's great-nephew, to sign a treaty. This agreement made Bijapur a tributary of the Mughal dynasty (although it also brought relief from the fighting on the northern front and allowed the kingdom to expand southward). After 1635, there is a discernible change in Bijapuri art. Most noticeably the increasing political presence of the Mughal Empire on Bijapur brought a growing Mughal influence to the art made from the 1640s onward. This study focuses on the progression of Bijapuri art over seventy years, from its initial development to the time when the "elixir of mirth and pleasure" became fully apparent and a visual identity for the sultanate and its court became codified.

The available artistic evidence further shapes the specific format of this book: five segments related to painting and four to architecture. Any study of Bijapuri art must remain flexible enough to accommodate indeterminate visual data, since the attribution and dating of much Bijapuri art is based on style rather than inscriptions or other seemingly incontrovertible evidence. And while certain artworks have the potential to reveal a great deal about the role and shape of the visual arts in Bijapur, there nonetheless remain large holes or gaps in the available evidence. My response to these circumstances is to take a "micro-view" of Bijapuri art. That is, I study in great detail a limited number of specific works, such as a monumental tomb, or groups of closely related works, such as paintings with identical subject matter, rather than attempting a complete survey of Bijapuri art from the period 1565–1635. This approach allows me to use the optimal visual evidence that does survive and at the same time acknowledge that this evidence is only the fragmented remains of a once-remarkable whole. Additionally, the format lets the artworks remain the focus. By concentrating on a limited number of works, the book can fully examine the intricacies of Bijapuri art, both its patterns and incongruities.

The chosen examples fit certain parameters. Specifically, the artworks must be confidently, if not absolutely, attributable to the court of Bijapur between 1565 and 1635 (although being able to attribute a work to a specific patron or artist is not essential).[4] While this means excluding many interesting and perhaps revealing works from the study, such prudence is necessary to avoid getting stuck in the quagmire of connoisseurship issues surrounding much of Bijapuri art. The included visual material also needs to be compelling; in other words, it has to have the potential to reveal something substantial about the nature of Bijapuri art. Early in my research, however, I made the decision to define "art" broadly—not to limit the scope of analysis to one medium or another.[5] This breadth allows the study to make use of the best material available, in whatever form it takes, and therefore to assemble a multifaceted body of evidence, one which presents a complex picture of the relationship between the visual arts and the Adil Shahi court. In the end, nine examples of painting and architecture suit the established criteria.[6]

Three chapters frame the nine studies loosely by date and subject. Chapter 2: Prosperous Beginnings addresses the question of why Bijapuri art began to blossom between 1565 and 1580. It discusses the building campaign of Bijapur city carried out between 1565 and 1568 by Ali Adil Shah I and his courtiers. The chapter also examines the late sixteenth-century tomb of Ali I and the *Nujum al-Ulum*, an unusual illustrated manuscript on magic and astrology, dated to 1570–71. By probing artistic development between 1590 and 1635, chapter 3: Developing Visual Metaphors scrutinizes the mystical metaphors and poetic illusions that pervade much of Bijapuri art. The chapter examines the *Pem Nem*, a mystical love story composed, copied, and illustrated between 1591 and 1604, and the numerous yogini paintings created in Bijapur. It also considers portraits of Ibrahim Adil Shah II and the building of a new capital city, Nauraspur, in 1599. Chapter 4: Meaning in Ornament analyzes the famous tomb complex, the Ibrahim Rauza, built in 1626, as well as the *abri*, or marbled, drawing of emaciated horses attributed to Bijapuri artists circa 1620–35. This fourth chapter, focusing specifically on the first half of the seventeenth century, examines the fully formed expression of Bijapur's courtly identity.

Each of the chapters, and indeed each of the nine examples housed within them, raises two themes: cultural interaction and courtly identity. From these two overarching themes comes the conclusion that artists and patrons helped shape an Adil Shahi courtly identity by cultivating a specifically Bijapuri character in the art. This courtly identity was based heavily on poetry, Sufism, and symbols of kingship drawn from a variety of sources. Additionally, it was closely linked with, and mapped onto, the physical shape of the capital city of Bijapur. The blending and juxtaposing of cultural elements created an identity for the Adil Shahi court that was encompassing yet select to the Deccan kingdom. In the same vein, the emphasis on visual metaphors drawn from poetry and Sufism allowed the court culture to be simultaneously inclusive and exclusive, a desirable characteristic due to the constant political shifting and diverse ethnicity of the nobility. The Adil Shahi patrons and artists aimed their artistic output primarily at a local audience who would recognize the intimacies of the visual language and share in the imagined ideal of Bijapur as a place of refuge where one might find an "elixir of mirth and pleasure." If much of the art of the Mughal dynasty, ruling to the north of Bijapur, fashioned a detailed, concrete material environment and history for the empire, then Bijapur's elite art crafted a courtly culture deliberately removed from the specificities of historical events.

Evidence and Scholarship

In contrast to its better known contemporaries, the Mughal and Safavid dynasties, from which a multitude of paintings, monuments, contemporary histories, and travelers' accounts survive, the kingdom of Bijapur offers far less evidence; however, the fragmentary visual and written evidence that does survive frequently provides valuable insights. The first task in any discussion of Bijapuri art, therefore, is to determine a corpus of reliable material. As one begins this investigation, it quickly becomes clear that the study of painting in particular is fraught with problems of attribution and connoisseurship. Although growing, the number of known Bijapuri paintings is relatively small. Additionally, only a few of the surviving Bijapuri single-page paintings or illustrated manuscripts are inscribed with either the date of creation, the artist's name, or the patron's name. As Robert Skelton has pointed out, in the best of contexts, the evidence on painting at Bijapur is circumstantial rather than absolute.[7]

Compared to painting, Adil Shahi architecture seems to offer a wealth of concrete information. The situation perhaps results from basic differences in the two media. Buildings cannot be moved about as easily as small-scale paintings, and thus the question of their place of origin is more readily concluded. Certainly, the chances of still unknown but key monuments nestled away in the corners of private collections are much less likely than of equally key paintings and manuscripts in the same position. Additionally, because large-scale building campaigns were considered public works, several surviving Adil Shahi dynastic histories provide important details regarding architectural projects. This same information does not exist for manuscript or album paintings, which, due to their size, were intimate visual forms, ones therefore not discussed in official state histories. To fully understand the situation surrounding our knowledge of Bijapur's painting and architecture, however, one needs to examine the history of post–Adil Shah Bijapur, including the earliest scholarship on the kingdom, which was firmly grounded in the colonial production of knowledge about India and which continues to shape our view of Bijapur.

The downfall of the Adil Shahi dynasty occurred during the reigns of Ali Adil Shah II (r. 1656–72) and Sikander Adil Shah (r. 1672–86), the eighth and ninth rulers. In 1658 Aurangzeb, fixated on defeating the Deccan kingdoms, became Mughal emperor and led his armies against Bijapur. At the same time, Shivaji, a dynamic Maratha warrior, came to power and began attacks on Bijapur. To make matters worse for the kingdom, Ali II died suddenly, leaving Sikander, a five-year-old boy, as his successor. Internal power struggles over the regency and a treasury emptied by constant warfare proved to be Bijapur's final afflictions. In 1686, Bijapur, already a Mughal tributary, completely fell, becoming a province of the empire. The victors took the young ruler, Sikander, prisoner, and he died in captivity in 1700.[8]

In the final battle of 1686, the Mughal army sacked Bijapur city. Traditionally the small amount of surviving Bijapuri painting is linked to that event. It is often assumed that the Mughal ruler Aurangzeb had most of Bijapur's wall paintings destroyed in a fit of religious zeal and that the Mughal armies, likewise, took or destroyed many of the album paintings and illustrated manuscripts in the wake of their victory. Some scholars, however, have begun to question the extent of the damage; the story of Aurangzeb's destruction of the wall paintings seems to be based on Aurangzeb's reputation as a zealot rather than any hard evidence.[9] Yet it is clear that some works of art must have been taken at the time of the Mughal victory. For example, the Bikaner royal collection contains at least one Bijapuri painting obtained by the raja of Bikaner while he served as a commander of the Mughal armies battling Bijapur.[10]

For the next 160 years, the rule of Bijapur passed back and forth as the Mughal Empire fragmented. When the nizam of Hyderabad declared independence from the Mughals in 1723–24, Bijapur became part of the nizam's territories until 1760 when the Marathas forced the nizam to cede Bijapur to them. In 1818 Bijapur fell to the raja of Satara, and then in 1848, the whole of the Satara kingdom, including Bijapur, passed into British control. This political instability, coupled with devastating famines that hit the region in the late eighteenth and early nineteenth centuries, allowed the monuments of Bijapur to be plundered and to fall into ruin. In fact, Salim al-Din Quraishi believes that this 160-year period is when the Bijapur royal library, housed in the Asar Mahal, was looted and much of the art destroyed—not by the command of Aurangzeb.[11] The writers of the *Gazetteer of the Bombay Presidency: Bijapur District* seem to have agreed when they wrote, "Under Moghal [*sic*] rule the palace and other buildings in the *Ark-killah* (citadel) remained as if their royal masters had left them the day before. With the Marathas matters were sadly different . . . all that could be pillaged or spoiled was carried away."[12]

Despite the political instability in the region, early on some figures recognized the historical significance of Bijapur. Attention first turned to the Adil Shahis' Persian court histories. In 1811, Mirza Ibrahim Zubairi, a scholar and resident of the Deccan, wrote a detailed history of Bijapur based on many original historical manuscripts from the Adil Shahi period, including some sources that no longer survive.[13] In 1829, a London firm published John Briggs's four-volume translation of Muhammad Qasim Firishta's seventeenth-century history, the *Tarikh-i Firishta,* under the title of *The History of the Rise of the Mahomedan Power in India*. Two years later Briggs helped edit a two-volume Persian text of the history published by the government of Bombay.[14] Briggs's nineteenth-century translation of Firishta's history remains not only the sole published version of Firishta but also the sole Bijapuri history to be fully translated into English.

As the nineteenth century progressed, interest in Bijapur's architecture grew. The restoration of Adil Shahi monuments began during the reign of the last Satara raja, Shahaji (r. 1839–48). Notably, Captain Philip Hart, an Englishman working for the raja, supervised the restoration of the Ibrahim Rauza.[15] The work included fitting the tomb with flying buttresses that remain today (fig. 4.3). Full-scale attention turned to the architecture in the late 1850s. In fact, when the British colonial government initiated a campaign to photograph and document the monuments of India, they focused on Bijapur first. The premiere photographic album was an 1859 survey of Bijapur's monuments entitled *The Architectural Illustrations of the Principal Mahometan Buildings of Beejapore*.[16] The second photographic study, sponsored by the British government of Bombay in 1866, also centered on Bijapur. The book, *Architecture at Bijapoor, an Ancient Mahometan Capital in the Bombay Presidency,* includes a detailed photographic account of the monuments along with an introduction to the city by Captain Phillip Meadows Taylor.[17] Taylor admired Bijapur so much that he penned two picturesque novels about Adil Shahi court life, *Tara* and *Noble Queen,* in which the central scenes take place in a vividly described Gagan Mahal, the audience hall built by Ali Adil Shah I in 1560–61.[18]

Other British commentators of the period shared Taylor's admiration for Bijapur's monuments. Lord Napier considered Bijapur's architecture in the same category with that of Granada, Constantinople (Istanbul), and Samarkand.[19] James Fergusson, who did many of the early studies of Indo-Islamic architecture, saw Bijapur as a "provincial style," but one of the best.[20] The British were charmed with the originality and ornament of Bijapur's architecture, as well as what they considered the city's picturesque state of decay. Even more, the engineering of the architecture impressed them. They were so in awe of the massive dome of the Gul Gumbad, the mid-seventeenth-century tomb of Muhammad Adil Shah, that the method of construction used in the dome, in which the lateral thrust was offset by weight added to the pendentives, became a model for dome designs in the colonial Indo-Saracenic style.[21]

Britain's role as imperial overlord of India grounded early British interest in Bijapur. Thus during the nineteenth century the ultimate purposes for studying Bijapur's architecture and history were to help create an appropriate Anglo-Indian colonial architecture style and to "master" the past—that is, as Thomas Metcalf has discussed, to define the past in terms that justified the present political situation.[22] Much of the early information collected and written on Bijapur displays a strong Orientalizing element, one that, while lavishly praising Bijapur, often stresses decadent descriptions and loquacious anecdotes over detailed analysis. Such exoticism served to assert British (and western) superiority over former rulers of India such as the Adil Shahis.[23]

In 1879, the colonial government began repairing some of Bijapur's picturesque ruins and even converted a number of Adil Shahi buildings to suit British administrative purposes. For example, local administrators turned the *serai* (inn) of Mustafa Khan, located outside of the city, into a district jail; the Bukhara mosque into a post office; and the Anand Mahal, built by Ibrahim Adil Shah II (r. 1580–1627) in 1590 to celebrate his accession, into the residence of the first assistant collector.[24] Such conversions, as well as the restorations carried out by the British government and the earlier local Indian rulers, were done without the care that preservationists of today demand. Thus, to the modern viewer, it is often unclear how much was altered or restored and with what degree of accuracy.

The strong attention given to Bijapur's architecture continued through the turn of the century. In fact, the architectural surveys completed by Henry Cousens between 1889 and 1916 remain the most extensive to date.[25] His works include detailed architectural drawings and plans for all of the major monuments in Bijapur city (see, for example, fig. 4.1 or 4.12). Cousens was interested not only in fully recording the various buildings and their ornament but also in establishing dates of construction, engineering methods, and a stylistic evolution for Bijapuri architecture. Adding to Cousens's base of information, during the 1930s Muhammad Nazim transcribed and translated Bijapur's architectural inscriptions, providing information on the construction of several key monuments.[26]

Despite this firm base, the study of Bijapuri architecture presents some difficulties, ones common to the study of premodern architecture. To begin with, many of the buildings survive in poor condition or have disappeared entirely—or have been restored with questionable accuracy.[27] Many building names, which appear at first to provide tantalizing clues about the monument, such as patron or function, are in fact later appellations, while often dates or other information that early colonial sources give as certain, upon further research, cannot be confirmed.[28] None of the wall paintings that originally decorated many of the monuments survive in good condition, and the beautiful gardens, furniture, and textiles that originally adorned the structures and added so much to their visual context disappeared long ago. Nevertheless, the early attention paid to Bijapur's monuments provides a solid basis for subsequent scholarship (for example, the early photographs, drawings, and plans often capture a building in considerably better state of repair than it is today). Recent studies on Bijapur's architecture have been able to draw on this early work, and with the addition of new observations, they have established a detailed understanding of the stylistic progression of Bijapuri architecture, which seems to have started with modestly decorated rubble-and-plaster buildings that drew on earlier Bahmani traditions, such as the use of decorative roundels flanking archways. The architecture grew larger over time before shifting at the beginning of the seventeenth century to more intimately scaled, highly ornamented, stone-carved structures, such as the Ibrahim Rauza, and then eventually returning, at about the midcentury mark, to large-scale rubble-and-plaster buildings.[29] Into this stylistic framework we can place any undated buildings with a fair degree of certainty.

In contrast to Bijapur's architecture, scholars did not turn their attention to painting until much later. To a large degree, lack of evidence caused the art historical neglect. Until the mid-twentieth century, collectors and scholars knew of only a few Deccani paintings, and those were mainly unsigned and undated works in ambiguous styles. The slight undoubtedly stemmed as well from a difference between the two media, painting and architecture. Small, intimately sized album and manuscript paintings did not have the direct political-propagandizing appeal of large-scale, imperially sponsored architecture. Such appeal was central to the early colonial studies of Indian architecture.

The first tentative discussions of Bijapuri painting appeared in the late 1920s and 1930s, by which point surviving works were scattered among museum and private collections throughout India, as well as across Britain, Europe, and North America. A precious few illustrated manuscripts remained intact; most examples were single-page paintings intermingled in albums and boxes with Islamic and Indian paintings from a range of locales. Scholars such as N. C. Mehta, Lawrence Binyon, Stella Kramrisch, and Basil Gray began the task of sorting out the Bijapuri works. In the following decades, studies by Moti Chandra, Douglas Barrett, Robert Skelton, Karl Khandalavala, and Jagdish Mittal added to the body of analysis.[30] Because of the lack of evidence on Adil Shahi painting, these discussions necessarily focused on issues of style, attribution, and dating. As more paintings came to light, art historians frequently had to reconsider attributions and dates of already known paintings.[31] More recent studies have continued this work.[32] From such scholarship and from the body of paintings now recognized, we are able to identify a distinct "Bijapur style" from the late sixteenth and early seventeenth centuries. This includes a distinctive palette of orange, pink, dark greens, reddish-brown, lapis blue, and gold, the last two colors particularly favored in the late sixteenth century when pigments seem to have been more thickly applied than they were in mid-seventeenth-century paintings. The dress and some of the physical characteristics of the figures in Bijapuri painting are also distinctive. Most notably, the clothes of both men and women are adorned with long scarves and sashes that flare out at the ends and seem to blow in the breeze. Of course, issues of dating and attribution continue to impact analyses of Bijapuri painting and probably will for some time to come, as we slowly uncover more paintings lying yet unstudied in various collections.[33]

Thus, while the problems of attribution in painting are much greater than in the architectural realm, the study of Bijapuri art is yet nascent. We continue to establish a body of datable, identifiable works and to present basic information. In some cases, even when dealing with the best-known and best-documented Adil Shahi buildings and paintings, seemingly "basic" issues such as the date of a work, the patron, and who or what is being represented in a painting need to be addressed. At the same time, select surviving monuments, illustrated manuscripts, and paintings, when viewed in conjunction with Adil Shahi courtly literature and the scholarship to date, can provide rich information regarding the roles that the visual arts played in Bijapur.

Cultural Interaction

A legacy of early scholarship on the Deccan was the foregrounding of Hindu/Muslim relations, or perceived notions of such relations, onto the history of the region. While a variety of colonial practices fed this preoccupation, one key event was the publication in 1900 of Robert Sewell's *Forgotten Empire*.[34] This important history of Bijapur's southern neighbor, Vijayanagara, vitally impacted how Bijapur and its art came to be viewed in the twentieth century. Sewell portrayed the kingdom of Vijayanagara as the great Hindu stronghold, militarily and culturally, against Muslim incursion in India. This placed Bijapur, as well as the other Deccan sultanates, in direct opposition to Vijayanagara and centered the issue of Hindu-Muslim relations. Bijapur's art began to be analyzed in terms of its "Muslim" and "Hindu" elements, as well as the degree of intermingling or separation between the two.

Perhaps influenced by regional pride or perhaps in reaction to the work of Sewell and other non-Indian scholars, local scholars such as Ghulam Yazdani, P. M. Joshi, H. K. Sherwani, and Nazir Ahmad, working from the 1930s and 1940s onward with the support of the last nizam of Hyderabad, stressed the high degree of cultural synthesis that existed in the Deccan Islamic kingdoms.[35] For example, Sherwani asserted that cultural interaction between Hindus and Muslims occurred in the Deccan long before it did in the larger and more celebrated Mughal kingdom of north India.[36] Eventually the focus shifted from establishing the existence of cultural interaction in the Deccan sultanates to addressing precisely *when* and *why* it occurred, and many of the inquiries centered on late sixteenth- and early seventeenth-century Bijapur. While such scholarship provides a different perspective than that of Sewell, it still serves to foreground Hindu and Muslim interaction, that is, it assumes a separation between Hindu and Muslim and a privileging of religious identity above all else, as found in Sewell's earlier work.

In the last few decades, important advances have taken place in our understanding of Hindu-Muslim relations. Most recently, studies such as those featured in David Gilmartin and Bruce Lawrence's edited volume, *Beyond Turk and Hindu*, have provided nuance and critically needed depth to our understanding of the ways in which religious identities were constructed in South Asia's medieval and early modern periods.[37] One advance has been the expansion of the terminology with which we discuss the issue. As Gilmartin and Lawrence explain, the terms *Muslim* and *Hindu*, so commonly employed, are fraught with modern connotations and religious limitations that obscure the range of ways in which identity was conceived in earlier periods. Therefore, they and others recently have adopted Marshall G. S. Hodgson's term *Islamicate* to refer to Islamic cultural and political practices that are not strictly religious and the term *Indic* for the corresponding South Asian norms. As they explain, "Both *Islamicate* and *Indic* suggest a repertoire of language and behavior, knowledge and power, that define broad cosmologies of human existence. Neither denotes simply bounded groups self-defined as Muslim or Hindu."[38] Such terminology proves particularly useful when discussing art, which incorporates a range of traditions that are rarely strictly religious.

These recent insights also pertain to three key issues cited in analyses of cultural and religious synthesis in Bijapur: namely, the switch from Shia to Sunni Islam that took place in Bijapur at the end of the sixteenth century, the impact on Bijapur of the fall of Vijayanagara in 1565, and the role of Ibrahim Adil Shah II. Each of these factors has, at one point or another, been credited with the syncretic atmosphere manifest in the visual arts of early seventeenth-century Bijapur. If we recognize that fixed religious identities did not necessarily operate in the way that we often perceive them to operate now, and that intercultural exchange had been a part of Bijapur since its inception, what, then, is the significance of the three factors, particularly to the court's artistic and cultural climate? And how should we situate the cultural and religious eclecticism dominating Bijapur's art?

When Ali Adil Shah I died in 1580 and the kingdom passed on to his nephew, Ibrahim Adil Shah II, the official state religion switched from Shia to Sunni Islam. This change is sometimes viewed as a turning point in Bijapuri culture, decreasing Persian influence (the reasoning being that the religion of the Persian heartland, Safavid Iran, was Shiism, which the Adil Shahs no longer practiced) and increasing Indic influence on Bijapuri art and culture. But how significant was the late sixteenth-century sectarian switch? The Adil Shahi sultans, in fact, shifted between the two Muslim sects seven times over the nearly two hundred years of their rule. When Yusuf Adil Khan (r. 1490–1510), governor of Bijapur province, broke away from the 150-year-old Bahmani dynasty and founded his own kingdom, one of his most important acts was to declare Shiism the official state religion. He was the first ruler in India to do so, and he did this in 1502–1503, less than a year after Shah Ismail had declared the newly formed Safavid dynasty in Iran a Shia kingdom.[39] The decision proved unpopular with Yusuf's contemporaries—the lingering Bahmani kingdom and the emerging Bahmani splinter states—so much so that they prepared a confederacy against Bijapur and forced Yusuf to convert back to the Sunni faith for a short while. In 1504, when the political climate had relaxed, he reintroduced the Shia creed to Bijapur. Then, in 1539–40, Ibrahim Adil Shah I (r. 1535–58), the fourth Adil Shahi ruler, changed the state religion to Sunni Islam. In 1558, less than twenty years later, Ibrahim I's son, Ali I, began his reign, immediately reverting back to Shiism. The state religion changed for the sixth time approximately 30 years later when Ibrahim II, who favored Sunnism, came to power. The final change came in the late 1650s, with the reign of the Shia sultan, Ali II. Despite such repeated sectarian turnabout, Yusuf's initial declaration forged a strong bond between Bijapur and Iran, one which historical evidence suggests remained strong even during the periods when the reigning Adil Shahis practiced Sunni Islam.[40]

Recent studies of Shiism in the Deccan have shown that political objectives often fueled adoption of one creed or another.[41] Externally, embracing Shiism could assist a sultanate in garnering support from the Safavid dynasty or help distinguish the kingdom from its neighbors. Yusuf Adil Khan may have considered both of these objectives when he declared Shia Islam the official religion of his new kingdom, the move signaling his split from the Bahmani dynasty while also getting the attention of the Safavid shah. Internally, a shift in official religion could work to shore up support with a particular faction of the Muslim nobility or, conversely, if the sultan wished, to limit the power of a growing group. Because of the strong divisions within the nobility of Bijapur, as well as the other Deccan sultanates, such courtly balancing acts were essential.

The primary split in the nobility, inherited from the Bahmani dynasty, was between the Deccanis, or Indian-born Muslims, and the Afaqis, or foreign-born Muslims. The Deccanis (including Muslims whose families had been in India for several generations and who spoke the local languages), Hindu-converts to Islam, and also Habshis (East Africans, primarily Abbysinians) tended to belong to the Sunni sect of Islam. The Afaqis, mainly Persian-speaking soldiers and administrators from Transoxiana, Iran, and the Persian Gulf, were primarily Shia Muslims.[42] Rivalry for influential positions at court, as well as cultural, linguistic, and religious differences, created animosity between the two groups. Although ultimately this split served to weaken the Deccan kingdoms, at times the sultans were able to exploit it to keep the power of the nobles in check. One of the ways in which they could alter power relations was by switching the official religion and, with it, the favored group of nobles.

Hence, personal choice, political concerns, and the influence of powerful courtiers all impacted Adil Shahi rulers' shifts between the two Muslim sects. Through all of the changes, both groups of nobles, Afaqi and Deccani, were present at court, though in varying numbers. Additionally, the majority of Bijapur's inhabitants, the lower classes as well as members of the kingdom's court and administration, followed some form of Hinduism and therefore must have been minimally affected by such shifts. With all of this in mind, it is difficult to gauge how much impact the late sixteenth-century switch from Shia to Sunni Islam had on the kingdom's cultural expressions.

Indeed, in my exploration of Bijapur's artistic development between 1565 and 1635, which includes both Shia and Sunni periods, I found only a few, rather subtle, examples of sectarian identities expressed in the art (see, for example, the discussion of Ali Adil Shah I's tomb in chapter 2). Certainly the overt Shia and Persian identity fostered in the visual environment of Hyderabad, the seventeenth-century capital of the solidly Shia Qutb Shahi dynasty to Bijapur's east, with its exquisitely tiled *ashurkhanas* (buildings in which the relics associated with the Shia martyr Imam Husayn are kept) and elaborate *alams* (standards associated with the Imam Husayn) is conspicuously absent from Bijapuri art produced during the periods when Shiism was the official religion.[43] Between the numerous politically motivated shifts from Shia to Sunni Islam and back, the overall religious and cultural diversity of the region, and the lack of sectarian emphasis in the arts, it seems clear that the late sixteenth-century Shia/Sunni shift cannot be as significant as some have thought.

Another theory regarding Bijapur's abundant intercultural exchange credits it to the 1565 fall of Vijayanagara and a subsequent influx of Hindu artisans and others from the fallen kingdom to Bijapur.[44] The defeat of Vijayanagara unquestionably had a major impact on Bijapur. The amount of land alone gained by the Adil Shahis significantly changed the character of the sultanate (map 1). However, the underlying assumptions in the above statement—that Vijayanagara was a purely Hindu kingdom religiously, politically, and culturally, and on the other hand, until 1565, Bijapur was equally exclusively Muslim—are faulty. Vijayanagara was a sophisticated composite kingdom that combined local south Indian practices with broader Sanskrit and Islamicate traditions in order to effectively operate at a variety of regional levels. Phillip Wagoner, for example, has shown that the Vijayanagaran elite consciously adopted Islamicate dress and titles in their external political interactions, while Catherine Asher has pointed out the Islamicate elements in Vijayanagara's courtly architecture.[45] Historical sources tell us that the Vijayanagaran rulers employed a number of Muslims in their service, particularly in their cavalry, enough so that they had a mosque constructed in the capital.[46] Some of Vijayanagara's composite nature undoubtedly came from the earlier Bahmani dynasty, of which it, like Bijapur, was a splinter state.

Bijapur certainly inherited patterns of cultural interaction from the Bahmani dynasty. One notable practice was the use of Maharashtran Brahmins and Marathi-speaking soldiers in the kingdom's administration and army. Because the number of Muslims in the Deccan was relatively small, the Deccan Islamic kingdoms depended on Brahmins, primarily from the Maharashtran region, for administration and tax collection. Early on, the Bahmani leaders developed a system in which *deshmukhs,* local landholders who controlled groups of villages, collected taxes for the sultan, of which they got a percentage. The same need to employ local talent occurred within the Deccan armies. The local soldiers, called Marathas, formed a large part of the armies in Bahmani dynasty.[47] They continued to do so in the successor states, particularly in Bijapur and Ahmadnagar, the two kingdoms whose boundaries included the Maharashtran region.[48] Thus, from the start, Marathas and Maharashtran Brahmins played vital roles in Bijapur's army and administration as well as in the development of the kingdom's culture. For example, Marathi, the language spoken by Marathas, became a component in the development of Deccani Urdu.[49]

The Adil Shahi rulers themselves were a mixture of Maratha and Persian blood and grew up familiar with both Maratha and Persian culture. Bijapur's founder, Yusuf Adil Khan was an Afaqi who had come to India from Central Asia around 1460 and then worked his way up in the Bahmani dynasty.[50] Yusuf spoke Persian and was shaped by Persian culture, even inviting scholars and poets from Iran to his court.[51] The new sultan, however, did not remain remote from the local culture. He married a Maratha princess, Punji Khatun, and their son was his successor, Ismail Adil Khan. Such historical evidence proposes that Bijapur was a site of intercultural exchange long before the Deccan sultanates' joint victory over Vijayanagara in 1565.

Finally, and perhaps most often, the remarkable cultural developments at the beginning of the seventeenth century are often attributed to the personality and greatness of Ibrahim Adil Shah II (r. 1580–1627). Both popular and scholarly accounts of Bijapur credit Ibrahim's personal religious eclecticism for the cultural synthesis, his interest in music, poetry, and Sufism for cultural advances in those areas, and his active patronage of the arts for the flourishing of painting and architecture during his reign.[52] Ibrahim unquestionably cuts a dashing figure in historical accounts of Bijapur, which emphasize him more than anyone. Bestowing himself with the Sanskrit title Jagatguru, "World Teacher"; beginning his poetry with invocations to the Hindu goddess Sarasvati and then shortly thereafter praising the Muslim Sufi saint Gesudaraz; wearing the *rudraksha* (dried berry) beads of the Hindu mystic; becoming lost in a trance when he listened to music—it is hard to imagine a more appealing, religiously open, romantic figure than Ibrahim II. Moreover, the surviving evidence suggests that the kingdom reached its cultural, including artistic, peak during his forty-seven-year reign. But was Ibrahim the *cause* or the *result* of the culturally eclectic effervescence of the age? And what is the larger effect of singling out Ibrahim II in Bijapur's history?

Carl Ernst has identified a trend—pertinent to this discussion—in writings on South Asian history in which prominent historical figures, typically princes or kings, are transformed into heroes or villains. He terms this transformation "historiomachy":

> Modern writers, following to some extent the depiction of medieval epics, have seized upon certain historical figures as heroes and villains of a drama that has finally culminated in modern times. These examples of historiomachy are only slightly exaggerated summaries of positions that are familiar to every student of Indian history.[53]

Ernst explains that the characterization of hero or villain tends to be based on whether or not the figure is perceived as religiously tolerant. He lists the Mughal emperor Akbar and the prince Dara Shikoh, both of whom had eclectic approaches to religion, as easily recognizable heroes in the history of India, and the Mughal emperor Aurangzeb, famous for his perceived religious zeal, as an equally recognizable villain. If Ernst's analysis is extended to art historical discussions of South Asia, such characterizations are clearly visible, with art often seen as flourishing under the guidance of the heroes and stagnating during the reigns of the villains. Bijapur is no exception. Not only do many popular and scholarly accounts cast Ibrahim II as the leading man in the story of Bijapur and its art, but they also place his predecessor, Ali Adil Shah I, in the role of villain. As one art historical account put it, Ali was too busy undertaking "a campaign of religious persecution" to be the "brilliant patron of music and the visual arts" that his nephew Ibrahim II was.[54] Such characterizations, which have little basis in historical fact, show the lingering power of the works by Sewell and other colonial scholars. Ibrahim II undoubtedly was an important patron of the arts, and the point is not to minimize his role in codifying an Adil Shahi courtly identity but rather to include as many factors as possible into the analysis in order to create a multidimensional reading of the past.

The problem with trying to account for the cultural syncretism in early seventeenth-century Bijapur is that the query itself is based on the assumption that the coming together of cultural traditions was so outside the norm as to *require* explanation. The norm is imagined to be cultural traditions existing in some sort of "pure" or "authentic" state. Yet such cultural purity was far from the reality of medieval and early modern South Asia. Another approach, then, is to replace the phrase "cultural syncretism," which implies a complete coming together of discrete practices to create something new, with "cultural interaction" or "intercultural exchange," phrases that encompass a range of actions—synthesis but also appropriation, competition, conflict, and even rejection. This substitution acknowledges that cultures continually interact and change and that such hybridity happens not only passively or gradually but also through the actions of individuals and groups for particular purposes. The focus of inquiry then shifts from measuring if, how much, and why cross-cultural contact occurred to investigating specific examples of interaction and how they related to the needs and beliefs of people at the time. Moreover, when the coming together of cultures is viewed as *within* rather than *outside* the norm, it grounds cultural interaction as an important part of the equation in understanding artistic development in Islamicate South Asia without foregrounding it as the cause and effect of all such development. Abandoning a dualistic approach to Indo-Islamicate art allows for the consideration of multifaceted social constructions and historical circumstances, and enables other questions, such as how painting and architecture contribute to the formation of dynastic identity, to rise to the surface.

Courtly Identity

The question of courtly identity shares with cultural interaction the thematic core of this book. Under the category of "court," I include the Adil Shahi royal family (men and women), nobles, administrators, and even the court artisans, who although typically low in standing, depended on the dynastic elite for their success and played central roles in creating representations of the court. The adjective *courtly* refers to various aspects of collective life at court, including the architectural environment of the capital city and newly acquired paintings and illustrated manuscripts that would have been shared with one's courtly companions but also the latest fashions in dress, popular poems and literary references, and knowledge of recently won (or lost) battles, economic conditions, and political intrigues, to name a few things. Courtly identity thus can be defined as the cultural (including artistic) practices and vocabularies, priorities and visions, as well as memories shared and shaped by the various groups listed above.

The comprehensiveness of the definition allows for consideration of a variety of people involved in the artistic process, not only patrons and artists but also intermediary figures such as the head of the *kitabkhane* (book workshop), who most likely oversaw the various artists, calligraphers, papermakers, and other artisans involved in the production of illustrated manuscripts. One intermediary figure repeatedly referenced in discussions of architecture by Bijapur's court historians is the *sar-i kar,* or supervisor of construction, typically a high-ranking noble appointed to oversee large-scale royal projects. Viewing the art as the product of a courtly environment allows the sar-i kar and other significant but often overlooked figures to be included in the analysis. It also brings into account the intended audience of the works, which typically included other members of the court. While a wide range of people viewed and benefited from very public monuments such as city walls and congregational mosques, a large amount of the art, particularly paintings, had a much more select audience. The courtly model includes the primary viewers of such artworks in any analysis and therefore is able to address the creation and the reception of both images and monuments.

Furthermore, incorporating all of the participants into the equation and thereby emphasizing the art as a joint effort of many people rather than the single vision of one person avoids an overemphasis on Ibrahim II (or any other ruler). While the sultan as the head of the court had an important, perhaps the most important, role in artistic development, he was only one factor in a larger courtly environment. As John Seyller has observed, the focus on Ibrahim II and his personality, particularly in regard to the development of painting, has become overly common (surely a practice related to the historiomachy phenomenon observed by Ernst). Making use of the comparative wealth of information on Ibrahim and his personality, scholars frequently credit Ibrahim's interest in poetry and music for the lyrical and melancholic character found in many Bijapuri paintings, even in cases when the work's patronage is unknown. In a similar manner, discussions of Mughal painting often link the lively and energetic personality of the emperor Akbar with the content and style of painting during his reign (1556–1605), but in this case, scholarship has begun to complicate the analysis. As Seyller explains, "Some recent studies . . . assign

Akbar a primarily initiatory role, citing workshop instructions and schedules as evidence of many levels of authority between imperial patron and artist."[55] Although we lack detailed evidence such as workshop schedules and artists' instructions for Bijapuri painting, we can assume a similar situation existed in the sultanate, with Ibrahim II and other royal patrons playing initiatory roles within a larger network of individuals involved in the process.

Again looking toward recent studies of Islamicate and Indic art for models, we find that scholars have begun to recognize the substantial roles played by nobles and female members of royal families. Such individuals were significant patrons, not merely mimicking the artistic patronage of the ruler but also shaping the character of the kingdom's art.[56] The ruler may have been a consequential patron, but he was far from being the only one. These conclusions can be equally applied to Bijapuri art, for which there is tangible evidence that nobles and wives of the sultans were important patrons.

Finally, and perhaps most crucially, analyzing Bijapuri art from the perspective of courtly identity fits the surviving evidence. Typically, in studies of Islamicate and South Asian art, the practice is to identify the patron, artist, and specific historical circumstances of the object's creation, locate as much information as possible regarding them, and analyze the work's appearance with this information in mind. While this is a fruitful way to understand an artwork within its original context, this approach often is not viable with regard to Bijapuri art, which therefore demands another avenue of analysis. The existing material regarding Bijapuri art is fragmentary; we lack the names and identities of most of the court artists, and often it is impossible to date a work more precisely than to within a quarter of a century. And while we have helpful information regarding patronage, we in fact know less than some discussions make it seem, as authors tend to assume Ibrahim II was the patron of most of the surviving art datable to his reign. In cases when the patron, artists, and precise dates of the work are not known or when the information is questionable, however, we can still safely analyze the art if we place it within its larger courtly context. This context does not rely on knowledge of a particular individual or historical event but rather develops out of our sum knowledge of Adil Shahi Bijapur; therefore, the model allows us to work with the optimal surviving evidence while acknowledging the existing gaps in our information.

At least one member of the Adil Shahi court appears to have viewed art explicitly through the lens of courtly identity and political power. Between 1608 and 1612, the Persian émigré and author Rafi uddin Shirazi (who served both Ali Adil Shah I and Ibrahim II) wrote a history of

Bijapur titled *Tazkira al-Mulk* (Memorial of kings). Toward the end of this work, Shirazi provides a fascinating account of the rock-cut monuments at Ellora, which he visited while serving as ambassador to Bijapur's northern neighbor, the kingdom of Ahmadnagar.[57] Visitors have long celebrated the remarkable sculpture enlivening all thirty-four Hindu, Jain, and Buddhist cave temples constructed at the site of Ellora between approximately 600 and 1000 CE, of which the monumental Kailasa Temple, intended as a representation of the Hindu god Shiva's home, Mount Kailasa, is perhaps the most famous. As Carl Ernst explains in his translation and analysis of Shirazi's description, the Muslim historian did not view the site in terms of religion or express shock at the numerous "idols" carved into the stone, but rather lavishly praised Ellora, which he saw in wholly political terms. He credited the legendary ruler Parchand Rao as commissioning the work so that it would be a permanent and famed memorial to his kingdom. As Ernst writes, "For [Shirazi], Ellora is a royal monument that depicts the court life of an ancient king of India, making it comparable to pre-Islamic Persian monuments such as Persepolis."[58] In fact, Shirazi interpreted the rock-cut temples and shrines as palaces, forts, and other court buildings, "things such as bachelor quarters, goldsmith shop, fountain shop, wardrobe, treasury, and the like." He perceived a carved figure of Shiva not as an image of a god but as a royal portrait. In a similar manner, he assumed that various other images of gods and their attendants were "servants, friends, and relatives, each in the proper places," as well as watchmen, musicians, athletes, swordsmen, and a multitude of other figures that one might find in attendance at court.[59] Indeed, Shirazi's description could easily fit the courtly environment of a Deccan Islamic kingdom from the seventeenth century or those of his homeland, Iran. Clearly Shirazi was interpreting Ellora from his own vantage point, and his perspective seems to have centered on courtly environments and monumental artworks consciously constructed to mark the wealth, prosperity, and good governance of a kingdom. Thus it seems entirely appropriate to view the art of the kingdom to which he belonged as operating in a similar light.

Two primary factors affecting Bijapur's courtly identity and its visual expression underlay all the others: the constant warfare that Bijapur faced and the legacy of the Bahmani dynasty. From its start in 1490, the sultanate came into conflict on all sides: from the weakening Bahmani dynasty, from the newly formed neighboring Bahmani splinter states of Golconda, Ahmadnagar, Bidar, and Berar, from the large and wealthy kingdom of Vijayanagara, and from the Portuguese at Goa. Bijapur would remain in an almost continuous state of warfare with one or more of these neighbors, as well as other powers, throughout most of its existence, until its ultimate defeat by the Mughals in 1686. Internal conflicts, notably between the Afaqi and Deccani factions at court, only served to amplify the environment of conflict and instability. Alliance and betrayal were common, with nobles frequently moving from one Deccan sultanate to another.

As the kingdoms surrounding Bijapur gradually fell or became unstable, more and more émigrés arrived at Bijapur and took up residence at court. Many had fled more than one location on their way to Bijapur. For example, as the economic and political environment in Safavid Iran became increasingly inhospitable, several of Bijapur's Persian court historians first sought refuge and employment at the court of Ahmadnagar. Then as Ahmadnagar's situation became more precarious (the kingdom fell to the Mughals in 1600–1601), the men moved south to Bijapur. All of this served to create a religiously, linguistically, and ethnically diverse nobility (made up of not only Afaqis and Deccanis but also local Hindu nobles) that was constantly shifting and frequently operating in an atmosphere of instability and conflict.

The other factor providing a strong foundation for the development of an Adil Shahi courtly identity was Bijapur's relationship to the earlier Bahmani dynasty. The Bahmani kingdom had lasted for 150 years and had covered a large area of land in central and south India; moreover, it had developed a potent administrative and cultural power base. Adil Shahi Bijapur, inheriting many Bahmani political and cultural legacies, was a successor dynasty in every sense of the term. Bijapur's court life reflects several Bahmani elements such as the split between Afaqi and Deccani courtiers as well as the reliance upon Maharashtran Brahmins and Marathi-speaking soldiers in the administration and army.

Perhaps the most crucial Bahmani legacy was the strong link between local Sufi saints and political legitimacy. Sufism, or Islamic mysticism, was popular in the Deccan with Hindus and Muslims alike. The Bahmani dynasty strengthened its power base by drawing on the support of Sufi saints revered by the local population. The rulers offered endowments in the form of villages, stipends, or buildings to the saints and their followers. In turn, the Sufis gave the rulers their endorsement, thus increasing popular support for the kingdom.[60] The Adil Shahis and their nobles followed this practice in Bijapur, fostering new links while continuing to build up and support saints' shrines associated with the Bahmani dynasty.[61] In this manner, the Adil Shahis were able to draw on the power of the Sufis as well as the legitimacy of the earlier Bahmani dynasty. Because Sufis were critically involved in the development of local languages, such as Deccani Urdu, and the corresponding literature, Sufism became central to the Adil Shahis' courtly culture on a number of levels.

The Adil Shahis' attitude toward the Bahmani dynasty was not always straightforward; it frequently fluctuated between conscious acts of linkage and rejection. For example, Bijapur's founder, Yusuf Adil Khan, declared Shiism the official religion, boldly marking his separation from the Sunni kingdom, yet he never formally declared independence from the Bahmanis. Although he had the *khutba*, or Friday prayer, read in his name as an act of autonomy, he—as well as his next two successors—retained the title of "Khan," a term used to refer to high-ranking Muslim officials in Central and South Asian courts. Bijapur's rulers did not take up the imperial title "Shah," meaning "king," until the Bahmani kingdom had completely ended in 1538, demonstrating that the Adil Shahis recognized the Bahmanis' lingering prestige.[62] This same dualism carried on into the Adil Shahis' relationships with the other Bahmani splinter states. Like siblings, the Deccan sultanates alternately squabbled and aligned together, reinforced their dependency and declared their separateness. All of this not only factored into Bijapur's courtly identity but also served to increase the importance of fostering a distinctively Adil Shahi identity.

Bijapuri art arose out of the post-Bahmani Deccan environment, and the art in turn shaped—and continues to shape—perceptions of Islamicate culture in the Deccan. A close study of Bijapuri visual remains can deepen our understanding of the ways in which intercultural exchange and identity formation operated in the region and in South Asia more generally. Our view of the art, however, is filtered through colonial interest in Bijapur, including deeply held notions of Hindu/Muslim interaction. The connoisseurship issues surrounding much of Bijapuri art and the gaps in the surviving evidence further affect our present understanding, yet in many ways these matters add to the richness of the surviving art. Works such as the Ibrahim Rauza or Chester Beatty yogini are potent not only because they are visually appealing but also because they force us to look anew at our approaches to art history and remind us of the multiplicity of meanings and influences embedded in artworks. Bijapuri art drew on Sufism, literary trends, poetic metaphors, Hindu religious practices, local Indic imagery, and Persianate royal traditions, among other things. Its development simultaneously responded to both the economic prosperity and political instability of the early modern Deccan, while individual artworks related to the needs and capabilities of specific patrons and artists, at the same time that they fostered a collective courtly culture.

Ultimately, courtly identity seems to have been the primary factor affecting the how and why of artistic development in Adil Shahi Bijapur. Bijapur's nobility was both diverse (its diversity encompassing religion, ethnicity, and language) and constantly shifting. Courtiers frequently changed alliance, moving from one sultanate to the next. The Deccan kingdoms, in turn, variously formed coalitions and engaged in battle with one another. Undoubtedly, in such an inconstant, conflict-ridden environment, it became crucial to foster a courtly culture that would simultaneously create a distinct identity for Bijapur distinguishing the kingdom from its neighbors, bind the nobility together, and allow the individual members to demonstrate their allegiance to the court, while promoting themselves within it. Art was only one part of this elite culture, but it played a central role by materializing, and thus communicating and codifying, a shared identity.

2
Prosperous Beginnings

Surviving visual evidence indicates that artistic output at the Adil Shahi court increased markedly in the late 1560s and early 1570s. Almost no pre-1570s Bijapuri painting survives; a fragment of a 1560s astrology manuscript in the Jagdish and Kamla Mittal Museum of Indian Art, Hyderabad, provides one of the few known examples. Yet there are at least six illustrated manuscripts or fragments thereof datable to the early 1570s.[1] Bijapur's architecture experienced a similarly timed expansion in construction. While examples of Adil Shahi buildings exist from the dynasty's beginnings in the late fifteenth and early sixteenth centuries, such early architectural works are modest and few in number. Attempts to enhance the urban environment on a more monumental level do not seem to have begun until the 1540s, and then they accelerated considerably in the mid- to late 1560s.

The seeming suddenness of the increased artistic production during the late 1560s and 1570s, corresponding with the latter half of Ali Adil Shah I's reign, begs the question of what happened. What change or changes occurred to cause this upsurge? Bijapur's victory over Vijayanagara in the 1565 battle of Talikota, the single event for which Ali's reign is most remembered, may seem like the obvious catalyst and, indeed, the military triumph played a key role in the sultanate's flourishing. However, Bijapur's emergence as an artistic center was directly related to the 1565–68 building campaign of Bijapur city carried out by Ali and his courtiers and the accompanying shift in the Adil Shahis' attitude toward their capital, evident in works such as Ali Adil Shah's circa 1580 tomb and the *Nujum al-*

Ulum, an original manuscript on kingship, astrology, and magic dated to 1570–71.

Ali, like the Adil Shahis before him, spent a good deal of his reign battling against various neighbors. What distinguishes Ali from his predecessors is that he achieved more military successes than they did. Shortly after coming to power in 1558, the sultan took several actions: he changed the state religion back to Shia Islam, welcomed Afaqi nobles at court, and formed a close alliance with the ruler of Vijayanagara, Ramraj. Ali even visited Ramraj to pay his condolences after the death of the raja's son. This association with Vijayangara led to a successful three-year war, from 1559 to 1561, against Bijapur's northern neighbor, the Nizam Shahs of Ahmadnagar. From the victory Ali gained the Sholapur and Naldrug hill forts and secured Bijapur's northern border. Eventually, however, in search of political betterment, Ali abandoned his alliance with Ramraj and joined a coalition of Deccan sultans, including the Qutb Shah ruler of Golconda and the Nizam Shah ruler of Ahmadnagar, against Vijayanagara. In 1565 they defeated the powerful southern state and killed Ramraj at the battle of Talikota.

The victory was the most significant of Ali's reign not only because he helped defeat the large and wealthy kingdom of Vijayanagara, securing his southern border, but also because Ali managed to obtain the best portion of the victory spoils for his sultanate. In particular, Bijapur gained the Raichur Doab, the region between the Krishna and Tungabhadra rivers rich in iron deposits, diamond mines, and fertile black soil in which cotton was grown for export. These resources provided Bijapur with major sources of income. For example, the kingdom and its merchants, with the aid of a 180-ship trading fleet constructed during Ali's reign, exported the cotton to various points around the Arabian Sea.[2] Although it took another eleven years to consolidate his power in the Raichur Doab, in the first seven years of his reign, Ali doubled the size of his kingdom (map 1). Its revenue also grew considerably, as did its army and civil bureaucracy, in turn increasing the control of the central government based in Bijapur city.[3] Although fighting, including an unsuccessful war with the Portuguese, continued after 1565, Bijapur was now wealthier and more secure than ever before.

In *The Venture of Islam,* Marshall Hodgson states, "While prosperity cannot assure cultural creativity, in the long run it is a presupposition for it."[4] Were urban enhancements, manuscript production, and other examples of "cultural creativity" only possible after Bijapur's wealth and standing reached a significant level? Was it the newfound prosperity and security brought about by Ali's military victories that led to Bijapur's artistic blossoming? Undoubtedly the 1565 victory and the subsequent political and economic boons transformed the kingdom, significantly augmenting its ability to undertake monumental artistic endeavors; however, this was only part of the equation. An analysis of the 1565–68 building campaign of Bijapur city carried out by Ali Adil Shah and his nobles demonstrates that how Ali and his nobles made use of their newfound prosperity proved to be as important as the prosperity itself to the kingdom's artistic development. Notably, the building campaign of Bijapur city, which was undertaken directly after the victory and which included the construction of city walls, waterworks, gardens, and a community mosque, transferred Bijapur's new affluence into a physical, tangible, and long-lasting form. In the process it established the urban environment necessary to promote cultural innovations. These physical changes occurred in tandem with an important shift in the Adil Shahi family's attitude toward their capital city—the two, dynasty and capital, becoming more closely linked. The shift is perhaps most evident in the location of Ali Adil Shah I's tomb, which was the first Adil Shahi mausoleum built at the capital. The newly enlarged kingdom, army, and administration all required effective rule, and these needs provided strong impetus for the development of visual forms that would aid in expressing, sustaining, and augmenting Bijapur's power. With its rich text and plentiful illustrations, the *Nujum al-Ulum* provides a multifaceted example of a work created with such objectives in mind.

In addition to illuminating the reasons behind Bijapur's artistic blossoming, when taken together, the building campaign of Bijapur, Ali's tomb, and the *Nujum al-Ulum* demonstrate the range of forms that the art took at this early stage in its development as well as how closely linked artistic production was to the court as a whole, not just the sultan. Moreover, they indicate the importance of the period to Bijapur's later art. The period between 1565 and 1580 not only marked the beginning of Bijapur's artistic flourishing, but the art created at the time also provided the foundation, in some cases literally, upon which subsequent Bijapuri art was conceived. Themes, motifs, practices, and urban patterns first developed during this period provided the focus of, and guidelines for, later painting and architecture, though expressed in increasingly elaborate and refined forms over the following decades.

The Building Campaign of Bijapur

Directly following their victory over Vijayanagara, Ali and his nobles embarked upon an immense building campaign. Between 1565 and 1568, they completed a massive six and a quarter mile wall around the capital of Bijapur, a system of underground canals and tanks to provide the city with water, and the foundation of three gardens.[5] Additionally, they began construction of Bijapur's monumental *jami masjid* (community or Friday mosque), the largest mosque in the Deccan. Although each of the four components could be considered a consequential task on its own, the court clearly conceived the works as one vast building campaign intended to dramatically restructure the urban environment of Bijapur.

It is evident that Ali and his nobles viewed the projects as a single monumental campaign because that is how the surviving dynastic histories present it. Firishta, Shirazi, and Astarabadi, three Persian émigrés to Bijapur during the late sixteenth and early seventeenth centuries, each wrote detailed histories of the Adil Shahi dynasty.[6] These accounts, which describe political intrigues at length, are for the most part either disappointingly vague or silent about the many artistic developments that took place throughout Adil Shahi rule. A notable exception is the building campaign, which the historians discuss in detail as a single event. Their accounts not only provide information about the project but, by doing so, they also make it clear that it was deemed momentous at the time. The author, Zubairi, also writing in Persian, based his 1811 history of Bijapur, *Basatinu's Salatin,* on these and other dynastic records, providing a useful compilation of Adil Shahi histories. Notably, Zubairi devotes an entire chapter to the building campaign, which he entitled "When Ali Adil Shah commanded the building of Bijapur's city walls with Qishur Khan as supervisor and the building of the jami masjid and the bringing of water into the city."[7] When the information in the seventeenth-century histories and Zubairi's nineteenth-century compilation of them are combined with travelers' descriptions of the city and the surviving architectural evidence, a clear picture of the building campaign's extensive scope and effect emerges.

Exploring the appearance of the city before the project further highlights the impact of the new construction. Bijapur is located on a basalt plateau consisting of a series of small depressions and rises that form a corrugated pattern on the mostly flat landscape, affording no natural protection to the city. The land is arid; the city's nearest major source of water is the Ramling River, running west of Bijapur, near the village of Torveh.[8] When Yusuf Adil Khan, the Bahmani governor of Bijapur province, rebelled in 1490, the city of Bijapur became his capital. He had mud walls built around the citadel, which presumably functioned as the center of the city's power in earlier times as well. The citadel, which is less than a mile in circumference and only a quarter of a mile in diameter, sits in a depression in the landscape rather than on a hill, as was common for defensive purposes.[9] Some sort of stone wall replaced Yusuf's humble mud one in 1493, but the citadel was not completely fortified until the reign of Ibrahim Adil Shah I. In 1546 he had a double wall and moat built (pl. 1).[10] At about the same time, Ibrahim replaced the old jami masjid, a modest structure of rubble construction built by Ismail Adil Khan in 1512, with a new mosque in the southwestern part of the city.[11] Ibrahim's mosque, with a triple-arched façade, two tall minarets, and no dome, is larger than the first mosque, but still small by contemporary standards for a Friday mosque.

It is difficult to establish the exact size of the city during the fifteenth and sixteenth centuries, but clearly it was expanding. A mercantile suburb, located northwest of the citadel on a hill near the Ramling River, was established in 1510 (map 2). Firishta states that in 1557 Ali Adil Shah named this suburb Shahpur in honor of the fact that he was crowned shah (king) there when returning to the city to claim the throne after his father's death.[12] Shahpur continued to be developed as a center for merchants and traders throughout Ali's reign.

From the beginning, Ali worked on enhancing his capital city. In 1560–61 Ali commissioned the Gagan Mahal, a two-story stone-and-timber audience hall facing onto a water tank in the northern part of the citadel, as the architectural centerpiece of his court (pl. 1).[13] To the left of the Gagan Mahal, Ali's workmen constructed a monumental entranceway, adorned with stone-carved lions and salutary inscriptions in Persian such as one reading, "May this threshold ever remain open in wealth and prosperity" (fig. 2.1).[14]

In a letter to the Provincial of the Jesuits in Goa, the Portuguese colony to Bijapur's west, the traveler Gomcalo Rodriguez describes the conditions of Bijapur city and citadel at the time of his visit in 1561. The Portuguese visitor recounts entering the royal palace area through a very rich portal "newly made by this king" and decorated with inscriptions in Persian, clearly referring to Ali's monumental gateway. From there he and his companions reached a terrace consisting of a garden and a large tank with waterspouts. Three palace buildings, one of which he calls the treasury (presumably referring to the Gagan Mahal) surrounded the terrace. From Rodriguez's description, it seems that there were already some sort of waterworks in Bijapur, as he states that the moat surrounding the citadel was filled with water from afar brought in by pipes. Overall, however, Rodriguez gives the citadel and its royal buildings only a mediocre review. He admits that they were "very rich" and "built in the fashion of the Moors," but he concludes, "Without any doubt those of the king of Ormuz or of king Ra'is Sharaf are better."[15]

His assessment of the citadel is kind, however, in comparison to his sharp criticisms of the rest of the city, which he describes as teeming with people but not built up. "This city of Bijapur is bigger than the one of Goa, but does not have 10 houses that are worthwhile, nor good streets nor planning. Many of these people live in small tents, torn and old."[16] Of course, as a Portuguese visitor to one of Goa's rivals, Rodriguez would have been predisposed to view Bijapur in a negative light or at least to record it that way in a letter to a Goan official. His comments relate his

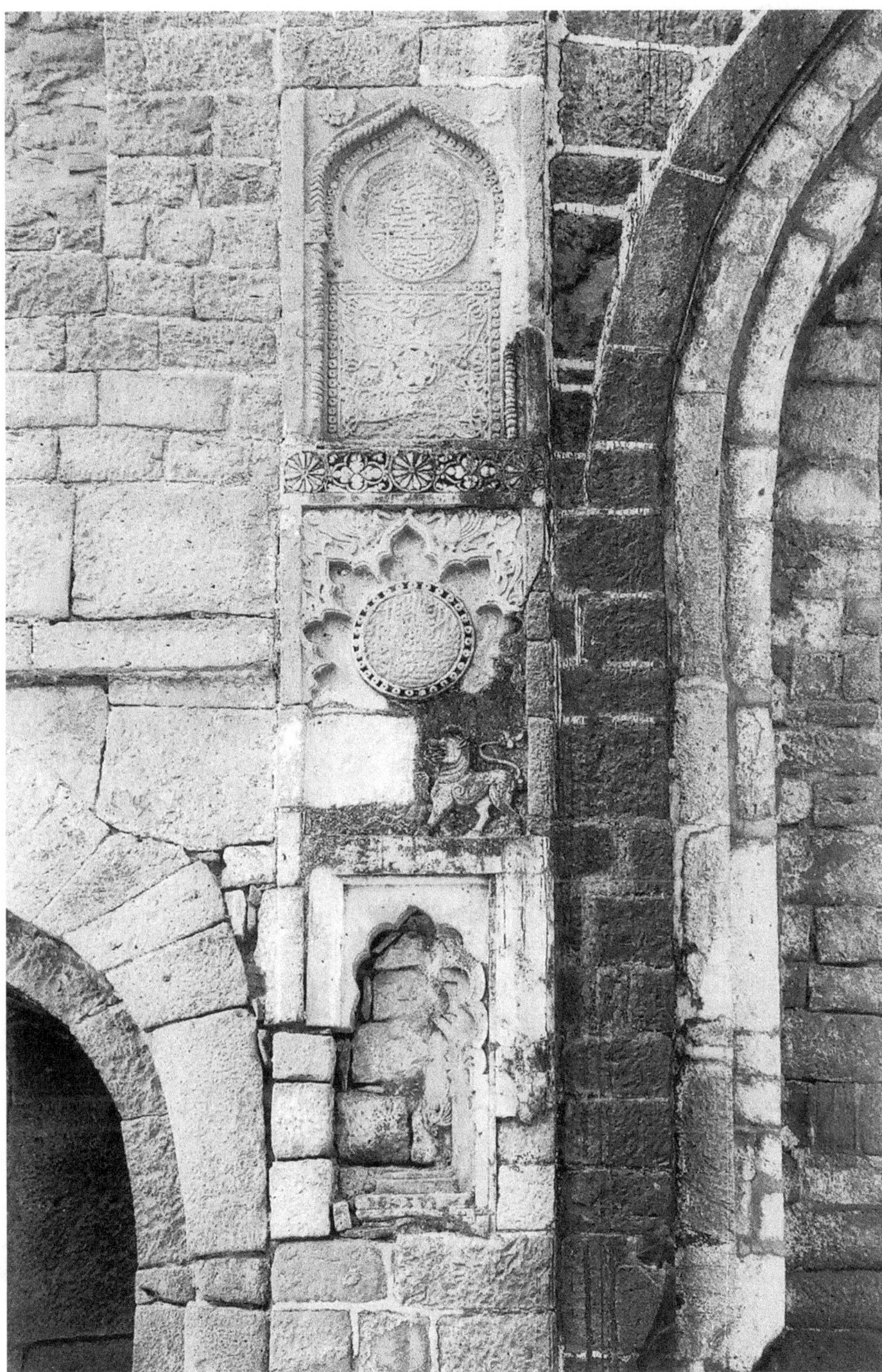

Figure 2.1. Detail of the stone-carved ornament from the entranceway to the citadel, 1560–61, as placed after nineteenth-century conversion into the All Saints Church, Bijapur. Photograph by author.

own political position as much as Bijapur's physical appearance. Yet much of what he records corresponds with what we know of Bijapur's state from other sources, written and architectural. At the time of his visit, the city was not walled, with only the small area inside the citadel affording protection from invading armies. Many of the nobles lived outside the city, and when they were in the city, they stayed in tents inside walled gardens, presumably within or near the citadel area.[17] Thus from Rodriguez's description and the surviving architectural evidence, it appears that by the early 1560s Bijapur was a populous provincial center, but one with little infrastructure to support it and only a few architectural monuments to distinguish it. By the end of Ali's reign, however, even Rodriguez would have had to admit that the situation had improved considerably.

Bijapur may have remained architecturally neglected for the first part of the dynasty because the early rulers did not see themselves as independent kings, as truly separate from the Bahmani dynasty. Indeed, Yusuf and his successors called themselves Adil Khan rather than Adil Shah (Khan was an epithet used by nobles as well as local rulers, while Shah was reserved specifically for rulers). Ali's father Ibrahim I adopted the title Shah only in the mid-1540s when the Bahmani dynasty finally ended. Perhaps the Adil Khans and their courtiers did not view Bijapur as an exalted capital to be built up in the same manner as Bidar or Gulbarga, the Bahmani capital cities. Certainly it is not coincidental that the wall around the citadel and the new mosque were built at exactly the same point that Ibrahim I began calling himself Adil Shah rather than Adil Khan.[18] Of course, the constant warfare with neighboring powers, shifting boundaries of the kingdom, and resulting instability for the first eighty years must have made extensive building difficult. Moreover, the lack of walls around the city undoubtedly discouraged building activity outside of the citadel, which offered the only area of protection and security.

Bijapur gained much wealth, stability, land, and status after the 1565 victory over Vijayanagara, and these changes undoubtedly facilitated the undertaking of the 1565–68 building campaign. The rapid population growth of Bijapur city after the victory, because of the increased army and administrative system, as well as immigrants arriving from neighboring kingdoms less secure than Bijapur, necessitated the architectural development of the city. Astarabadi and Zubairi both begin their accounts of the building campaign by explaining, "When Ali Adil Shah had obtained a spacious kingdom and the best army of all, many people from all parts of the world journeyed to the court of this king."[19] Both historians call Bijapur *shahar-i pana,* "the city of refuge." They go on to explain that although Bijapur was more secure than the surrounding kingdoms, the threat of invasion still existed, and so it was decided to construct city walls. For this important task, begun in 1565 and finished less than two

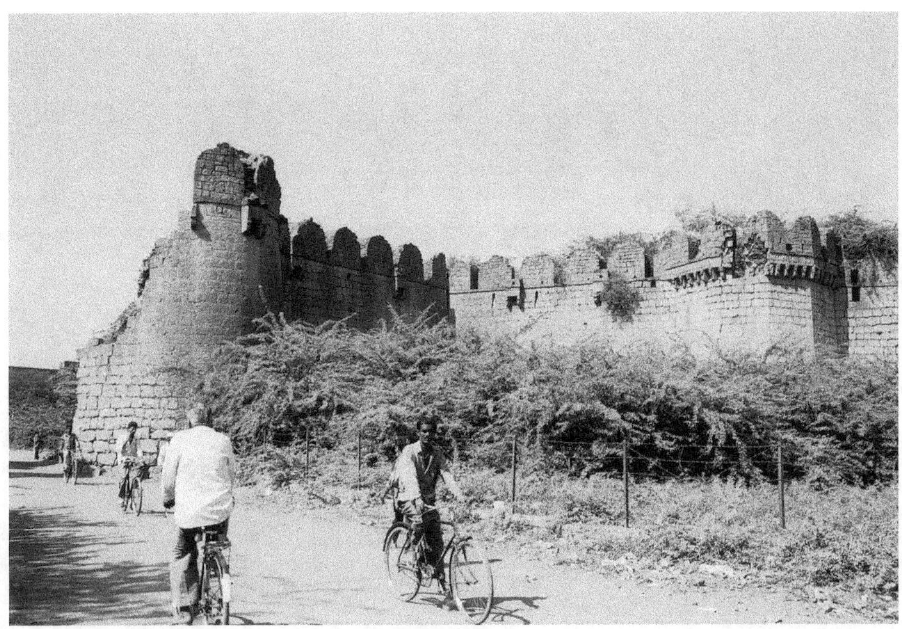

Figure 2.2. City walls, 1565–68, Bijapur. Photograph by author.

and a half years later, "expert builders and sculptors were recruited from all sides."[20]

The resulting walls, six and a quarter miles in circumference with ninety-six bastions and five gateways, are impressive (fig. 2.2). They encompass an area of about two and a half square miles and form an irregular ellipse with the older citadel at the center (map 3). Major roadways connected the older citadel with each of the five new gates (fig. 2.3): the Mecca Darwaza on the west side, the Shahpur Darwaza at the northwest corner, the Bahmani Darwaza on the north side, the Allahpur Darwaza to the east, and the Fateh Darwaza, also called the Mangoli Darwaza, at the southeast corner.[21] The ninety-six bastions are semicircular in plan, and the distance between each ranges between 50 and 130 yards. Additional bastions flank each of the five gateways. The curtain walls between the bastions vary in height from thirty to fifty feet, with an average thickness of twenty feet.[22] A platform, protected by a battlemented breastwall, runs around the top of the whole wall and once held the lighter cannons and guns, while heavier armaments were placed on the bastions (fig. 2.4). Finally, a moat, approximately forty to fifty feet wide (no longer extant), surrounded and further fortified the walls.

In addition to their strength, the walls are notable for the speed with which they were completed and the variations in height and width that add character to the walls' overall appearance. These features directly

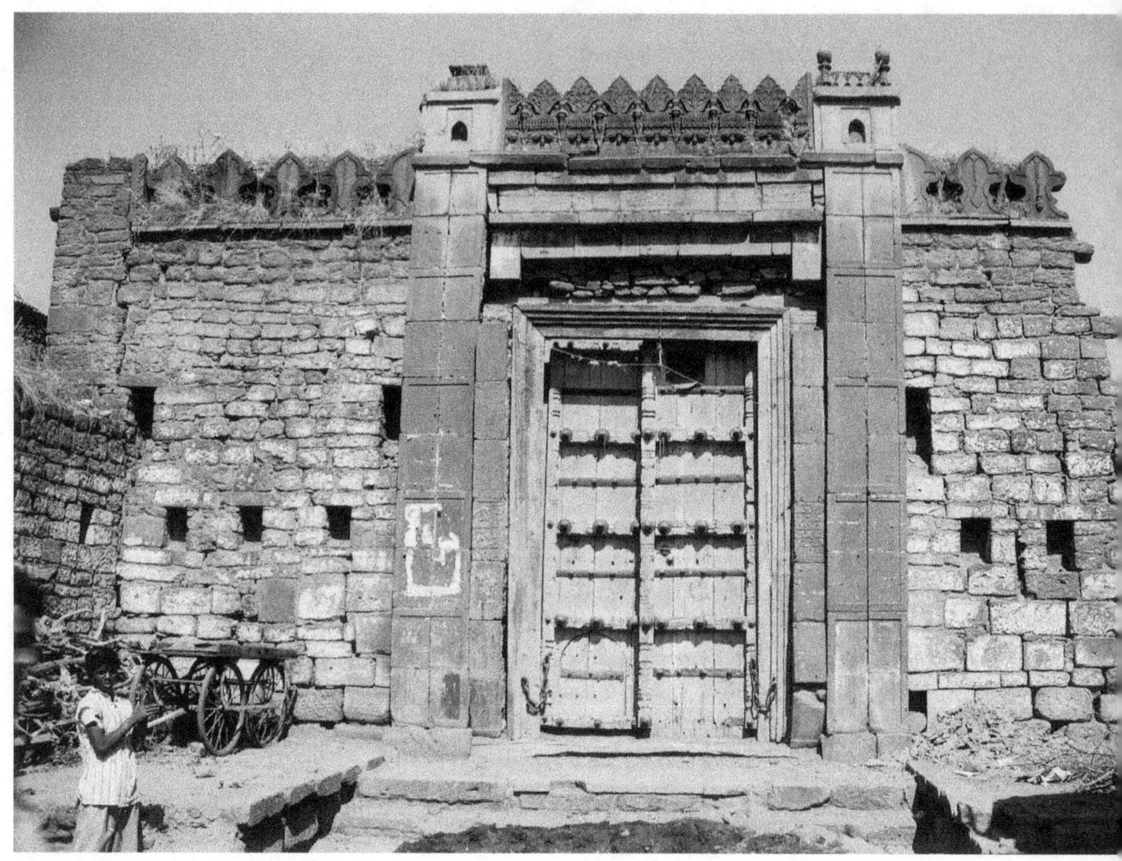

Figure 2.3. Gateway, 1565–68, Bijapur. Photograph by author.

resulted from the patronage system under which they were constructed. Zubairi writes that each noble of the court was responsible for building a portion of the curtain wall and the corresponding bastions.[23] A few surviving inscriptions on the gateways indicated that nobles were put in charge of building those as well. For example, an inscription over the inner gate of the Shahpur Gateway states that it was constructed "by the efforts of the great Khan Murad Khan, the Ghazi, the minister of finance." Other inscriptions list the courtiers Pandi Nand Ji and Baghrash Khan as patrons of various wall segments.[24] The variety in the walls' appearance indicates that the nobles and their workmen had some degree of independence. Yet the synchronization of the wall segments, the gates, the surrounding moat, and the battlemented platform dictated careful planning as well. In order to coordinate the project, Ali appointed his vizier, Qishur Khan, to act as *sar-i kar,* "head of the work," or supervisor of construction.[25]

The patronage system chosen was effective. Not only did it guarantee quick and sound construction of the walls, but it also spread out the

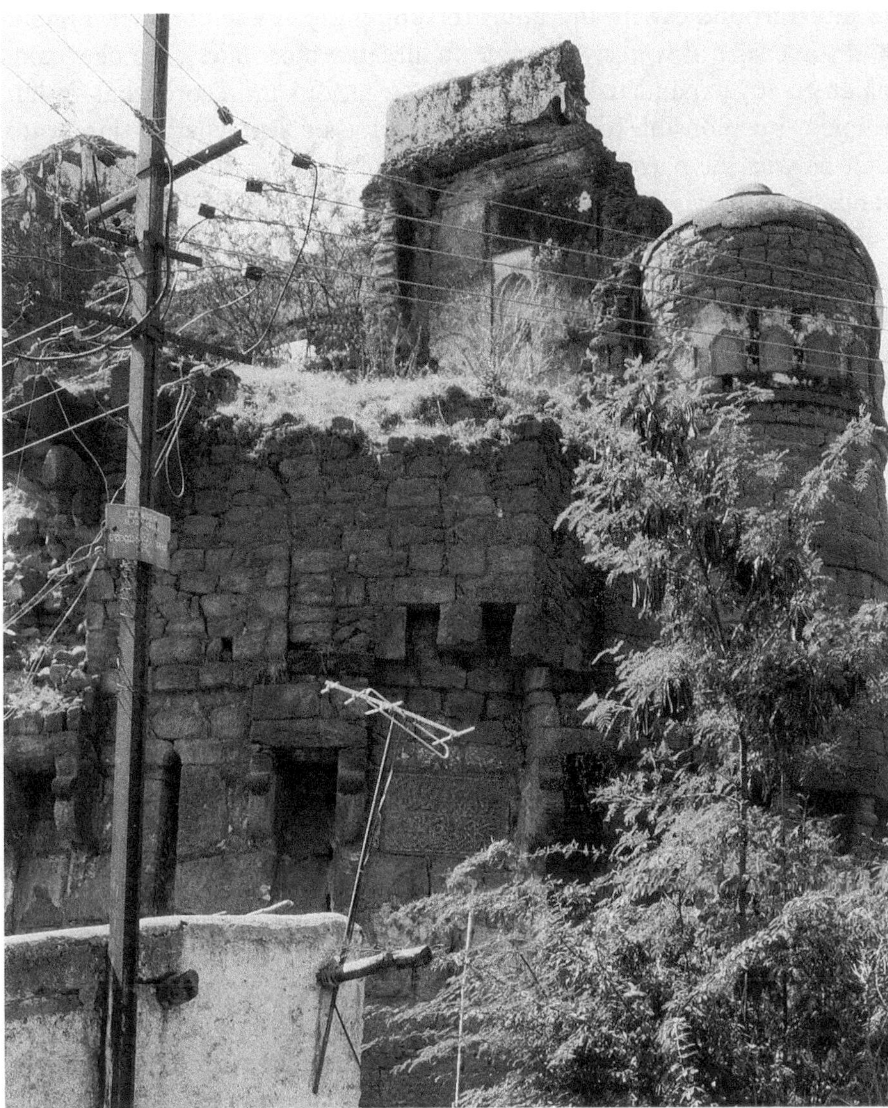

Figure 2.4. Bastion, 1565–68, Bijapur. Photograph by author.

building expenses. At the same time, asking nobles to patronize wall segments bestowed honor upon them by allowing them to demonstrate their rank at court. Furthermore, building the walls figuratively bound the nobility to the Adil Shahi capital. They now had considerable investment in the economic and political welfare of the city as well as in its architectural growth. Indeed, after the completion of the walls, many of the nobles built palace and garden complexes within the city, taking advantage of the city's new security, adding to its urban environment, and linking themselves to it even further.[26]

The second stage of the building campaign involved the construction of underground canals and tanks to supply the city with water. Bijapur had some sort of waterworks system already; most likely, the new campaign greatly expanded the existing structure. Zubairi records that Qishur Khan was responsible for the waterworks. It is unclear whether this means that he was the patron, paying for the construction out of his personal funds, the supervisor of the project, as he was for the city walls, the designer/engineer of the system, or some combination of the above. Certainly the project, essentially a variant of the *qanat,* a type of subterranean aqueduct system whose design originated in the Iranian highlands around 500 BCE, was expensive, complicated, and must have involved a large number of people.[27] Workers built a masonry dam near Torveh, a village west of Bijapur, in order to create a combination lake/large tank fed by the Ramling River (map 2). From there they dug a three-mile underground channel to carry the water into the city. In some places the channel reached sixty feet below ground, with periodic shafts connecting the channel to the surface. At the city walls, the canal split into two parts, one of which supplied the western part of the city while the other went southeast to supply the citadel moat and, eventually, the new jami masjid (map 3).[28] Workers dug the underground canal out of the basalt stone forming the plateau and, when necessary, also lined it with bricks. The density of the basalt rock allowed the water to be carried over the long distances without it being absorbed into the ground, while simultaneously helping to keep the water clean, elements appreciated by the Persian historians who greatly praise both the purity and constant supply of water.[29]

In his study of Iranian cities, Heinz Gaube stresses the significance of the qanat to the settlement pattern and social structure of medieval Central Asian cities. Both their construction and maintenance were costly, so only the rich and prospering communities could afford them. Once built, they became a primary determinant of later settlement patterns in the area.[30] This proved true in Bijapur as well. Although already existing structures such as the citadel and its moat influenced the paths of the canals through the city, the new canals then determined the location of subsequent monuments. For example, the Ibrahim Rauza, built in 1626, sits directly on the path of the channel as it comes from Torveh, just before it reaches the city walls and splits into two. The mosque and tomb of the saint Ali Shahid Pir, the Mihtar-i Mahal mosque, and the Anda mosque all are situated on or very near the channel leading to the jami masjid. Nobles placed their palace and garden complexes near the channels as well. The gateway to the courtier Mustafa Khan's complex, built about 1581, is just north of the Mihtar-i Mahal and jami masjid. The walled enclosure of Mustafa Khan, no longer extant, contained palace buildings, gardens, a mosque, and a large square tank fed by the canal.[31]

Not only the upper classes benefited from the waterworks. The second stage of the post-1565 building campaign included the construction of a large tank, called Hauz-i Shahpur, in the suburb of Shahpur, which was connected to the newly walled city by a large road leading to the Shahpur Darwaza.[32] The water from the tank presumably supplied not only the local inhabitants' needs but also those of the *caravan serais* (inns) and *hammams* (baths) built for the travelers who frequented the mercantile suburb. In fact, Zubairi credits the new building project with an increase in the prosperity of Shahpur. He claims that during this period merchandise from all parts of the world could be found there.[33]

The third stage of the building campaign involved laying out three gardens inside the city. These gardens, according to the historians, were named the Alawi Bagh, the Bagh-i Ali, and the Dwazdah Imam. The last garden also was known as the Bagh-i Darwaza because it was built near the Mecca Darwaza, the gateway on the west side of the city.[34] Unfortunately, no physical evidence of the gardens remains. Thus, apart from the Dwazdah Imam, whose name records its location in the western section of the city, the precise sites of the gardens are uncertain. Likewise, the gardens' appearances and sizes are unknown. We can assume, however, that the gardens were generally located in the southwest section of the city. One of the newly built channels fed that section of the city, and water would have been necessary to supply the many fountains and plants adorning the gardens. Even today local inhabitants consider the southwest part of the city the section of gardens and graves. The Persian historians record that the gardens took years to mature, but eventually were filled with a variety of vines, flowers, and plants. Then, thanks to the gardens and the constant supply of fresh water, the air of Bijapur reached "a state of perfection."[35]

The construction—or rather, the start of construction, as it was never completed—of a new, monumental jami masjid (fig. 2.5), replacing the older and smaller mosque built by Ibrahim Adil Shah I, concluded the building campaign.[36] The new congregational mosque, located in the southeast quarter of the city, remains the largest religious structure in the Deccan.[37] It is also the only mosque in Bijapur to be built on the orthodox hypostyle plan consisting of an open courtyard enclosed by walls with a sanctuary on the west side and arcades on the remaining sides (fig. 2.6). The usual plan of Bijapur mosques consists simply of a three- to six-bay sanctuary with a triple-arched façade placed within a walled enclosure. In this more typical plan, the surrounding arcades are missing and the sanctuary is much smaller than in the orthodox hypostyle plan. The new jami masjid, using the hypostyle plan, consists of a courtyard over forty-seven meters square with seven arches forming the arcades on each of two sides (the third and final side was never completed). In the midst of the spacious courtyard a square cistern for ablutions originally provided water from the newly constructed underground canal. Piers divide the prayer chamber on the west side of the

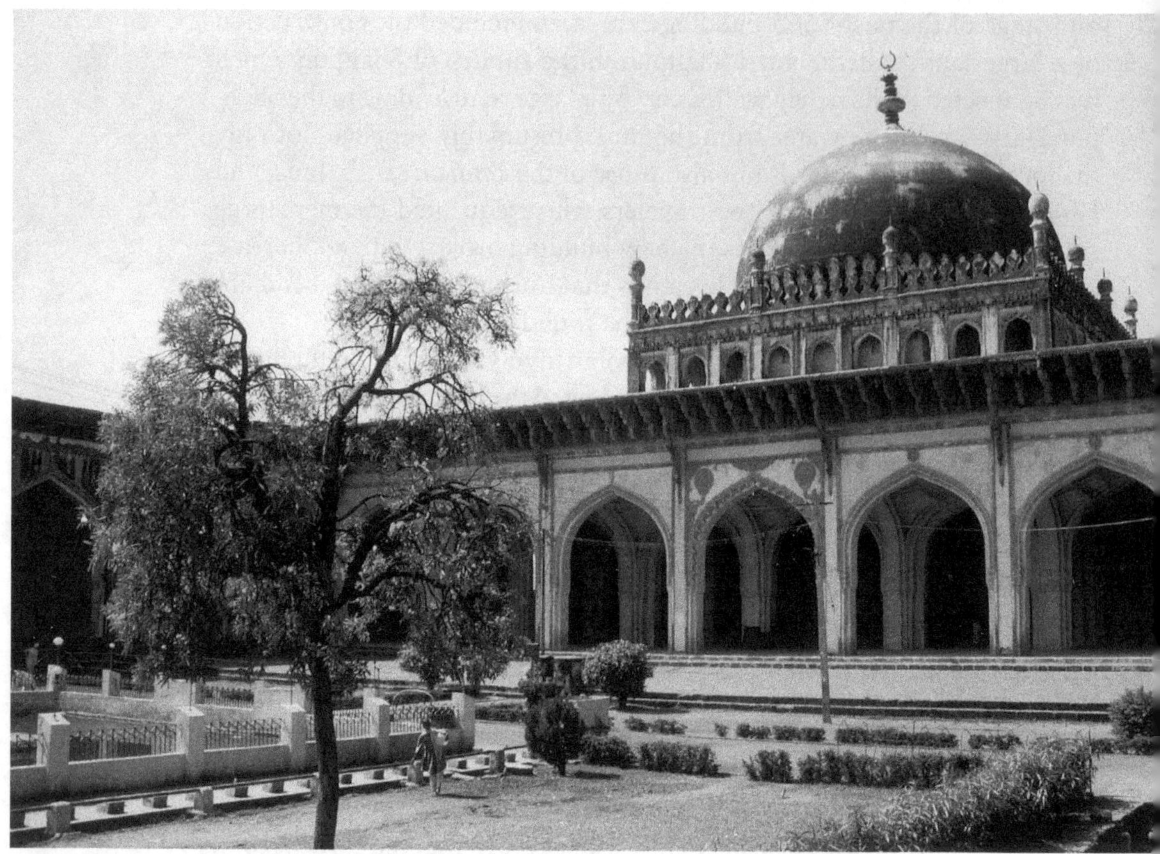

Figure 2.5. Jami masjid, begun ca. 1568, Bijapur. Photograph by author.

courtyard into forty-five bays (nine aisles and five bays). The segmental dome, which rises above the middle of the sanctuary, employs intersecting pendentive arches in the zone of transition. Overall, the mosque has very little ornament. The primary embellishments, apart from the brilliant *mihrab* added in the mid-seventeenth century, are limited to decorative plasterwork flanking the central arch of the façade and colored tiles edging the arches of the central space under the dome.

The mosque's size, use of the orthodox hypostyle plan, and date of construction led Henry Cousens to view it as a victory monument commemorating the battle of Talikota.[38] Others see these characteristics, particularly the use of the hypostyle plan, as evidence of Sultan Ali's "austere religious nature."[39] It is difficult, however, to draw many conclusions from the design of the mosque, except to say that its large size was clearly a statement of Bijapur's new status. The contemporary historians make no reference to it being either a victory monument or a marker of Ali's religious nature. In fact, they fail to comment on any of the particularities of

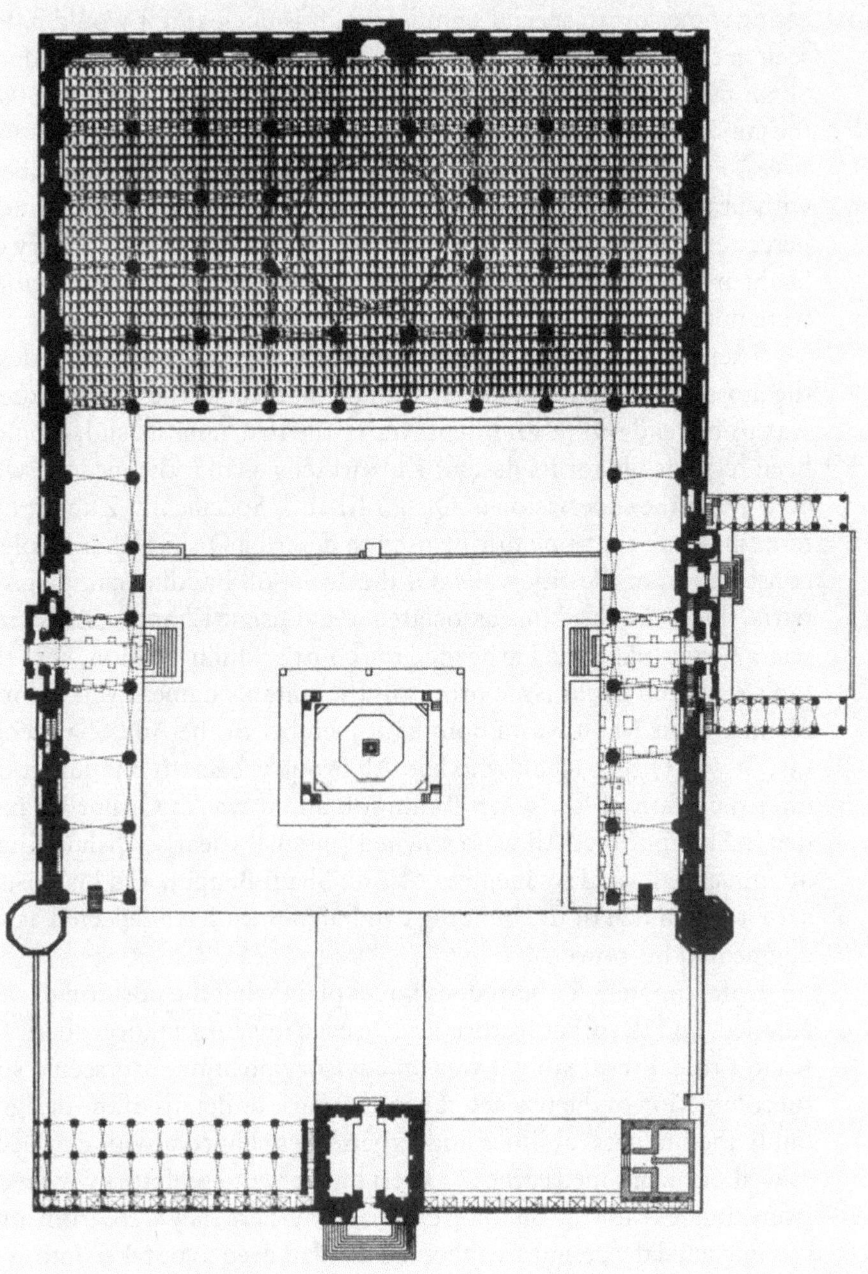

Figure 2.6. Jami masjid, begun ca. 1568, Bijapur. Plan from Henry Cousens, *Bijapur and Its Architectural Remains: With an Historical Outline of the Adil Shahi Dynasty.* Archaeological Survey of India, New Imperial Series 37 (1916; reprint, Delhi: Bharatiya Publication House, 1976). Reproduced by kind permission of the Archeological Survey of India.

its design. They present its construction merely as part of the larger campaign to build up the city.

While the mosque's plan strikes us today as atypical and thus indicating some sort of special significance, it is unclear if it would have been seen in the same way when it was built. Most of Bijapur's abundant Adil Shahi period mosques had yet to be constructed in the late 1560s when the jami masjid was begun. What we now identify as the typical "Bijapuri style," including the intimate triple-arched façade mosque plan embellished with profuse ornamentation, was not fully developed at that time. Our perception of the mosque is filtered through the subsequent history of Adil Shahi architecture, while the builders' and original users' perceptions of it were not.

There is also the question of who was responsible for the design of the mosque. While it might be assumed that Ali, as the ruler whose name was to be read out in Friday prayer at the new jami masjid, would have been responsible for its design, Zubairi tells us that the mosque was created under the supervision of Qishur Khan.[40] Specifically, Zubairi uses the term *sar-i kar,* the same title he used to describe Qishur Khan's role in the construction of the city walls. Of the 1565–68 building campaign's four parts, this is the third one associated with Qishur Khan. As Ali's vizier, he was a powerful figure. He headed the court's administration, kept the sultan's seal, and could issue orders in the sultan's name. Even before Ali's reign, Qishur Khan was a dominant member of the Adil Shahi court. In fact, it was Qishur Khan who had Ali brought back to Bijapur from exile after the death of his father, Ibrahim I, and it was in Qishur Khan's garden in Shahpur that Ali was crowned sultan.[41] Clearly, Qishur Khan was an influential, wealthy member of Adil Shahi Bijapur, and his position as sar-i kar in much of the building campaign must have reflected as well as augmented his power.

Unfortunately, Zubairi does not explain what the position of sar-i kar entailed, and the other historians give even less information about Qishur Khan's role. Presumably it was an advisory position, overseeing successful completion of the project, if not also various details of the design. Certainly the builders' abilities and experiences shaped any design decisions as well. As mentioned earlier, "expert builders and sculptors were recruited from all sides" for the building campaign. Where they were from and how this impacted the design are other factors that need to be taken into account; however, the names and origins of the artisans do not seem to have been recorded. In the end, what is clear is that it was a complicated patronage and building system with many levels of input at work. Thus the design of the jami masjid, as well as the whole building campaign, should not be viewed as the vision of one person or another. Rather, it can be read more accurately and fruitfully as a joint effort of many people with sometimes disparate, sometimes overlapping ideas about what cities and mosques should look like—in other words, a product of Bijapur's courtly culture.

If we view the post-1565 building campaign of Bijapur within the larger context of Islamicate urban development, it becomes apparent that the objective of Ali, his nobles, and the builders was to transform Bijapur into a proper capital city. Gaube in his study of Iranian cities lists four primary functions of an Islamicate capital city: to act as the seat of government, the center of the intellectual and religious life, the locus of economic activity, and the dwelling place of the population engaged in these functions.[42] The physical form of the city developed to fulfill these functions. Thus the typical Islamicate city was centered on a citadel, which was the seat of government. The city, usually walled to protect the population, had either four or five gates from which the major roads led to city center. Along a major artery of the city would be located the jami masjid, the center of religious life. The space within the city walls was divided into various quarters of economic activity, and if need be, suburbs outside the walls accommodated growth.[43] A prosperous city also was expected to have monuments, gardens, and waterworks to enhance the appearance of the city as well as the lives of its inhabitants. The urban environment of pre-1565 Bijapur fulfilled some of these functions but not all of them and not adequately.

The 1565–68 building campaign added the architectural elements needed to fulfill these functions: city walls along with five gateways and roads connecting them to the city center, an extensive waterworks system, gardens, and a monumental jami masjid located on a major roadway. The building campaign enhanced Shahpur, the economic center of Bijapur, and led to the construction of more monuments in the city, such as the palace complexes of the nobles.

The campaign also created the basic urban structures that continued to shape Bijapur's appearance throughout subsequent periods. The walls, although shored up during the reigns of Muhammad Adil Shah (r. 1627–56) and Ali Adil Shah II (r. 1656–72), were never expanded.[44] They control the boundaries of the city even today to some degree. The city's major arteries stem from the five gateways in the city walls. These roadways, along with the underground canals, influenced where builders located later monuments. The waterworks system also allowed for more tanks to be built and gardens to be watered. During the reign of Muhammad Adil Shah, another underground canal system from a water source south of the city was built, but the waterworks system of Qishur Khan was not abandoned until long after the fall of the Adil Shah dynasty. The jami masjid was expanded but never replaced. Adil Shahi Bijapur had at least three Friday mosques in the first 80 years of existence, but only one for the remaining 150 years.

In effect, in an approximately three-year period, the city of Bijapur transformed from a provincial center into a true capital city. This urban transformation directly resulted from Bijapur's political and economic advances gained through successful military offensives; however, the urban development in turn further enhanced Bijapur's political and economic situation by allowing the city to better fulfill its functions, including affording a secure environment and attracting people and commerce. This, in turn, led to more architectural development of the city, undoubtedly aided by the fact that builders, who needed to be recruited for the original building campaign, were now readily available. The movement of the nobility and flurry of construction brought craftsmen, shopkeepers, and servants to the city, creating a dynamic, fast-growing, and prosperous capital. Moreover—and this point is significant for understanding the development of Bijapuri art—the new concentration in the city of wealth, skilled artisans, and members of the royal court created the environment necessary for the arts to flourish. In medieval and early modern Islamicate culture, the major creative developments in architecture and painting as well as the other decorative arts, poetry, and music took place largely in cities, political and commercial centers with concentrations of both artists and wealthy patrons.

Thus the importance of the building campaign of 1565–68 is fivefold. It marked the Adil Shahi dynasty's emergence as a political and economic power. It transformed Bijapur from a provincial center to a true capital city. Conceived and carried out as a collective effort of the nobility under the guidance of the sultan and his vizier, it served to link the courtiers to the capital and led to further monumental construction projects. It also created the basic urban structures that continued to shape Bijapur's appearance throughout subsequent periods. Finally, and perhaps most significantly in terms of this study, the building campaign produced the urban setting needed for Bijapuri art to develop, reminding us that artistic endeavors not only reflect larger cultural changes but also help effect them.

The Tomb of Ali Adil Shah I

The tomb of Ali Adil Shah I (fig. 2.7), constructed circa 1580 in the southwest quarter of the recently walled city, manifests Bijapur's transformation from a populous provincial center to a true Islamicate capital city as well as the affiliated shift in the Adil Shahis' attitude toward the city. Yet, after a quick glance, the modern visitor to Bijapur might be tempted to pass over the structure, which is rather small, simple in design, lacking ornamentation, and today is in a poor state of repair.[45] Despite its humble appearance, the tomb is significant, for it influenced later burial pat-

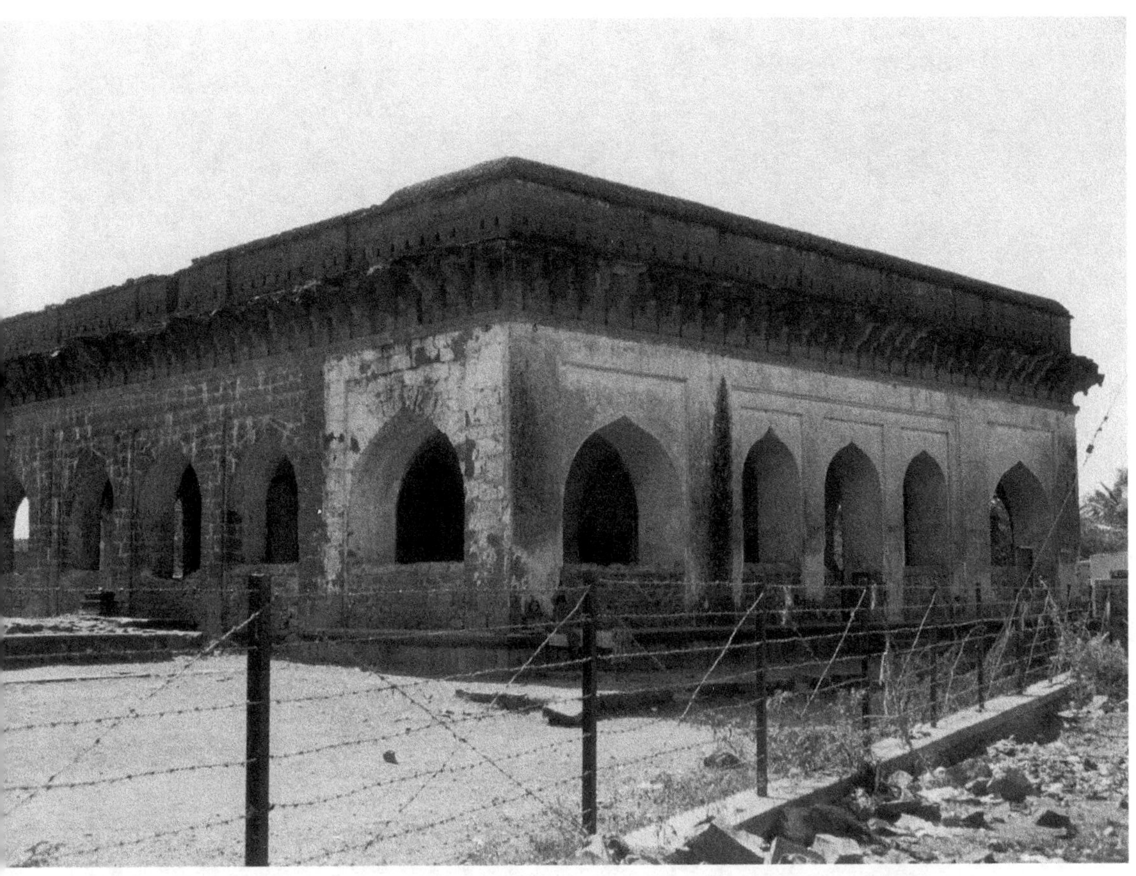

Figure 2.7. Tomb of Ali Adil Shah I, ca. 1580, Bijapur. Photograph by author.

terns of the Adil Shahs, marking a dramatic shift in the relationship between the dynasty and the capital city. From the point of its construction onward, the Adil Shah royal family, by building their tombs at various locations in or around the capital, chose to map their memory and identity directly onto the physical form of Bijapur city. The legacy, location, and design of Ali's tomb also reveal aspects of the relationship between Shiism and Sufism at Bijapur.

Although no evidence survives regarding the exact date or patronage of the tomb, we can date it to within a decade or so of Ali's death in 1580 based on stylistic comparison and historical mention. We also can assume either Ali or a close relative planned its construction and had some degree of influence over its design.[46] An arcaded corridor surrounds the austere, rectangular, vaulted tomb chamber containing Ali's cenotaph (fig. 2.8). Five arched openings mark each side of the arcade, with the two corner arches being wider than the middle three. The structure bears only a simple cornice and is conspicuously missing several distinctive Bijapuri architectural

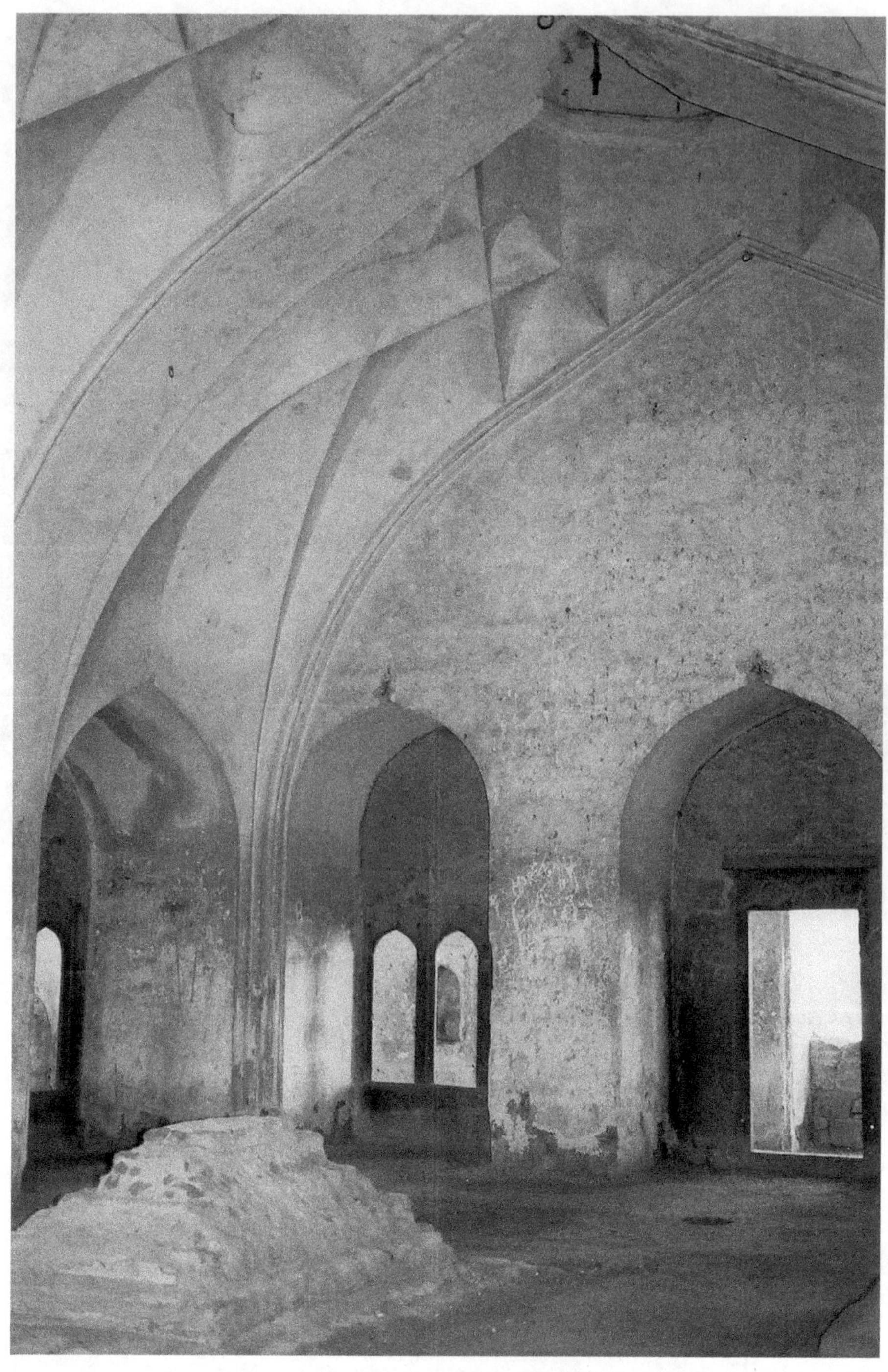

Figure 2.8. Interior of tomb of Ali Adil Shah I, ca. 1580, Bijapur. Photograph by author.

elements present in earlier and contemporary buildings. Chiefly, it has neither the bulbous dome with lotus petal base nor the rosette spandrel decorations, either of stucco or carved stone, found on many of the sixteenth-century monuments in Bijapur, including the recently built jami masjid. In fact, the tomb lacks any prominent dome to mark its presence on the skyline (it does have three small domes carried on transverse arches, but these are not visible from the ground). The building's surviving decoration is limited to painted geometric designs around the windows piercing the tomb chamber and painted inscriptions around the north doorway leading to the tomb chamber (pl. 2).[47] The calligraphy is faded but legible, bearing the Shia profession of faith, the throne verse from the Koran, and the words "Allah and Muhammad (his) apostle." Just as with the orthodox hypostyle plan of the jami masjid begun as part of the 1565–68 building campaign, scholars have linked the tomb's simplicity to Ali's "austere religious nature."[48] Although I am wary of drawing too many links between the ruler's character and the building's design (particularly when we don't know the details of its patronage), it does seem that Sultan Ali's tomb, with its Shia invocation and consciously humble design, was intended to mark his religious faith.

The tomb's plan of a central chamber surrounded by an arcade, while simple, elaborates that of the Adil Shahi dynastic tomb structure built during the first half of the sixteenth century at the small site of Gogi (fig. 2.9). The earlier royal mausoleum, containing the cenotaphs of all previous Adil Shahi rulers, consists of a rectangular, domed chamber with a veranda on one side. Ali's tomb expands the veranda to all four sides, creating an arcade completely encasing the central chamber. This plan can be found in Indo-Islamic Sufi saints' tombs of the period, the outer arcade allowing for circumambulation around the saint's cenotaph.[49] Ali's tomb, perhaps intentionally, mirrored this structure type.

Despite its simplicity, the building's plan influenced later architecture. Ali's tomb was the first royal tomb in the Deccan to follow the arcade-wrapped central chamber plan, and several subsequent Bijapuri tombs, including the celebrated Ibrahim Rauza, copy this design.[50] Another influential innovation proved to be the tomb's location. Built in Bijapur city's southwest section, the area where most likely Ali had three gardens laid out during the building campaign and which was fed with fresh water from the new underground canal, it became the first Adil Shahi royal tomb situated at the capital city, signifying a crucial change in the Adil Shahis' relationship with Bijapur.

The early Adil Shahi rulers, Yusuf, Ismail, Mallu, and Ibrahim I, had chosen to be buried away from the city in the dynastic tomb at Gogi, a remote site located in the district of Gulbarga, the former Bahmani center. The site housed the grave of a Sufi saint, Hazrat Chanda Shah Husani,

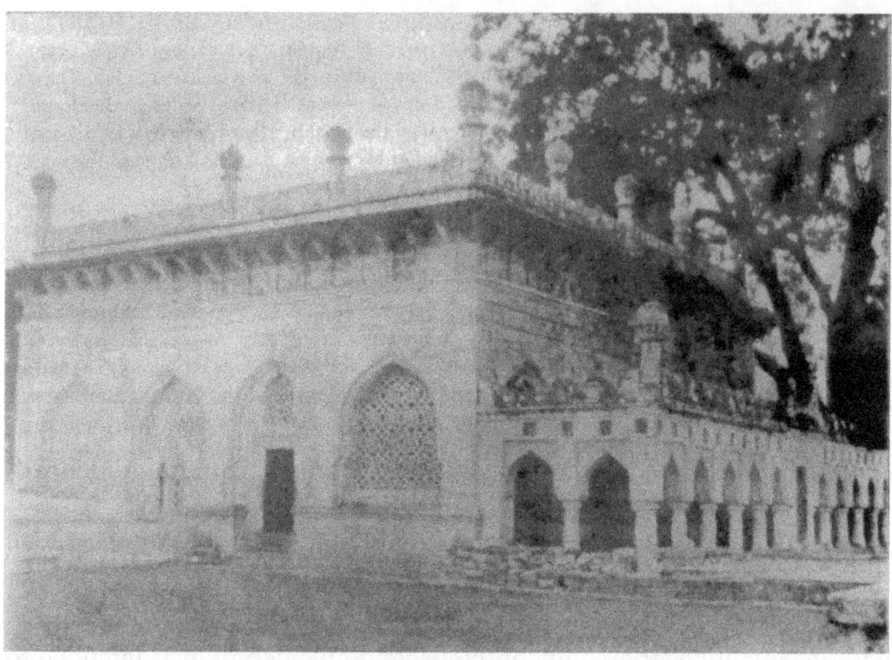

Figure 2.9. Adil Shahi royal mausoleum, sixteenth century, Gogi. Photograph from Henry Cousens, *Bijapur and Its Architectural Remains: With an Historical Outline of the Adil Shahi Dynasty.* Archaeological Survey of India, New Imperial Series 37 (1916; reprint, Delhi: Bharatiya Publication House, 1976). Reproduced by kind permission of the Archeological Survey of India.

revered by the Adil Shahis.[51] The Adil Shahi royal tomb, built near the Sufi's grave, served to demonstrate their allegiance to the saint and to link the dynasty to his power—both his spiritual power, his *baraka,* contained in his grave, and his more earthly power, his popular appeal. Additionally, and perhaps even more significantly, being buried in the Gulbarga region connected the Adil Shahis to the lingering power of the Bahmani dynasty.

Thus when Sultan Ali was buried at Bijapur rather than at Gogi, an important shift occurred, one that signaled Bijapur's emergence as an important urban space and true capital of the kingdom. Ali's predecessors may have seen fit to rule from Bijapur, but they certainly did not choose it as their eternal resting place. Instead, they chose a remote location close to the old Bahmani center of power, emphasizing their links to the earlier kingdom. In contrast, Sultan Ali's final resting place forever links him with his own capital, while also creating a memorial to the individual ruler rather than to the dynastic line as a whole.

In doing these two things, Ali's tomb began a pattern. The subsequent Adil Shahi rulers (except for the last, Sikander, who died in Mughal captivity) were all buried in or around Bijapur in tombs linked to their individual reigns. For example, the Ibrahim Rauza, built by Ibrahim's wife Taj Sultana on a site outside the western gateway, contains the graves of Ibrahim Adil Shah II, Taj Sultana, and several of their children. The massive tomb popularly called the Gul Gumbad, located just inside the eastern border of the city, honors Muhammad Adil Shah, while the unfinished tomb of Ali Adil Shah II, which would have surpassed even the Gul Gumbad in size if completed, sits in the northern part of the city. Each generation's memorial reaffirmed the Adil Shahi dynasty's rule over their capital city and simultaneously distinguished each ruler from their predecessors by associating them with a specific section of the city or environs (and not to mention featuring increasingly grand designs). These tombs mapped the identity and visual legacy of the Adil Shahis directly onto Bijapur's urban shape.

Ali's tomb not only broke early Adil Shahi tradition by being located at Bijapur rather than at Gogi, it also was built within the city walls of Bijapur. This is significant because until this point, only Sufi saints were buried within the city, a tradition inherited from the Bahmani dynasty. For example, at Gulbarga, the royal tombs spread out south and east of the city, and at Bidar, the Bahmanis' second capital, the sultans are buried at Ashtar, a site a few miles east of the city.[52] If a ruler wanted to connect himself with a Sufi saint, he typically chose a saint buried at a location outside the city. Whoever decided the location of Ali's tomb must have been aware of the import of the choice, which seems to suggest that Ali had a special bond with the city of Bijapur or in some other way merited the special location.

The placement of Ali's tomb within the city also allowed his grave to be physically close to the Sufis buried in the vicinity.[53] In Sufism, after a saint dies, his baraka, or potent spiritual power, resides in his tomb, and those buried near him benefit from the Sufi's baraka throughout eternity, bringing them closer to God. By placing Ali's tomb in the southwest section of the city, which even today is considered by local residents to have strong ties to Sufism, the tomb's patron, whether Ali himself or a close relative, was ensuring Sultan Ali would receive the baraka of Sufi saints.[54] Several nearby Sufi structures bear possible direct links to his tomb.[55] Most significantly, the tomb complex of Pir Shaikh Hamid Qadiri (d. 1602) and his brother Latif Allah Qadiri (d. 1612) sits just a bit to the west of Ali's tomb. The complex (fig. 2.10) contains the unfinished tomb of the two Sufis, a mosque, the remains of a step well, and two more unidentified tombs. Stylistic and historical evidence dates the central tomb to the first decades of the seventeenth century, after Ali's death and about the time of the two Qadiri brothers' deaths, while an inscription records that Fatima Sultana, one of Ali's widows, patronized it. Fatima Sultana also paid for the construction of the step well, the Gumat Bauri, built on the site in 1562, before

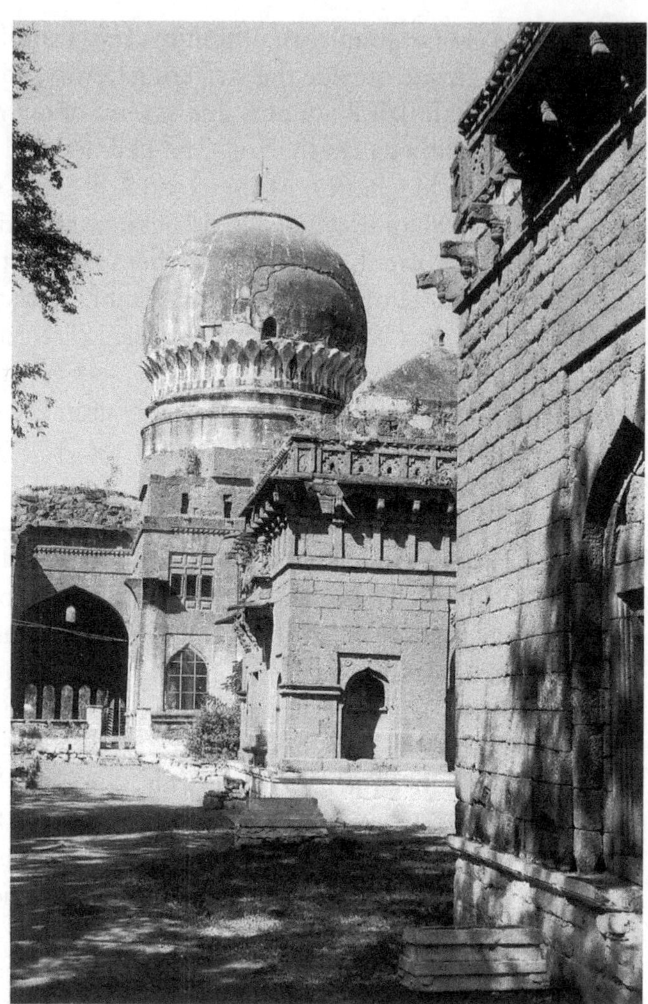

Figure 2.10. Tomb of Pir Shaikh Hamid Qadiri and Latif Allah Qadiri, ca. 1602–12, Bijapur. Photograph by author.

Ali's death, leaving open the possibility that planning of the tomb complex began at that time.[56] The Qadiri brothers' tomb, never completed, was intended to be of the same plan as Sultan Ali's tomb, a central chamber surrounded by an arcaded corridor; however, unlike Ali's, a high dome embellishes the Qadiri brothers' arcaded tomb. The proximate locations of the two tombs, the similarity in design, and the patronage of the Sufis' tomb by Ali's widow in sum suggest a consciously intended link between them. By constructing the Qadiri brother's tomb near her husband's, Fatima Sultana provided Ali with another connection to the baraka of Sufi saints.

An inscription at a Sufi complex in Miraj, a small site outside of Bijapur, states that in 1558 Ali had himself crowned at the tomb of a local Sufi, Shams al-Din "Shamna Miran," a disciple of Zayn al-Din Shirazi.[57] Such evidence demonstrates that Ali consciously sought to align himself with

Sufism in life; his tomb suggests that he wished to be linked with the power of Sufism in death as well. In many respects, this is not surprising. Mysticism was popular in the medieval and early modern Deccan with Hindus and Muslims alike, and it played an important role in the development of Islamicate Deccani culture. From the Bahmani dynasty onwards, the Deccan sultans patronized Sufi shrines and tombs. For example, Yusuf Adil Khan, the founder of the Adil Shah dynasty, built a large two-story entrance, serving also as a *madrasa* (school) and *serai* (inn), to the shrine of Hazrat Shaykh Siraju al-Din Junaidi at Gulbarga.[58] And the location of the first Adil Shahi royal mausoleum connected the family to the tomb of the Sufi saint, Hazrat Chanda Shah Husani, whom they patronized. It was politically expedient for sultans to align themselves with local saints, who, because of their baraka, were perceived to have a special link with God. Sultans, who were secular rulers, did not possess such a divine connection. They therefore depended upon associations with popular religious figures, past and present, for spiritual legitimacy.[59]

In another respect, however, Ali's link with Sufism is noteworthy. It is often believed that, historically, Shia Muslims have been less accepting of Sufism than Sunni Muslims. Shiism and Sufism share many characteristics, such as an emphasis on esoteric knowledge and a preservation of the religion's spiritual sense, and the two movements influenced each other during their formative periods; however, a sense of antagonism eventually developed between the two. One of the primary reasons for this was a tension, almost rivalry, between each one's concept of the perfect man, *qutb* in Sufism and *imam* in Shiism, which could not allow for the recognition of the other.[60] The history of the Adil Shahis' contemporaries, the Safavids of Iran, makes particularly visible the conflict that developed between Sufism and Shia Islam. Although originally arising out of a Sufi brotherhood, by the late sixteenth century the Safavid court was seeking out and persecuting Sufis. In fact, the increasing lack of patronage by the Safavid dynasty led many Sufis to immigrate to India, including Bijapur, during the late sixteenth and seventeenth centuries.[61] It is often assumed that the hostility toward Sufism in Safavid Iran existed in other Shia regions as well, including the Deccan; however, Ali's tomb expresses visual links to both Sufism—through its location and appearance—and Shiism—through its inscription—at the same time and without apparent conflict.[62] Perhaps Shiism in the Deccan, like Islam in general, took on distinct regional characteristics in response to local cultural needs.

Thus, under close examination, Ali's tomb reveals itself as a significant structure. The painted ornamentation around the doorway contains the Shia profession of faith, the location and plan of the tomb links it to Sufism, and its conscious simplicity conveys both Ali's religious and mystical devotionalism. Through these attributes, the tomb displays Ali's Shia and Sufic identities simultaneously, suggesting one did not have to be compromised in favor of the other. Moreover, it highlights the importance of Sufism in Bijapur to both Sunni and Shia Muslims. The tomb proved innovative and influential to later Adil Shahi memorial architecture. It was the first royal tomb in the Deccan to employ the plan of a central chamber surrounded by an arcaded corridor; several later structures follow this plan. The location of Ali's tomb at Bijapur rather than at the dynastic tomb site at Gogi impacted later royal mausoleums as well. All subsequent Adil Shahi tombs were built either inside or just outside the city, linking the dynasty with its own capital rather than the former Bahmani centers of power. Moreover, by locating the tomb at Bijapur, the patron, whether Ali or someone close to the ruler, reinforced Bijapur's emergence as an important urban space and true center of the Adil Shahi dynasty. Ali's tomb thus stands as a simple but potent marker of the changes that were taking place in late sixteenth-century Bijapur.

The *Nujum al-Ulum*

Mysticism and kingship, two themes expressed in Ali Adil Shah I's tomb, also play central roles in the *Nujum al-Ulum,* or "Stars of the Sciences." The *Nujum al-Ulum,* today housed in the Chester Beatty Library, Dublin, is an original treatise, written in Persian, on esoteric and cosmological knowledge as it relates to kingship and effective rule. It contains 348 folios and nearly 800 illustrations, the style of which links its production to Bijapur.[63] Inscriptions on three separate folios date the manuscript to 978 AH (1570–71 CE), making it one of the earliest surviving examples of painting from Bijapur, as well as one of the few securely dated.[64] The work, with its extensive illustrations and lengthy original text, confirms Bijapur's emergence as a cultural center after 1565. The manuscript's noteworthy text/image relationship, extensive and varied examples of intercultural exchange, emphasis on Sufism and other esoteric practices, and overriding concern with kingship provide considerable insights into Adil Shahi courtly culture as it existed in the latter half of the sixteenth century as well as the factors affecting Bijapur's artistic development.[65]

The inscriptional evidence providing the manuscript's date gives neither its place of production nor the names of its author, patron, and artists. We link its production to the Adil Shahi court based on the style of the paintings, which correspond with other illustrated manuscripts connected to 1570s Bijapur, and the extensive scope of the project, indicating that it must have been the product of a courtly *kitabkhane* (library and book workshop) with a large staff and ample resources. In the *Tazkira al-Mulk,* Shirazi gives a description of Sultan Ali's kitabkhane that not only corresponds with the environment necessary to produce a manuscript like the

Nujum but also suggests that such a book would have been appreciated by the sultan, if he was indeed the patron. Shirazi explains that Ali had "a great inclination toward the study of books and he had procured many books connected with every kind of knowledge, so that a colored library had become full."[66] He further states that Ali's kitabkhane employed nearly sixty people, including calligraphers, gilders, bookbinders, and illuminators, with Waman Pandit bin Anant Pandit Shesh, a Sanskrit scholar and local Maratha, appointed as the chief librarian.[67] Production oversight by a Sanskrit scholar would help explain several noteworthy aspects of the *Nujum,* such as the familiar use of Sanskrit terms in portions of the Persian text and the accurate depictions of Tantric Hindu earth forces in the illustrations accompanying the last section of the manuscript. And certainly the *Nujum al-Ulum* would have fit well in a collection of books "connected with every kind of knowledge."

An inscription on the book's first folio provides another piece of evidence linking the *Nujum* to Bijapur, although not necessarily to Ali's patronage. It states, "The book of 'the Stars of the Sciences' by order of the king of Bijapur, Ibrahim *jagatguru,* bought by Nawab Sayyid Rustam Khan." The inscription is ambiguous—from whom and why the Nawab purchased the manuscript is unstated. Nevertheless, it indicates that the manuscript was at Bijapur's court during the reign of Ibrahim Adil Shah II, called Jagatguru, "World Teacher," who came to the throne only ten years after the manuscript's production.

Whoever the patron was, whether Ali Adil Shah, a Bijapuri noble, the *Nujum*'s author, or someone else, it is clear that the *Nujum al-Ulum* was an appreciated work in Bijapur's elite circles. Ibrahim II stamped a page of the book with his royal seal of approval, and at least two later copies of the *Nujum al-Ulum* survive. Sometime during the 1660s and 1670s, Bijapuri artists produced a slightly less lavish but equally heavily illustrated version of the manuscript, which, like the original, is currently housed in the Chester Beatty Library. The Wellcome Library, London, contains another apparent copy, a partial manuscript (missing its beginning and end) datable to the seventeenth or eighteenth century and featuring illustrations identical in content and composition to those of the *Nujum.*[68] Such later attention suggests that the manuscript, and thus its articulations of kingship, resonated with the Adil Shahi court.

The main thesis of the *Nujum al-Ulum*'s anonymous author, who Linda Leach has theorized was most likely a high-ranking Adil Shahi courtier, is that supernatural forces govern worldly affairs.[69] The author states that he was attempting to compile information on these forces as found in older sources, and addresses his description of them to an unspecified ruler, perhaps Ali Adil Shah or perhaps just a theoretical, ideal figure. The author believes that if the sultan is able to understand the cosmos and the various supernatural powers at work, he then can exert proper control over the affairs of his kingdom.

The body of the text begins by describing the Islamic orders of heavenly angels, with the accompanying images illustrating the various types (fig. 2.11). A report of the northern constellations paired with their anthropomorphized images follows. Next comes the longest section of the text, which also contains some of the most carefully rendered paintings. This section lays out the planets, signs of the zodiac, *nakshatras* (ancient Indian star groupings), and degrees of the zodiac, creating an astrology system that covers the whole year. Each of the six planets has two zodiac signs associated with it, and each zodiac sign has 30 degrees. Thus the twelve signs and their degrees add up to 360 degrees total, equaling a full circle and approximately a year's time. The artists divided the illustrations into color-coded subsections consisting of one planet, two zodiac signs, six to eight nakshatras, and 60 degrees. For example, the illustrations of the planet Venus, the signs Taurus and Libra, the corresponding six nakshatras and 60 degrees are associated with the color white; therefore, the artists placed the figures on white backgrounds (pl. 3). The images present the planets, as well as the Sun and Moon, and various zodiac signs in anthropomorphic form (pls. 4 and 5; fig 2.12). Emblematic objects, such as a house or pair of bed legs, illustrate the nakshatras, with identification given in a cartouche above each image. Simple scenes depict the degrees, each of which roughly corresponds with a day of the year. For example, 6 degrees of the sign Taurus are portrayed as a man tugging his beard, a patch of grass, a Muslim woman praying, a man riding on an antelope, a collection of scarves, and a woman washing herself (pl. 3). The pictures suggest correspondence with specific charms or spells for each day or perhaps activities to be carried out; however, the text does not fully explain their meanings.[70] Small cusped roundels frame these curious scenes, while inscriptions enclosed in cartouches placed above each one provide labels.

Comparatively brief discussions of the southern constellations and talismans such as stones to be used as charms follow the long discussion of the astrological system. The author next documents magic spells for summoning Islamic spirits from the heavens and hell. The corresponding illustrations portray a "Master of Invitation" performing the various spells (fig. 2.13). The text then moves onto a long and heavily illustrated explanation of the ideal objects surrounding a ruler and the supernatural powers of these items (fig. 2.14; pl. 6). The section contains the only full-page painting in the entire manuscript, indicating the subject's importance. Notably, the illustration, which depicts a ruler atop his seven-storied throne, is also the page that bears Ibrahim Adil Shah II's seal, further highlighting its import. The section also includes descriptions of ideal fort designs, such as a circular fort, a bow-shaped fort, and a fort in the form of a Hindu

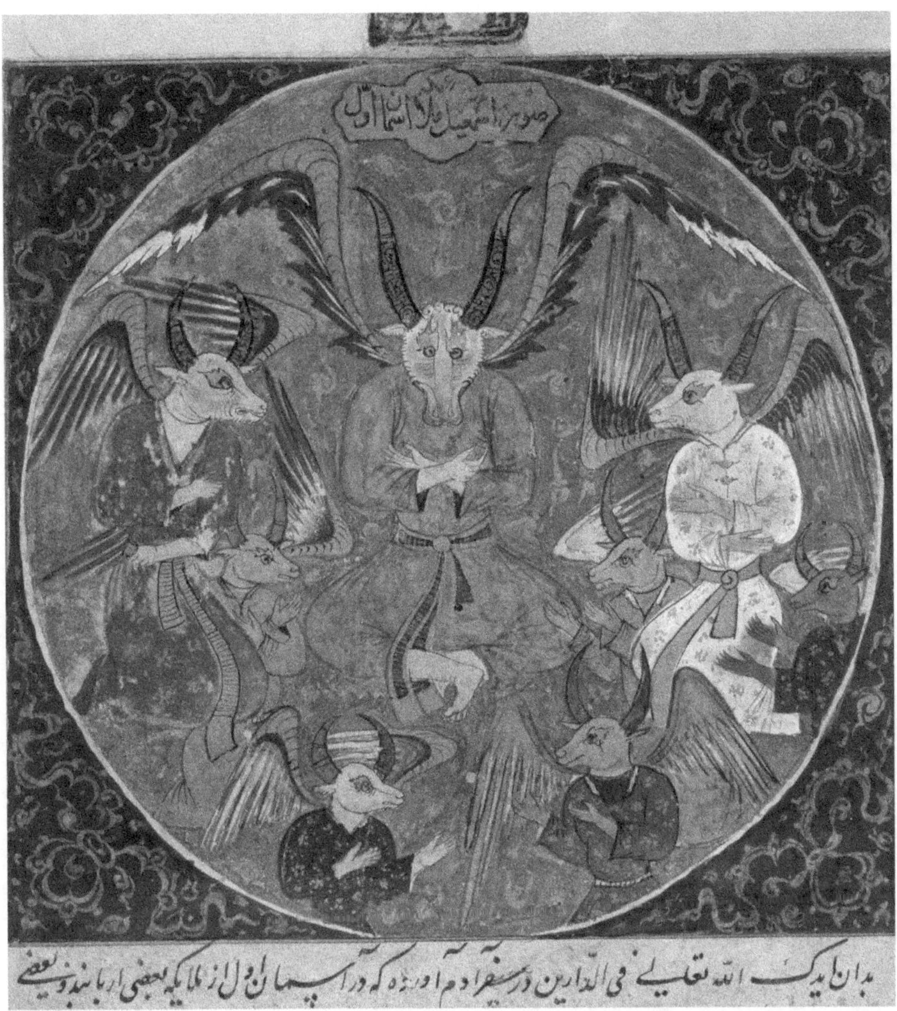

Figure 2.11. Order of cow-headed angels with the angel Asmail in the center, *Nujum al-Ulum,* 1570–71, Bijapur. Chester Beatty Library, Dublin, MS. 2, folio 5v. Reproduced by kind permission of the Trustees of the Chester Beatty Library, Dublin.

altar. Next comes perhaps the most unusual portion of the text. In it, the author describes 140 *ruhanis,* or Hindu earth forces (fig. 2.15; pl. 7). The illustrations depict the Tantric goddesses and their attributes precisely as described in the text. Diagrammatic depictions of the ruhanis accompany these illustrations. The *Nujum* ends by cataloging types of horses, elephants, and weapons. Curiously, in the final section the illustrations do not follow the text closely at all, contrasting sharply with the close relationship between text and image displayed in most of the manuscript.[71] It may have been that this final section was completed when time or interest in the project was waning.

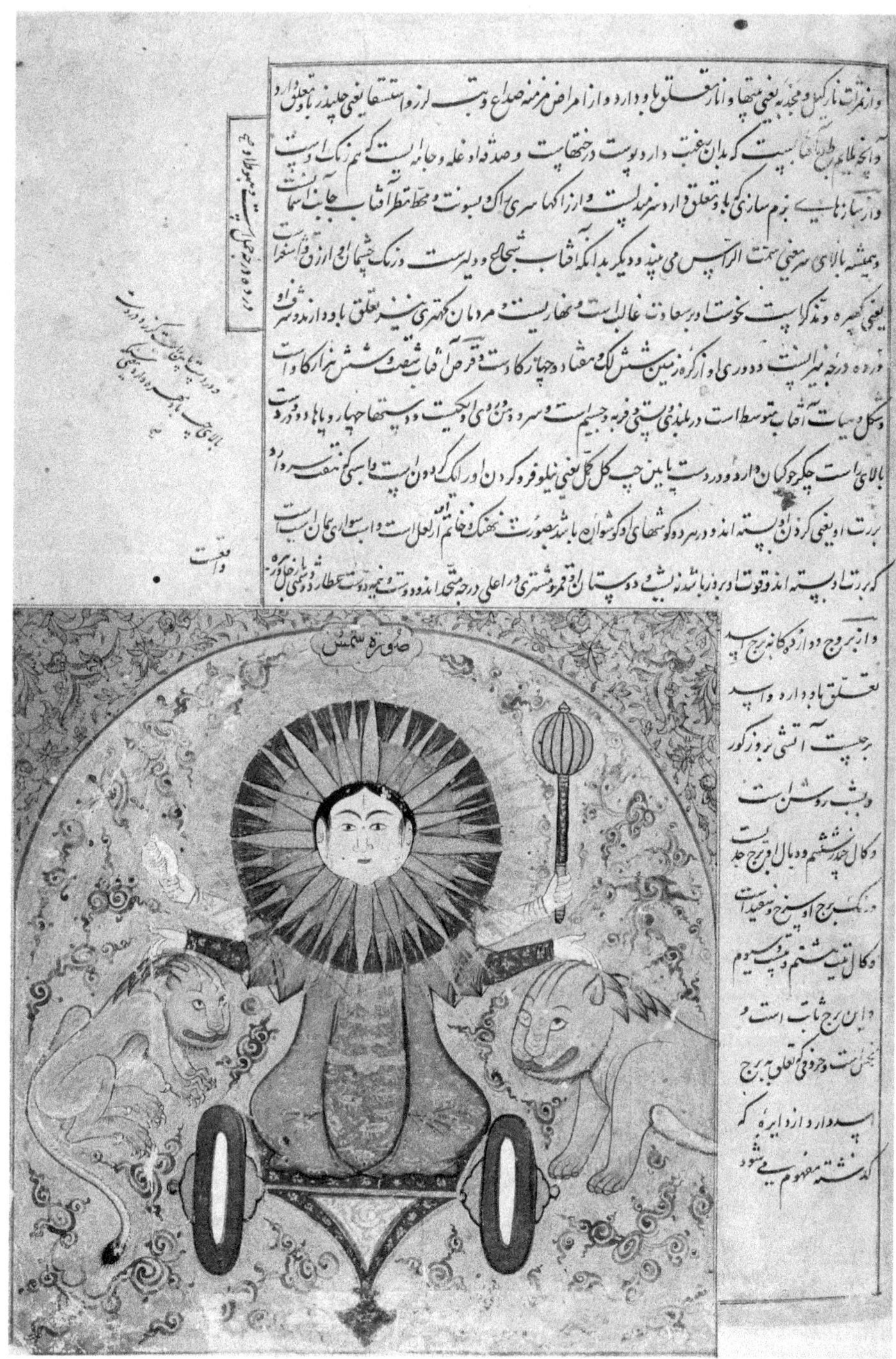

Figure 2.12. The Sun, *Nujum al-Ulum,* 1570–71, Bijapur. Chester Beatty Library, Dublin, MS. 2, folio 22. Reproduced by kind permission of the Trustees of the Chester Beatty Library, Dublin.

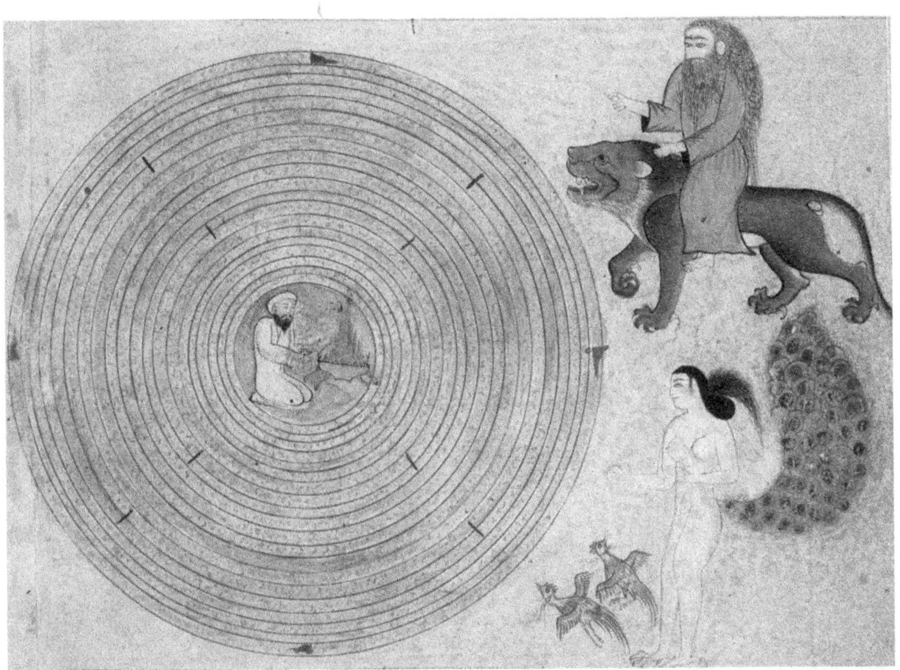

Figure 2.13. The Master of Invitation summoning up a man riding a lion and a naked woman with a peacock tail, *Nujum al-Ulum,* 1570–71, Bijapur. Chester Beatty Library, Dublin, MS. 2, folio 125v. Reproduced by kind permission of the Trustees of the Chester Beatty Library, Dublin.

Overall, the illustrations adjoining the text are numerous, often quite small, yet very bold in both color and design. Usually a single page contains two to seven paintings incorporated with text. Occasionally many small paintings compose a full page without text. As stated, only once in the whole manuscript does a single painting take up an entire page. The paintings have little or no settings, but small cloudlike swirls or gilded foliage fill the spaces surrounding the main figures in many of the paintings, giving them a decorative quality unusual in scientific treatises. The addition of decorative details indicates that the manuscript was meant to be a lavish one. Yet the quality of the images varies greatly. The artists rendered with care many of the paintings, such as those representing the planets, zodiac signs, and their degrees; however, they haphazardly illustrated other sections, such as the brief one on talismans and the final pages detailing types of horses, elephants, and weapons.

In general the *Nujum al-Ulum*'s paintings correspond stylistically with those of other surviving illustrated manuscripts from the period. However, upon close study, a number of distinct styles, apart from variances due to quality, emerge among the *Nujum*'s many paintings, or more precisely in the figures depicted in the paintings. Specifically, I identify three

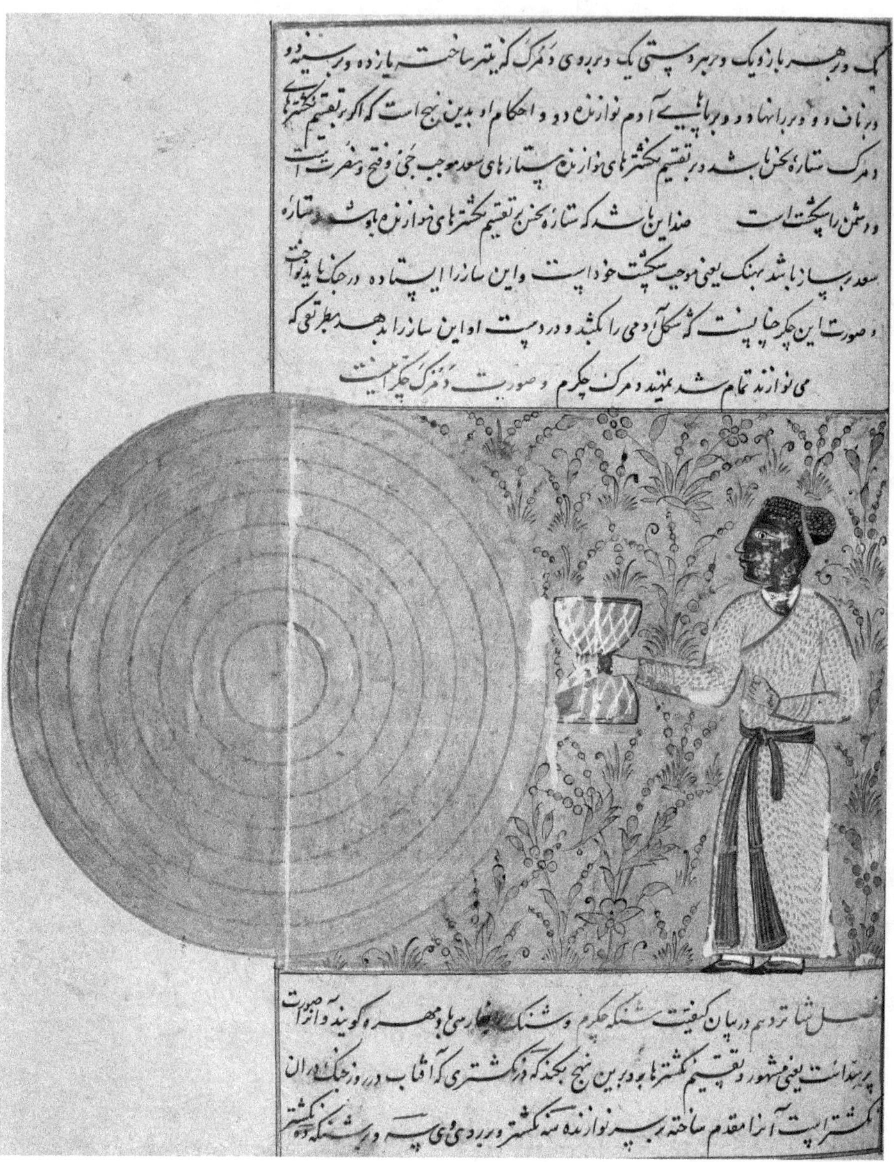

Figure 2.14. A man holding a drum from which sound waves reverberate, *Nujum al-Ulum*, 1570–71, Bijapur. Chester Beatty Library, Dublin, MS. 2, folio 213. Reproduced by kind permission of the Trustees of the Chester Beatty Library, Dublin.

stylistic categories into which the figures can be divided. The stylistic variations are not absolute—there are inconsistencies and subtleties among the paintings that make perfect categorization impossible, and the backgrounds of all the illustrations share many of the same decorative elements. In general, however, the styles of the figures seem to correspond with textual variations in a manner suggesting the artists or supervisor of the project

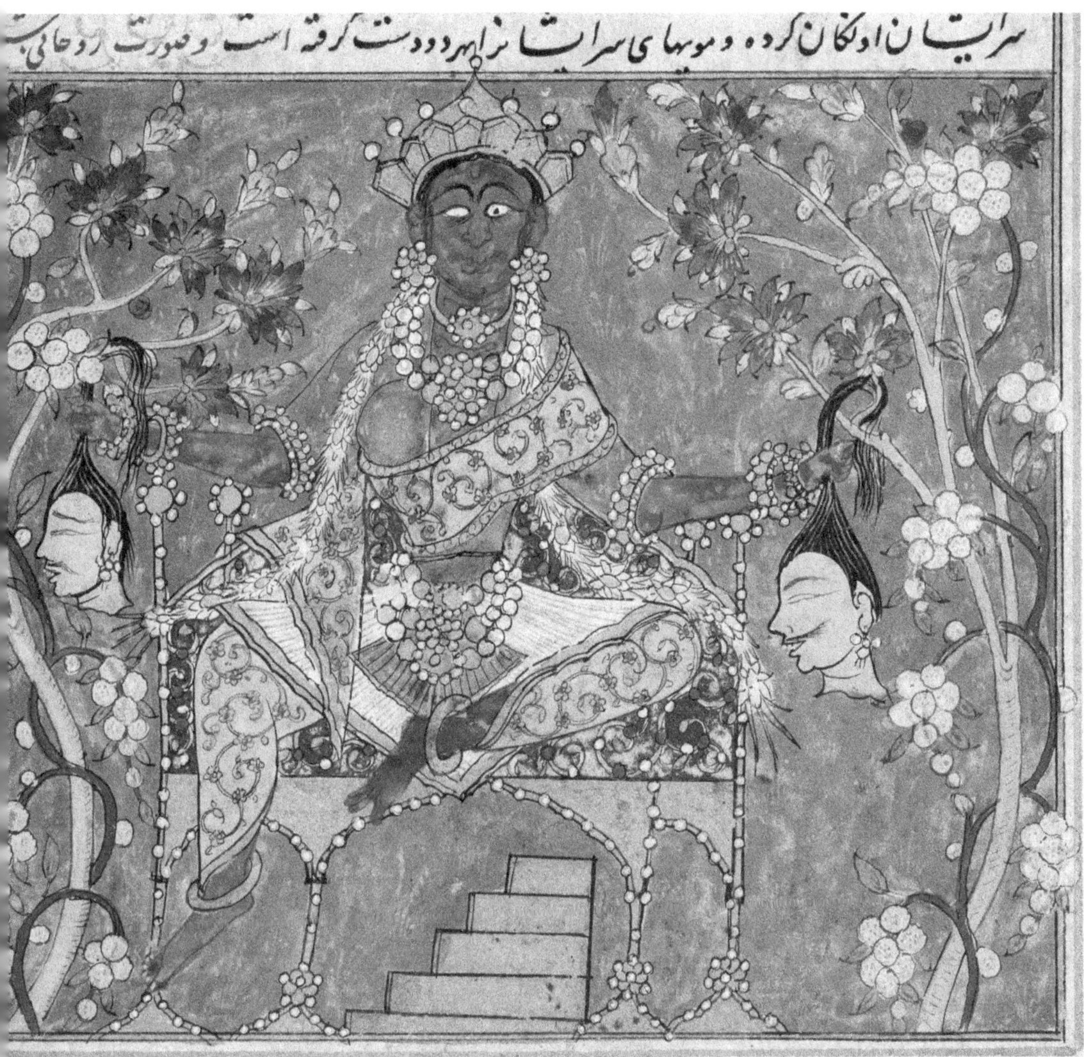

Figure 2.15. The ruhani Chalandhari, *Nujum al-Ulum,* 1570–71, Bijapur. Chester Beatty Library, Dublin, MS. 2, folio 241v. Reproduced by kind permission of the Trustees of the Chester Beatty Library, Dublin.

coordinated styles to fit with the text. Such parity indicates that stylistic variations were not the accidental by-products of assigning work to available artisans, but rather that Bijapuri patrons and artists understood the potential of visual languages.

The first stylistic category might be labeled archaic Persian, in that it seems to draw on older Persianate painting styles. The *Nujum*'s paintings of this style display an attention to detail, emphasis on anatomical proportion, compositional harmony, and static quality not found in the manuscript's other illustrations.[72] Most of the examples of the archaic Persian style occur at the beginning of the manuscript in the sections devoted to the constellations and orders of angels, such as one image on folio 5v depicting an order of cow-headed angels (fig. 2.11). Some of the zodiac and anthropomorphized-planet illustrations also fall into this category. The author based these portions of the text on earlier Persian and Arabic astronomy treatises. For example, the first chapter of the *Nujum al-Ulum* discussing the heavenly angels and northern constellations, whose illustrations all follow the archaic Persian style, comes directly from the Arabic work of the thirteenth-century Iranian author al-Qazvini.

Copies of al-Qazvini's work seem to have been widely available in Bijapur. A Persian translation of his treatise, the *Ajaib al-Makhluqat wa Gharaib al-Mawjudat* (Wonders of creation and oddities of existence), was completed in Bijapur in 1547, and several folios survive from an illustrated copy of the same manuscript made in Bijapur circa 1570.[73] The India Office Library, London, houses an Arabic copy of the manuscript, copied and illustrated in 1571–72 for the patron Ibn Kamal al-Din Husayn, an Adil Shahi courtier.[74] Significantly, the two illustrated examples of al-Qazvini's work created about the same time as the *Nujum al-Ulum* also follow older Persian rather than local painting styles. In other words, the artists illustrated these texts, which were relaying centuries-old information, in older, "classic" painting styles. They seem to have viewed the archaic Persian style as befitting the text, highlighting in a vague but visible way the origins of the information. In fact, at this time in much of the Islamic world, it was standard practice to adopt earlier styles when illustrating earlier scientific treatises. Moreover, by the sixteenth century, scholars were writing very few new astrological works. The study of cosmology had become static, and copying old, well-known works, such as al-Qazvini's thirteenth-century treatise, was customary.[75] In this respect, the *Nujum* was following the norm.

What was innovative about the *Nujum al-Ulum,* therefore, is not that it compiles earlier works on astrology, nor that some of its illustrations copy older practices, but rather that it also incorporates information, whether Islamic, Hindu, or Indic, not normally found in Persian or Arabic scientific treatises. These innovative textual sections contain the paintings of the second stylistic category (see, for example, fig. 2.13 or pls. 5 and 6). This category, into which the majority of the *Nujum*'s illustrations fall, combines Indic and Persian stylistic elements and can be classified as the emerging Bijapuri style found in other original illustrated manuscripts from the period. For example, the *Javahir al-Musikat,* a book on music and dance attributed to Bijapur circa 1570, displays the same bold, angular, stylized figures and energetic compositions as most of the *Nujum al-Ulum* illustrations.[76] The *Nujum*'s paintings in this second style also display the widest range in quality, perhaps as a result of its "emerging" nature. Many of the paintings in the emerging Bijapuri style employ the distinctive palette of bright orange, moss green, brownish red, and royal blue that becomes the hallmark of later Bijapuri painting.

Two notable sections devoted to information uncommon for scientific treatises and illustrated in the developing Bijapuri style are those describing Sufic magic spells to conjure up spirits and the objects surrounding the ideal ruler. The portion of the text specifying spells for calling up Islamic spirits is highly unusual, if not unique, among surviving Persian and Indian illustrated manuscripts, and the content of the illustrations, which follow the text closely, are original as well. The author precisely describes the rites, the point of which was to invoke certain Islamic spirits in the hope of gaining assistance in various situations. He identifies the person presiding over the ceremonies as the Master of Invitation.[77] All fourteen illustrations in the section portray the Master of Invitation as a bearded old man, presumably representing a Sufi saint, as such saints were considered to have special powers, and people often visited them in the hopes that the Sufi would use his magic to help them. In one spell, the Master of Invitation sits in the center of a large, circular area and in front of a fire burning in a metal brazier (fig. 2.13). He has called up a bearded man riding a lion and a naked woman with a peacock tail as well as two birds. The two human figures are probably *jinns,* spirits with special powers (a man riding a lion is a reoccurring image in Sufism with his dominance over the beast indicating his power).

Although such mystical spells conjuring up beings from the heavens and hell were common throughout the Islamic world, they were considered secret and not normally written down, much less illustrated.[78] Thus the *Nujum al-Ulum*'s detailed discussion of them is striking, as is the specific way in which the spells are articulated in the text and images. To describe the circular and square areas in which the rites are carried out, the author, writing in Persian, employs the word *mandal* or *mandala,* a Sanskrit term that entered the South Asian Persian lexicon at some point. In Sanskrit, *mandala* refers to a figure or diagram created as a focus for ritual, usually in Buddhist or Hindu Tantric practices. In his Persian-English dictionary, Steingass defines the term *mandal* as "an enchanter's circle, described on the ground, in which they sit when endeavouring to conjure up demons or spirits," a meaning very close to the original Sanskrit one.[79] Such overlap in terminology speaks to the extent of religious interaction, particularly in terms of mystical practices, in South Asia by the early 1570s. The artists carefully depicted the geometric areas, thus conveying their importance to the enactment of the spells. For example, the mandala takes various shapes depending on the spell, and the artists painted small spikes at the edges of the circles and squares to indicate the cardinal directions.

Like the section on Sufic spells, the text devoted to the objects surrounding the ideal ruler is unusual for Islamicate illustrated manuscripts and employs both Indic concepts and terminology. Specifically, the author describes the items as the *chakra* of objects surrounding the ruler. *Chakra* is a Sanskrit term literally meaning "wheel" but also referring to a paradigm, ideal, or energy source, and as Leach has observed, the objects described in this section correspond with the Indic idea of the *chakravartin*, the Universal Ruler, a notion with a long history in South Asia.[80] The early Indian ruler Ashoka (r. circa 269–32 BCE) was considered a chakravartin, as was the Buddha. Jain and Hindu conceptions of rule employ the chakravartin ideal as well.[81] The Universal Ruler, who would bring with him peace and prosperity, had seven "Treasures" or kingly attributes. The Seven Treasures differ in various accounts, but in general they include the perfect consort, minister, general, horse, and elephant. The *Nujum al-Ulum*'s discussion of the chakra of objects surrounding the ideal ruler refers to these, although it incorporates additional items, such as the ruler's allegorical seven-storied throne (pl. 6), musical instruments (fig. 2.14), a fan, a fly whisk, and even a palanquin for carrying the ruler. In some instances, the artists also created diagrams (typically charts of various geometric shapes divided into boxes bearing Persian terms or letters) of the ideal objects and in one case a diagram of an ideal man. While the chakravartin was a widespread, long-standing ideal in South Asia, the concept's corresponding objects, such as the seven-storied throne, were rarely illustrated in such detail, and thus the *Nujum*'s paintings are exceptional. Moreover, the paintings in this section are among the finest in the whole manuscript, reiterating the importance of the kingship theme to the work.

The sections on Islamic spells to conjure up spirits and the objects surrounding the ideal ruler demonstrate that, as with the archaic Persian style, the artists seem to have purposefully employed the emerging Bijapuri style in specific portions of the text that it was deemed to suit. The unusual subject matters of these sections, for which there must not have been many illustration models to follow, allowed, or perhaps demanded, a new style. And just as the painting style combines familiar Persian and Indic elements to create something new and distinctly Bijapuri, the text does as well. The material upon which the text draws, whether of Persian, Indic, or combined origin, is not presented as odd or foreign but as something that would be familiar to readers. For example, the Persian author uses the Sanskrit terms *chakra* and *chakravartin* without explanation, as if he assumes his readers would be familiar with them. The material in these portions of the *Nujum* may have been unusual in the larger tradition of Islamicate scientific treatises and therefore innovative, but it was not foreign to Bijapur. Both the wording of the text and the style employed in the paintings serve to convey both its freshness and familiarity.

The third stylistic category, which we might classify as an archaic Indic style, is limited to the section toward the end of the manuscript that describes the 140 ruhanis, almost all of which are female (although the section describes several *yogis* as well). The ruhanis also can be considered *shaktispithas,* or Tantric goddesses associated with places of pilgrimage.[82] Tantrism, regarded by some scholars as an ancient movement that arose as a reaction to the stratification and elaborate rituals of the Vedic religion, parallels Sufism, Islamic mysticism, in several regards. Both were open to all members of society and provided a contrast to the more formal, restrictive religions from which they sprang.[83] Both also included rites and beings believed to have the ability to bestow special powers upon their practitioners. In general, one would appeal to ruhanis in order to gain their help in destroying one's enemies. The *Nujum*'s author discusses the ruhanis' power chiefly in terms of their influence over a ruler's success in battle, suiting the author's overall purpose in writing the manuscript.[84]

The illustrations in this section portray the ruhanis as well as their corresponding diagrams of magnetism, or chakras. Many of the ruhanis bear characteristics, such as tridents or cups of blood, associated with the Hindu deities Kali and Shiva, considered the founder of Tantrism. Some of the figures, such as the ruhani Chalandhari (fig. 2.15), sit on thrones, while others ride vehicles such as buffaloes and peacocks, and all are large and powerful. For example, the artists depicted the ruhani Lhanas as a giant lion-bird beast carrying helpless soldiers in her hands (pl. 7). Not all of them, however, are depicted in such a ferocious manner. The goddess Subhapgi nurses a baby while attendants hold a parasol over her, fan her with a fly whisk, and massage her feet, as if she were royalty.

Islamic astrological treatises occasionally contain a section devoted to describing demons and other destructive forces. For example, the *Kitab al-Bulhan,* a fourteenth-century Arabic manuscript on astrology, catalogs a selection of Islamic demons.[85] These forces are portrayed in a similar manner to the *Nujum al-Ulum*'s ruhanis (though in a very different style): large, powerful figures clutching tiny, defenseless enemies and depicted with careful attention to their identifying attributes. What makes the *Nujum*'s forces distinctive, therefore, is not that they are destructive and powerful but rather that they are no longer male and Islamic in nature. They are now largely female and Hindu.

The painting style employed to portray the ruhanis is devoid of overt Persian features and seems to follow older south Indian painting traditions rather than the emerging local Bijapuri style. The goddesses wear flower garlands and oversized gold jewelry, including large disklike earrings that often are as large as their heads. Most have ample breasts that contrast strongly with their small waists. The artists depicted the figures, some of which are placed in niches, as fierce and dynamic, and disregarded both scale and anatomic proportion in order to convey the energy of these goddesses. Some elements of the paintings seem almost sketchlike in their lack of attention to detail, but the artists paid careful attention to the ruhanis' identifying attributes, even depicting the hand gestures, or *mudras,* described in the text.[86] In fact, the illustrations in this section precisely fit the text, which is devoted to articulating the goddesses' attributes and poses.

In contrast to other Indic material in the *Nujum,* the author presents the ruhanis and their powers as foreign information. He explains the appearance of each goddess in detail to his readers and specifically states that his material is taken from Hindu sources, perhaps trying to vouch for its accuracy.[87] In this instance it seems that the author did not assume his audience would be familiar with the subject. This is the only section the author presents in this manner, and it is also the only section whose illustrations fall into the third stylistic category, archaic Indic. The style is distinct enough from the other two styles present in the book to suggest that the artists employed in this section had different training and backgrounds from the painters working on the rest of the manuscript. In fact, both Linda Leach and Hermann Goetz have suggested that the artists of the ruhani section were perhaps recent immigrants from Vijayanagara, the south Indian kingdom that Bijapur helped defeat in 1565.[88] Once again, the style seems to have been specifically chosen to fit the text. It also may have been that the material, devoted to describing the Tantric goddesses and their attributes in detail, required artists familiar with the ruhanis in order to depict them with the accuracy expected in a scientific treatise.

In addition to style, the *Nujum al-Ulum*'s creators also manipulated and blended iconography to correspond with the message of the text. A striking example of this is the small illustration on folio 27v, in the section laying out the yearly astrological system, that depicts the planet Mars in anthropomorphic form (pl. 4). Traditionally Islamic astrological treatises conceptualize Mars as an invincible warrior and associate the planet with a ram. In keeping with that, the *Nujum* presents Mars as the legendary Persian warrior Rustam riding on a ram. A viewer familiar with Persian traditions can easily recognize Rustam by his leopard-head helmet, beard, and distinctive dress. Yet one aspect of the image gives it a distinguishing twist: Rustam has four arms that hold a sword, dagger, mace, and trident, the last of these being the attribute of the Hindu god Shiva. Thus the artist of the painting bestowed upon Mars not only the fortitude of Rustam but also the invincible power of Shiva in warrior mode, and in doing so conceived an ingenious composite form.

The strength of this representation is that it operates as a multivalent signifier, an image endowed with multiple paths to arrive at its meaning. In other words, the artist who created this image combined two disparate visual traditions in order to suggest the same reading—in this case, the planet Mars personified as a stalwart, undefeatable warrior—to different viewers. A Persian viewer familiar with Rustam immediately would recognize him and thus would read the planet Mars as the mighty warrior; however, if the viewer were unfamiliar with that tradition, the connection could still be made through Mars's multiple weapon-bearing arms, suggesting the superhuman power of a Hindu god. If the viewer were aware of both traditions, then the meaning of the image would just be strengthened. In a four by five centimeter space the artist cast Mars as a fully Persianate, Shiva-incarnate, ram-riding Rustam and, in doing so, demonstrated that Bijapuri artists not only consciously employed but also ingeniously blended visual traditions for specific purposes.

The anthropomorphic painting of the Sun (fig. 2.12) combines a similar iconographic juxtaposition in order to operate in the same manner as the Mars illustration. Islamic astrology typically presents the Sun as a figure pulled in a chariot by lions. Again, the *Nujum*'s Sun follows this traditional portrayal. The figure even sports a distinctively Central Asian Islamicate Sun face. Yet, once again, the artist added multiple arms as found on images of Hindu deities. Two of the Sun's arms rest on the lions pulling the chariot (the lions are awkwardly positioned off to the sides, making it seem as if the Sun is petting them), while the other two hold a conch shell and a mace, the attributes of the Hindu god Vishnu. Vishnu's role as the preserver of the world connects with the Sun's continual restoration of the earth as it travels across the sky each day, and so once again, by combining two disparate visual traditions in a way that conveys a similar meaning, the artist has created an effective multivalent signifier. Such multivalence must have been useful, if not vital, in the composite, constantly shifting environment of the Adil Shahi court.

If, as in the Mars and Sun portrayals, some paintings mix easily recognizable iconographic elements in order to create images meaningful to a wide range of possible viewers, then other paintings create new iconography in order to imbue the scenes with a specifically Bijapuri character. The illustration of the planet Jupiter provides an excellent example of the conscious appropriation of three visual elements, iconography as well as artistic style and the clothing worn by figures in the painting, to tie the illustration to Bijapur (pl. 5). Islamic astrological tradition typically personifies the planet Jupiter as an old man reading.[89] In contrast, the *Nujum al-Ulum*'s illustration, done in the emerging Bijapuri style, portrays Jupiter as a Deccan sultan. He remains a bearded old man and carries a book in one hand, as a nod to the traditional depiction of Jupiter (and revealing that the artists were aware of the standard depiction and their departure from it), but clearly he has been transformed into an Indo-Islamic monarch. He sits on horseback surrounded by his royal attendants. The seven attendants carry many of the usual objects demarcating kingship in India: parasol, fanning cloth, and royal standard bearing the Persian inscription *Kaukab-i mushtari ast* (This is the star Jupiter). Most of the figures wear Persianate dress and small white turbans, as many Adil Shahi courtiers, particularly the Afaqi, would have. The first two attendants, however, are clad differently. The bare-chested men wear pants and tall, conical caps. They carry swords and shields indicating their status as soldiers. Armbands, anklets, and animal tails attached to their belts and shields as evidence of their prowess further adorn the two warriors. As Phillip Wagoner has noted, their attire is similar to that worn by figures in wall paintings from Vijayanagara and seems to be a combination of local south Indian and Islamicate dress.[90] Just as in the other Deccan kingdoms, men from a variety of backgrounds made up the Bijapuri army, including a large number of Marathas and other local Deccan Hindus who may have dressed in a manner similar to Vijayanagaran soldiers. In fact, this procession probably mirrors an actual procession of a Deccan sultan at the time of the *Nujum*'s production.[91]

Presenting Jupiter in the guise of a Deccan sultan creates a deliberate visual link between Bijapur and the information presented in the *Nujum al-Ulum*. The illustration drives home the point that by understanding the supernatural forces at work, it is not just any ruler but specifically Bijapur's ruler who will be able to effectively govern worldly affairs. Additionally, the comparison between the powerful planet Jupiter and the king in royal procession alludes to the might of Deccan sultans, which in the wake of the 1565 victory over Vijayanagara would have held immediate historical allusions for the Bijapuri viewers. The composition, bright colors, effective use of gold, and careful execution make the painting one of the most striking in the manuscript. It also is considerably larger than any of the other planet illustrations, suggesting that the *Nujum*'s creators viewed it as a particularly significant image, undoubtedly due to its local slant and emphasis on kingship.

Another important *Nujum* painting relating to kingship that employs iconography to link the image specifically to Bijapur is the depiction of the chakravartin's allegorical seven-storied throne (pl. 6). The painting, located on folio 191, is the sole full-paged painting in the entire manuscript and thus provides the climax not only of the section devoted to the objects surrounding the ideal ruler but of the entire manuscript. The page, which contains the imprint of Ibrahim Adil Shah II's royal seal and which also appears worn out (the paint having flaked away on the lower portions of the page) in this otherwise pristinely preserved manuscript, must have been a favorite of the manuscript's readers, no doubt due to its subject matter.

At the top of the golden throne, the ruler, whose dress casts him as a Deccan sultan, sits cross-legged in the middle of a lapis-colored eight-petal lotus flower and beneath a lotus canopy. On the second level, his two female consorts stand in front of a row of palm trees. The king's subjects, including a tribal family on the left side, villagers on the right, and two urbanites seated on a carpet in the center, populate the third level. Next come the sultan's courtiers, depicted as six men in conversation. A pair of horses pulling chariots, a pair of *mahouts* (drivers) on their elephants, and two seated men fill the fifth level, while the sixth and seventh levels consist of tiny heraldic lions in gold and lapis lazuli. At base of the diagram, in front of a stone arcade, kneeling courtiers alternate with gold lions standing atop elephants. More gold heraldic lions march around the edges of the throne, and a lapis blue eight-petal lotus flanked by peacocks occupies the center of the composition.[92]

The objective of the seven-storied throne was to illustrate the various elements bolstering the chakravartin's power, a concept related to his Seven Treasures. His ideal consorts, one of his Seven Treasures, stand directly below the king to support him. Next in line are his subjects, followed by his courtiers. The elephants, horses, and two seated men (presumably his generals) represent the kingdom's military strength and also make up three more of the Seven Treasures. The text accompanying the illustration refers to the throne as the *simhasana chakra,* literally "ideal lion seat." As in many other regions of the world, in South Asia from early times onward, the lion symbolized kingship. For example, the Mauryan emperor Ashoka, who was considered a chakravartin, employed the imagery of both lions and wheels when erecting the famous monumental sandstone pillars on which his edicts were written. The carved lions perched atop the pillars combined with images of the wheel illustrated the idea of the universal ruler. By drawing on this potent symbolism, the Ashokan pillars provided a visual reminder of Ashoka's power.[93] In the same vein, the many heraldic lions populating the *Nujum*'s throne painting visually express the idea of the simhasana chakra. Like the ruler's Persianate dress, which serves to situate the Indic concept of the seven-storied throne within a Bijapuri context, the pose of the heraldic lions imbues the image with a specifically Deccan flavor. The artists depict each of the lions with one upraised paw, which, as Mark Zebrowski has argued in his study of Indo-Islamic metalwork, was a feature particular to Deccan representations of these royal felines, whose imagery probably evolved from *yalis,* South Indian mythological winged lion-beasts.[94]

Just as the lions relate to the idea of the chakravartin, so do the lotus flowers. The lotus, a popular image in South Asian art, symbolizes creation and prosperity. In terms of the chakravartin concept, the eight-petal lotus holds special significance, as demonstrated by its repeated use in the seven-storied throne. As Linda Leach explains, the eight petals symbolize the eight spokes of the wheel around which the universe spins smoothly during the reign of a chakravartin.[95] The eight-petal lotus flanked by peacocks at the center of the throne thus symbolizes the wheel smoothly turning at the center of the kingdom.

Notably, the two most repeated symbols in the throne painting, the lotus flower and the heraldic lion, are found throughout Bijapuri art from earlier, contemporary, and later periods, demonstrating that these motifs held immense appeal for the Adil Shahis. For example, the distinctive design of a stylized lotus budlike dome resting on a ring of lotus petals provides one of the most characteristic elements of Adil Shahi architecture. One of the earliest surviving Adil Shahi mosques, commonly referred to as "Yusuf's old jami masjid," bears a dome with lotus petal base, and the lotus bud and petal combination became increasingly popular over time. As architectural ornament became more profuse, lotus buds and petals began appearing everywhere: capping minarets and cornices, dripping off brackets, delicately carved into lintels, posed as perky finials (stylized lotus bud finials even augment the top corners of the *Nujum al-Ulum*'s golden throne). The peculiar lion standing atop an elephant combination repeated at the base of the throne painting also can be found in Bijapur's architectural decoration; some of the delicately carved brackets ornamenting the gateway to the seventeenth-century Mihtar-i Mahal mosque bear the lion/elephant pairing (fig. 4.17).[96] Heraldic lions and lotuses also are common decorations in the surviving examples of Adil Shahi metalwork. For example, the Bijapur Archeological Museum contains a ten-inch high brass object (possibly an incense burner) composed of four heraldic lions supporting an opened lotus flower that is surrounded by birds and small lotus buds.[97] The lions, with their slender waists, opened mouths, and slightly angry expressions bear striking similarity to the stylized gold and lapis lions in the throne painting.

The heraldic lion seems to have been a particularly popular motif during Ali Adil Shah I's reign. A lion, who, like those in the throne painting, has a slender waist, opened mouth, and upraised paw, appears on the 1560–61 gateway leading to the Gagan Mahal built for Ali (fig. 2.1). The Portuguese visitor Rodriguez describes the entrance to the royal palace as flanked by tents decorated with "two lions for arms, such as he [Ali Adil Shah] usually bears on the field." The court historian Firishta states that in 1566–67 Ali presented his vizier, Qishur Khan, with a standard on which was embroidered "an angry lion."[98] The popularity of the motif during Sultan Ali's reign presumably was due to the fact that the lion also serves as a symbol of the Shia imam Ali, who often is referred to as "the lion of God." The heraldic lion thus would have alluded to Ali Adil Shah's Shia faith and, because his name was Ali, the sultan himself.

The lion and lotus were potent symbols because both held multiple connotations. The lion could reference the Shia imam Ali; if depicted with one upraised paw, it held specifically Deccan associations; in certain circumstances it could refer to the simhasana, the throne of the ideal ruler; and underlying all of these associations is the fact that images of lions operate as general symbols of kingship throughout many regions of the world. In South Asia, the lotus symbolizes creation and prosperity. As a plant that grows in water, it also connotes lush gardens, greenery, and an abundance of water, all conditions that the builders of Bijapur were working diligently to create. Because the lotus is not an anthropomorphic image, it could be used freely as a motif on any object or building, including mosques, tombs, or other Islamic religious buildings, in which images of humans or animals are not allowed. Thus the lion and lotus were effective visual symbols of kingship, implying good leadership, prosperity, and royalty to a wide range of viewers. Recognition of their generality and popularity, however, should not eclipse their roles as links to the Indic ideal of the chakravartin. Their repeated use in the *Nujum al-Ulum*'s illustration of the ruler's seven-storied throne unequivocally establishes the emblems' connection to the chakravartin concept and signifies that the bond was a conscious one to at least some Adil Shahi artists, writers, patrons, and manuscript viewers.

The throne painting, with its lions and lotuses, operates largely on a symbolic level. It combines a range of visually simple, yet highly recognizable, potent forms to represent complex concepts that of themselves have no visible form. This emphasis on putting things into visible form, whether spirits, hidden energy sources, or theoretical concepts that are not typically experienced visually, can be found throughout the *Nujum al-Ulum*'s illustrations and provide one of the underlying characteristics of the manuscript. For example, diagrams of the ruhanis' forces of energy accompany the physical depictions of the goddesses. The paintings convey the ruhanis' power through their ferocious appearances, while the diagrams, through the use of abstract forms, present the energy underlying the physical prowess. The diagrams thus provide a link between the seen and unseen.

A small painting of a drummer accompanied by a circular diagram perhaps best exemplifies the link between the visible and invisible created in many of the *Nujum*'s illustrations (fig. 2.14). The painting, one of the many illustrations of musical instruments, is part of the collection of objects surrounding the ideal ruler and depicts a drum being held by a court musician. The diagram on the left side of the painting, extending out from the drum, consists of a series of concentric circles. The point of the circles seems to have been to convey the expanding sound reverberations that the drum makes when hit. Thus, by including the simple diagram along with the figural painting, the artist created a conceptual representation of the drum's sound. While the meaning of the drum diagram is fairly obvious, many of the other diagrams, including the diagrammatic representation of the seven-storied throne and eight-petal lotus, are more obscure and require the viewer to already possess some understanding of the subject matter to fully grasp the significance of the renderings. As Leach explains, "Many compositions have some symbolic level which is frequently expressed by a partial diagrammatic arrangement. The pictorial thus verges into the conceptual, and the viewer requires explanation of the underlying philosophy presented in order to establish the intended relation between certain miniatures."[99]

The *Nujum al-Ulum* is a complex manuscript conveying a broad range of knowledge with multiple levels of meaning at work, undoubtedly not all of which are apparent to modern viewers and readers. Yet, even from our current perspective, a careful reading of the illustrated manuscript brings into focus much about the shape and role of the arts in 1570s Adil Shahi Bijapur. First, the work's size and scope make apparent that courtly artistic production was flourishing by the time of its production in 1570–71. Second, while the text reveals an intense interest in knowledge aimed at increasing a ruler's effectiveness, including ensuring the military success and prosperity of his kingdom, the *Nujum*'s images demonstrate recognition of the substantial role that the visual arts could play in augmenting such effectiveness. The stylistic variations and manipulations of iconography in many of the paintings present further evidence of a sophisticated understanding of the capabilities of visual language.

Third, the examples of intercultural exchange found throughout the text and images illuminate the specific forms and purposes that it embodied in Adil Shahi visual culture. In some instances, such as the illustrations of Mars and the Sun, the artists combined disparate iconographic traditions in order to create multivalent signifiers, images with multiple paths to arrive at the intended reading, allowing a variety of viewers to grasp the significance of a form. At other times, the artists seem to adopt already existing emblems with broad, varying associations across cultural traditions, like the lion and the lotus flower, to allow for a wide range of possible readings. And yet, in other instances, the artists seem to have brought together style, iconography, and even dress in order to link a concept or piece of information specifically to Bijapur—the specific composite nature of the depiction reflecting, and thus easily recognizable as, the composite nature of the Islamicate Deccan. All three reveal a conscious recognition of the diverse makeup of Bijapur.

Finally, the *Nujum al-Ulum* exhibits themes and motifs that are central to later artworks, providing a foundation from which to understand Bijapur's artistic development. The common motifs include such things as the heraldic lions and lotus flowers, while the shared themes encompass mysticism and kingship as well as a proclivity to put into artistic form things that are not normally experienced visually. In the *Nujum,* the tendency to visually express the unseen relates to the desire to understand the supernatural forces at work in the cosmos, while later artistic examples tend to focus more on poetic allusions. Recognizing this inclination, whatever form it takes, is key to understanding much of Bijapuri art.

When we place the *Nujum al-Ulum* alongside the post-1565 building campaign of Bijapur city and the tomb of Ali Adil Shah I, it becomes apparent that the period between 1565 and 1580 witnessed the formation of the groundwork upon which Bijapur's later artistic production built. The 1565 victory over Vijayanagara dramatically increased Bijapur's wealth, standing, and stability. The post-1565 building campaign carried out by Ali Adil Shah I and his nobles transferred this new affluence into a tangible and long-lasting form that in turn helped transform Bijapur city from a regional center into a proper Islamicate capital. This created the urban setting needed for the flourishing of courtly artistic production, including the creation of manuscripts like the *Nujum al-Ulum.* The *Nujum* reveals that Bijapur's courtly culture was a vibrant one, drawing on a wide range of traditions and fully cognizant of the power of visual forms. The manuscript, along with Ali's tomb, establishes the strong link that existed between mysticism and kingship, even during the reign of a Shia monarch, while the construction of Ali's tomb further began a tradition in which the Adil Shahi rulers mapped their identity and legacy directly onto the physical form of Bijapur city, the capital of their kingdom and home to their court. Viewed through these three examples, the period of 1565–80 truly appears as a time of prosperous beginnings.

3
Developing Visual Metaphors

There are different languages;
But there is one emotional appeal,
Be he a Brahmin or a Turk.
He is only fortunate on whom
The Goddess of learning smiles.
O Ibrahim, the world only seeks knowledge—
Serve and meditate upon with steadfast heart
The power of words.

This verse from the *Kitab-i Nauras,* a collection of poems/songs composed in Deccani Urdu heavily laden with Sanskrit vocabulary and attributed to Sultan Ibrahim Adil Shah II, speaks eloquently to the courtly culture developing in Bijapur in the late sixteenth and early seventeenth centuries.[1] Freely drawing on Indic and Islamicate traditions, Bijapur's blossoming courtly culture centered largely on language—on the growth of Deccani Urdu, but also on individual words, literature, and poetry tailored to fit the composite nature of the Deccan kingdom as well as the mystically oriented, learned environment promoted in courtly circles. Indeed, knowledge became so esteemed at the Adil Shahi court that in 1603–1604, Ibrahim II officially changed the name of Bijapur (or Vijayapur), meaning "City of Victory," to Vidyapur, "City of Learning."[2] In the City of Learning, music flourished, Sufis from the Chishti, Qadiri, and Shattari orders found receptive followers, and courtiers created original poems, literary works, and historical accounts.[3]

Art played an integral part in Bijapur's courtly culture. Patrons and artists created numerous original works aimed at transforming "the power of words" into visual form. Their results helped create a distinct visual identity for the sultanate. The translation from word to image/object was achieved largely through the development of visual metaphors drawn from Sufism and court poetry. For example, the *Pem Nem,* a Sufic romance written and illustrated in Bijapur circa 1591–1604, displays an intriguing relationship between its text and images. In some respects, the paintings are amateurish, illustrating the text in a simplistic, inconsistent manner. In other ways, however, the paintings are innovative, employing novel elements in an effort to convey the depths of love and longing expressed in the tale. Late sixteenth- and early seventeenth-century paintings of *yoginis,* Hindu female ascetics, like the *Pem Nem*'s illustrations, are closely linked with the ideas of mysticism as expressed in literature of the period. The yogini images, however, are single-page paintings and thus refer to literature and poetry without directly illustrating a text, allowing them to operate on more symbolic levels. Like the yogini paintings, portraits of Ibrahim Adil Shah II from the same period visually refer to poetry—poetic accounts of the sultan as well as general ideals of kingship as expressed in poetic sources. The poetic conduit is so strong that the paintings are perhaps better understood not as portraits of Ibrahim II but rather as visualizations of poetic ideals regarding Ibrahim II. The foundation of Nauraspur in 1599 as a twin capital with Bijapur demonstrates that the development of visual metaphors was not limited to Bijapuri painting. Ibrahim, his courtiers, and builders conceived the palace-city as an architectural embodiment of *nauras,* a many-layered poetic term that had become central to the court's collective identity.

Ali Adil Shah I's prolific twenty-two-year rule came to an abrupt end in 1580 when one of the sultan's servants murdered him.[4] Since Ali had no children of his own, it was left to his nine-year-old nephew, Ibrahim II, to succeed him. During Ibrahim's adolescence, Ali's widow, Chand Bibi, acted as dowager queen while a series of power-hungry regents vied for control of the kingdom. Various intrigues, including a plot to murder Chand Bibi, threw Bijapur into chaos. In 1588 the Nizam Shahs of Ahmadnagar took advantage of Bijapur's weakened state to attack. In 1590, when Ibrahim became old enough to take the throne fully, his kingdom was still fighting off Ahmadnagar, a conflict not resolved for another three years.[5] No paintings survive, or at least have been dated to, the 1580–90 period, and one of the few major pieces of architecture from the period is the Sat Manzil, a palace commissioned by Ibrahim II in the citadel's royal compound. The lack of significant artistic production most likely resulted from the turbulence of Ibrahim's first decade of kingship.

With Ibrahim II's maturation and an end to the major political strife, courtly art once again seems to have proliferated. If, as the surviving evidence suggests, the early 1570s saw a burst of illustrated manuscript production in Bijapur, then the next onset of painting seems to have occurred in the 1590s. The surviving works from the 1590s onward, however, are primarily single-page paintings rather than illustrated manuscripts (although a few manuscripts, such as the *Pem Nem*, were produced). Architectural projects, likewise, once again increased in number. When the young ruler ascended the throne in 1590, the ceremony was held at the newly constructed Anand Mahal, designed to emulate its neighboring palace, the Gagan Mahal of Ali Adil Shah. Nine years later, Ibrahim II even founded a new city west of Bijapur, Nauraspur, to showcase the blossoming Adil Shahi court.

Although Ibrahim was not nearly as active politically or militarily as his uncle, Ali, there were significant political developments during his reign. Ibrahim changed the state religion for the sixth time since the beginning of the dynasty; he declared the kingdom's official religion to be Sunni Islam and favored Deccani, rather than Afaqi, nobles at court. The role of Maharashtran bureaucrats also grew.[6] In 1619 Bijapur annexed the kingdom of Bidar, which included the wealthy and fertile area of Berar, further enhancing the size and revenue of the kingdom.[7]

A new threat from the north, however, appeared at the beginning of Ibrahim's reign. The Mughal dynasty, under the leadership of the emperor Akbar, began to look southward. In 1600–1601, the Mughals defeated the Nizam Shah kingdom of Ahmadnagar, Bijapur's northern neighbor. Ibrahim II managed to put off the growing danger for Bijapur by arranging a marriage alliance between his daughter, Begam Sultana, and one of Akbar's sons, Prince Daniyal.[8] Bijapur's relative security in comparison to its northern neighbor led many scholars and courtiers, such as the Persian poet Zuhuri, who had been residing at Ahmadnagar, to migrate south, substantially enriching the ranks of the Adil Shahi court.[9] After the death of Akbar in 1605, the Mughal threat to Bijapur diminished somewhat, although it remained strong enough that Ibrahim felt the need to request the Safavid Shah's diplomatic intervention with Jahangir, the newly crowned Mughal ruler, on behalf of Bijapur.[10]

Another danger to Bijapur emerged when the Habshi general Malik Ambar, determined to resist the Mughals, came to power in Ahmadnagar. Initially, Ibrahim II and Malik Ambar joined forces; however, their relationship quickly deteriorated, leading to a war between Bijapur and Ambar's forces. In 1624, Malik Ambar and his armies destroyed Ibrahim's beloved new city, Nauraspur, reminding us that the ideal, learned, peaceful environment promoted in the court's art did not necessarily reflect the political reality.[11]

The *Pem Nem*

A 1590s illustrated romance, the *Pem Nem,* parallels the *Nujum al-Ulum* in several key ways, making it a valuable resource regarding Adil Shahi courtly culture. Specifically, both illustrated manuscripts remain largely intact, and they are among the most concretely attributable examples of painting from late sixteenth-century Bijapur. Adil Shahi courtiers wrote each work. They are original, yet they draw on older literary sources, and both manuscripts exhibit revealing relationships between text and image. In contrast to the *Nujum,* however, the *Pem Nem* reveals little, at least directly, about Adil Shahi conceptions of kingship and more about the role of mystical romances in the courtly culture. The manuscript's illustrations act both individually and as a whole to augment the emotions and goals of Sufism as positioned within the context of elite life.

The *Pem Nem,* housed in the British Library, London, contains 239 folios and thirty-four illustrations, all but three of which occupy a full page.[12] Hasan Manjhu Khalji, who adopted the pen name Hamsa, states in the introduction that he completed the story in 1591. Hamsa goes on to praise not only Ibrahim Adil Shah II and the city of Bijapur but also the city of Nauraspur, which was not founded until 1599, and Ibrahim's prized elephant Chanchal, which the sultan gave to the Mughal emperor Akbar in 1604. These references indicate that the author and artists completed the illustrated manuscript at some point after the tale's original penning in 1591, but before 1604.[13] Hamsa wrote the entire text, which unfortunately has yet to be fully translated, in an early form of Deccani Urdu employing many Persian, Arabic, and Marathi words, and composed the body of the work in poetic verse. The romance centers around Ratan Sen, the prince of Chittor, and Padmavati, the princess of Simhala (Sri Lanka).

Although the *Pem Nem* (variously translated as *The Toils of Love* or *The Law of Love*) is a unique manuscript, the story is based on a common Sufic allegory of love and longing in which the lover, in this case the prince of Chittor, sets out to find his beloved, with whom he is finally united at the end of the tale.[14] Usually this type of Sufic romance begins with two lovers being separated for some reason or with the lover having a vision of, or chance encounter with, an anonymous beloved. The lover then goes off in search of his beloved, during which he endures great suffering that only intensifies his longing, before finally being united with his beloved. Sometimes the stories end in death or annihilation rather than earthly union. This literary type, often called *Prem Marg* (Path of Love), serves as an allegory. The lover represents the Sufi seeking union with God, and the beloved symbolizes God. This type of Sufic love story is particularly widespread in Urdu literature in which often one or both of the main characters are Hindu, as they are in the *Pem Nem.* The text typically takes the form of a *masnavi* (a long story composed in poetic verse), the South Asian development of which seems to have coincided with the evolution of Urdu language. The earliest example of *Prem Marg* is the 1379 tale *Chandayan,* written in Urdu by Maulana Daud, a disciple of a Chishti Sufi saint and a member of an Indo-Islamic court near Awadh in northern India, one of the regions central to the development of Urdu. Creating the model followed by later poets including the author of the *Pem Nem,* Daud combined the conventions of Persian masnavis, such as beginning the poem with a formal prologue that praises God, the prophet Muhammad, the author's royal patron, and his Sufi spiritual guide, with Indic motifs and aesthetic practices. Both literary type and language thus emerged out of cultural interaction and in turn provided fertile ground for more such intercultural exchange.[15]

The fictional main characters in the *Pem Nem,* Padmavati and Ratan Sen, along with the romance's Sri Lankan setting suggest a link between it and an earlier, well known Urdu tale of love, Malik Muhammad Jayasi's *Padmavati,* composed in 1540. The story, which David Gordon White describes as "a beautiful yogic allegory of the wooing of Padmavati, princess of Simhala, by a prince-turned-Nath Siddha [yogi] named Ratansen," most likely provided the basis for the *Pem Nem,* but the latter clearly incorporates its own twists and turns.[16] Specifically, in Jayasi's *Padmavati,* the story begins with the couple's marriage, during which Ratan Sen presents himself as a yogi, an ascetic. Only later does he reveal himself to Padmavati as a prince. Conversely, the *Pem Nem* begins with Ratan Sen's journey and ends with the couple's marriage. Throughout the *Pem Nem*'s illustrations Ratan Sen remains a prince, and the story serves as a Sufic rather than yogic allegory. Toward the beginning of the text, however, Ratan Sen does encounter a yogini, a female Hindu ascetic. In fact, this event, which appears to be the catalyst for the prince's search, is the subject of the manuscript's first illustration on folio 46, in which Ratan Sen and an attendant listen to the yogini play her *veena* (pl. 8).[17]

The *Pem Nem*'s next four illustrations, occurring on folios 47, 49v, 69, and 70v (fig. 3.1), depict Ratan Sen sitting or walking in the countryside. Eventually in his travels, the prince meets up with a king. Folio 75v depicts the prince and king conversing on a carpet, with the king's procession in the background. The king then invites the prince back to his palace, shown on folio 80. At the palace, the prince sees his beloved (presumably the king's daughter). In folio 82v's illustration, Ratan Sen has fainted upon seeing her (pl. 9). The following fourteen paintings, spread out between folios 87 and 178v, show the prince pining for the princess while he continues to stay at the palace and the princess in turn longing for Ratan Sen as she takes part in various harem activities. Eventually a

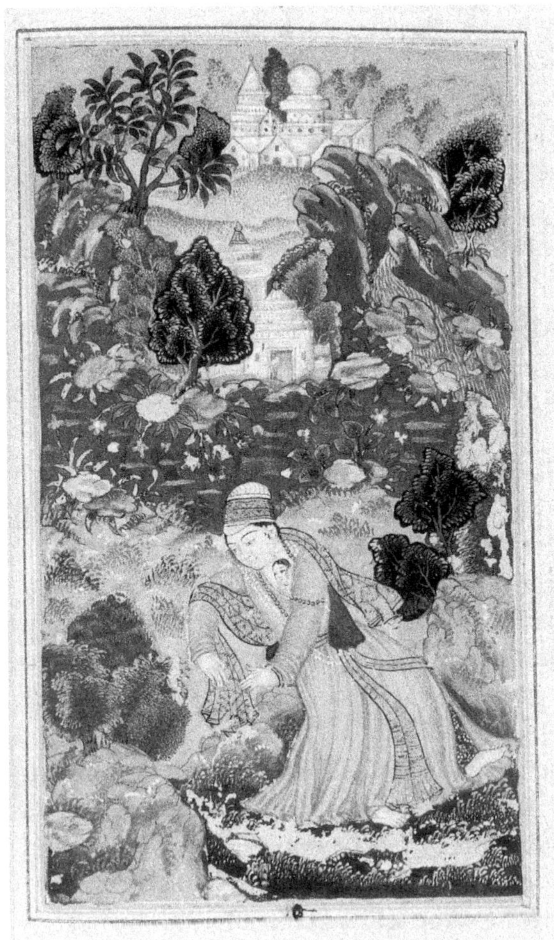

Figure 3.1. Prince in landscape, *Pem Nem*, ca. 1591–1604, Bijapur. British Library, London, Add.16880, folio 70v. By permission of the British Library.

marriage between the prince and princess is arranged, and the remaining twelve illustrations occurring between folios 181v and 232 depict the wedding festivities in detail before concluding with the lovers together, finally united.

In the *Pem Nem*'s illustrations, the figures move through lush countrysides with white palaces perched atop craggy hills in the distance, a feature repeatedly found in later Bijapuri paintings, or they sit within white, multistoried domed palaces highlighted with pink pigment and adorned with flowered carpets. The skies are covered in thick gold pigment, and in some paintings, the artists have added a second sky, a blue strip enlivened with white clouds and birds, above the golden atmosphere. In the middle ground of the illustrations, the artists painted dense foliage dark green with orange and gold highlights. Overall, the colors in the paintings—dark green, orange, pink, and gold—make up the characteristic Bijapuri palette. Throughout the manuscript Ratan Sen is clothed in typical

Bijapuri fashion: a small turban with a sash across the middle, a voluminous robe, and long, flowing scarves decorated with geometric ornament.[18] The other male characters in the *Pem Nem* dress in this manner as well, while the women wear saris and much gold jewelry. The architecture and dress along with the paint palette in the illustrations serve to situate the tale of a prince from Chittor and princess from Sri Lanka in a wholly Bijapuri visual environment, thereby ensuring its familiarity to its intended audience, members of the Adil Shahi court.

Despite Bijapuri-related stylistic continuities, there are clearly observable differences among the folios, leading art historians to identify three "hands," or individual artists who worked on the manuscript.[19] "Hand A," who seems to have been responsible for fourteen to eighteen of the paintings—including the first illustration (pl. 8)—is the most accomplished of the three. In fact, the artist has been linked stylistically to several other key Bijapuri paintings, most notably the circa 1605 yogini painting in the Chester Beatty Library, Dublin (pl. 16).[20] "Hand B" appears to have been the least skilled of the three artists, with some of his fourteen or fifteen paintings appearing almost clumsy, amateurish (see pl. 11), while "Hand C," credited with only a few of the illustrations, falls in the middle (see fig. 3.1).

Perhaps due to the varying skill of the three artists, there are marked inconsistencies among the thirty-four illustrations. The disparities include not only the quality of the images but also the appearance of the main characters and even the scale employed in the scenes. In most of the paintings, the various figures occupy the same scale, but in a few, the artist has drawn the main character much bigger than the rest of the figures. For example, in folio 87 (pl. 10) the prince towers over the court musicians to whom he is listening, and in folio 138 (pl. 13) the princess dwarfs her attendants. This type of scaling, employed to emphasize the importance of the main characters, can be found frequently in both Persian and Indian paintings, but not typically in the same manuscript in which proportional scaling also is used. Moreover, it appears as if the artists expended little effort to coordinate the appearance of the main characters. Their dress differs from scene to scene, and even their physical characteristics vary so much, from slim-faced to round-faced to chinless, that if they were not the main characters in the scenes, it would be difficult to recognize them.

At the same time that these discrepancies score the illustrated manuscript, a close consideration of the images reveals some intriguing consistencies as well, beyond a mere conformity to the developing Bijapuri painting style. Most notably, in every depiction of Ratan Sen the artists have painted the face of his beloved on his chest, as if to express the metaphorical sentiment that she and his heart are permanently joined.[21] The artists may not always have adeptly or gracefully depicted her head in the small space exposed above the *V* of Ratan Sen's robe, but the motif nonetheless succeeds in being a highly original, endearing device that visually conveys emotions, in this case undying love, usually expressed through words.

Several other paintings also contain elements that visually express feelings of love and longing typically found in poetry. For example, in folio 90v (pl. 11), the prince, who sits on a rock in the countryside, is crying. His tears fall down to form a stream that runs between him and his attendant. The image thus conveys the depths of Ratan Sen's sorrow and longing by literally depicting him crying a stream of tears. In another instance, folio 119 (pl. 12) illustrates the prince and princess alone together for the first time and carrying on an intimate conversation. The artist has depicted gold spray coming out of Ratan Sen's mouth, as if to represent his words or voice as he expresses the depths of his love for Padmavati. Folio 138 (pl. 13) portrays the princess with her female attendants playing water games. The women frolic around a fountain and douse one another with water in a chaotic yet friendly scene. Padmavati occupies the middle of the space, not really taking part in the activities but sitting pensively with her head resting on her hand. An attendant has just poured water over her, but instead of being soaked like some of her attendants, golden flames rise from Padmavati. The painting seems to be saying that not even water can extinguish the flames of her passion for Ratan Sen, about whom she is thinking despite the cacophony around her.

Persianate painting, meaning painting from areas included in the greater Persian cultural sphere, from the early modern period typically relied on visual conventions to convey emotion rather than using facial expressions, as European art from the same period did. For example, Persian artists conveyed wonder or surprise by placing a character's finger at his or her mouth rather than, say, widening the character's eyes. They also sometimes employed specific landscape elements to accentuate the emotion in a scene, such as using entwined cypress and flowering trees to symbolize love or dead tree trunks to convey death and sorrow. Moreover, the practice of creating visual elements that mirrored poetic metaphors was fairly common in Persianate painting, as exhibited by the youthful beauties in Safavid album pages whose appearances precisely match the moonfaces and rosebud lips praised in poetry of the period.[22] While related to such practices, the *Pem Nem*'s particular use of visual metaphors is unique. The manuscript's artists were creating wholly new visual metaphors to fit the *Pem Nem*, which was an original work rather than an oft-copied classic. Additionally, the innovative elements, like Padmavati's face drawn on Ratan Sen's chest, are not subtle. They do not blend in with the rest of the scene as, say, entwined cypress and flowering trees positioned behind a pair of lovers in a garden would. The *Pem Nem*'s innovations stand out as clearly extraordinary elements, as if to drive home the point that they were written metaphors that had been put into visual form.

The *Pem Nem*'s visual metaphors, furthermore, all relate to emotions, whether longing, sorrow, desire, or joy, that would have been central to the poem's *rasa,* its "juice" or "flavor." As Aditya Behl explains, the "poetics of rasa" was a uniquely Indic tradition brought to the masnavi literary form by South Asian authors.[23] To be *rasavat,* full of rasa, a work had to convey a range of emotions that could be deeply felt by the cultivated reader, the *sahrdaya,* or by the connoisseur, the *rasika,* and that would move them to appreciate the work on a number of levels. The *Pem Nem*'s illustrations are intertwined with the literary practice of rasa. The illustrations highlight and reinforce the emotions conveyed by the author's words, and in doing so provide the readers with a second opportunity to position themselves as connoisseurs, this time through their appreciation of the emotions conveyed by the images rather than by the verses. That the visual strategies employed by the artists to convey the *Pem Nem*'s rasa are so striking and seem to have been created specifically for this manuscript suggests the centrality of rasa in Bijapur's developing courtly culture.

In addition to the repeated use of innovative visual metaphors to convey the depths of feeling in the poem, the *Pem Nem*'s illustrations display a consistent, though not absolute, spatial progression that is revealing. When one considers the paintings in terms of their settings, they fall loosely into five groups, which I have labeled "The Search," "Transitional Scenes," "Harem Scenes," "Palace Scenes," and "Wedding Scenes" (see appendix B). These groupings advance from open outdoor spaces toward increasingly confined or intimate spaces. Notably, this progression parallels the movement of a Sufi closer to his goal of union with God, which is phrased in Sufic literature as the movement from the outer world, the *zahir,* to the inner essence or truth, the *batin.*[24] Thus the illustrations' settings, when viewed in sequence, reinforce the mystical significance of the romance.

In the first five paintings, "The Search," Ratan Sen is moving through an open landscape, and in four of the five illustrations, he is the sole figure in the scene. The only architecture depicted is a distant white palace, and the landscape is craggy, with hills and trees, in addition to the palace, marking the background. The next seven paintings are transitional, depicting Ratan Sen moving from one space and one segment of his quest to another. In three paintings, folios 75v, 82v, and 90v, the prince is still in the countryside, although the palace no longer remains in the distance and a variety of figures now crowd the scenes, with the main characters often framed by a carpet spread out on the ground. In two paintings, folios 80 and 89v, Ratan Sen is just outside the king's palace, denoted by a pinkish-white building on the left third of each page. In the remaining two paintings, on folios 87 and 119, the prince is inside the palace, the walls and floors of which

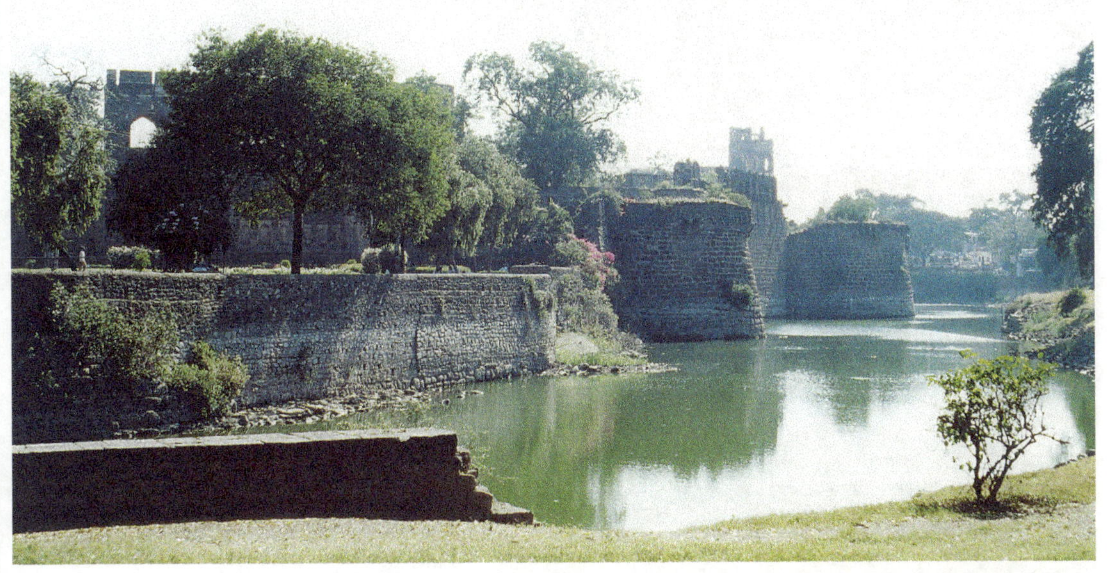

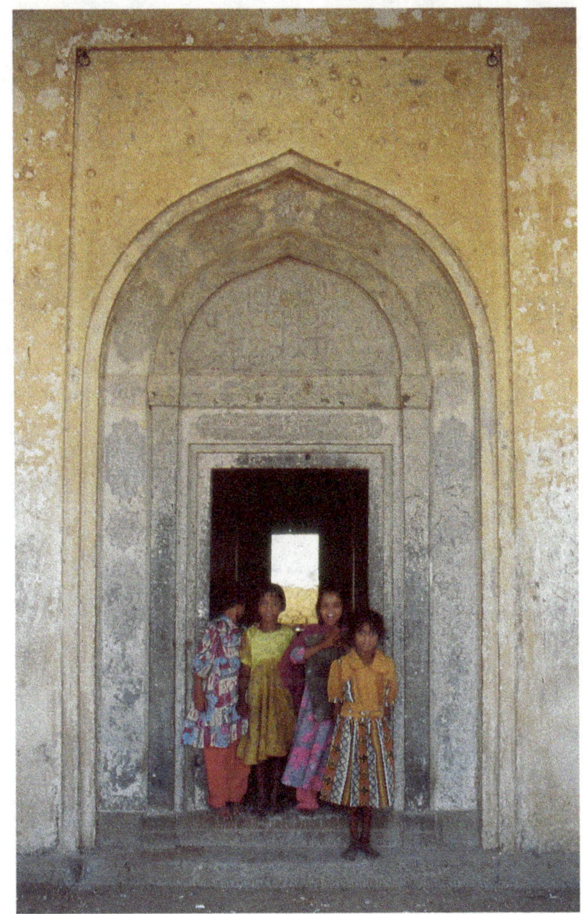

Plate 1. *Above:*
Gagan Mahal and citadel moat, mid-sixteenth century, Bijapur. Photograph by author.

Plate 2. *Right:*
Doorway with painted inscriptions from the tomb of Ali Adil Shah I, ca. 1580, Bijapur. Photograph by author.

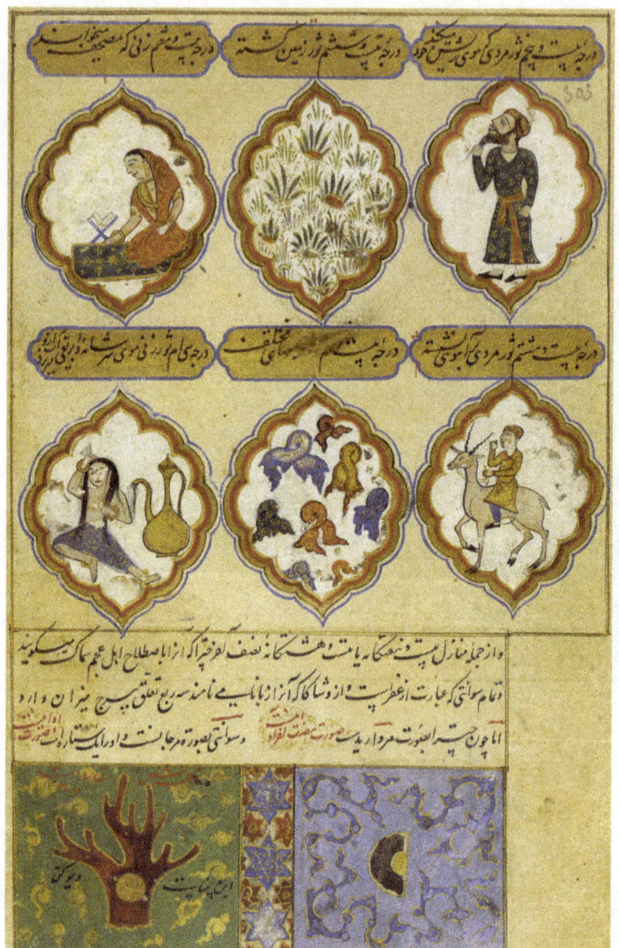

Plate 3.
Six degrees of the sign Taurus, *Nujum al-Ulum,* 1570–71, Bijapur. Chester Beatty Library, Dublin, MS. 2, folio 45v. Reproduced by kind permission of the Trustees of the Chester Beatty Library, Dublin.

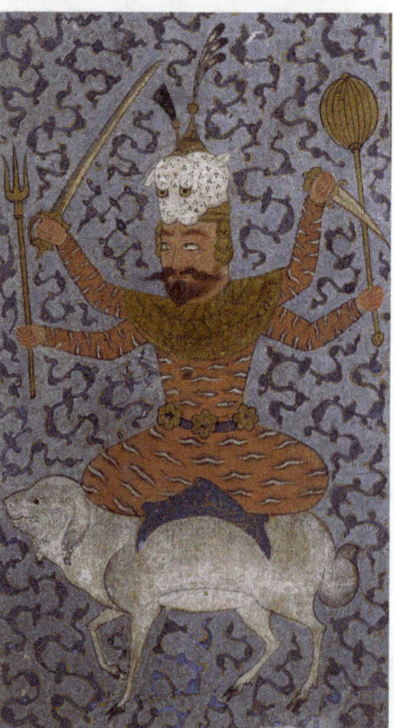

Plate 4.
The planet Mars, *Nujum al-Ulum,* 1570–71, Bijapur. Chester Beatty Library, Dublin, MS. 2, folio 27v. Reproduced by kind permission of the Trustees of the Chester Beatty Library, Dublin.

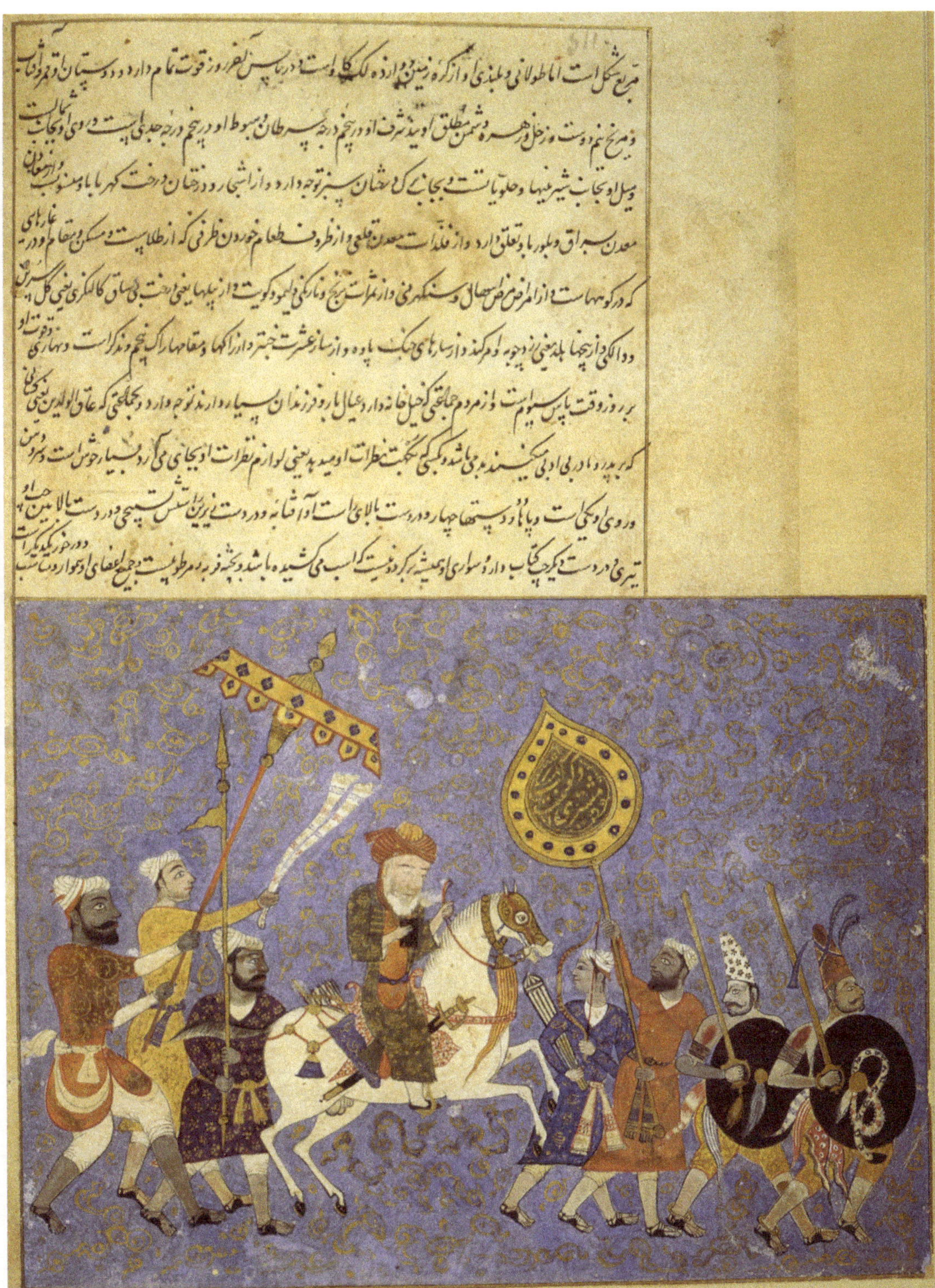

Plate 5. The planet Jupiter, *Nujum al-Ulum,* 1570–71, Bijapur. Chester Beatty Library, Dublin, MS. 2, folio 37v. Reproduced by kind permission of the Trustees of the Chester Beatty Library, Dublin.

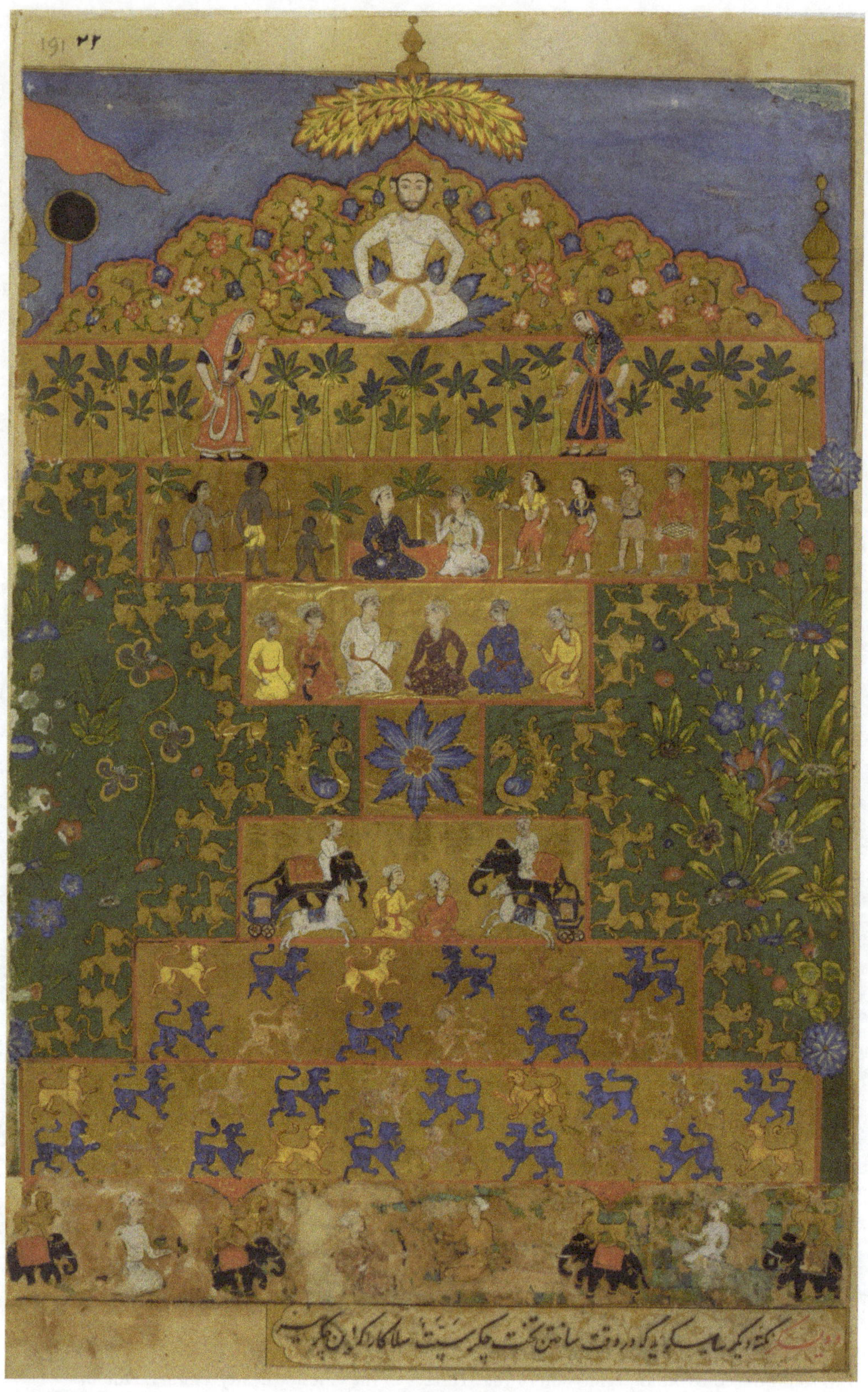

Plate 6. Seven-storied throne, *Nujum al-Ulum*, 1570–71, Bijapur. Chester Beatty Library, Dublin, MS. 2, folio 191. Reproduced by kind permission of the Trustees of the Chester Beatty Library, Dublin.

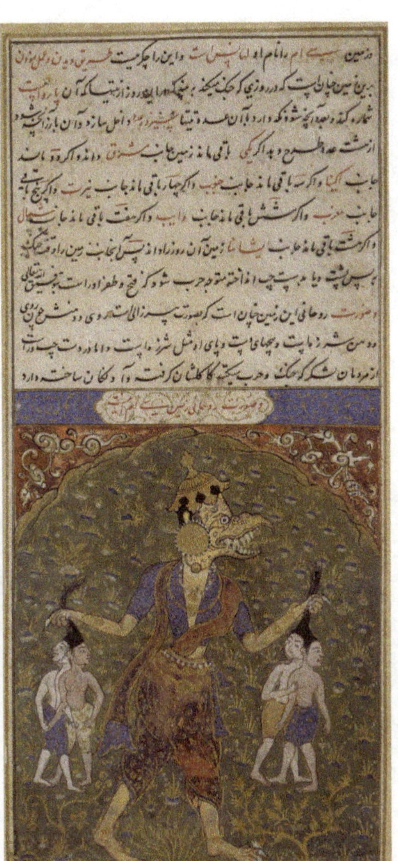

Plate 7. The ruhani Lhanas, *Nujum al-Ulum,* 1570–71, Bijapur. Chester Beatty Library, Dublin, MS. 2, folio 255. Reproduced by kind permission of the Trustees of the Chester Beatty Library, Dublin.

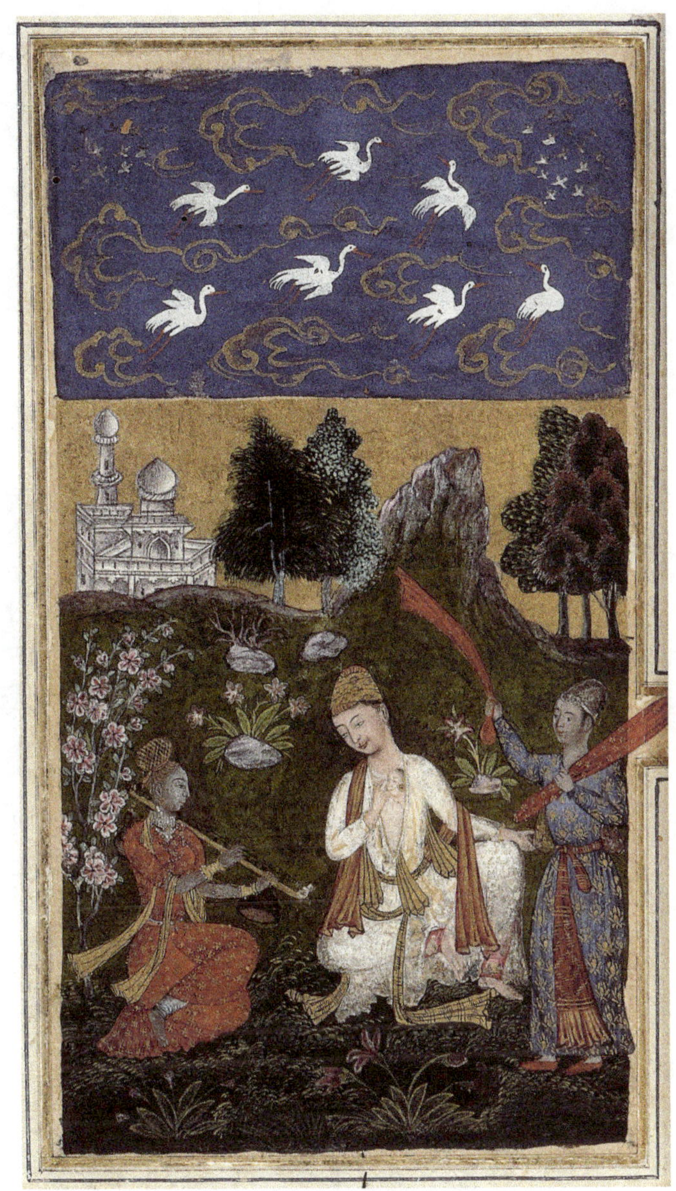

Plate 8. Prince listening to a yogini play music, *Pem Nem,* ca. 1591–1604, Bijapur. British Library, London, Add.16880, folio 46. By permission of the British Library.

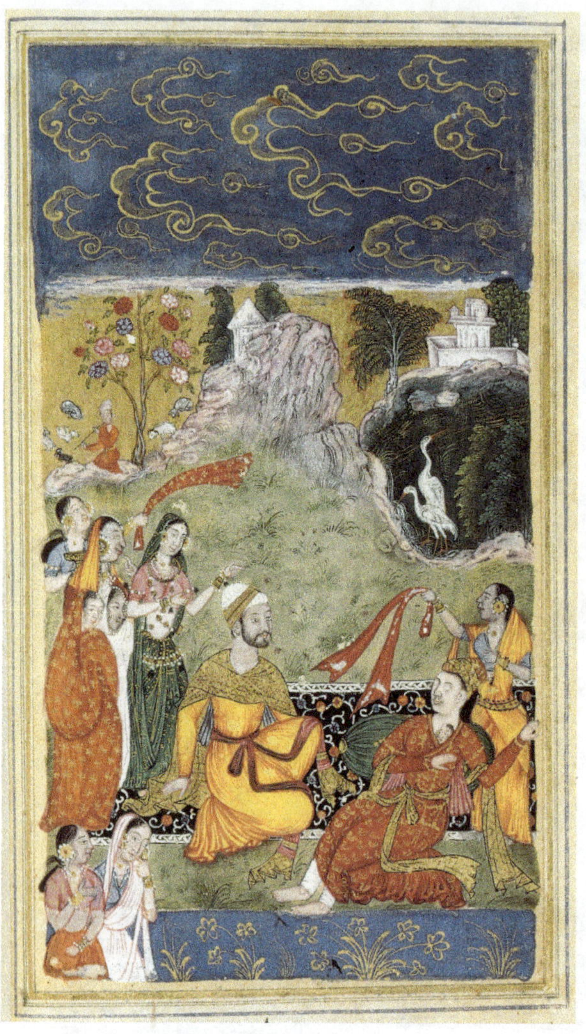

Plate 9. Prince, on carpet with king, fainting at the sight of his beloved, *Pem Nem,* ca. 1591–1604, Bijapur. British Library, London, Add.16880, folio 82v. By permission of the British Library.

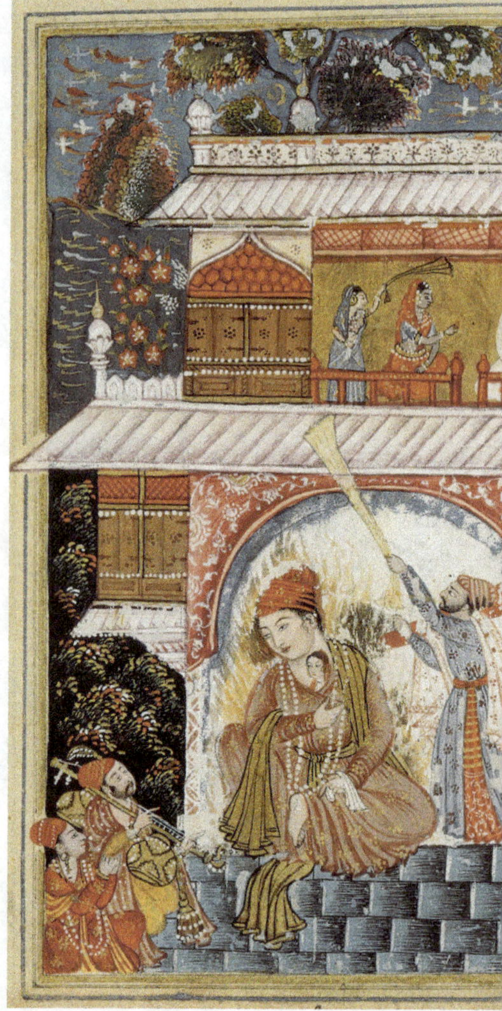

Plate 10. Prince listening to court musicians, *Pem Nem,* ca. 1591–1604, Bijapur. British Library, London, Add.16880, folio 87. By permission of the British Library.

Plate 11. *Facing page:* Prince sits on rock in landscape with attendant and cries, *Pem Nem,* ca. 1591–1604, Bijapur. British Library, London, Add.16880, folio 90v. By permission of the British Library.

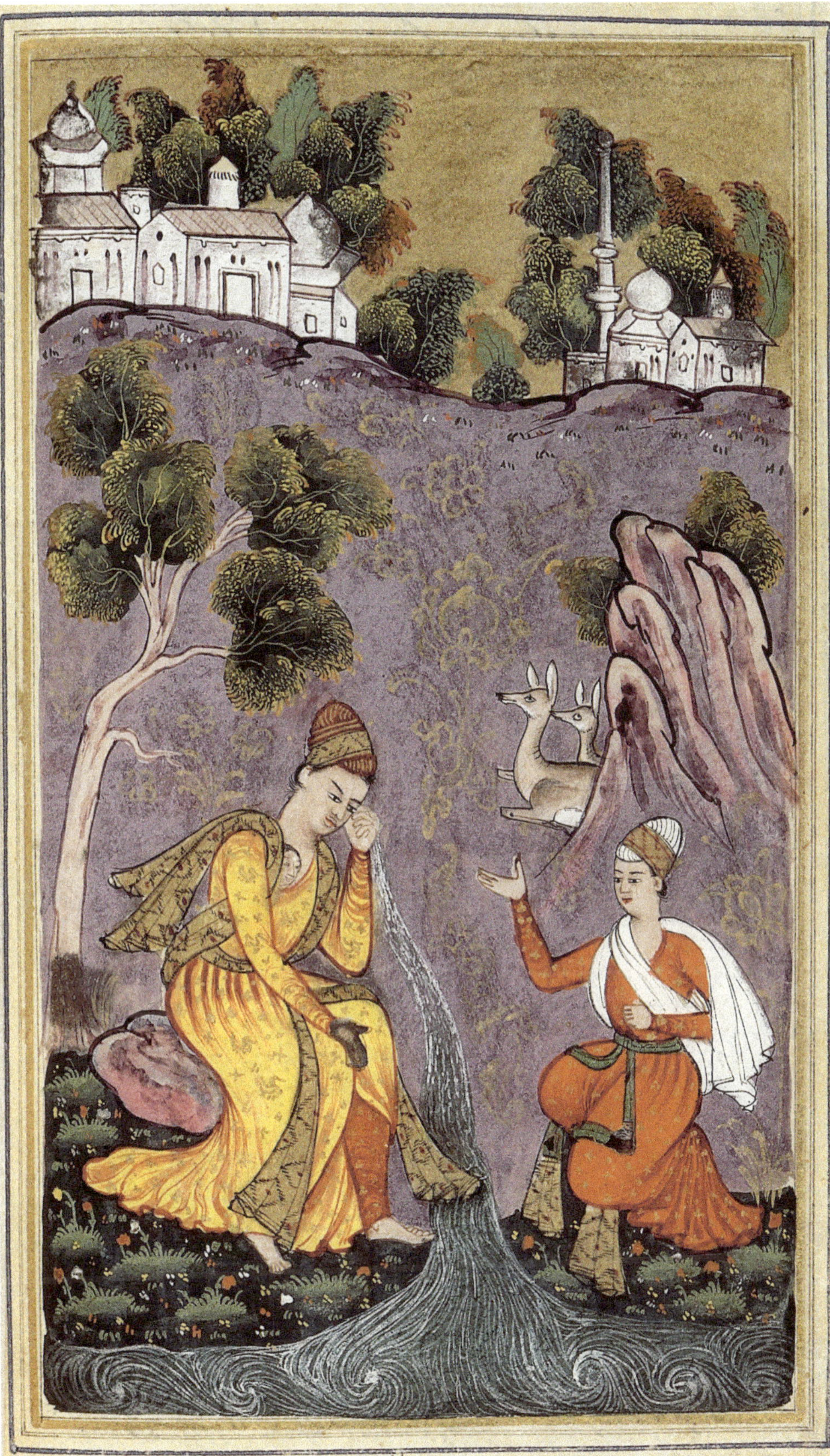

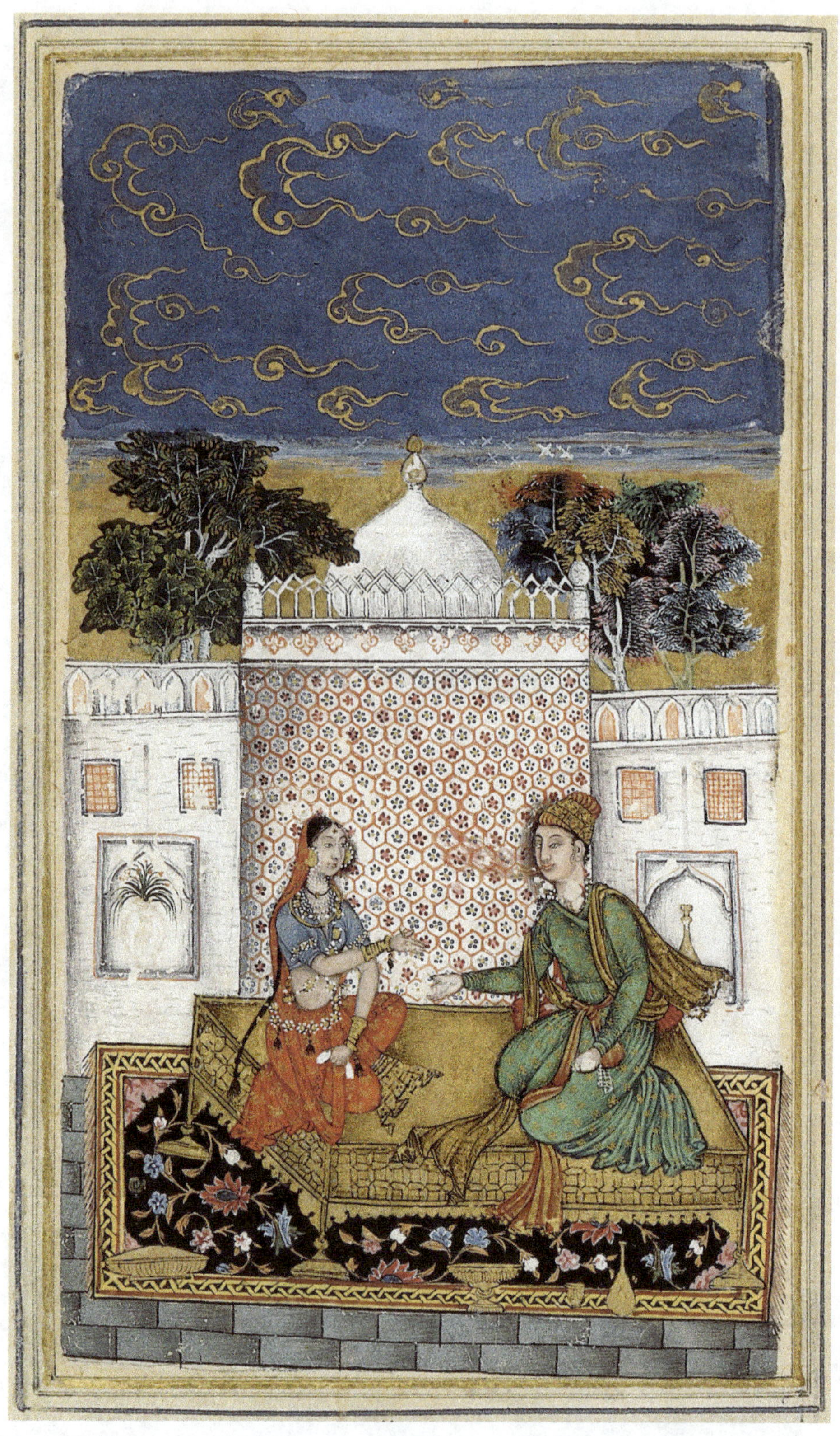

Plate 12. Prince and his beloved sitting on throne, *Pem Nem,* ca. 1591–1604, Bijapur. British Library, London, Add.16880, folio 119. By permission of the British Library.

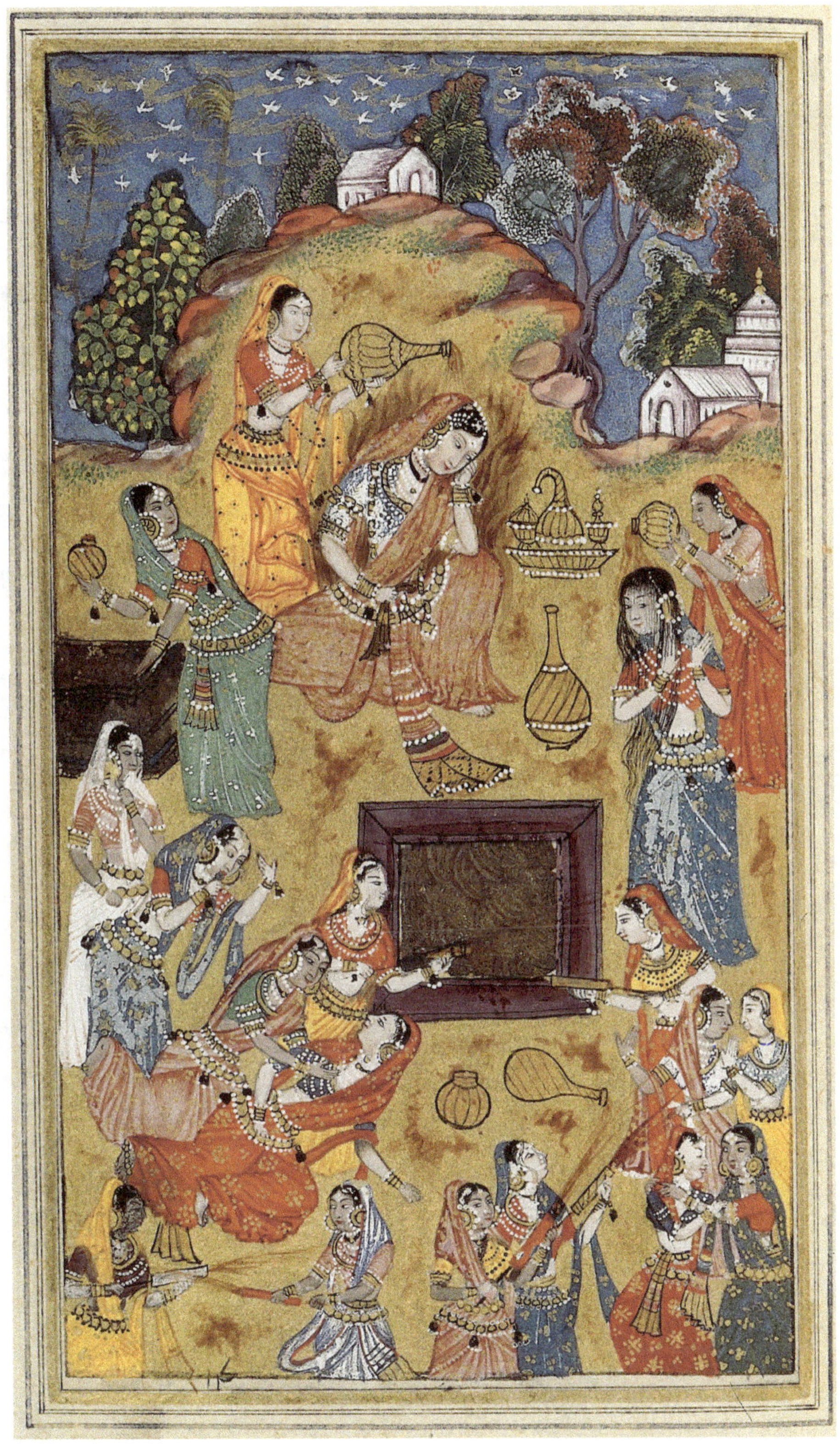

Plate 13. Princess with court women playing water games, *Pem Nem,* ca. 1591–1604, Bijapur. British Library, London, Add.16880, folio 138. By permission of the British Library.

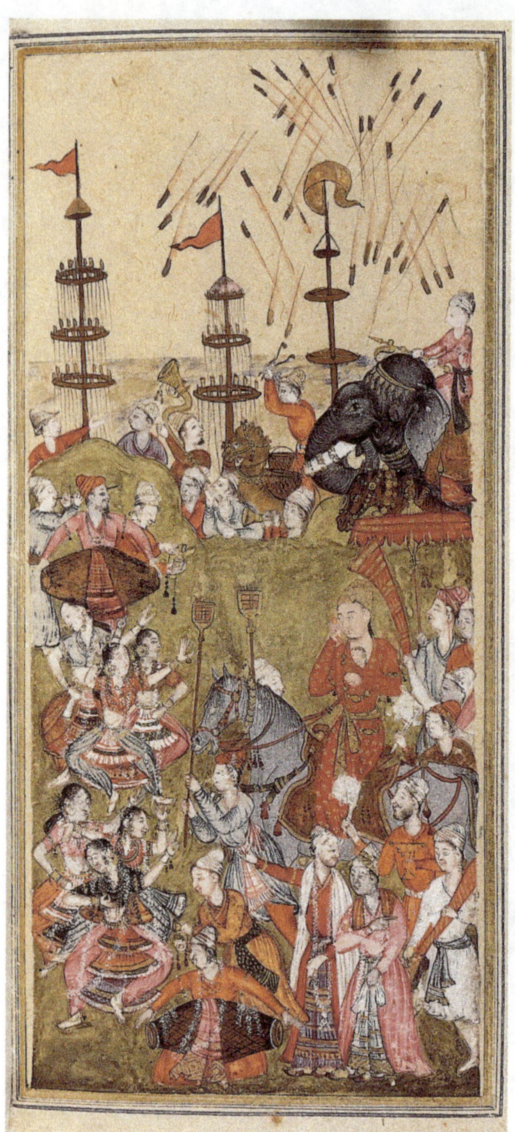

Plate 14. Prince riding horse in wedding procession, *Pem Nem,* ca. 1591–1604, Bijapur. British Library, London, Add.16880, folio 197v. By permission of the British Library.

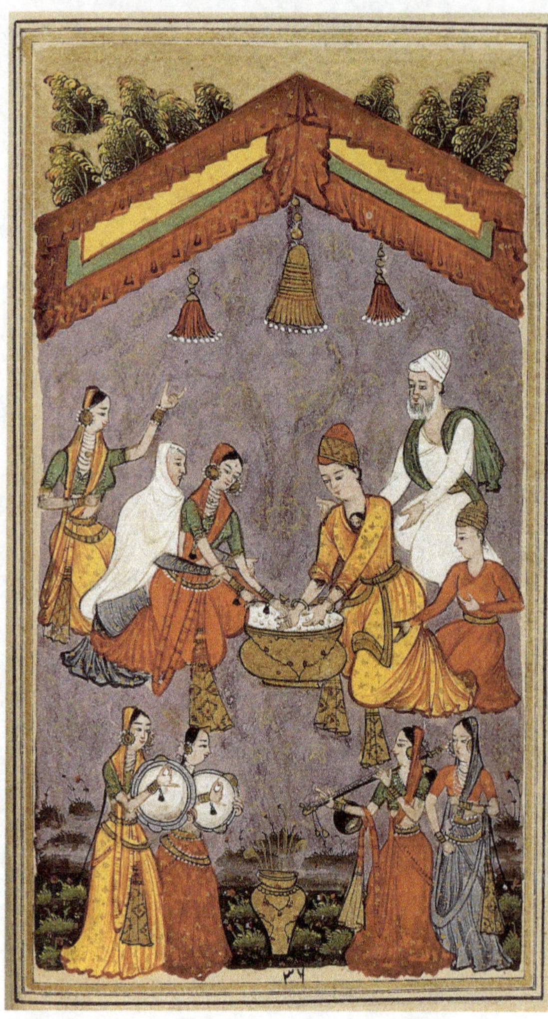

Plate 15. Prince and princess washing hands together in basin, *Pem Nem,* ca. 1591–1604, Bijapur. British Library, London, Add.16880, folio 224v. By permission of the British Library.

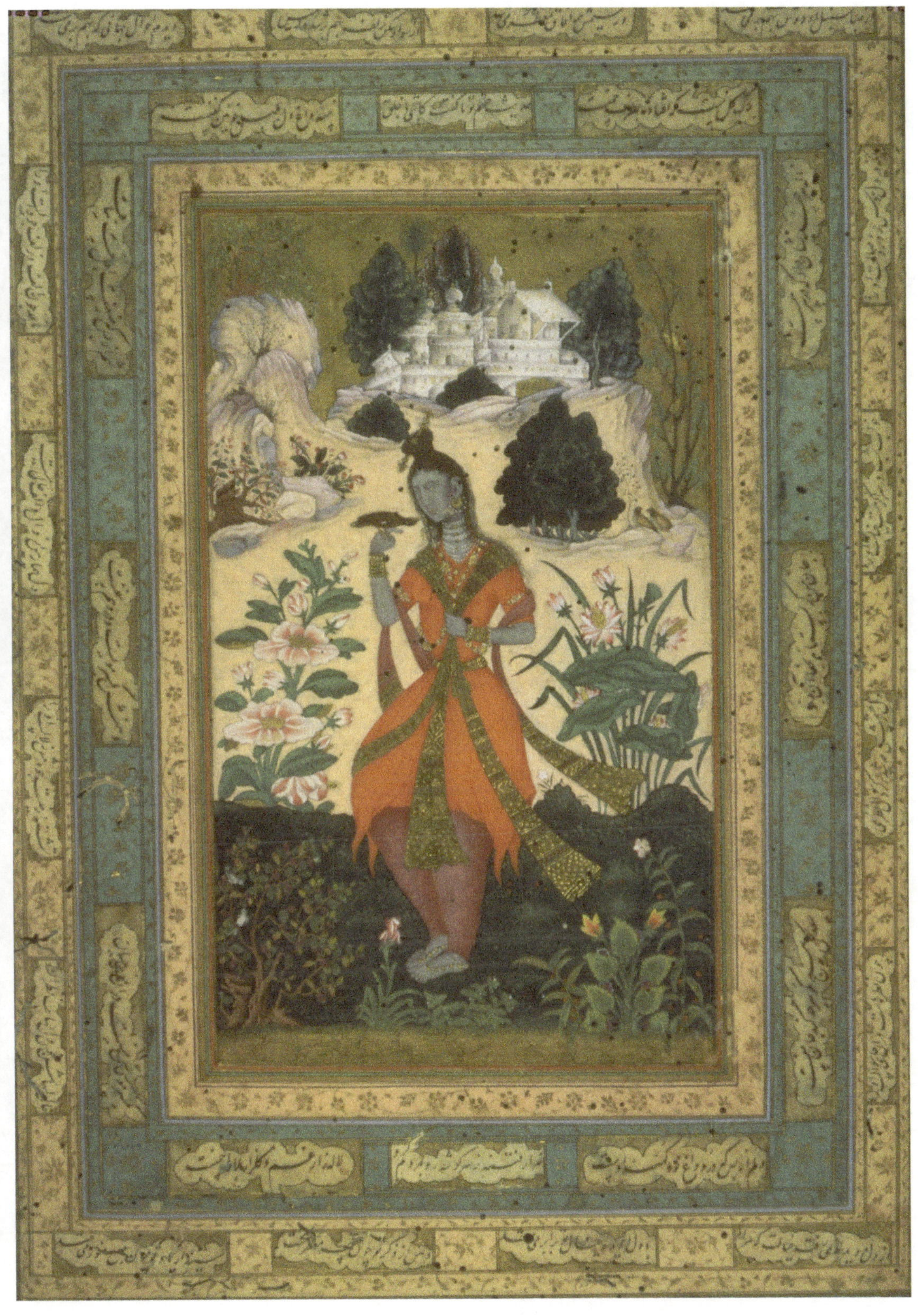

Plate 16. Yogini holding myna bird, ca. 1605, Bijapur. Chester Beatty Library, Dublin, MS. 11A, no. 31. Reproduced by kind permission of the Trustees of the Chester Beatty Library, Dublin.

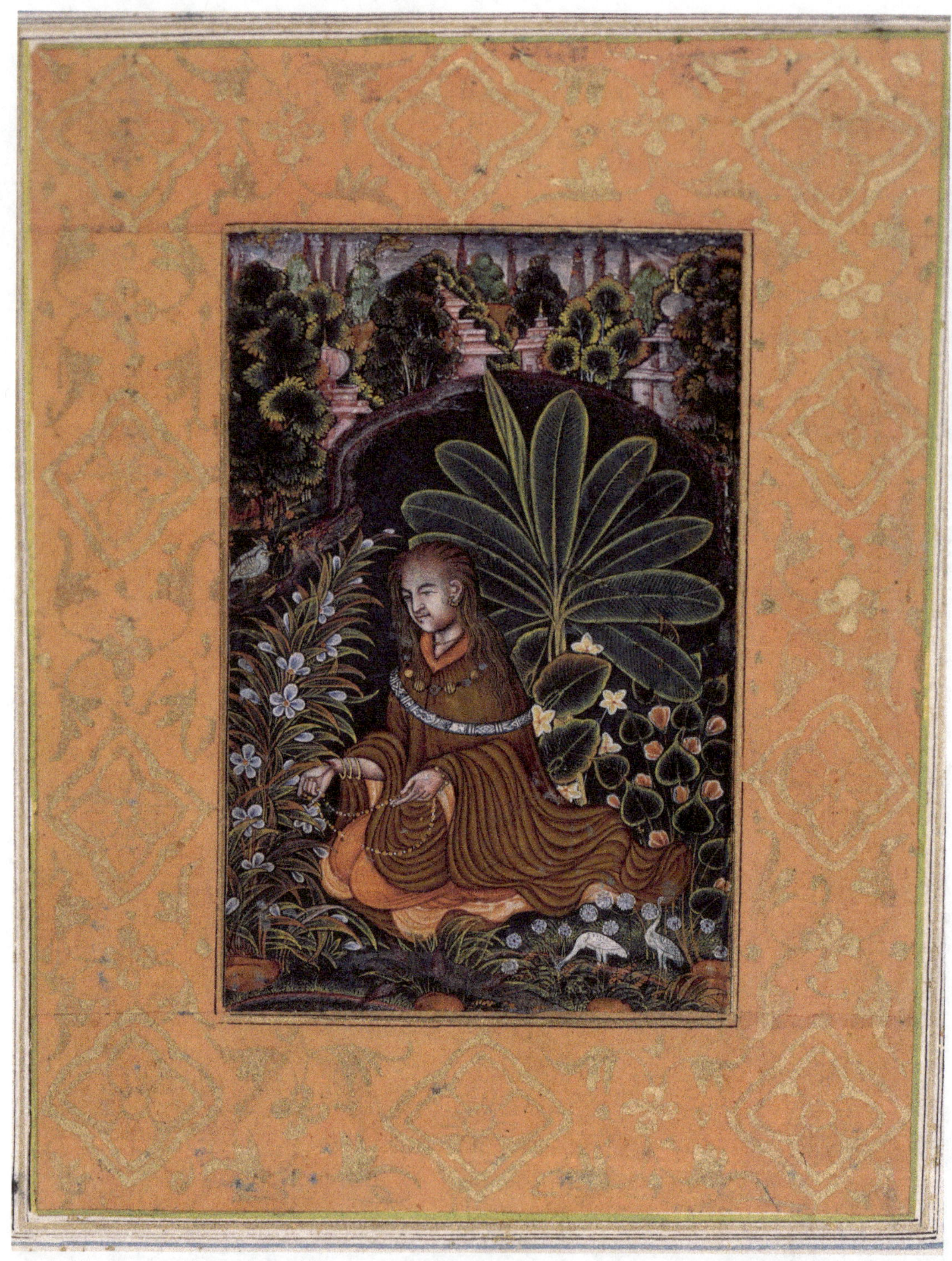

Plate 17. Yogini by a stream, ca. 1605–40, Bijapur. Victoria and Albert Museum, London, IS 133:56-1964, folio 56a. V&A Images/Victoria and Albert Museum Picture Library.

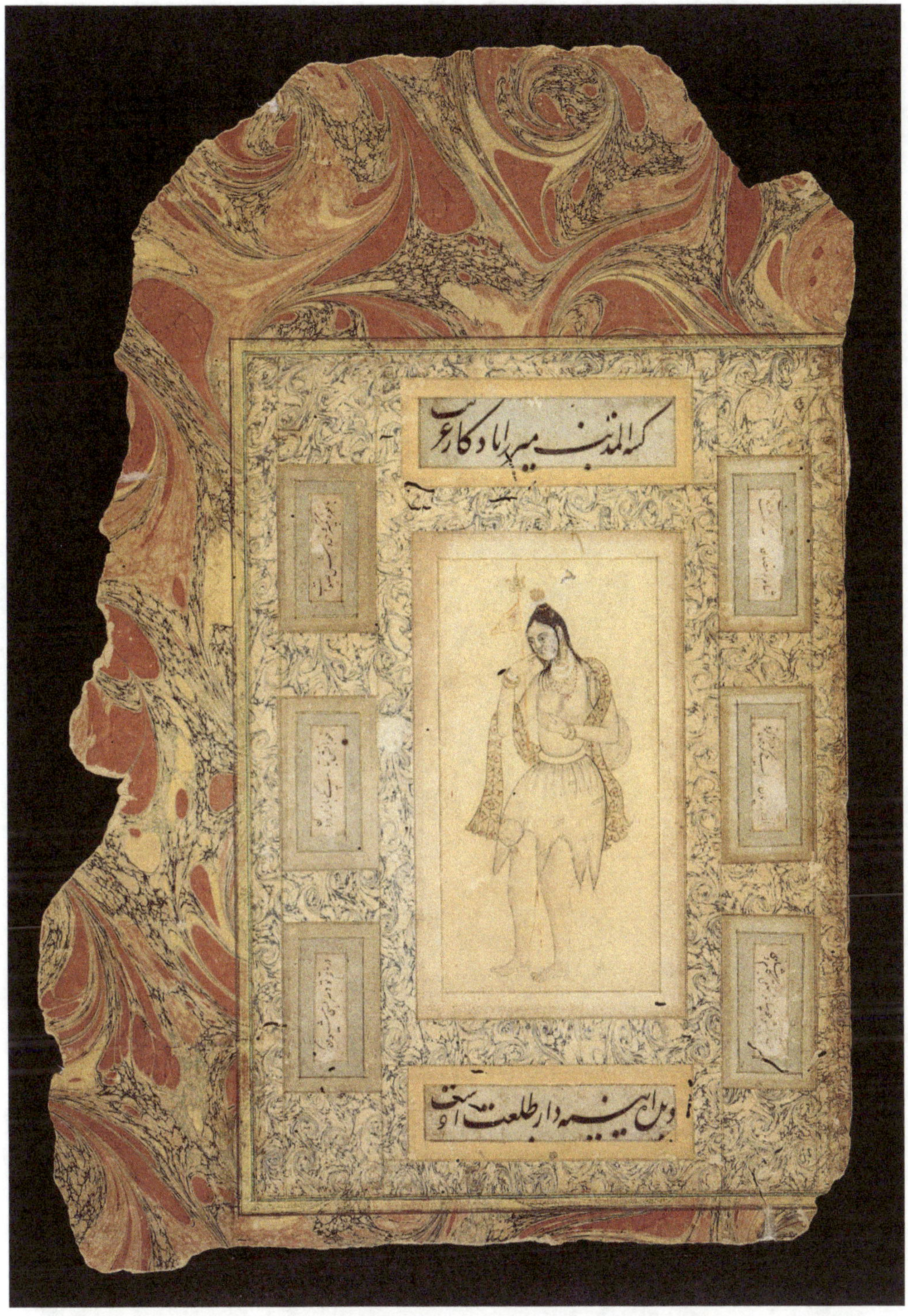

Plate 18. Female ascetic, ca. 1605–40, Bijapur. Sheet: 36.83 × 25.72 cm. Image: 13.34 × 6.99 cm. Los Angeles County Museum of Art, Los Angeles, M.90.141.3. Bequest of Edwin Binney III. Photograph copyright 2005 Museum Associates/LACMA.

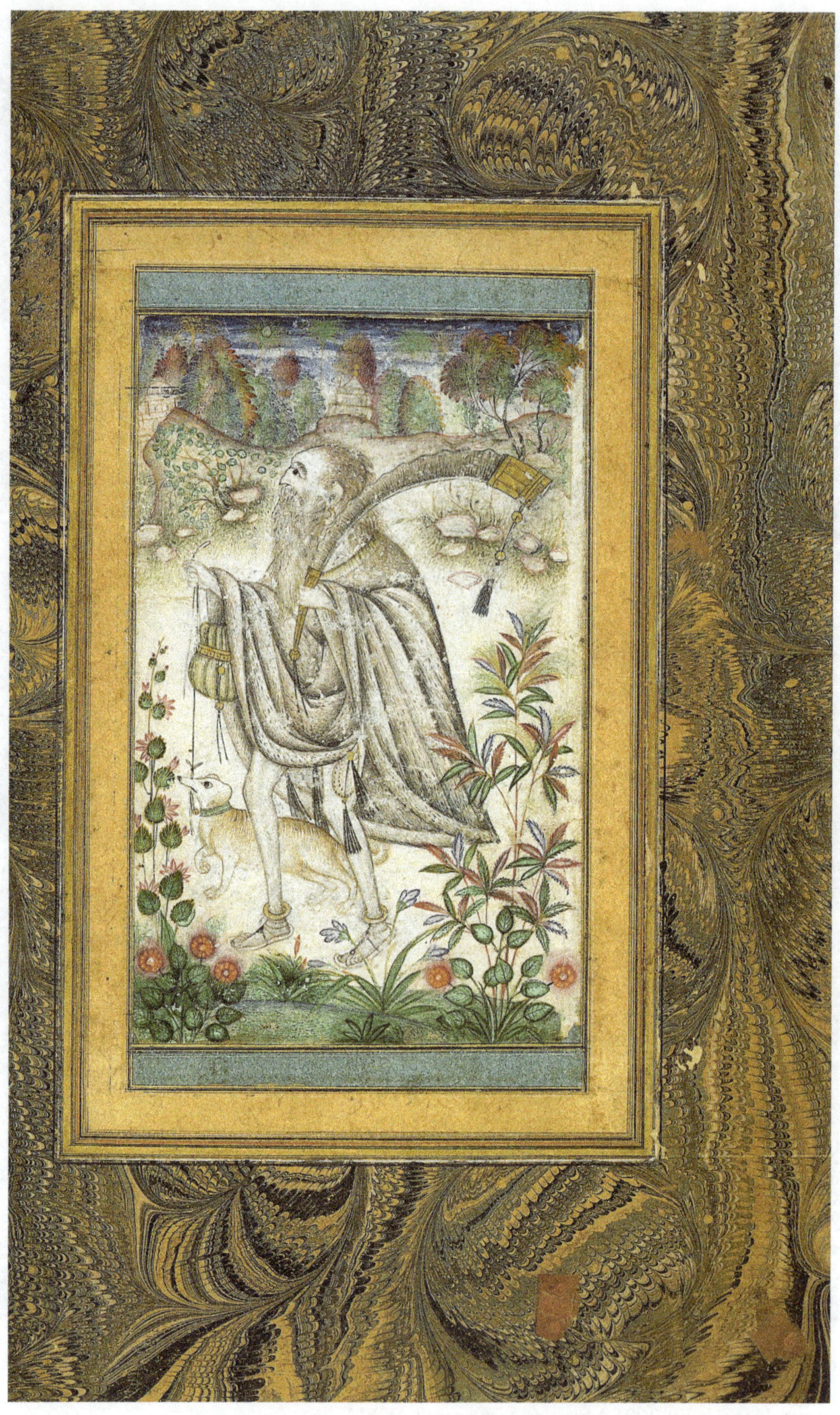

Plate 19. Dervish wandering with his dog, ca. 1600, Bijapur. Collection, Israel Museum, Jerusalem, O.S. 5374.11.77. Photograph copyright The Israel Museum, Jerusalem/Nahum Slapak.

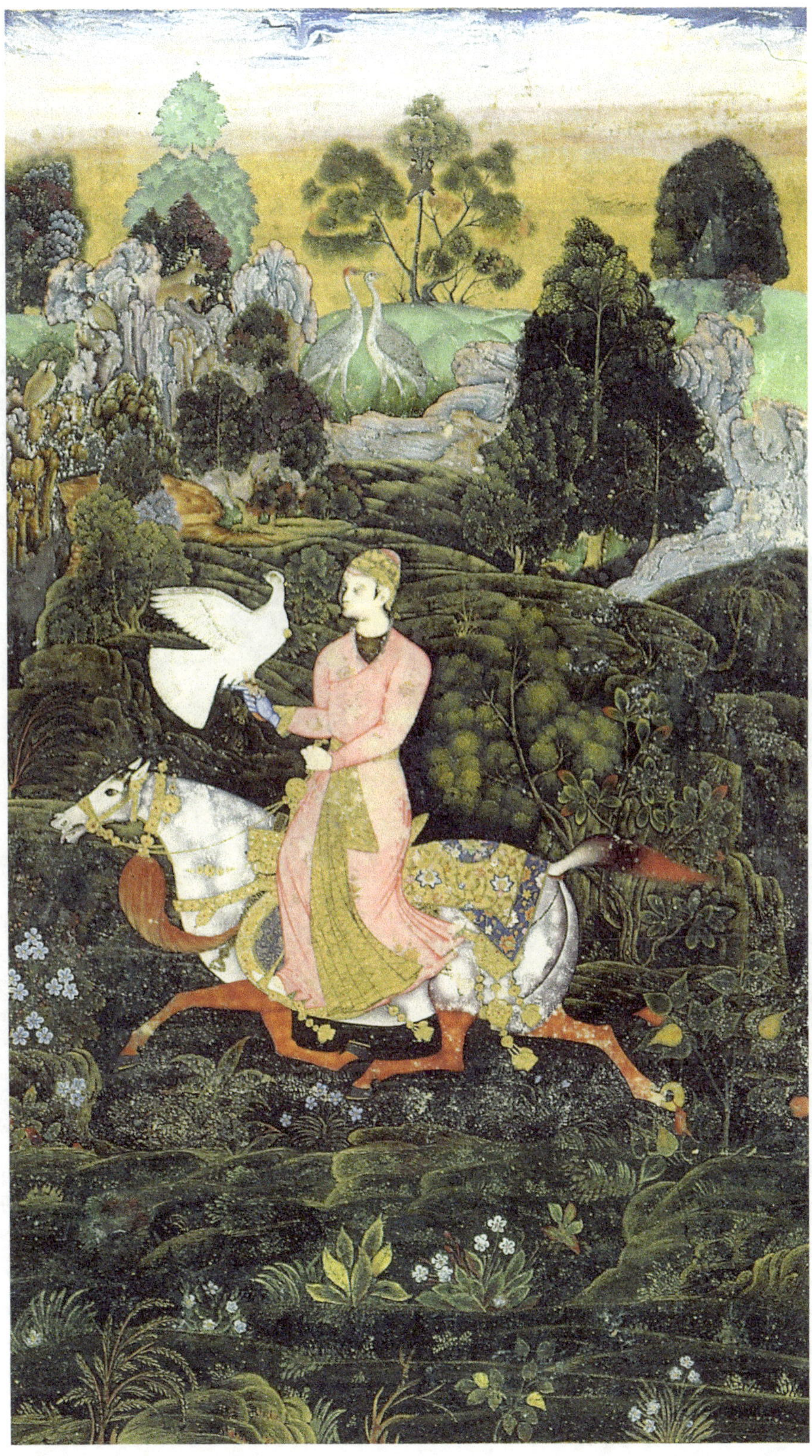

Plate 20. Ibrahim Adil Shah II hawking, ca. 1598–1600, Bijapur. Institute of Oriental Studies, Russian Academy of Sciences, St. Petersburg, MS. E. 14, f. 2.

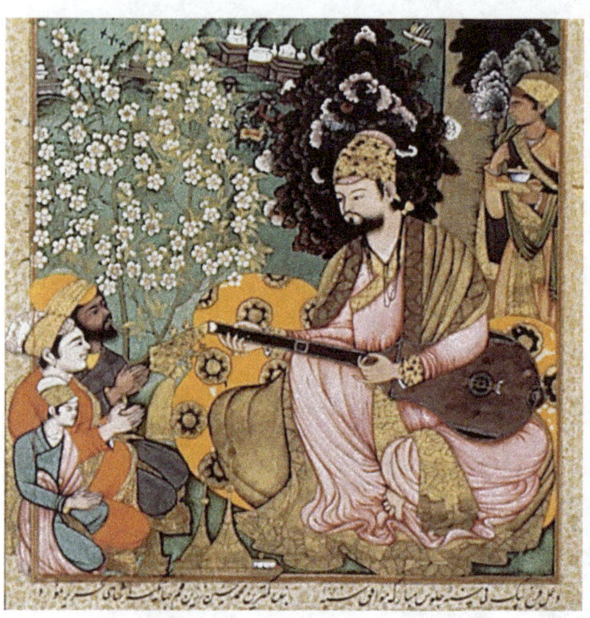

Plate 21. Sultan Ibrahim Adil Shah II playing the tambur, ca. 1600, Bijapur. Naprstek Museum of Asian, African, and American Cultures, Prague, A. 12182. Courtesy of Naprstek Museum, Prague.

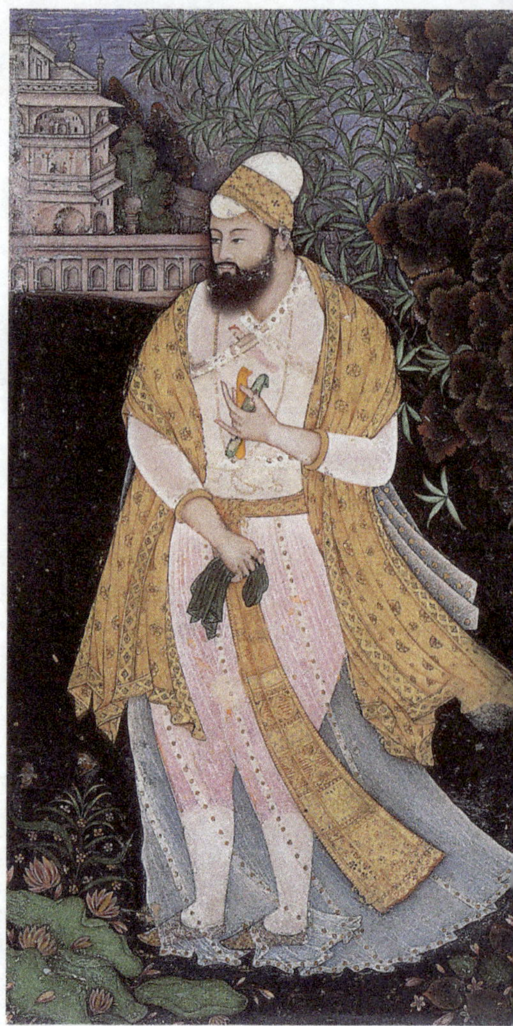

Plate 22. Ibrahim Adil Shah II holding castanets, ca. 1610, Bijapur. The British Museum, London, 1937 4-1002.

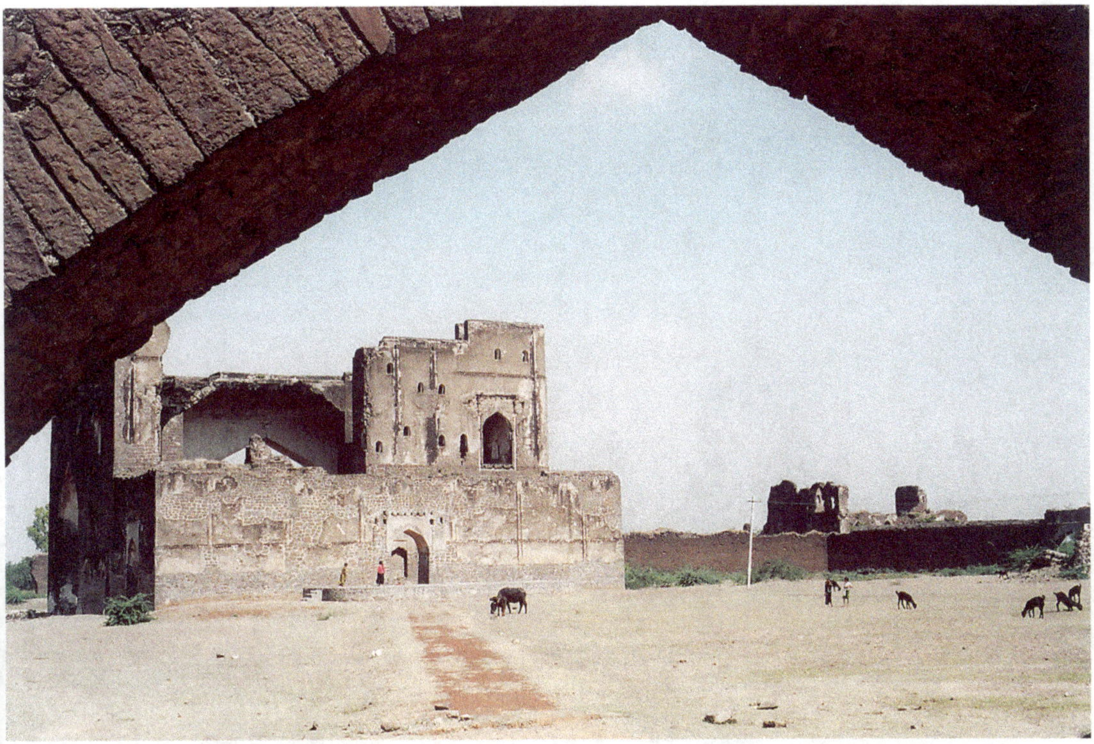

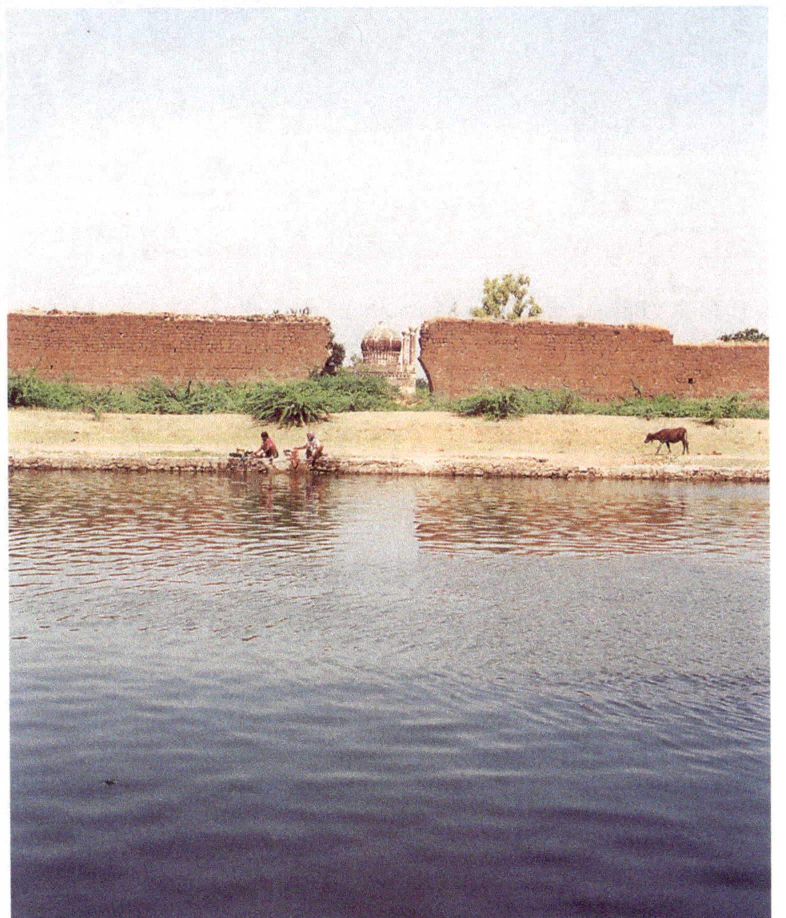

Plate 23. *Above:*
Rear of Nauras Mahal,
1599, Nauraspur.
Photograph by author.

Plate 24. *Left:*
Mosque, as viewed from the
second story of the Nauras
Mahal, 1599, Nauraspur.
Photograph by author.

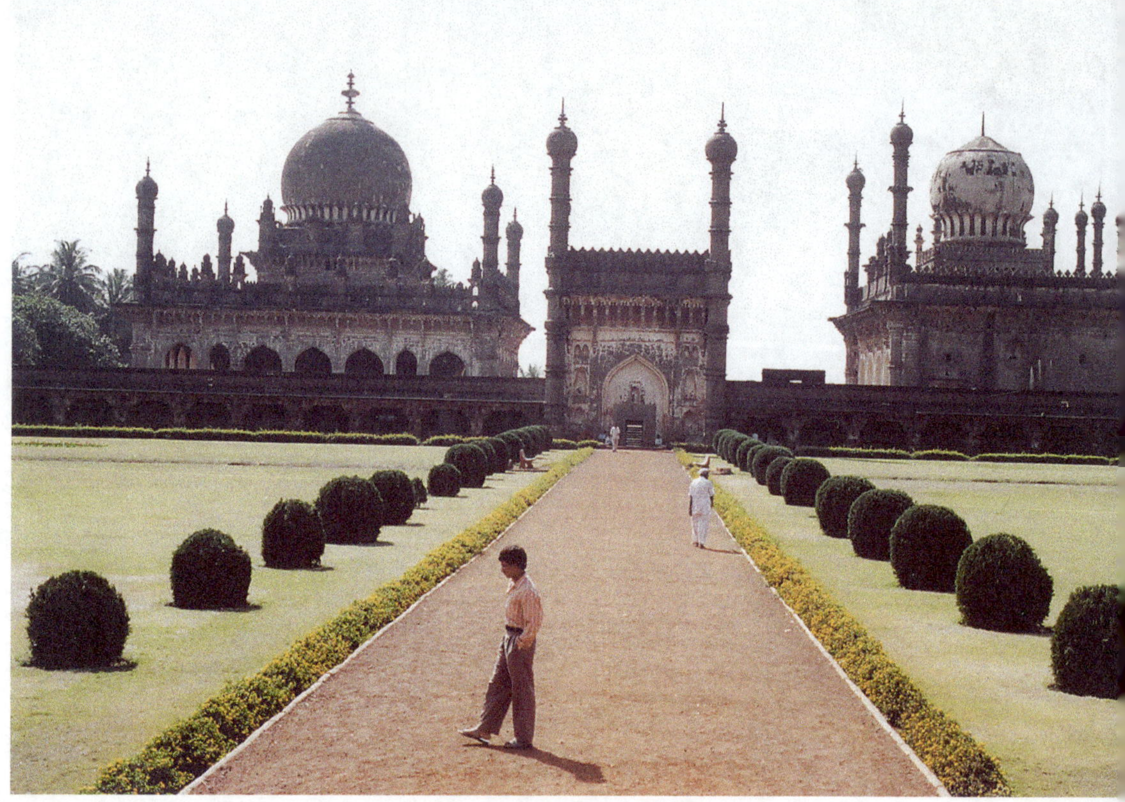

Plate 25. Ibrahim Rauza complex, 1626–33, Bijapur. Photograph by author.

Plate 26. *Facing page:* Ibrahim Rauza, tomb façade and fountain, 1626–33, Bijapur. Photograph by author.

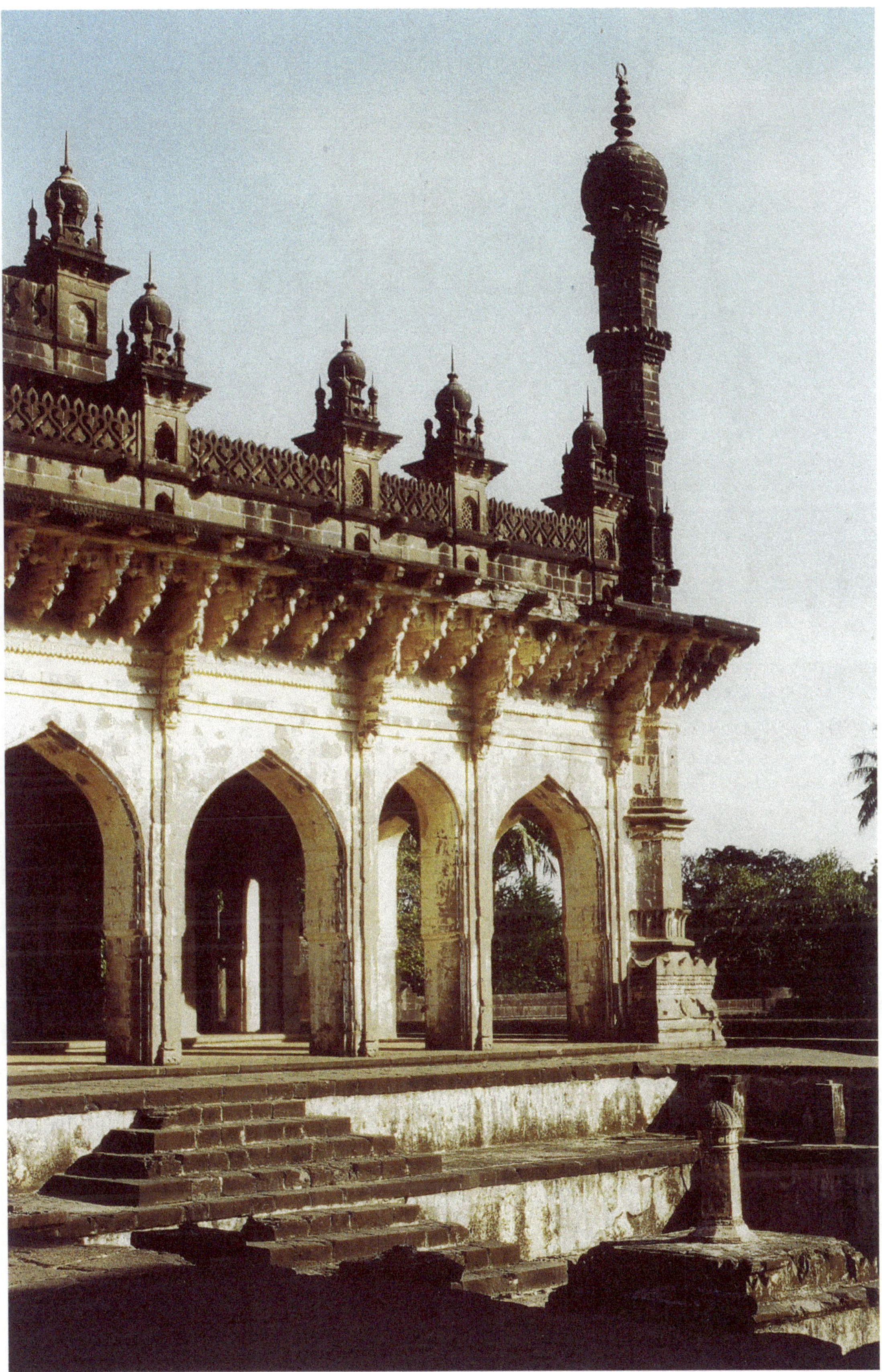

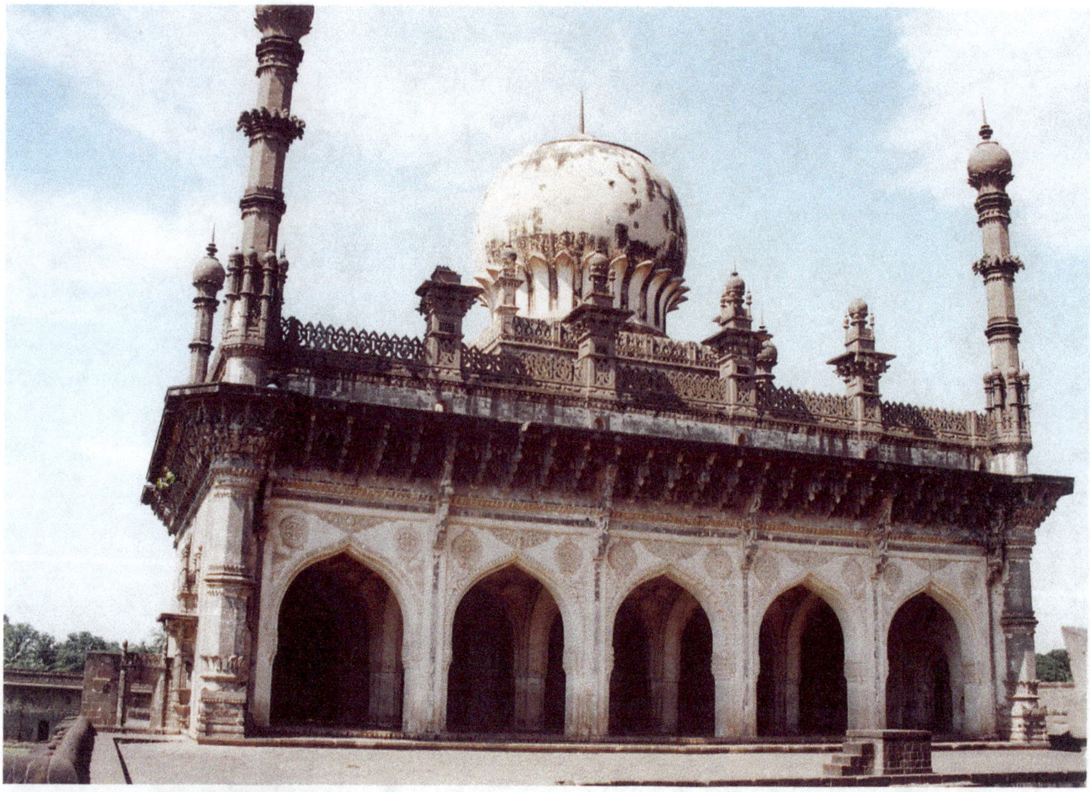

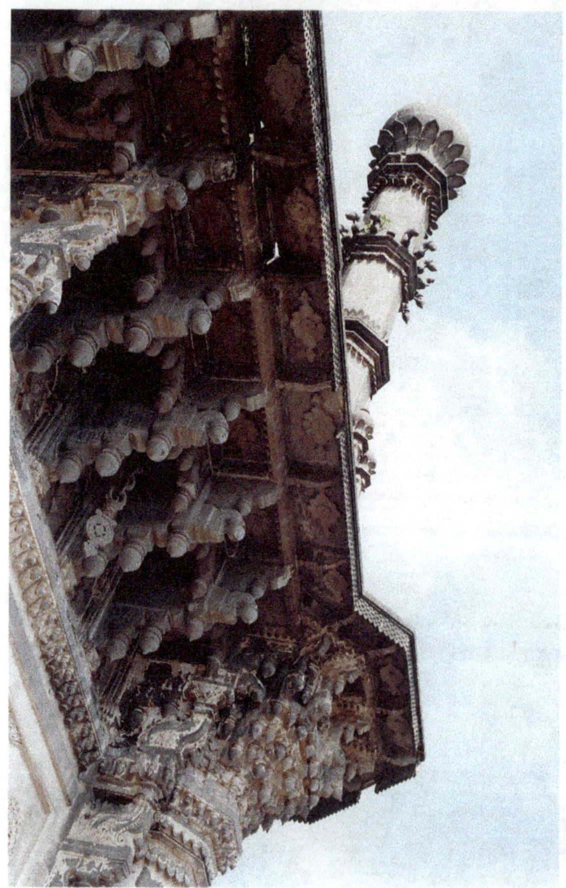

Plate 27. *Above:*
Ibrahim Rauza mosque, 1626–33, Bijapur. Photograph by author.

Plate 28. *Left:*
Detail of stone medallion and chain on the Ibrahim Rauza mosque, 1626–33, Bijapur. Photograph by author.

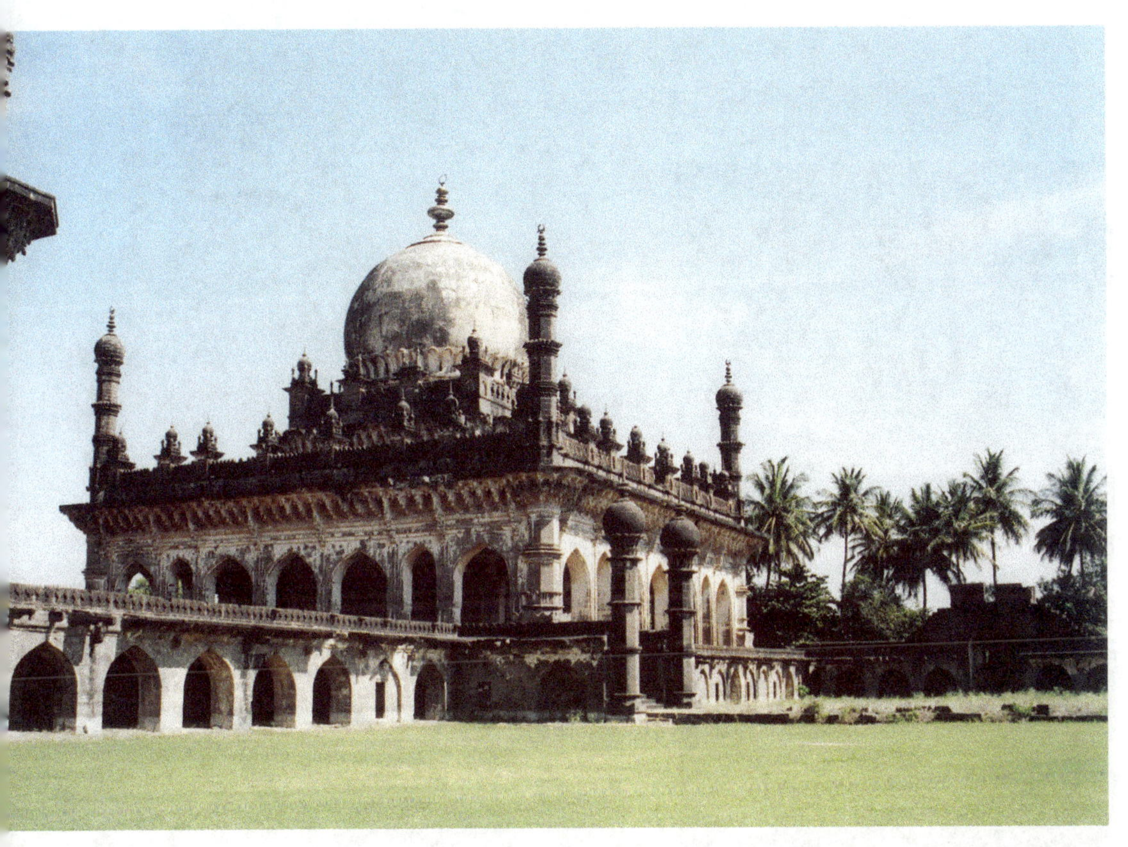

Plate 29. Ibrahim Rauza, 1626–33, Bijapur. Photograph by author.

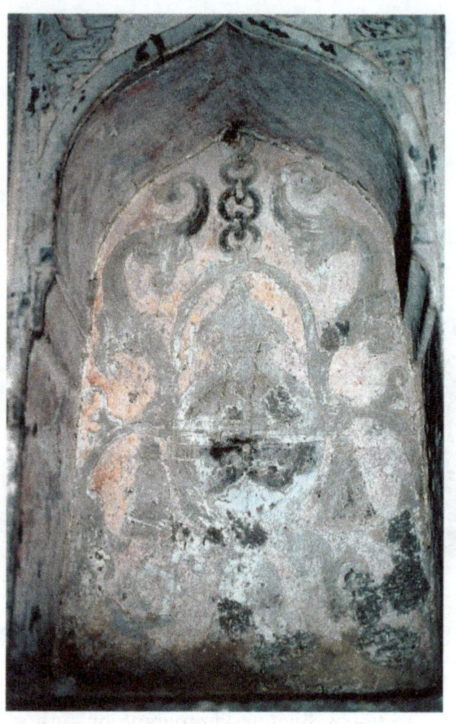

Plate 30. Painting of lamp in exterior niche of the Ibrahim Rauza's arcade, 1626–33, Bijapur. Photograph by author.

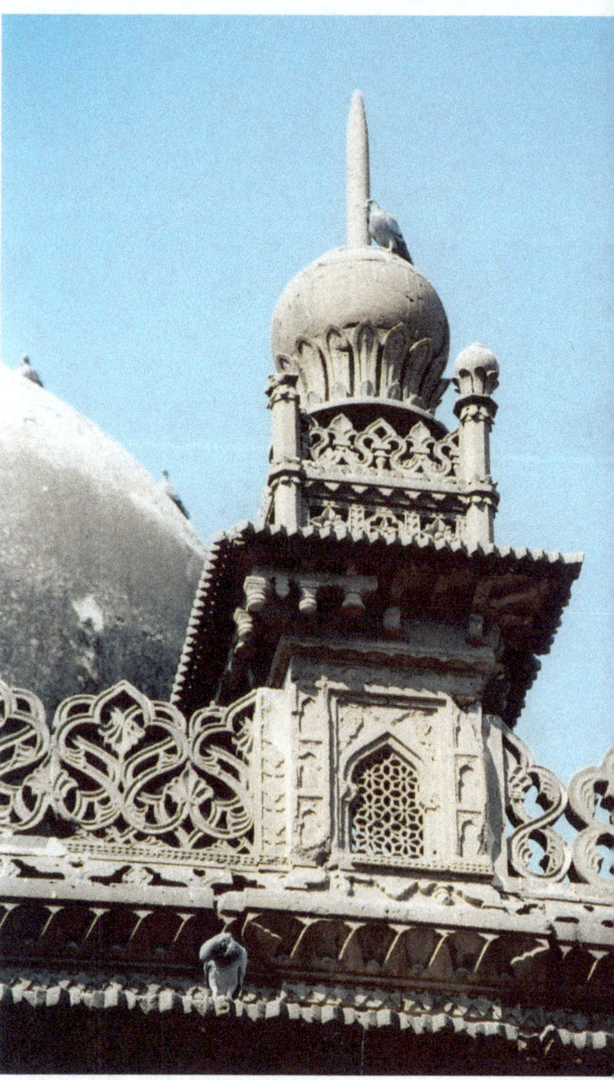

Plate 31. Guldasta, Malika Jahan mosque, ca. 1590, Bijapur. Photograph by author.

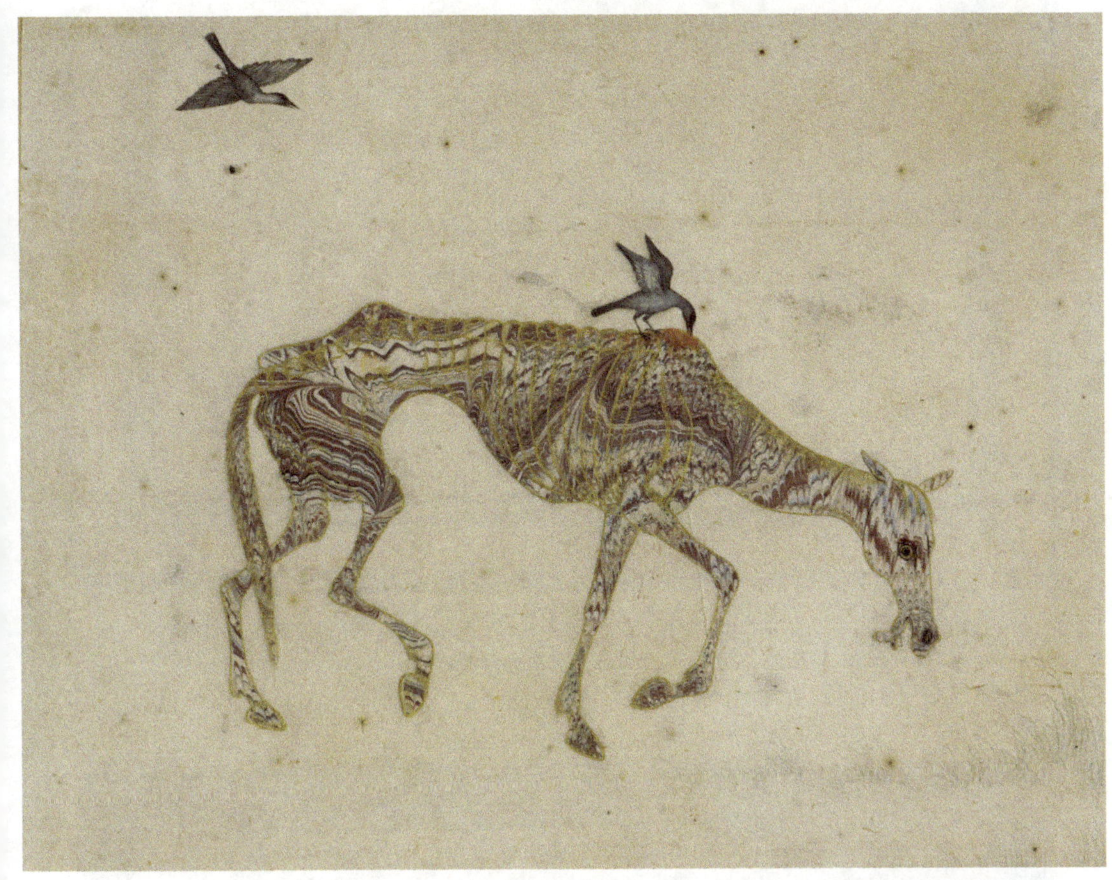

Plate 32. Birds attack a dying nag, ca. 1620–35, Bijapur. 13.2 × 16.6 cm. Sackler Museum, Harvard University, Cambridge, 425.1983. Courtesy of the Arthur M. Sackler Museum, Harvard University Art Museums, Private Collection. Photo by Katya Kallsen.

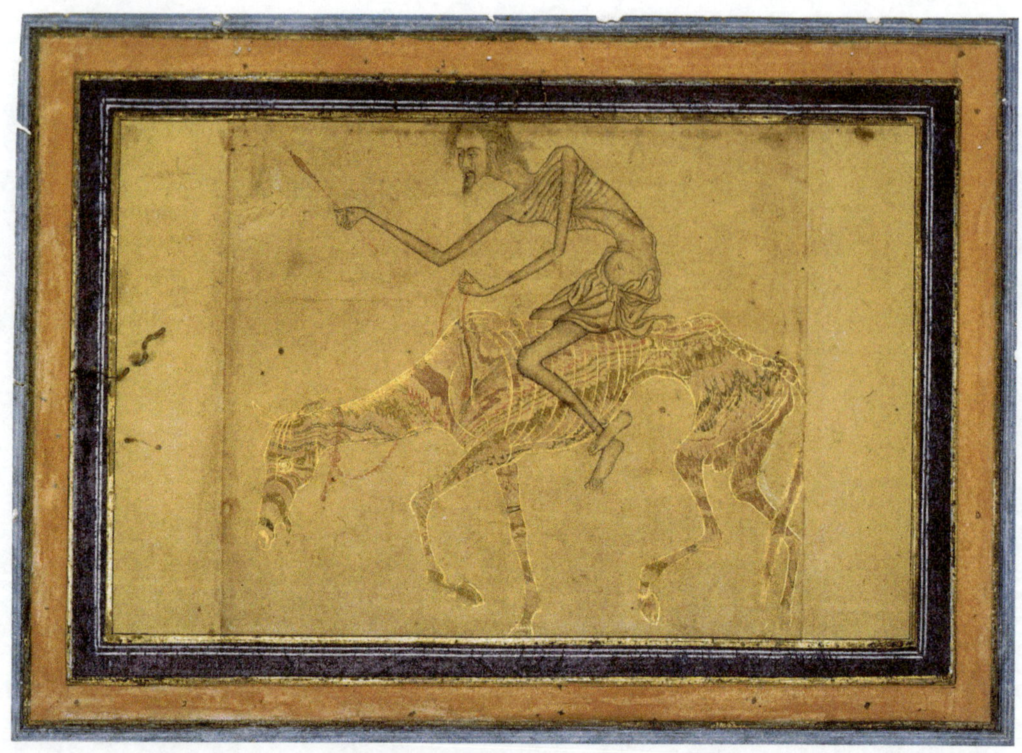

Plate 33. Rider on a nag, ca. 1620–35, Bijapur. 10 × 11.7 cm. Metropolitan Museum of Art, New York, Rogers Fund, 1944, 44.154. Photograph copyright 1996 The Metropolitan Museum of Art.

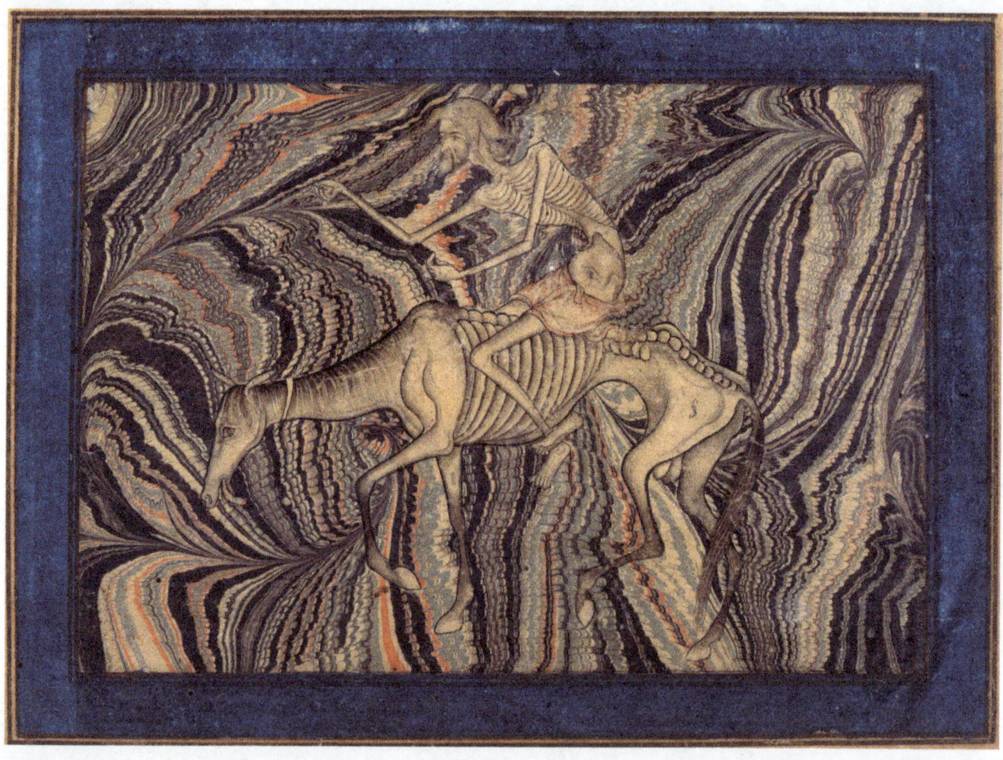

Plate 34. Ascetic riding a nag, ca. 1620–35, Bijapur. The Pierpont Morgan Library, New York, MS. M.458, folio 30V.

function as the illustrations' backdrops. In terms of action, this is the high point of the story, when the prince meets the king, is invited into the palace, faints upon seeing his beloved, and talks to her for the first time. The variety of action is indicated not only by the scenes themselves but also by the scenes' settings, which vary more in this grouping than in any of the others.

The following three paintings depict Princess Padmavati with her female attendants, enjoying different festivities. In folio 135 four women play a board game, while others attend to pet birds perched on stands or placed in cages. Folio 138 depicts the women playing water games, and in folio 147 the women set off fireworks (or perhaps burn incense). All three scenes take place in a landscape, but rather than being an open countryside, it appears to be a garden (one indication of the garden setting is the fountain in folio 138). I have labeled this grouping "Harem Scenes," for the images depict activities that the royal women would have enjoyed when they were alone, not in the larger company of the court. These scenes can be understood, therefore, to be set within the confines of the palace, and thus they provide a link with the next grouping of paintings, "Palace Scenes." This fourth group includes seven paintings, all except one of which are set inside or in front of the palace.[25] In them, the palace takes up a large amount of space and almost dominates the compositions. For example, in folio 172, the prince kisses the feet of the princess, who sits on a throne in the palace (fig. 3.2).

The final twelve paintings depict the wedding ceremony, including the traditional postwedding events: the bride hands betel leaf to her new husband and he places her in a covered palanquin. All but two of these scenes take place in very confined space, under a canopy within the palace enclosure.[26] In some instances the artists rendered the canopy as an upside-down *V* with trees peaking out behind it, as in folio 224v. In other cases, they painted it as just a straight, tasseled band crossing the top of the page. In one instance, in folio 206 (fig. 3.3), portraying Padmavati's attendants adorning her with wedding jewelry, orange and green curtains hanging from a white archway replace the canopy, but the resulting space is still an intimate one.

This final grouping suggests that the illustrations' spatial progression was not merely a by-product of the narrative but a consciously constructed visual element. The artists did not have to depict the wedding scenes in such a confined, intimate space. The wedding festivities could have taken place in the general palace setting as the scenes in the previous two sections did; however, the artists chose to situate the wedding events under the canopy and thus distinguish them spatially from the previous illustrations. The groups, therefore, can be read as purposely moving from large outer spaces to increasingly confined, or inner, spaces.

This movement from the outer to the inner was precisely the goal of

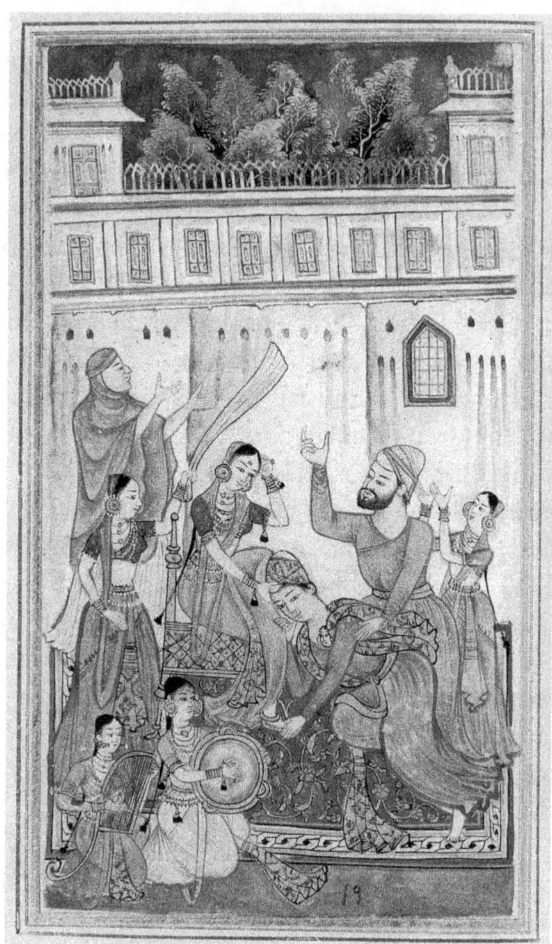

Figure 3.2. Prince kisses feet of princess, *Pem Nem,* ca. 1591–1604, Bijapur. British Library, London, Add.16880, folio 172. By permission of the British Library.

the Sufic path, the *tariqa.* It was also what was being symbolized in Urdu love masnavis when the lover sets off in search of his beloved. Peter Gaeffke has found that Deccani authors often turned traditional Indic stories into Sufi parables in which the garden became a central theme. In the stories Gaeffke examined, the authors employed different types of gardens to stress or symbolize different parts of the quest.[27] In the *Pem Nem*'s illustrations, it is as if the palace, rather than a garden, represents the goal of the search. Perched on a far-off hill, it is just a distant view in the first few paintings, but as the hero moves closer to his goal, he moves closer to the palace as well. Eventually he is just outside the palace, then he reaches the inside of the palace, and finally he crosses into the most confined space—under a canopy within the palace, where he is united with his beloved. Thus the evolution from open landscapes to the innermost confines of the palace represents the main character moving closer to his goal of union with the beloved as well as the corresponding movement from the outer

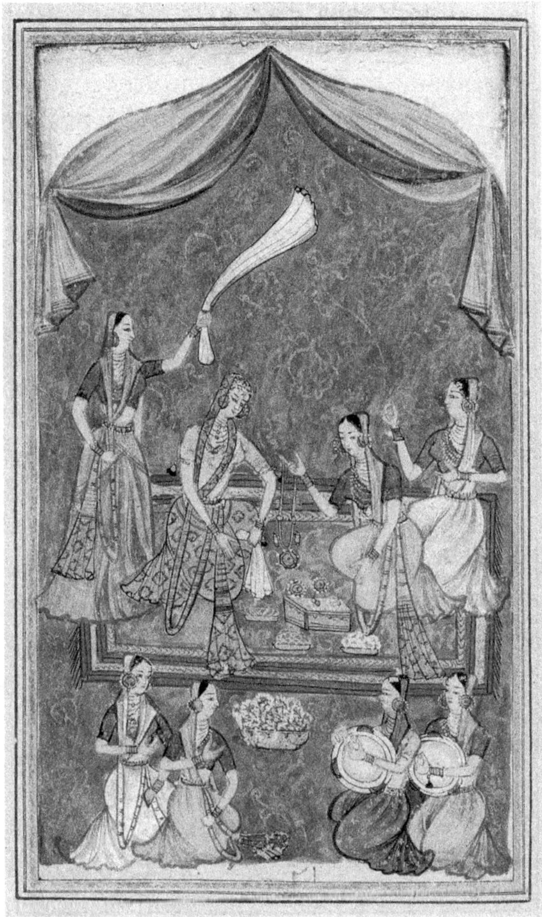

Figure 3.3. Princess puts on wedding jewelry with help of attendants, *Pem Nem,* ca. 1591–1604, Bijapur. British Library, London, Add.16880, folio 206. By permission of the British Library.

world, the zahir, to the inner essence, the batin. The spatial settings translate the underlying mystical concepts into visual form while also mirroring the story's plot.

In fact, the hero's journey is more fully conveyed through the spatial progression than it is through the action depicted in the images. Overall, the paintings' subject matter emphasizes courtly life and its rituals rather than Ratan Sen's actions. For example, while only a handful of illustrations depict his journey, and these just typically show him sitting or walking in a landscape, twelve of the thirty-four images portray the wedding ceremony, making this final portion of the text the most heavily illustrated. Moreover, in contrast to the rather generic, sometimes repetitive, paintings of the prince's quest in the first third of the manuscript, the artists depicted each step of the wedding with careful attention to detail. For example, folio 197v (pl. 14) shows the wedding procession with Ratan Sen riding a gray horse accompanied by dancers, musicians, torchbearers, elephants, camels, and flag-bearers. In folio 206 (fig. 3.3), female attendants take the wedding jewelry from a chest and place it on the princess, while court musicians play in the foreground. Another illustration depicts the prince sitting on a golden throne while female attendants hold a curtain in front of the princess. When the two lovers are finally married, they first wash their hands together in a large gold basin, as shown on folio 224v (pl. 15), and then the princess, in her new role as wife, presents her husband with betel leaf, depicted in the manuscript's final painting on folio 232.

Such visual emphasis on the material goods and ceremonies of elite palace life may seem at odds with the asceticism and renunciation of worldly goods often associated with mysticism, but clearly in the *Pem Nem*'s illustrations, the courtly setting is as central to the story as the Sufic path is. This dual emphasis is not, however, another of the manuscript's inconsistencies. Rather, it is a significant, purposeful aspect of the illustrated romance, one that serves to align the spiritualism of Sufism with the materialism of courtly life. The combination of Sufic and courtly settings, which as Behl explains have "distinct yet interlinked protocols of reception," is a common aspect of the *Prem Marg* genre and one of the conventions drawn from traditional Persian masnavis.[28] The linking of mysticism and courtly life in the *Pem Nem* thus would have been both familiar and appealing to the Bijapur elite audience, who perhaps would have seen their own mystical and material values and aspirations mirrored in the manuscript.

When one considers the paintings' patterns, inconsistencies, and innovative visual elements all together, it seems that the artists were less concerned with coordinating the external appearances of the main characters than they were with fulfilling other goals. In fact, the illustrations seem to have had three primary functions, beyond depicting the basic plot elements: namely, expressing the emotions, conveyed in text, communicating the essence of the Sufic quest for union with the beloved, and situating the mystical romance in a courtly environment similar to that of Bijapur. The first, the visual expression of poetically conceived emotions, relied on the creation of visual metaphors such as the face of the beloved drawn on the prince's heart. The second, conveying the Sufi's quest, was achieved through the spatial progression of the paintings from the outer to the inner. The third, placing the story in an Adil Shahi–like setting, rested on the style, dress, and architecture in the paintings, as well as on the emphasis on the details and rituals of courtly life.

Literary scholars generally consider early Deccani Urdu verse, such as that in which Hamsa wrote the *Pem Nem,* as less refined than that of later Urdu literary works from the seventeenth and eighteenth centuries.[29] Likewise, art historians may consider the *Pem Nem*'s illustrations to lack the lyricism and mastery of subsequent Bijapuri paintings, but it is precisely the developing nature of the paintings that makes them so revealing. The

Pem Nem's illustrations are early experiments in the themes that reach their full flowering in the ensuing decades and, as such, speak to the process of Bijapur's artistic development, which seems to have centered on concepts first and aesthetic concerns second. Moreover, the point of the *Prem Marg* genre of literature was to depict the depths of love, and particularly longing, experienced by the Sufi on his quest for union with God, and from this point of view, the *Pem Nem*'s illustrations are successful, despite any visual clumsiness. The images not only depict the story's basic plot elements, such as the prince meeting the king and then seeing his beloved for the first time, but they also convey the emotions that make up the heart of the story and the spiritual development that underlies it.

Ehsan Yarshater, while exploring the link between Persianate painting and poetry, explains that both the medieval Persian artist and poet were more interested in conveying typical and everlasting abstractions than in reflecting external realities.[30] This observation fits the *Pem Nem* artists as well, at least to some extent. Yarshater goes on to explain that the Persian poet and artist often drift from the main theme of the work in order to pursue less relevant details that please him, such as the carefully painted tiny flower in the case of painting. This pursuit helps create the perfect, "sensuous," imaginary world whose depiction is the ultimate point of their work.[31] In this respect, the *Pem Nem* seems distinct. Details such as the face of the beloved etched on the prince's heart were not extraneous elements added merely to please the artists; rather, they were relevant to the essence of the story. The *Pem Nem*'s paintings do depict a privileged, courtly environment, and in this manner the artists were creating a type of perfect, imaginary world—a key aspect of the romance, to be sure. But they were doing more than that. Through details such as the flames surrounding the princess and through their use of space, the artists were trying to go beyond reality, to find ways of illustrating what cannot typically be seen. In this way, the *Pem Nem* compares to the *Nujum al-Ulum*, whose artists through the use of abstract diagrams, such as the concentric circles representing the reverberations of a drum, were attempting to depict that which is not usually experienced visually. In the *Nujum al-Ulum*'s case, the objective was scientific, aimed at increasing the power of the king, rather than poetic, intended to show the power of words and communicate the work's rasa, as in the *Pem Nem;* yet both resulted in the development of new visual forms, and both demonstrate the vigorous, highly original nature of art at the Adil Shahi court.

Yogini Paintings

David Kinsley gives two definitions for the term *yogini:* a female associated with magical powers, and a female practitioner.[32] The first definition refers to a type of Hindu female deity usually associated with Tantrism, and the second refers to women who follow the Hindu ascetic path, typically linked with devotion to the god Shiva. A number of solitary yoginis positioned in single-page paintings attributable to Bijapur from the late sixteenth through mid-seventeenth centuries survive. These images depict yoginis of the second type—women following the ascetic path and who, whether indicated by their up-knotted hair, ashen skin, or some other detail, are devotees of the god Shiva. Significantly, the creation and production of yogini images of this type seems to have been limited to the Deccan and Lucknow areas of South Asia during the sixteenth through eighteenth centuries, periods and regions in which both Urdu literature and Sufism flourished.[33] Indeed, close analyses of six such paintings from Bijapur demonstrate that these images of Hindu female ascetics intimately relate to the Sufic ideals of the lover and the beloved as expressed in literature and poetry. In this way, they compare to the *Pem Nem* illustrations, but unlike those images, the single-page yogini paintings refer to literary and mystical ideas without directly illustrating a text. They operate symbolically rather than narratively, at least overtly (the informed viewer may ultimately apply narrative associations to the images). As such they require the viewer to bring many of the references to the viewing experience. In this way, in their original context, the paintings served to promote a collective, composite, mystically oriented culture at Bijapur's court.[34]

The production of the six paintings discussed here covers about a half century of Bijapur's artistic development. The two earliest paintings are attributable on stylistic grounds to the early 1590s, approximately the same time that artists were producing the *Pem Nem*'s illustrations. Another image is datable to circa 1605, and the remaining three images, again based on style, seem to have been produced sometime between about 1605 and 1640. While none of the six images bear inscriptional evidence relating to their production, all are characteristic of Bijapuri painting in coloring, composition, dress, and the handling of details.[35] In fact, because their imagery is so similar, when taken together, they provide an excellent reconstruction of Bijapuri painting's stylistic progression between 1590 and the 1630s, which seems, in part, to have moved from paintings layered in thick pigment, particularly dark greens, combined with oranges and golds, to works featuring less pigment and more ink-rendered details. The similarities and clear stylistic progression of the paintings also suggest a pattern in which Bijapuri artists developed meaningful motifs and then revisited, often artistically reworking, them over the subsequent decades.

The two earliest paintings, datable to the early 1590s, include an image of a yogini in the collection of the British Museum, London (fig. 3.4), and another in the Jagdish and Kamla Mittal Museum of Indian Art, Hyderabad (fig. 3.5). Several areas of pigment in the British Museum yogini paint-

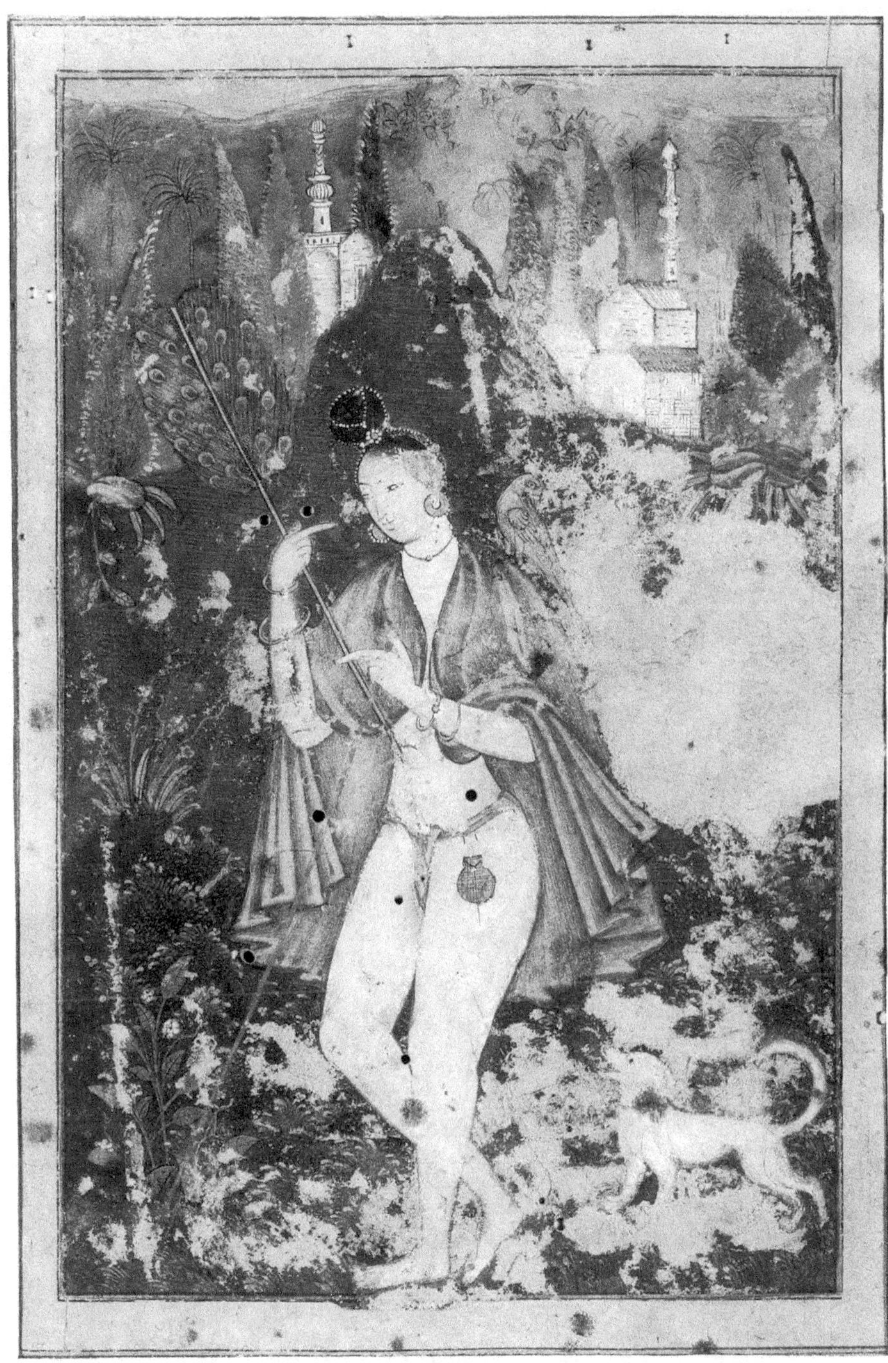

Figure 3.4. Yogini holding peacock fan, ca. 1590, Bijapur. The British Museum, London, 1943-10-9-073.

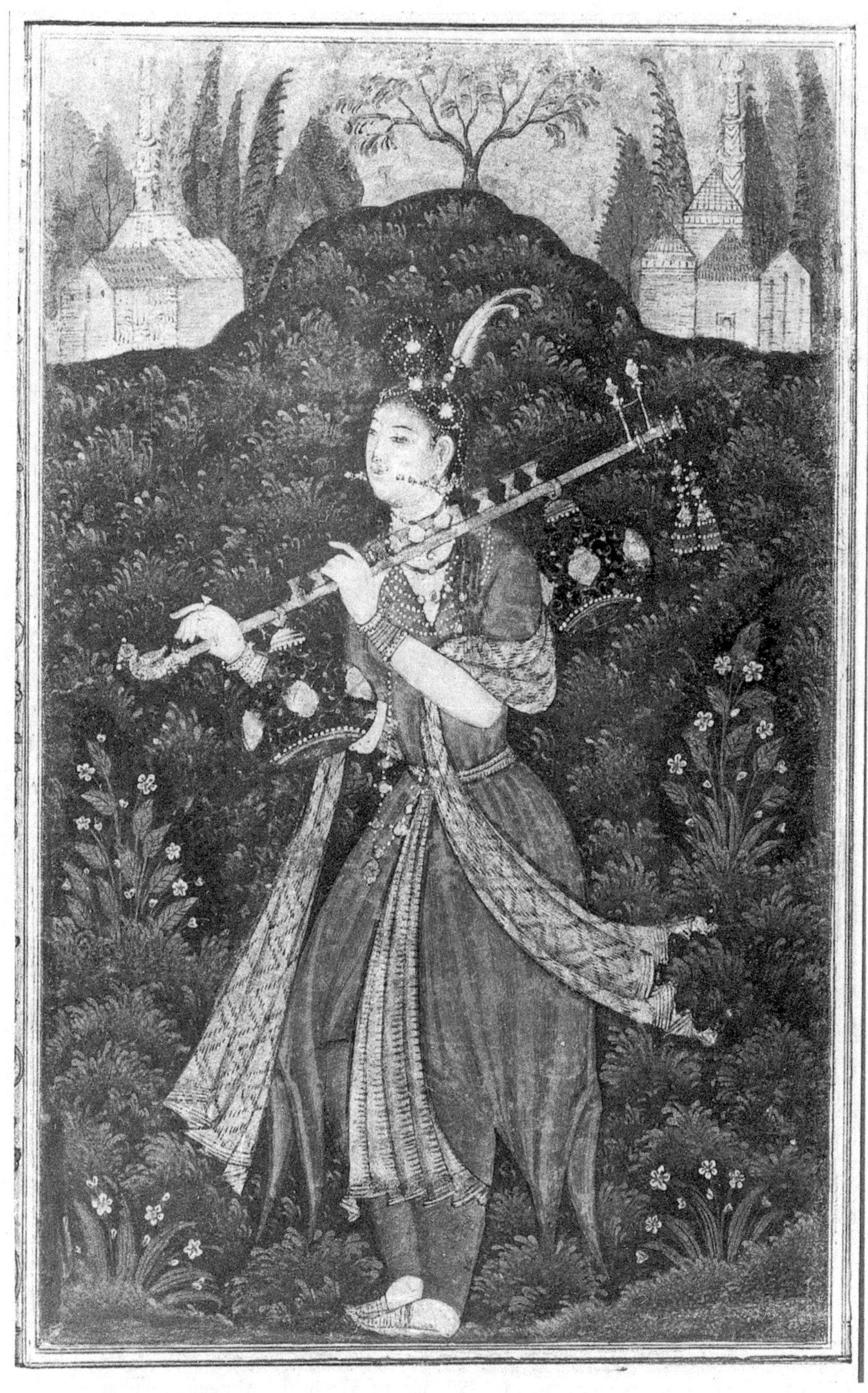

Figure 3.5. Yogini with veena, ca. 1590, Bijapur. Jagdish and Kamla Mittal Museum of Indian Art, Hyderabad, 76.404.

ing have flaked off, but the image is still clearly discernible. A scantly clad young woman with her hair in a topknot stands in three-quarter view, holding a peacock feather fan and walking through the countryside with a dog at her heels, a parrot on her shoulder, and white palace buildings in the distance. The Mittal yogini, like the British Museum yogini, stands in a flowering, hilly landscape with multiple white palaces in the background. She also wears her hair in a topknot, but is fully clothed in a *sawar camise* and plays a veena. Close stylistic similarities between the two images, including the distinctive hatching on the distant palaces, suggest that the same artist produced both paintings.

The well-known painting housed in the Chester Beatty Library, Dublin, and commonly called the "Chester Beatty yogini" is datable to circa 1605 (pl. 16). Once again, the yogini, a beautiful young woman dressed in a sawar camise with long, flowing scarves, stands in a lush landscape with a white palace marking the distant hills. In this case, she also holds a myna bird. The Victoria and Albert Museum contains an image of a yogini situated in an equally verdant scene to that of the Chester Beatty painting. The V&A yogini (pl. 17), whose matted hair flows over her shoulders rather than being knotted above her head like the other yoginis, kneels in the abundant landscape, with a pair of white herons at the base and pinkish-white palaces in the background. The young female ascetic, clothed in a long brown cloak, holds rosary beads and appears to be praying. The oversized foliage, distant palace, and face of the figure link the painting to other Bijapuri works datable to circa 1605–40.[36]

The remaining two yogini paintings, one in the Los Angeles County Museum of Art (pl. 18) and the other in the Islamisches Museum, Berlin (fig. 3.6), are also datable to circa 1605–40, again based on stylistic grounds. Both images combine painting and drawing and have finely marbled paper adorning their borders, in a manner similar to other Bijapuri works from the first half of the seventeenth century. The LACMA album page depicts a young female ascetic standing in front of a largely blank background. She wears an animal skin, holds a trident, and has placed one finger at her mouth in a gesture of amazement. The Islamisches yogini, dressed in an exquisitely detailed sawar camise, carries a musical instrument as she walks through a somewhat abstracted landscape, indicated only by a few plants at the painting's base and outlines of mountains or clouds at the top.

The women portrayed in the paintings are identifiable as ascetics of the Shaivite sect (worshippers of the Hindu god Shiva) by their general appearance and dress, as well as by the type of accoutrements they carry. The LACMA figure holds a trident, while the British Museum yogini carries a *morachhal,* a peacock feather fan, both clear Shaivite links. Most of the women have their hair pulled up in a topknot, as a yogi would. Sev-

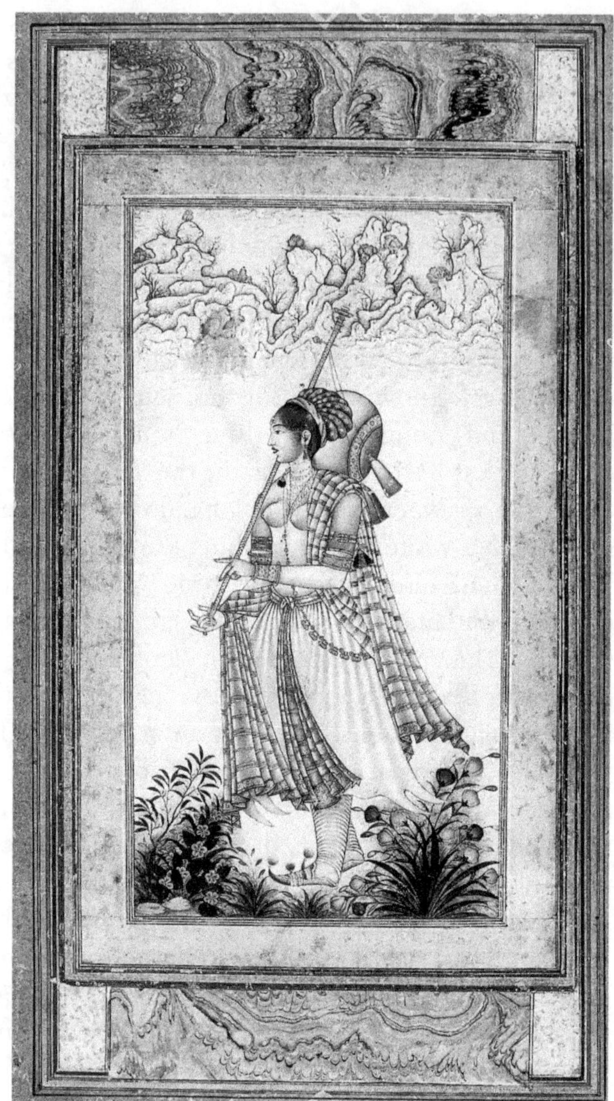

Figure 3.6. Yogini playing a tambur, ca. 1605–40, Bijapur. Staatliche Museen zu Berlin, Islamisches Museum, Berlin, T. 4591, folio 13.

eral have ashen complexions, representing ash smeared on their bodies, another distinguishing yogi marker. The British Museum yogini is scantly clad in only a loin cloth and shawl draped over her shoulders, just as male ascetics often are depicted, while the LACMA yogini wears an animal skin garment and carries a bag over her shoulder in the manner of a wandering ascetic. Two play musical instruments, another holds a beaded rosary, and several wear saffron-colored garments, all visual elements further suggesting their yogini status.

The images share other characteristics as well. The yoginis are the sole characters in each of the paintings, though sometimes accompanied by animals, and their figures dominate the compositions. All are young, attractive women, five of the six depicted in three-quarter pose and the remaining one in profile. They stand against a bare backdrop or in an open landscape, typically consisting of distant white palaces perched atop craggy hills in the background with lush foliage and oversized flowers in the foreground. All the images are single-page paintings, rather than folios from illustrated manuscripts, as indicated by their nonnarrative content and the elaborate borders framing some of them. Two paintings, the Chester Beatty and the LACMA yoginis, even have verses of poetry adorning their borders.[37]

Most likely, at some point in their histories, the pages were part of albums exhibiting examples of painting, poetry, and calligraphy.[38] The Chester Beatty yogini, when acquired by Sir Alfred Chester Beatty for his collection, was bound in exactly such an album, consisting of fifteen folios, fourteen bearing poetry and one displaying the yogini painting. David James has argued that the album actually contains fragments of two earlier albums, both of them made for Muhammad Quli Qutb Shah of Golconda. James believes the first album, containing examples of calligraphy by famous Persian calligraphers as well as local Deccan scribes, was assembled in 1591, while the second album, featuring poetry written by Muhammad Quli Qutb Shah himself, dates to 1605.[39] The second album held the Bijapur yogini image, which was presumably gifted to the sultan or somehow obtained by him shortly after the painting's completion.[40]

In Indo-Islamic painting, single-page paintings of solitary figures tend to be reserved for portraits, either of individuals (usually historically prominent people such as a sultan, prince, or courtier) or of types of people. A type portrait depicts not a specific person but rather a single figure standing in for a type of person, a dancer or courtly lady, for example. Though not portraying an individual, these images can be considered portraits in a broader sense. Just as a portrait of an actual person carefully depicts characteristics of the person's appearance in order to represent the subject, a type portrait illustrates the significant attributes of the type with the same careful attention to detail. Based on this definition, we can classify the six yogini paintings as type portraits; they represent the female ascetic as a type, rather than portraying actual, individual ascetics. The type portrait functioned in one of two primary ways or in a combination of the two. It could act as a sort of genre scene, representing a common but interesting figure that one might encounter in the physical environment, or it could act on a symbolic level. In the latter case, the artists intended the type portrait to invoke powerful ideals and feelings associated with the figure, who may or may not have been a common sight in the environs.

The wandering male ascetic, whether Hindu or Muslim, was one popular type that operated on both levels, corporal and symbolic. A painting of an ascetic, most likely a dervish (Muslim male mystic), housed in the Israel Museum, Jerusalem, and attributed to circa 1600, furnishes a Bijapuri example (pl. 19). The dervish, depicted in profile, provides the focal point of the painting's composition. He wears a large shawl and holds some sort of elephant tusk or horn container along with a small bag.[41] A dog accompanies him as he travels through an open landscape consisting of white palaces behind hills in the background and oversized plants in the foreground. The open landscape, his dress, the small bag that he carries, even his canine companion (the dog implies the man's status as beyond the norms of society)—each of these elements clearly conveys the figure's status as a wandering ascetic. He represents the male Muslim ascetic as a type of person. Such men, we imagine, must have been somewhat commonplace sights in Adil Shahi Bijapur, which housed a growing number of Sufis at the turn of the seventeenth century. The painting also operates on a symbolic level, and in many ways the symbolism lies at the heart of the image. The figure represents one who has forsaken worldly possessions and his position in society in order to follow the Sufic path, to go off in search of Truth or union with God. He thus invokes the intense Sufic feelings of love, longing, the pain of separation, just as the *Pem Nem* and its illustrations would have done through its allegorical romance between a prince and princess. He also reminds the viewer of the struggles involved in following the Sufic path. The single image, by sensitively portraying key attributes that define and distinguish a wandering ascetic, conveys with it all the feelings and associations surrounding such figures and Sufism in general.

In many respects the dervish image and the yogini paintings mirror each other. The dervish image and the two 1590s paintings, the British Museum yogini and the Mittal yogini, in particular bear striking similarities. In fact, the similitude in the specific accoutrements carried by the ascetics and various stylistic details, including the distinctive hatching on the background palace, suggest the same artist produced the three images. All seven images, however, relate to each other on a broader level. They share similar compositions—a single figure occupying most of the page and positioned in front of a blank backdrop or open landscape with palatial structures marking the distance. Their dress and accoutrements also match. Thus, in precisely the same manner as the Israel Museum dervish, even using many of the same visual signifiers, the yogini paintings represent the wandering ascetic.[42] More than that, they all function as type portraits intended to represent someone who has given up worldly positions to follow the mystical path in search of union with God, and thereby convey associations with love, longing, and spiritual seeking as specifically related to Sufism, Islamic mysticism. The poetic verses placed around the Chester Beatty yogini painting, which extol the beauty of the beloved as longed for by the lover, confirm the reading of the yogini paintings as Sufic symbols.[43] The Sufic theme, ubiquitously framed as the lover in search of the beloved, was a popular one throughout the Islamic world. What makes the Bijapuri images unique is that they employ female Hindu ascetics to stand in as the lover in search of the beloved. Typically in Persianate painting a male Muslim, such as a Sufi, poet, or wandering prince, represented the lover.

The use of a female Hindu ascetic to symbolize the Sufic lover in search of the beloved connects these images to local literary trends. In Deccani literature, including that from Bijapur, it was common for the figure in search of union with God to be portrayed as Hindu or female. For example, in Urdu masnavis such as the *Pem Nem,* one or both of the main characters often were Hindu. In the *Pem Nem*'s case, the lover was Ratan Sen, the Hindu prince of Chittor. Another Bijapuri Sufic work, *Khabushnama,* employs as its main character a girl named Khabush who was a devotee of God and detached from worldly things.[44] The Sufi saint, Shah Miranji, also called Shams al-Ushshak (d. 1563), the first writer of Deccani Urdu in Bijapur, composed the feminized Sufic story. Shah Miranji's son, Shah Burhan al-Din Janam (d. 1583), carried on the tradition, also writing Deccani Urdu poetry that employed female characters as the lover yearning for the beloved.[45] The incorporation of Hindu and female figures into Sufism's repertoire of the tortured lover in search of God reflects the strong influence of Hinduism on Sufism in the Deccan at this time. Deccan Sufis often incorporated local traditions in their teachings and writings, particularly when they were writing in Deccani Urdu, a language that developed as a combination of Persian and local Indic vocabulary and imagery. Bijapuri poets actively embraced this trend, liberally employing Hindu philosophy and terminology in their writings.[46]

In her discussion of "the feminization of Sufism in India," Annemarie Schimmel notes that Sufi poets, particularly those in Gujarat and Bijapur, took up the Indic tradition of representing the soul as a longing woman thanks to the influence of *bhakti.*[47] Like Sufism, bhakti is a mystical movement based on the concept of the lover devoted to God, but in the case of bhakti, the lover is typically cast as female.[48] However, the sentiment of longing and pain of separation felt by the lover is the same in both traditions. In Persian Sufism, this sentiment is called *firaq-i yar* and is often expressed in a *ghazal,* a type of poem written in the male voice, while in bhakti it is called *viraha* and typically expressed in poetry using a female narrator. Carla Petievich has pointed out that the traditional canon of classical Urdu poetry developed by scholars largely excluded Deccani Urdu ghazals from the sixteenth and seventeenth centuries because the Deccani ghazals are written in the female voice rather than the male voice. Instead of revealing the literary weakness of the poems, as some scholars have viewed this trait, Petievich sees it as highlighting the Deccan poets' ability and freedom to combine traditions. They chose to write in ghazal format but employed the female voice to express the torment of the lover, and thus created a distinctive Perso-Indic strand of poetry.[49]

The wide incorporation of Hindu traditions and imagery into Sufism in the Deccan demonstrates that the yogini images would have readily suggested Sufic concepts to a Bijapuri audience familiar with such poetry and accustomed to religious and cultural interaction. Moreover, the extent to which the yogini images drew on contemporary literary traditions would have echoed with their Adil Shahi viewers, attuned as they were to "the power of words." Yet the use of female figures must have appealed in other ways as well. Notably, the artists portrayed the women as youthful beauties. This contrasts with the typical depiction of yogis and dervishes as older, worn figures (see, e.g., the Israel Museum dervish). The yoginis' beauty when paired with their gaze off into the distance rather than directly at the viewer and the compositional emphasis on their bodies indicate that the viewer was meant to admire them. In this manner, the women function as the beloved, the one adored and longed for, thereby allowing the viewer to take on the role of the lover and experience the emotion of longing for themselves. The yoginis thus effectively connote both the lover and the beloved (the verses adorning the Chester Beatty yogini reflect this, as they can be read alternately from the perspective of the yogini or of the viewer). As figures who have given up their place in society to follow the spiritual path, they represent the lover. As beautiful young women who are to be longed for, they represent the beloved. This dual functionality undoubtedly added to the resonance of the images.

Some of the material details that augment the beauty of these women—jewelry looped around the topknots of their hair, long flowing scarves, bangles on their arms—propose a further reading of these images, one that ties them even more specifically to literary developments and gives an intriguing twist to their symbolism. M. L. Nigam first noted peculiarities in the Deccani yogini images that he linked to a strand of Urdu literature. Nigam observed that the paintings contain details that do not quite fit with the straight reading of these women as Hindu ascetics.[50] For example, in all of the paintings, an abundance of jewelry, including necklaces, bracelets, earrings, and hair ornaments, adorns the women. A few of the figures, such as the V&A yogini, also wear *selhis,* distinctive long necklaces worn over the right shoulder. The Chester Beatty and Mittal yoginis' scarves are rich in gold and black geometric decoration. The Islamisches yogini even sports richly embroidered slippers. Such opulence belies an ascetic lifestyle. Additionally, several of the women wear *pyjamas* with tight-fitting bodices and full four-pointed skirts as well as long *dupattas,* scarves. Pratapaditya Pal in his discussion of the LAMCA yogini views this type of dress as Muslim-like and concludes, like Nigam, that the women are not truly Shaivite ascetics.[51] Finally, birds, specifically a myna bird and a parrot, accompany two of the women. South Asian literature often associates both types of birds with noble women, who kept them as pets and/or shared secrets and tales with them, the *Tutinama* (*Tales of a Parrot*) being perhaps the most prominent example of this.[52] Taken together, these visual elements suggest an aristocratic status for the women, yet a profusion of other details, from tridents to ashen complexions, indicate their status as Shaivite ascetics.

Based on these paradoxical features, Nigam connects the yogini images of the Deccan with a type of Urdu literature popular in eighteenth-century North India.[53] In this genre, noble women, largely Muslim noble women, disguise themselves as yoginis in order to escape the confines of *purdah* (seclusion) and go off in search of their beloved. The purpose of this type of Urdu romance was to promote Sufic ideas, in the same manner that the *Pem Nem* promoted such concepts. The stories stress the pains of separation from one's beloved and also serve as an allegory for the tariqa, the Sufic path, just as other masnavis do. The women's disguises and furtive escapes add twists and turns to the journey and take the overcoming of obstacles to new levels. Their "racy" behavior also, undoubtedly, serves to augment the adventuresome and romantic aspects of the tales.

If we apply Nigam's reading of the Deccani yogini images to the specific Bijapuri paintings examined here, it explains the seemingly contradictory visual details and deepens the symbolism of the images without fundamentally changing their import. They still represent the lover and beloved, just with an additional layer of meaning. Moreover, the opposing visual elements can be understood as deliberate visual clues incorporated by the artists to lead the viewer to that deeper level. For example, let us reconsider the Chester Beatty yogini in this light. Her saffron-colored garment, ashen complexion, and hair gathered up in a topknot characterize her as an ascetic follower of the god Shiva, but her abundance of jewelry and fine golden scarves reveal to the viewer her hidden aristocratic identity, while adding to her mysterious beauty. She looks at a myna bird perched on her right hand, and the bird tilts its head to look back at her, suggesting an intimacy between the two. Their shared look almost seems to indicate the shared knowledge of her disguise. The open landscape around her represents her journey on the Sufic path. At the same time, the oversized flowers, pink hills, and golden sky create an otherworldly landscape, intimating that the painting expresses something extraordinary. The white palace in the background perhaps illustrates the royal home that she has left, or perhaps it embodies the destination of her search, as I suggested the palace in the *Pem Nem*'s illustrations symbolized. The young woman is clearly in the midst of a journey, made all the more adventurous by the clandestine nature of her appearance. Every aspect of the painting is lush and luxurious, begging the viewer to admire its beauty and that of the yogini.

In the words of Evelyn Underhill, an effective mystical symbol "will use to the utmost the resources of beauty and passion, will bring with it hints of mystery and wonder, bewitch with dreamy periods the mind to which it is addressed."[54] Viewed from this perspective, the solitary noblewoman-disguised-as-yogini is the ideal mystical image. The beautiful female figure is both the lover and the beloved, and as such she arouses intense emotions. She also alludes not only to Sufic concepts but also to specific types of Urdu literature with which the viewer was assumed to be familiar, ones filled with expressions of passion and longing. Finally, her dual status, as both lover and beloved, but also as both a noble lady and one who has forsaken society's norms, heightens her romantic appeal and adds a sense of mystery to the scene.

One specific Urdu work, *Sihr al-Bayan,* an eighteenth-century Lucknowi masnavi written by Mir Hasan and considered one of the most popular Urdu romances of all time, provides an excellent example of a noble woman disguising herself as a yogini to aid in the search of the beloved. The plot of the story is typical of its genre: a prince and princess fall in love, they are separated by unforeseeable events, and only after a long, painful ordeal are they finally united. In Mir Hasan's tale, there are two royal couples, Princess Badr-i Muni and the prince of Sangaldip, as well as Princess Najm al-Nisa and the fairy prince, whom Najm al-Nisa charms when disguised as a yogini. The following passage describes the Princess Najm al-Nisa disguising herself as a yogini in order to go off to rescue the princely lover of her friend, Princess Badr-i Muni. Thus in this instance she is acting as an intermediary for other characters. The passage is notable for the detail with which it describes her transformation.

> She took off all her ornaments, and threw all her decorations and finery in the dust, then having somewhat collected her senses and understanding, she put, on that delicate body, the clothes of a female yogi, and burning several seers of pearls, rubbed her face with the ashes. Over her shoulders and round her waist, she tied a shawl of white brocade, and hid her bodice in a hundred ways; she made the rose-leaves of the garden of beauty resplendent with fresh greenness, and placed on her head a pretty ring made of gold, which made glorious the bed of spikenard; she then, tying in knots the ringlets of her hair, let them hang loose over her bosom and shoulders, and let slip from her hand the reins of the horse of beauty. She made her eyes red with the smoke of sighs, and filled them with the blood of her heart; round her hand she wore a rosary of emeralds, and placed a been [veena] on her shoulder; she also tied round her neck a thread necklace, and put on a wrapper of a red colour. After this she arranged her beads, and put them in their proper places, and dis-

guising herself completely in the clothes of a female yogi, took the road to the forest.[55]

Her ashen complexion, the shawl, the "ring of gold" placed in her hair, the jeweled rosary, the veena she carries, her taking to the road—all these details accord with the appearances of the yoginis in the Bijapuri paintings. This resemblance gives credence to the theory that the young beauties in the Bijapuri paintings represented noble women disguised as yoginis. Of course, the *Sihr al-Bayan* dates to about 150 years after the Bijapuri paintings and belongs to another part of India, Lucknow, far from the Deccan.[56] Therefore, an earlier literary source is needed to confirm this interpretation, probable as it is.

The *Pem Nem,* which has yet to be fully translated, provides an interesting possibility in this regard. The manuscript's first painting depicts Ratan Sen listening to a yogini play her veena. The artist depicted her in a manner similar to the women in the single-page Bijapuri paintings as well as the description of Princess Najm al-Nisa in the above passage. She is identifiable as a female ascetic follower of the god Shiva by her up-knotted hair and ashen-colored skin. At the same time, she is young and attractive, wearing a sawar camise and adorned with jewelry. There is also an intriguing artistic connection between the *Pem Nem*'s yogini and the single-page yogini paintings. Based on stylistic comparison, the same artist, "Hand A" of the *Pem Nem,* appears responsible for both the manuscript's illustration and the best-known single-page yogini image, the Chester Beatty yogini. Moreover, the two paintings were produced less than a decade apart, marking the start of the yogini images' production. Perhaps future studies of Deccani literature will uncover more definitive connections.

There are several reasons to assume that such a symbolic twist would have been appealing in an elite Bijapuri context. First, her "hidden" identity as a noble woman provides the image with multiple layers of meaning that the viewer can then uncover. This layered effect functions like poetic metaphors and suggests the concept of the batin, the inner, hidden essence or truth in Sufism. Second, the painting represents someone taking on the guise of mysticism in order to achieve her goals. A noble woman is confined by purdah, but as a yogini, she can go out in the world in search of her beloved. In the end, she returns to her former life and identity, thus accomplishing her goals while maintaining the order of society. Her use of mysticism seems to parallel the larger role that Sufism, whose popularity transcended class, religion, and ethnicity while ultimately supporting the existing power structures, played as a unifying agent in Bijapur during the sixteenth and seventeenth centuries.[57] Third, the woman's status as both a noble and an ascetic provides an important link between courtly life and ascetically oriented mysticism in the same way that the

Pem Nem's emphasis on courtly ritual does. On a purely visual level, the paintings' juxtaposition of humble ascetic elements, such as animal skins or matted hair, with hints of luxurious finery, such as earrings or embroidered slippers, achieves these ends. Finally, by drawing on ideas expressed in literature without directly illustrating a text, the yogini paintings not only denote the power of words in Bijapuri culture but also suggest the development of a particular type of visual language. To be literate in this visual language, viewers had to be conversant in the intricacies of Sufism, poetry, and Deccani Urdu literature, helping to foster a unified, learned culture at court. Yet, because the images and literature featured extensive religious and culture interaction, the courtly culture was *inclusive* as well as *exclusive*.

Despite lingering questions about the exact literary origins and meanings of these intriguing figures, the larger connotations of the yogini paintings are clear. The beautiful young women function as visual metaphors for both the lover and the beloved, as well as for the longing and pain of separation connecting the two. They also denote the struggles along the Sufic path. The paintings were bound tightly to literary developments of the period yet seem not to have been created for a particular work. They thus refer to literature without directly illustrating it. To Adil Shahi courtly viewers, the images would have brought to mind related mystical poems and stories with which they were familiar—perhaps a whole genre of literature would have been suggested by just one yogini painting. The images reinforce the "feminization of Sufism" that was happening in the Deccan and serve as visual examples of the cultural and religious interaction that was taking place. Above all else, they demonstrate the profound role that mysticism played in the development of the Adil Shahi visual identity.

Portraits of Ibrahim Adil Shah II

Paintings of Ibrahim Adil Shah II, the sixth ruler of Bijapur, are portraits of an individual, rather than portraits of a type, as the yogini images are. Yet depictions of the sultan exhibit characteristics normally associated with type portraits. While the images do convey his distinctive physical traits, such as a slightly hooked nose and beard, and aspects of what we assume to be his personal interests and character, they do so through the filter of poetry and poetic ideals. The paintings closely coordinate with contemporary written descriptions of Ibrahim, but more than that, in the manner of a type portrait or panegyric verse, images of Ibrahim employ visual details to suggest qualities belonging to larger categories, whether accomplished Persianate prince, mystic, lover, or Deccan sultan. Finally, like poetry, depictions of Ibrahim *allude* to meaning, in this case his identity, status, and quality of kingship, rather than delineate actions or events that would directly convey it.

Because portraits of Ibrahim, like most Bijapuri single-page paintings, bear minimal inscriptional evidence, art historical analyses of the images have focused primarily on issues of identification, attribution, and dating. For example, only three of the eight images to be examined in this case study contain inscriptions identifying them as portraits of Ibrahim, only three feature the name of the artist, and none bears a date of production. We have had to rely on stylistic analysis aided by historical framework, the few inscriptions that do exist, and Ibrahim's appearance in the paintings to classify the works. For example, one common method employed to estimate the date of a painting has been to base it on the apparent age of Ibrahim in the portrait.[58]

The other main approach to the portraits has been to analyze what the images reveal about Ibrahim's character as well as his role in Bijapur's artistic development. In this regard, we are assisted by the many references to Ibrahim in various written sources: court histories, panegyric poetry, verse attributed to Ibrahim himself, as well as a few visitors' accounts. These sources provide a solid body of evidence for comparison and reveal a close correlation between textual and visual descriptions of the sultan. For example, several of the portraits depict Ibrahim with musical instruments, and correspondingly, many written sources attest to Ibrahim's love of music. Asad Beg, a Mughal ambassador who visited Bijapur in 1604, recorded a conversation between himself and Ibrahim during a musical performance in which the sultan questioned Asad Beg about Tansen, a famous musician at Akbar's court. Ibrahim then asserted, "Music is such that it should be heard at all times and always. Musicians should be kept happy."[59] In the same vein, in one verse of the *Kitab-i Nauras,* a collection of songs attributed to the authorship of Ibrahim, the sultan writes that the two most pleasant things in the world are a tambourine and a beautiful woman.[60] The *Kitab-i Nauras,* composed in Deccani Urdu interspersed with Sanskrit vocabulary, begins with an invocation to Sarasvati, the Hindu goddess of learning, and follows with praise for the prophet Muhammad, as well as for the Deccan Sufi saint, Gesudaraz.[61] In the work, Ibrahim calls himself Jagatguru, "World Teacher."[62] The book thus revels in examples of religious and cultural interaction and stresses both learning and mysticism, and these things, likewise, pervade visual depictions of the sultan.[63] It is no wonder, then, that the paintings are so closely linked to Ibrahim's perceived character, but I believe the paintings embody more meaning than simple revelations of Ibrahim's interests or the centrality of his role in shaping artistic production at Bijapur. The close relationship between text and images, even when not physically connected, provide further evidence of the "power of words" in Adil Shahi courtly culture, as well as the strength of that shared culture in establishing an identity for the sultanate.

The eight portraits examined here, chosen because they are clearly identifiable as portraits of the sultan, feature Ibrahim Adil Shah II alone or positioned with a few other figures, and all are single-page paintings dating from the 1590s through the 1630s.[64] As a group, they are contemporary with the yogini images examined in the previous section, and in fact they exhibit the same stylistic development: from pages swathed in heavy pigment, particularly gold, in the early paintings, to tinted drawings and increasingly precise details in the later paintings. Additionally, like the yogini paintings, portraits of Ibrahim show the development of a visual theme, artists revisiting and reworking the subject matter over several decades.

Bust Portrait of Ibrahim, circa 1590, and *Ibrahim in a Procession with Courtiers*, circa 1595, two of the earliest surviving portraits of the sultan and both today in a private collection, share many stylistic similarities and were most likely created by the same artist.[65] The first of the two works features a close-up of Ibrahim's head and shoulders. The artist painted the background a vivid lapis blue and depicted the sultan as a slightly smiling young man with a wispy beard. He wears a large emerald necklace and gold turban with an unusually wide sash decorated with Persianate flowers. The distinctive conical turban appears in all the portraits of Ibrahim and seems to have been a Bijapuri fashion, for courtiers in paintings from the same period wear similar turbans.[66] The sash of this turban is further adorned with a *nastaliq* inscription, translated from Persian as follows:

> Khadiv of the world, the king of his age, enthroned under an auspicious sign, the fortunate king, light of the heart and of the eyes of the happy, the benefactor of the soul of the generous.
>
> He is Khalil, the oystershell of the heavens contains nothing like thee, Faridun and Jam have no son like thee, Solomon.[67]

The second line of the inscription begins by referring to Ibrahim as Khalil, a title meaning "friend of God" and referring to the Koranic prophet Abraham (Ibrahim in Arabic). This is an obvious play on Ibrahim's name, one that also can be found in Zuhuri's poetry. For example, one of the three works in Zuhuri's *Sehr Nathr* (the title given to the collective trilogy of his works) devoted to listing the glories of Ibrahim is called *Khan-i Khalil*, or "The table of the friend of God."[68] Mark Zebrowski further links the portrait to Zuhuri's poetry by comparing the rosy-cheeked, youthful sultan in the painting to a passage in which the poet claims "the sultan, as beautiful as Joseph, has cheeks as red as the fire into which Abraham was cast" and "a letter of bondage [has been written] to his newly grown beard."[69] Thus Ibrahim's portrayal here is filtered through poetry in two ways. First, the painting physically incorporates verse that not only praises the sultan, and thereby conveys the quality of his rule, but also alludes to his identity through the title Khalil. Second, specific aspects of Ibrahim's depiction—rosy cheeks and wispy hint of a beard—mirror written descriptions of the young ruler. Ibrahim may have indeed looked like this when the portrait was made, but his youthful appearance was equally important as a poetic ideal that connected him to the likes of Joseph.

The second portrait depicts Ibrahim clutching a cane and walking at the head of a procession of seven nobles, perhaps just generic men-in-waiting figures or perhaps representations of actual Adil Shahi courtiers.[70] One figure holds a fanning cloth over Ibrahim, partially covering a gold crown with tassels that hovers symbolically above the sultan's head. The men wear heavy gold-embroidered garments, with Ibrahim's robe and scarves being particularly voluminous and lavish. The artist placed the figures on a gold background, with a grassy base and clouds at the top to hint at a setting. Ibrahim dominates the center of the painting, and the courtiers, shown much smaller in scale than the sultan, pile up behind him on the page's left side.

In both this portrait and the previous, which focuses on Ibrahim's head and shoulders in a highly unusual "close-up," the artist seems to have been experimenting with composition, and his experiments resulted in effective royal images. Without the representation of any explicit courtly setting the paintings still convey Ibrahim's royal stature and the affluence of his court. For example, in the portrait of the sultan with courtiers, Ibrahim's lavish garments, the fanning cloth and crown over his head, his dominant size, and his placement at the head of the procession display his power and status, while the extensive use of gold pigment embodies the wealth of the court. The lack of specific settings or any real action allows the portraits to exist outside the scope of a particular moment in time, imbuing the paintings with a sense of universality. At the same time, certain visual details give them the specificity needed to function as portraits of Ibrahim. Thus the paintings balance the general and specific in the same manner that one of Zuhuri's panegyric verses does so. For example, in one portion of the *Sehr Nathr,* Zuhuri praises Ibrahim at length as a fair-minded ruler and generous patron, as well as an accomplished musician, poet, calligrapher, painter, and chess player. Details of this description seem to fit what we know of Ibrahim's personality, and yet overall it casts him in the generic, often hyperbolic mode of the well-rounded, refined ruler.[71]

Two turn-of-the-century portraits, *Ibrahim Adil Shah II Hawking,* in the Institute of Oriental Studies, St. Petersburg (pl. 20), and *Ibrahim Adil Shah II Reading,* in the Gulistan Library, Tehran, present the sultan in the guise of the accomplished Persianate prince. Farrukh Beg, the well-known Persian-turned-Mughal painter who spent several years at the Adil Shahi court, was most likely responsible for both. John Seyller has identified a tiny inscription on the painting of Ibrahim hawking that reads *amal-i Farrukh Beg ast,* "This is the work of Farrukh Beg," and appears to be in the artist's own hand. The inscription sits in the upper right corner next to a larger inscription identifying the image as a portrait of Ibrahim.[72] The painting features a young, smooth-shaven Ibrahim on horseback and holding a hawk. A luxurious landscape is filled with fantastic rocks in the manner of Safavid painting, dark green foliage, and a golden sky. The painting bears strikingly similarities to the Gulistan Library image of Ibrahim reading, which depicts the sultan with a long gold sword resting on his lap, holding a book in one hand and the end of his sash in the other.[73] Ibrahim wears the same bright pink robe and wide gold sash in both images, and the landscapes compare as well. In the latter case, the eroded, Safavid-inspired rocks circle the gold throne on which Ibrahim is sitting instead of remaining off in the distance. Because of the overwhelming stylistic similarities, Seyller has attributed both works to Farrukh Beg and dated them to circa 1598–1600, toward the beginning of the period when the artist likely resided at the Adil Shahi court.[74]

Notably, both portraits depict Ibrahim as a slim, beardless youth. Earlier scholars used his appearance as a clue in dating *Ibrahim Adil Shah II Hawking*—suggesting, it was believed, a pre-1590 date, when Ibrahim was still young and beardless.[75] But as the inscription reveals, Farrukh Beg painted the work, and surviving Mughal evidence points to 1596 as the earliest date that Farrukh Beg could have arrived in Bijapur.[76] Thus Farrukh Beg must have created the image after 1596, even though Ibrahim probably sported a beard by that time. The question then becomes how to account for Farrukh Beg's portrayal of Ibrahim.

If we understand the depictions not as records of his actual appearance but rather as images arising out of the artist's objectives, it becomes clear that Farrukh Beg's aim was to portray Ibrahim as the ideal princely figure as imagined in Persianate traditions. In Persian painting, the accomplished prince or other courtly figure was typically shown as a tall, slim, and barefaced youth, as Ibrahim is in the two paintings. Farrukh Beg, while still reproducing enough of Ibrahim's physical attributes to convey his identity, deliberately shaped aspects of his appearance to further the impression of Ibrahim as the ideal, refined, youthful, royal, Persianate figure. *Ibrahim Hawking* depicts a young, attractive ruler dressed in a brightly hued robe, holding a brilliant white hawk and riding a magnificent hennaed horse through a fantastic landscape. Hawking and riding were activities at which all good rulers were expected to excel, and here Ibrahim is doing them beautifully. *Ibrahim Reading* likewise presents Ibrahim in the guise of the erudite Persianate ruler. The golden sword, throne, turban, and scarves convey his royal status, while the book suggests a princely penchant for poetry and literature. Visually portraying Ibrahim adeptly engaged in such royal pursuits is akin to the poet Zuhuri describing the sultan as a masterful musician, poet, painter, calligrapher, and chess player. It may or may not have been true, but that was hardly the point. The objective was to present Ibrahim as a talented ruler within the accepted idioms of the culture and age.

The style of the paintings further places the sultan within a Perso-Indic landscape, so to speak, of courtly traditions. The fantastic, coral-like rocks hark back to the glories of Safavid painting under Shah Tahmasp (r. 1524–76), reflecting the artist's background. Farrukh Beg, a Persian émigré to the Mughal Empire, came from Kabul to India in 1585, when he was forty years old. Thus he would have been a young artist-in-training during Tahmasp's reign, and he most likely painted the portraits shortly after his arrival in Bijapur.[77] Perhaps he sought to exhibit his connection to the Safavid court through the employment of recognizable Persian visual devices and thereby add to his prestige in Bijapur. The painting also bears Mughal stylistic elements, displaying the artist's link to that court. Most notable is the use of atmospheric perspective, which gives the background landscape depth, something not found in Bijapuri painting until this point. Farrukh Beg also incorporated Bijapuri elements into the painting. The color scheme, with its dark greens, pink, orange, and gold, and the oversized, precisely painted foliage in the foreground, fit with the developing Bijapuri style. Farrukh Beg seems to have drawn on the various styles with which he was familiar in the hopes of gaining favor with his patron, and the Adil Shahi court at large, by exhibiting his own skill and at the same time portraying Ibrahim as a capable Indo-Persian monarch.[78] A reference by Zuhuri indicates that his efforts were successful; while listing Ibrahim's six most esteemed courtiers, the poet mentions a master artist by the name of Maulana Farrukh Husain, presumably referring to Farrukh Beg. Zuhuri writes, "Maulana Farrukh Husain . . . whose painting nothing better can be imagined. The expert painters take pride in being his pupils, and having adopted the outline of his plain sketch as their model put their lives under obligation."[79]

Farrukh Beg created a third, slightly later portrait of Ibrahim, *Sultan Ibrahim Adil Shah II Playing the Tambur,* housed in the Naprstek Museum, Prague, and datable to circa 1600 (pl. 21). A Mughal inscription on the border, added after the painting's completion and long believed to be erroneous, states that Farrukh Beg executed the work. In light of the newly uncovered inscription on *Ibrahim Hawking* that confirms Farrukh Beg's residency at the Adil Shahi court, the attribution now appears accurate.[80] The painting depicts Ibrahim lounging on pillows and playing the tambur. On the left three courtiers listen and clap to the music. The artist has pictured Ibrahim much bigger than the rest of the figures, who themselves have been rendered at various scales. A servant, several tiny elephants, and a white palace atop hills fill the background.

If we compare this painting to the two earlier portraits of Ibrahim by Farrukh Beg, differences emerge that indicate a shift in artistic intent. In this image, Farrukh Beg situates the sultan within specifically Adil Shahi idioms of kingship as they were being defined during Ibrahim's reign, rather than within the broader category of the accomplished Persianate ruler as the other two paintings do. Clearly in the short amount of time that Farrukh Beg had been in residence at Bijapur, he had become familiar with the courtly culture, visual as well as literary. Not only does the landscape take on a more Bijapuri feel due to the absence of the Safavid-style rocks and the addition of a distant white palace, but now Ibrahim sports a beard and wears *rudraksha* beads, the dried berry rosary associated with Hindu ascetics. These last two aspects are characteristic of all portraits of Ibrahim by local Bijapuri artists after 1594. Moreover, the painting seems to specifically reference Ibrahim's own written descriptions of himself in the *Kitab-i Nauras*. In one of the most revealing passages of the work and one that parallels this image in several regards, Ibrahim describes himself as a Hindu god, complete with attributes and a mount:

> In one hand he has a musical instrument, in the other, a book which he reads and sings songs related to the Nauras. He is robed in a saffron-colored dress, his teeth are black, the nails are . . . red and he loves all. Ibrahim, whose father is god Ganesh and . . . mother, pious Sarasvati, has a rosary of crystal round his neck, a city like Vidyapur [Bijapur], and an elephant as his vehicle.[81]

Farrukh Beg portrays Ibrahim singing songs and holding a musical instrument. In fact, several scholars have speculated that the instrument Ibrahim plays is his prized tambur called Moti Khan in his poetry.[82] Ibrahim also appears here with darkened fingernails, recalling the line in which he describes himself with red nails. The architecture and elephants in the background relate to Ibrahim's attributes, the city of Bijapur and an elephant, described in the last line. It seems Farrukh Beg recognized the importance of the emerging Adil Shahi courtly identity as expressed through poetry and art and quickly adapted his paintings to suit it.

Ibrahim Adil Shah II Holding Castanets in the British Museum, London (pl. 22), by an unidentified artist, seems to have been created circa 1610, at about the midpoint of the images examined here, and it demonstrates how artists revisited and visually refined the theme. In this painting Ibrahim wears elaborately embroidered golden scarves and a diaphanous white robe over saffron pants. He holds two castanets in his left hand, a third is tucked into his robe, and his right hand grasps a green handkerchief. A breeze blows at his garments, and he looks out into the distance. Lush trees and

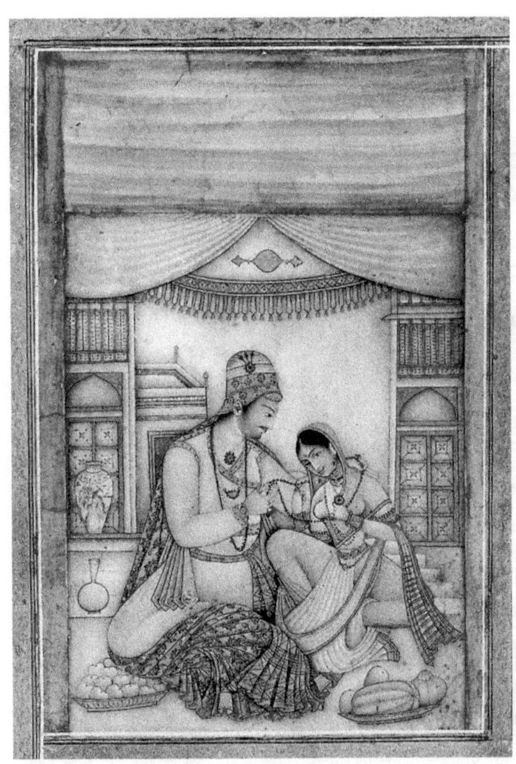

Figure 3.7. Sultan Ibrahim Adil Shah II presenting a necklace to his lover, ca. 1620–35, Bijapur. Victoria and Albert Museum, London, IS 48-1956, folio 1b. V&A Images/Victoria and Albert Museum Picture Library.

a white palace bearing thin Bijapuri minarets capped with lotus bud finials adorn the background, while two butterflies hover above pink lotus flowers in the foreground. As in the other images, Ibrahim, a large figure dominating the composition, stands in an unspecific, somewhat simple setting, yet the painting clearly conveys his royal stature as well as several particulars about him. The castanets indicate his love of music and the dried berry necklace his interest in mysticism. His lavish robe and scarves suggest his royal status, as does the green handkerchief, which Zebrowski has identified as "an old Islamic symbol of kingship" (the Bijapuri court historian Shirazi describes the holding of a handkerchief as a specifically Deccan gesture).[83] The lotus flowers in the foreground and the style of the palace in the background connect Ibrahim to Bijapur and Adil Shahi visual metaphors of kingship. At the same time, like the other portraits, the image connects Ibrahim to larger poetic ideals. Based on the manner in which the composition mirrors that of several of the yogini images as well as the scenes of the prince's quest in the *Pem Nem,* this particular image seems to present Ibrahim as a wandering figure off in search of his beloved and/or union with God. The poetic ideal, Sufic seeker and lover rather than Persianate prince or Deccan sultan, differs from that presented in the other portraits, yet it is equally common in literature of the period.

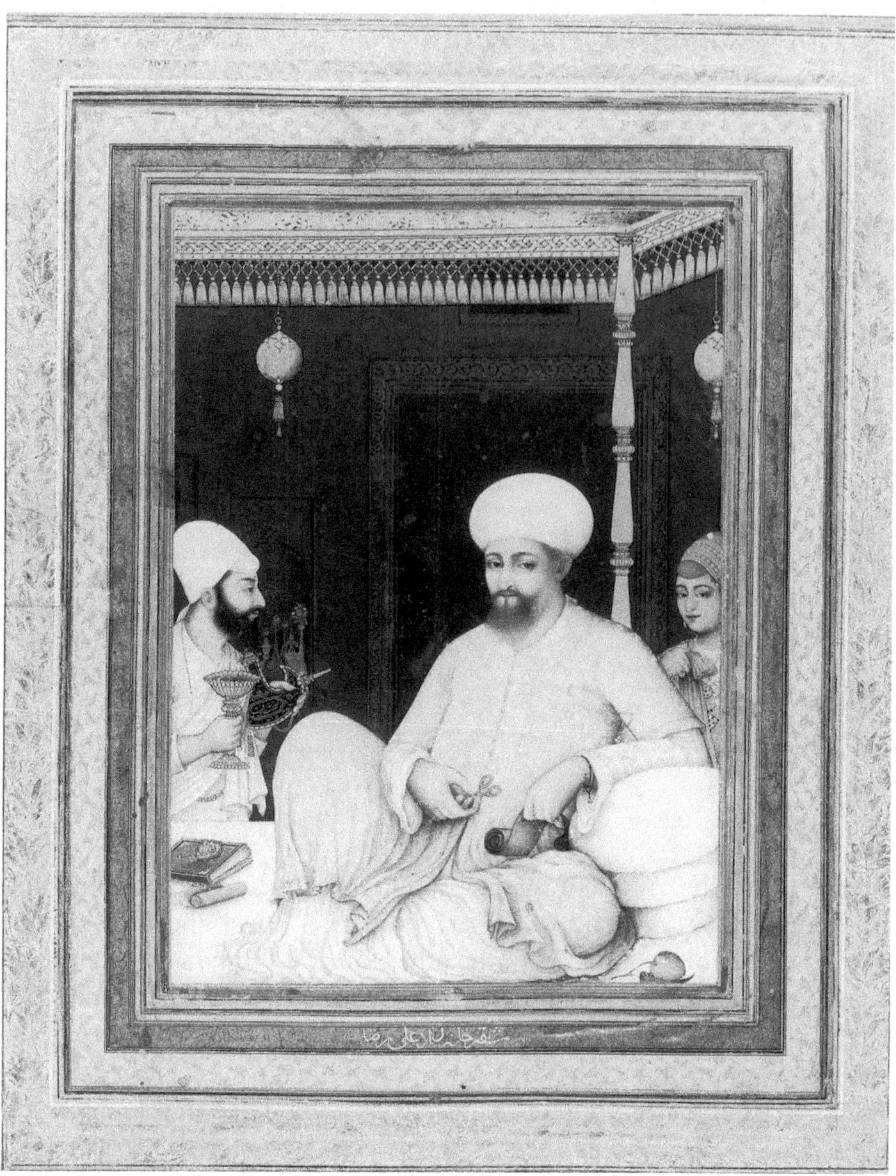

Figure 3.8. Ibrahim Adil Shah II venerates a Sufi saint, ca. 1630, Bijapur. The British Museum, London, 1997, 1108.01.

The final two portraits, based on stylistic analysis, seem to date to the 1620s or 1630s, several decades later than the other paintings, and they exhibit visible stylistic and compositional changes.[84] One image, a tinted drawing housed in the Victoria and Albert Museum, London, depicts Ibrahim presenting a lapis lazuli necklace to a female companion (fig. 3.7). He looks at her lovingly while she gazes off into the distance. The pair sits in a palace setting adorned with curtains and wooden panels set in niches, one of which holds a large vase. Abundant trays of fruit lay in the foreground. The second painting, in the British Museum, London, portrays Ibrahim venerating a Sufi saint (fig. 3.8). Ibrahim is pictured on the left holding a gold cup in one hand and a flask with a Persian inscription reading "Health and Prosperity" in the other.[85] The Sufi, holding a scroll and a pair of pinchers, lounges on a pillow, while a servant stands behind him. A book and a small gold plaque lie between Ibrahim and the Sufi. All three figures are located under a tasseled canopy from which hang ostrich eggs. The assortment of objects in the painting hints that the portrait may have functioned as an allegorical image of sorts.

In fact, both paintings display precise details that make the settings much more complete than in any of the portraits. This leaves the viewer with a sense of ambiguity as to whether the paintings represent actual events, ones that took place at specific times and places, or generic scenes of Ibrahim as the grand lover and patron of Sufis. For example, in *Ibrahim Presenting a Necklace to His Lover,* the setting appears to be illustrating the interior of a typical, if not actual, Adil Shahi palace. It is unclear whether the image of the woman is a portrait of an actual woman, such as one of Ibrahim's wives or mistresses, or a general representation of a beautiful, courtly lady. This sense is felt again when viewing *Ibrahim Venerating a Sufi.* The Sufi saint takes up the center of the painting and—like Ibrahim's companion in the previous image—looks directly at the viewer. In fact, the Sufi seems to be the subject of the portrait as much as or more than Ibrahim does. Again, the question arises of whether or not the image of the Sufi was a portrait of a real person. Moreover, one wonders if the portrait depicts an actual meeting between Ibrahim and a contemporary Sufi saint, an allegorical representation of Ibrahim venerating a popular local saint such as the Bahmani-era Gesudaraz whom the sultan praises in his poetry, or a generic scene of Ibrahim with a Sufi in order to visually reinforce the sultan's ties to Sufism. Revealingly, only with these two later portraits do such questions even arise. These two images depict Ibrahim within a much more specific sense of time and place than any of the other paintings. Even *Ibrahim Playing the Tambur,* which depicts the sultan involved in a particular activity, does not convey a sense of definite time or place. The differences in scale among the figures and the ubiquitous Bijapuri landscape with the tiny elephants and distant white palace, as well as the regularity with which Ibrahim playing music probably occurred, clearly indicate that the scene was an emblematic one.

A comparison with portraits of Ibrahim's contemporary or near-contemporary Indo-Islamic rulers in North India and the Deccan accentuates the lack of specificity in the Bijapuri portraits. While many images of these Islamicate rulers in front of simple or unarticulated backdrops do survive, so do images of them in specific settings. For example, surviving portraits of Abdullah Qutb Shah of Golconda (r. 1626–72) show him in detailed *darbar* (audience) scenes in which he is enthroned and surrounded by his numerous courtiers, as he would have been for public audiences. The 1565 illustrated history *Tarif-i Husain Shahi* depicts the Ahmadnagar ruler Husain Shah (r. 1554–65) in battle against the kingdom of Vijayanagara as well as enthroned with his wife. The well-known images from the *Akbarnama* portray the Mughal emperor Akbar (r. 1556–1605) in various actions—visiting saints' shrines, leading battles, supervising building projects. Portraits of his successor, Jahangir (r. 1605–27), include images of him at specific court celebrations, and the buildings depicted in the background correspond with actual Mughal palaces.[86] In contrast, when all of the surviving portraits of Ibrahim are considered, even those tentatively identified as portraits of Ibrahim but not discussed here, we find no detailed darbar scenes, no battle scenes, no images of holiday celebrations, not even a single painting of him at Nauraspur, the newly founded city so lavishly praised in the contemporary histories. The closest that images of Ibrahim come to recording specific events are *Ibrahim Presenting a Necklace to His Lover* and *Ibrahim Venerating a Sufi,* which are ambiguous at best.

This evidence suggests that portraits of Ibrahim are poetic rather than historical in essence. Rather than depicting Ibrahim in terms of a recorded historical event or specific, identifiable place, the portraits place him in generalized or abstract settings and then add details, such as rudraksha beads, castanets, lavish robes, and handkerchiefs, to relay Ibrahim's identity, stature, and personality. In one case, the artist added poetry itself to Ibrahim's turban in order to convey his identity. The paintings, like poetry, evoke ideas as much as, or more than, they record explicit scenes. The connection to poetry goes beyond just the essence of the images, for the activities and attributes depicted correspond closely to those described in contemporary poetry. Playing the tambur, venerating a Sufi, enjoying the company of a beautiful woman—the *Kitab-i Nauras* mentions each of these activities. The dark nails, dried-berry necklace, rosy cheeks, and reference to Khalil also correlate with poetic descriptions of the sultan. Even the two paintings by Farrukh Beg that portray Ibrahim in the guise of the accomplished Persianate prince correspond with poetry; Zuhuri's praise of Ibrahim in the *Sehr Nathr* essentially describes Ibrahim as the model of the ideal Persianate ruler.

The close correspondence between poetic and visual depictions of the sultan parallels the intimate relationship between written and visual metaphors found in the *Pem Nem* manuscript and the yogini images. All three examples reinforce the central role that poetry played on the development of Bijapuri painting. When taken together, the paintings establish a relationship between words and images that goes beyond a physical connection on a single piece of paper or manuscript and pervades the cultural interests of the time. Additionally, all three suggest that the producers and viewers of the works had to be conversant in the metaphors expressed. If we assume that members of the court sponsored and viewed the *Pem Nem*, yogini paintings, and portraits of Ibrahim, it suggests that a shared, elite culture existed in Bijapur, one largely revolving around poetry and Sufism, as well as both Persianate and more specifically Bijapuri images of kingship. Moreover, these examples demonstrate that this culture was being expressed and reinforced through artistic production tailored to highlight the "power of words" in Adil Shahi Bijapur.

The Founding of Nauraspur

In 1599 (1008 AH) Ibrahim Adil Shah II founded a new capital city, named Nauraspur or "city of nauras," *nauras* being a multilayered poetic term translatable as "nine flavors" or "new arrival." Ibrahim and his advisors conceived Nauraspur as a spacious garden city that would function as a dual capital with the older city of Bijapur, just four miles east. While practical concerns and political motivations impacted the decision to found a new capital, Nauraspur also emerged as a response to, and affirmation of, the developing courtly identity. In fact, Ibrahim and his advisors seem to have designed the city principally as a physical embodiment of, and space in which to enact, the prevailing courtly culture centering around poetry, music, knowledge, and above all else, words. In this case, one particular word, *nauras,* provided the focus of both the courtly culture and the new city. Through what survives of its physical form and information gathered from historical accounts, Nauraspur illustrates that the development of visual metaphors was not limited to Bijapuri painting but extended to architecture and city planning as well.

Nauraspur's construction was a monumental endeavor. The Adil Shahi court historian Shirazi states that 20,000 workmen, including stoneworkers, plasterers, and carpenters, were engaged in its building. The workmen constructed multiple palaces, city walls, along with a broad road lined with shops connecting the new city with its companion capital, Bijapur.[87] Nauraspur's walls, if completed, would have encompassed an area one and a half times as large as that of Bijapur, as indicated by surviving fortification traces (map 2).[88] The glorious new capital, however, was never finished, and only twenty-five years after its founding it was completely demolished. In 1624 the Abyssinian leader of Ahmadnagar, Malik Ambar, led his forces in battle against the Adil Shahis, and his armies destroyed Nauraspur, whose unfinished walls afforded no protection.[89]

As a result of the city's short life, history has largely forgotten Nauraspur. It is no longer included on most maps of the early modern Deccan, and Henry Cousens published the last scholarly study on it in 1916.[90] This neglect results largely from the dearth of surviving evidence; the remaining architecture is scanty, and that which has survived has not been fully excavated, nor are the buildings being protected from falling into further ruin. Fortunately, several contemporary court histories, including those by Shirazi and Astarabadi, as well as the later history by Zubairi, discuss the founding of Nauraspur.[91] When we combine the information in these histories with that provided by the extant architectural evidence, clues to the city's conception begin to emerge. Like much of Bijapuri art, what we uncover are only fragments of a once-remarkable whole; nonetheless, these pieces allow us to discern aspects of Nauraspur's conception, including how it related to the formation of an Adil Shahi identity.

The founding of Nauraspur, like the creation of most new cities, was in part a response to practical needs. By the end of the sixteenth century the city of Bijapur had grown populous, and water supplies were always a concern on its arid plateau. Bijapur received its water primarily via underground canals originating at a large tank called the Surang Bauri, adjacent to the village of Torveh four miles west of the city and fed by water from the nearby Ramling River.[92] Torveh was a fertile green area thanks to its proximity to the river, and undoubtedly wanting to take advantage of the spot's natural greenness and plentiful water, Ibrahim chose it as the location for Nauraspur. In their accounts of the new capital, the court historians explain that Nauraspur was meant to be spacious, airy, and filled with gardens of all sorts. They take particular pains to praise the water at Nauraspur.[93] Their records also make it evident that Nauraspur was to function as a twin city to Bijapur rather than supplant Bijapur altogether. The historian Zubairi explains that Adil Shahi nobles, though obligated to construct residences in the new city, continued to build in Bijapur.[94] Architectural evidence in Bijapur confirms this. The western half of Bijapur city, the section closest to Nauraspur, holds the majority of the surviving monuments constructed between the 1590s and the 1620s (map 3). The west side contains both the Mecca Darwaza, the gate which led to the newly built road connecting Bijapur to Nauraspur, and the Shahpur Darwaza, the northwestern gate leading to Shahpur, the mercantile suburb northwest of Bijapur and northeast of Nauraspur (map 2). The construction of Nauraspur, therefore, created a three-pronged network of commercial, courtly, and residential hubs. The network included the cities of Bijapur and Nauraspur, the important commercial center of Shahpur, the roadways connecting the three points, and the subterranean canal system that supplied water to the inhabitants of each area. Building a new city at Torveh provided a practical plan for expansion, one that took advantage of natural water resources and, at the same time, complemented Bijapur and its infrastructure rather than detracted from it.

Political motivations also underlay Ibrahim's decision to found a new capital. A number of his contemporary sovereigns had created new capitals during the late sixteenth century. In 1571, the Mughal emperor Akbar founded Fatehpur Sikri, and in 1591, Ibrahim's neighbor Muhammad Quli Qutb Shah founded Hyderabad.[95] Then in the mid-1590s, the Safavid emperor Shah Abbas moved his capital to the city of Isfahan and began an extensive building campaign there. Ibrahim would have been keenly aware of these events and surely would have wanted to join the ranks of his fellow rulers. In fact, the historian Astarabadi in his account of Nauraspur's construction compares Ibrahim and the city to a list of other contemporary Persian or Indo-Islamic rulers and their cities. His list mentions Akbar, Muhammad Quli Qutb Shah, and Shah Abbas, but also earlier rulers such as Sher Shah Afghan in North India and Shah Tahmasp in Safavid Iran.[96] Through this comparison, Astarabadi was demonstrating that by founding a new city, Ibrahim ranked among the group of celebrated Perso-Islamic monarchs.

In a similar vein, both Firishta and Shirazi, writing during Ibrahim's reign, give extensive accounts of the Deccan city of Firuzabad, a planned palace-city constructed between 1399 and 1406. The founder, Firuz Bahmani, was one of the most esteemed rulers of the Bahmani kingdom, the earlier Deccan sultanate from which Adil Shahi Bijapur sprang. The historians give detailed descriptions of Firuzabad, including, for example, asserting that Firuz built nine separate *mahals* (palaces) in which he kept nine women who spoke various languages so that he could practice his linguistic skills. Such detailed accounts show that the practice of founding capitals was regarded as an important aspect of a monarch's rule, even when devoted to private pleasure rather than public protection.[97] Even more locally and recently, Ibrahim must have been aware of his predecessor Ali's 1565–68 building campaign in Bijapur city, which gave the capital its walls, canal system, gardens, and *jami masjid,* transforming the urban environment.

In other words, Ibrahim had plenty of examples to remind him of the significance of city building both in the larger Islamicate world's conceptions of kingship as well as in the more immediate Deccan environment. To rule well, and to be remembered in history, one needed to build, preferably on a large scale. Zubairi begins his account of Nauraspur by writing, "When all affairs were in order, the fortunate, blessed, and powerful Padshah, Ibrahim Adil Shah, assented to his heart's desire to found a city."[98] Nauraspur can be read as Ibrahim's attempt to leave his mark on history and display his status as a glorious, powerful sultan in the same manner as countless rulers before him had.

Nauraspur's founding responded to historical precedents, and its location answered practical concerns. What we know about the form of the city as well as the meaning embedded in its name makes it clear that the capital also emerged as a manifestation of the court's shared identity and, moreover, was intended by Ibrahim and his advisors to further assert that identity. The legend repeated in the contemporary histories regarding the city's name claims that one day Ibrahim visited the site to see how construction was coming along. While he was there, a wine merchant gave him a cup of a sweet wine made from a local recipe of nine juices or flavors, *noh ras* in Deccani Urdu. Ibrahim found the mixture so delicious that he decided to name the new city "City of Nine Flavors," or "Nauraspur," in honor of the local wine.[99] Other literary references, however, suggest that the Adil Shahi court favored the word *nauras* before 1599 and the alleged wine-tasting episode.[100]

The popularity of the term *nauras* undoubtedly stemmed from its poetic nature, and like any good poetic term, it has a multitude of connotations. *Nauras* means not only nine juices or flavors. It also can refer to the nine *rasas,* or nine moods that make up traditional Indian music. Additionally, the word translates from Persian as "new arrival." It can also imply "new flavor" or a new fashion. When understood as "new rasa," the term refers to a new emotion or essence, such as that which a masterful artwork or poem would convey to the educated viewer or reader. It should be noted that in Persian, *nine* and *new* are pronounced and spelled slightly differently—*noh* and *nau,* respectively (Nauraspur is spelled with *nau* rather than *noh*); however, contemporary writings, such as the following passage by Zuhuri, make it clear that in Bijapur the words were used interchangeably. In this quote, Zuhuri is explaining why Sultan Ibrahim named his collection of songs the *Kitab-i Nauras.*

> The reason why the book is called by this name is that the Indians call a mixture of nine juices "nauras," and if the Persians believe it to be the fresh fruit of the tree of his learning and perfection, it is appropriate; and in this sense also that this beloved of perfect beauty has newly appeared on the stage of existence from behind the curtain of invisibility, if it is called "nauras," it is also right.[101]

Zuhuri's quote reveals that its Bijapuri users not only recognized but in fact celebrated and encouraged the various connotations of the term. Indeed, the multiple meanings probably led to the adoption of the term in the first place. Like the images of yoginis, which also draw on differing traditions and contain layers of meaning that rely on a prerequisite of poetic knowledge, the term *nauras* aptly suited the cultivation of a shared courtly identity at Bijapur by being both inclusive and exclusive. Moreover, *nauras*'s meanings were varied enough to ensure its easy application in a variety of contexts. As Nazir Ahmad explains in his analysis of Bijapuri poetry, "When-so-ever the term [*nauras*] be used, it goes to testify to the fine taste of the prince who happened to choose a word so elastic as to be employed to convey various senses."[102]

The whole Adil Shahi court seems to have been obsessed with the word *nauras*. Nazir Ahmad has identified seventeen items named *nauras*.[103] These include the *Kitab-i Nauras* and the city of Nauraspur already mentioned, as well as nauras, the sweet wine tasted by Ibrahim. Add to this *amal-i Nauras,* the act of drinking the nauras wine. Zuhuri titled one of his three celebrated poems the *Naurasnama,* while two other Bijapuri poets adopted the word as their pen name—Abdul Qadir was known as Naurasi, and Rashid Qasvini just as Nauras. The central building in Nauraspur was called the Nauras Mahal, and Ibrahim's personal secretary, Shah Nawaz Khan, named part of his palace in Bijapur the Nauras Bahisht. A particular musical note was given the title Naghma-i Nauras, and there was a group of musicians called the Kaschkar-i Nauras. Various aspects of the official royal court took on the term as well. The administrative and revenue department became the Nauras, while the department of justice received the title of Kisab-i Nauras. There was also the *alam-i nauras,* the royal flag; the *nishan-i nauras,* the royal emblem of yellow color; and *hun-i nauras,* gold coins minted during Ibrahim's reign and bearing the inscriptions "Nauras Mahur-i Adil Shahi" and "Jagatguru dad Ilahi," referring to Ibrahim's title of "World Teacher." Last but not least, the court created a new holiday called the Id-i Nauras. Zubairi states that the Id's festivities included daylong performances by professional storytellers and musicians.[104] In addition to the utter omnipresence of the word *nauras,* the number nine took on special significance. For example, the court celebrated the Id-i Nauras whenever a Friday fell on the ninth day of a month, and Zuhuri's poem *Gulzar-i Ibrahim,* "The Rose Garden of Ibrahim," lists the virtues of Ibrahim as, of course, being nine in number.[105]

What survives of the city's physical form suggests that it too celebrated, and was shaped around, the word *nauras* and its various connotations. The aptly named Nauras Mahal, a two-storied palace with an arched façade looking out over a large tank, functioned as the city's architectural centerpiece as well as its physical center (fig. 3.9). The palace sits in the center of a spacious courtyard/garden enclosed by a nine-sided wall pierced by nine broad archways (pl. 23)—an obvious architectural pun on the word *nauras*. Clearly the Nauras Mahal was the most important structure in the new city. It is one of the few buildings singled out for mention in the Persian histories and the only one mentioned by its proper name. It also happens to be the best-preserved building in Nauraspur, having been minimally restored at some point in the twentieth century.[106] Next to the Nauras Mahal stands another palace, much more in ruins (fig. 3.10). The

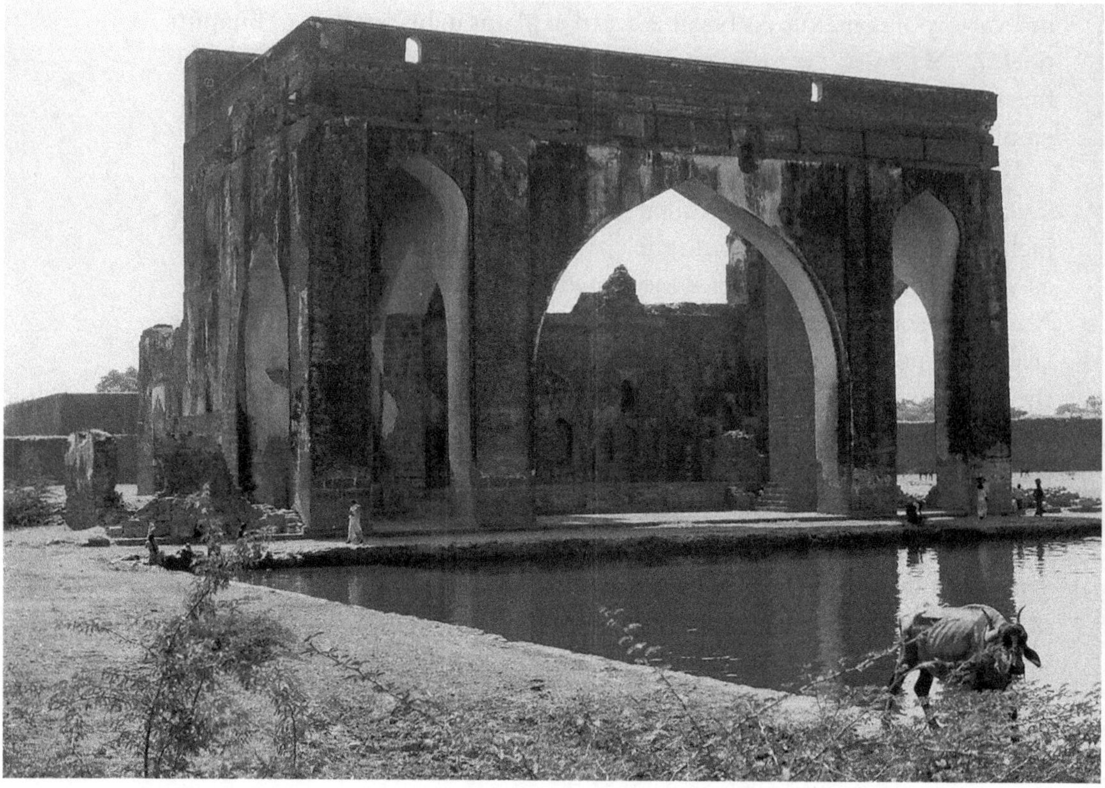

Figure 3.9. Nauras Mahal, 1599, Nauraspur. Photograph by author.

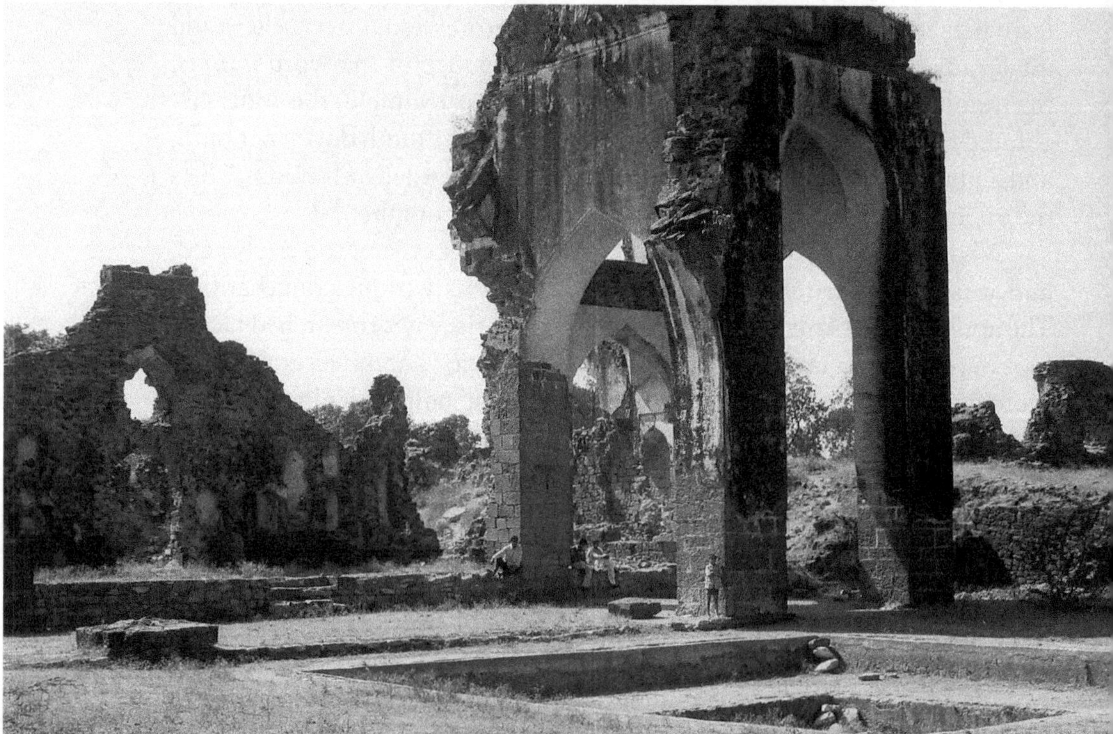

Figure 3.10. Remains of a palace, 1599, Nauraspur. Photograph by author.

palace seems to have been of the same design as the Nauras Mahal, with a two-storied arched façade and tank. This building, built on a slightly smaller scale than the Nauras Mahal, sits within a rectangular enclosure, the principle gateway of which adjoins one of the nine archways leading to the Nauras Mahal (fig. 3.11). One can discern the foundational remains of a third palace on another side of the Nauras Mahal suggesting that perhaps originally a series of palaces and other courtly buildings circled the Nauras Mahal, forming a royal center for the capital.

Both the Nauras Mahal and its neighboring building copy earlier palaces, specifically the Gagan Mahal and the Anand Mahal, both in Bijapur. Ali Adil Shah commissioned the Gagan Mahal in 1561 as the centerpiece of his court, and then in 1590 Ibrahim had the Anand Mahal built nearby as a matching monument. As Henry Cousens explained, these palaces served the "twofold purpose of a royal residence and council chamber."[107] The two Nauraspur palaces presumably functioned in a similar dual public and private manner. Façades with immense central arches flanked by narrow arches originally comprised all four structures—and remain intact in three of the four buildings. The central arch of the Gagan Mahal, which is the largest of the structures, measures sixty feet, nine inches. The wide arch spanned the whole front of the darbar hall, the public portion of the building, allowing it to be open to the view in front, which in each case originally included a reflection pool. The buildings' second floors, reached by stairwells in the back walls, held the more private apartments. In each structure, the second floor did not extend to the front of the central arch, but it did to the two smaller flanking arches, forming a U-shape that looked down on the central audience hall area. Massive wooden pillars originally supported the upper stories in front. The arrangement, including the wooden pillars, is still visible in the slightly later Asar Mahal, built in Bijapur in 1646 to house a relic of the prophet Muhammad (fig. 3.12).[108] In fact, the well-preserved Asar Mahal with its tank and pillars provides an excellent example of what Nauraspur's two surviving palaces would have been like in their original forms. The layout of these buildings, with the two-storied façades looking onto tanks and U-shaped upper stories looking down onto the public spaces, are similar to those of Persian palaces from the same period.

The two other prominent architectural remains found in Nauraspur today are a small mosque and the fragment of a multistoried structure. The mosque, located just outside of the Nauras Mahal's nine-sided enclosure, directly across from the tank, is a small, three-bay structure (pl. 24). A ubiquitous Bijapuri dome with lotus petal base along with a pair of thin minarets capped by lotus bud finials embellish the structure, and plasterwork decorates the fairly simple *mihrab* (prayer niche). The mosque's location and intimate size suggest that the royal court used it, perhaps as a private prayer hall. The ruin of a multistoried building sits a short dis-

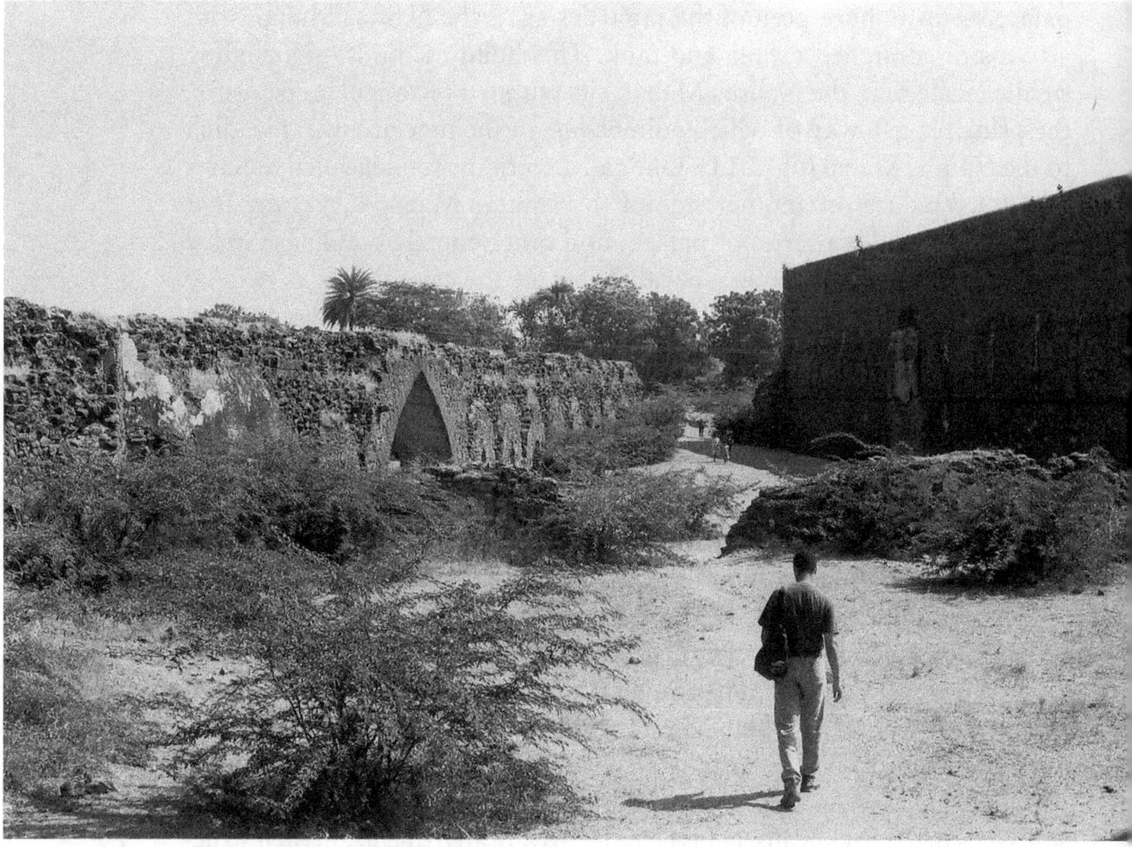

Figure 3.11. The Nauras Mahal's nine-sided enclosure adjoining the rectangular enclosure of another palace, 1599, Nauraspur. Photograph by author.

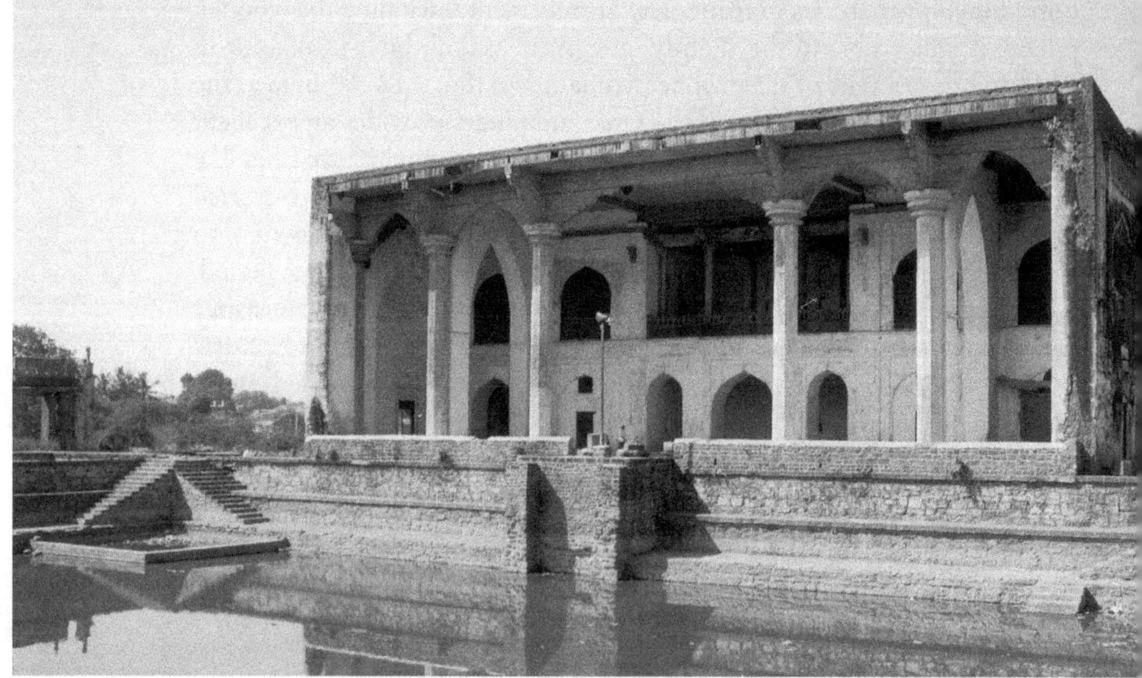

Figure 3.12. Asar Mahal, 1646, Bijapur. Photograph by author.

tance away from the Nauras Mahal in what is now a tamarind tree grove. It appears to have been a secular structure, such as the mansion of an Adil Shahi noble or wealthy merchant, both types of figures we know to have built residences in Nauraspur. The historian Zubairi records that "as customary, the princes, nobles, merchants, and wealthy were ordered to erect heavenly and commendable buildings and stately mansions" in the new city. He further praises these buildings as "lofty" and grand and singles out the residence of Shah Nawaz Khan for commendation. Zubairi describes it as having a rare and artistic form, being excessive in spaciousness and grandeur, and creating descriptions of astonishment from its visitors.[109] Shah Nawaz Khan acted as Ibrahim's private secretary and appears as one of the six top nobles praised by the poet Zuhuri, who lauds Khan for being, among other things, an excellent mathematician.[110] One early twentieth-century history states that Ibrahim placed Shah Nawaz Khan in charge of supervising the construction of Nauraspur, perhaps explaining why his palace was so commodious and singled out for mention in the histories.[111]

All of Nauraspur's surviving buildings, or fragments thereof, are made of stone rubble covered in plaster, and the limited surviving architectural ornament is plaster as well. During roughly the same period that Nauraspur was being conceived and constructed, the very late sixteenth and early seventeenth centuries, in the older capital city of Bijapur, patrons and artisans were beginning to build a number of monuments using solid stone and featuring elaborate carved-stone ornamentation. The new technique allowed the buildings to be more extensively ornamented, delicate in form, and refined in appearance than the older, heavier rubble method of construction. It is striking to note, then, that the extant buildings of Nauraspur, a city whose name can mean "new fashion," do not feature this new technique, but rather replicate older forms and methods; the Nauras Mahal essentially reproduces a nearly forty-year-old building, the Gagan Mahal. There are numerous reasons why this may have been the case. Perhaps dating of the new style is off, and it did not become common until the first decade of the seventeenth century, after Nauraspur's founding. Alternately, perhaps the carved-stone construction was too time-consuming for the rate at which Ibrahim wanted the new city constructed, or perhaps the rubble-and-plaster construction suited the wide, open arch form deemed appropriate for palaces. Of course, it should be noted that Nauraspur's palaces were not originally ornamented with plaster alone, but rather in their pristine forms would have been much more lavish than they appear today. Perhaps the other forms of decoration, now gone, conveyed the court's richness and "new fashion."

Zubairi writes that wood, gilding, lapis lazuli, and "various paintings in different styles" embellished the architecture of Nauraspur.[112] Henry

Cousens, who visited the Nauras Mahal in the late nineteenth century when its roof was still somewhat intact, noted the heavy timber beams and carved brackets found in the building, thus confirming that wood originally enhanced the palace.[113] Windows also would have been adorned with wooden frames and, in some instances, elaborately carved projecting balconies.[114] Although none of Nauraspur's wall paintings survive, some idea of their range can be gleaned by looking at surviving examples of Bijapuri wall painting from other locations. Such comparisons suggest that a variety of paintings, including floral, gilded, figural, even European-influenced scenes, would have graced the walls of the Nauras Mahal and other palaces.

For example, to the east of Bijapur and Nauraspur, at a pleasure resort of the Adil Shahis called Kummatgi, one finds wall paintings datable to the mid-seventeenth century. The interior of a rectangular pavilion pierced with arched openings bears an image of a sultan conversing with a Sufi in a style very similar to album and manuscript paintings from the same period or slightly earlier. Cousens describes several other paintings that he saw in the pavilion while visiting it, including a representation of a polo game with four horsemen depicted over one archway and a hunting scene with nobles on horseback chasing tigers, leopards, and deer over another. He also noted representations of European figures, which he speculated could be "possibly portraits of envoys or ambassadors who visited the Bijapur Court."[115] Other surviving Bijapuri wall paintings depict foliage, urns, vases, and fruit. In the interior rooms of the mid-seventeenth-century Asar Mahal, well-preserved gilded paintings of foliage and vases survive.[116] Blue flowering vines cover the walls of one of the mahal's rooms, whose niches bear painted vases filled with blue flowers. Similar paintings can be found in niches around the arcade of the Ibrahim Rauza, datable to circa 1626–33. These paintings, which are much faded, depict vases, urns filled with fruit, and lamps suspended from chains (pl. 30).

One of the most interesting pieces of evidence regarding painting and Nauraspur comes from a somewhat unexpected place. The archives of the Dutch East India Company contain several letters written between 1608 and 1617 by a painter named Cornelius Claesz Heda. These letters, written from Nauraspur, reveal that Heda worked for Ibrahim Adil Shah II as a court painter for about a decade at the beginning of the seventeenth century. No paintings by the Mannerist-style artist Heda survive (or, at least, have been identified) either in India or in Europe, but he does record completing a painting of "Venus, Bacchus, and Cupid," which, he claims, so enthralled Ibrahim that the sultan gazed at it for two hours. Heda seems to have been pleased with his appointment at Nauraspur because in one letter he comments on the wealth of the city and suggests that other Dutch artists might do well there.[117] Indeed, at the beginning of the seventeenth century Bijapur was a rich, cosmopolitan kingdom, whose markets were "filled with rare goods, such as are not seen or heard of in any other town," to quote the Mughal ambassador Asad Beg.[118] Due to its diamond mines and its proximity to the Portuguese ports of Goa, Adil Shahi Bijapur had extensive trade contacts with both Europe and Asia. Fragments of Chinese or Chinese-inspired blue-and-white ceramics can still be found among the rubble of Nauraspur's architectural remains, and the markets of Bijapur even had tobacco, imported from Europe and China, before the markets of the larger Mughal dynasty did.[119] We can imagine that such exotic goods would have appealed to a court enamored with "new flavors," and likewise, we can speculate that the incorporation of exotic images, such as those Heda would have produced or inspired, into the mixture of Nauraspur's architectural adornment would have fulfilled Ibrahim and his court's desire for "new flavors" or fashions—in other words, for nauras.

Notably, Heda addressed his letters from Nauraspur, not Bijapur, making it clear that he was living at the new capital. In contrast, the Mughal ambassador Asad Beg's account of his visit to Bijapur in 1603–1604, just a few years before Heda arrived at the kingdom, describes his residence as the city of Bijapur (although he does mention visiting Nauraspur in passing). This distinction, when taken together with the surviving architecture and references in court histories, suggests that Nauraspur acted as a center for the arts and courtly pleasures, while Bijapur continued to function as the more formal, political capital of the kingdom. For example, the plan of Nauraspur seems to have been divided into sections, with one building, if not whole quarter, of the city specifically marked for the residence of musicians. The poet Zuhuri states, "And in Nauraspur, a building has been newly erected and furnished for the residence and accommodation of the expert musicians," while Asad Beg mentions visiting Tarababad, a newly constructed quarter of Nauraspur where musicians and dancers lived.[120]

Nauraspur's apparent lack of official religious structure supports its role as a pleasure capital rather than a political one. Although the cityscape must have included numerous private mosques, such as the one still extant near the Nauras Mahal, as well as Hindu temples, there is no indication of a large-scale jami masjid or any sort of monumental religious space among Nauraspur's ruins, nor do the historical accounts of the city mention one. Instead, the surviving plan of the city and written descriptions of it emphasize palatial architecture, such as the Nauras Mahal. This contrasts sharply with written accounts of the 1565–68 building campaign of Bijapur city carried out by Ali Adil Shah and his nobles, which include descriptions of the massive, stately jami masjid, as one of the four key parts of that building project.[121] This aspect of Nauraspur's conception contrasts equally powerfully with the plan of Hyderabad, the new capital of the Qutb Shahis of Golconda. Hyderabad, founded just nine years before Nauraspur, included not one but three large-scale religious monuments: a Friday mosque as well as the Charminar, the monumental centerpiece to the city celebrating the Qutb Shahi's Shia affiliation, and the royal *ashurkhana,* an elegant storehouse for the court's Shia *alams.*[122] In fact, it is Hyderabad's religious structures that provided, and continue to provide, the city with its identity.

V. K. Bawa, in his study of Hyderabad's architecture, posits that the Qutb Shahis and their builders designed Hyderabad to highlight the rulers' Shia affiliation and the kingdom's close Persian links, thereby helping to create a distinctive identity for the Deccan sultanate.[123] Likewise, Nauraspur can be understood as embodying a specifically Adil Shahi courtly identity. The city's concept, however, rather than drawing on specific religious or regional links, centered around the word *nauras* and the courtly culture it embodied, one based heavily on music and metaphors, poetry and pleasure, and seeped in examples of intercultural exchange. Indeed, what survives of the architectural environment suggests that Ibrahim and his advisors designed the center of Nauraspur foremost as a space in which to enact what we might term the culture of nauras. The monuments marking the city were palatial rather than religious—lofty homes for the ruler and his court adorned with gilding, lapis lazuli, and a wide variety of wall paintings. The planners chose the location of the city to ensure that it was filled with lush gardens and plentiful sweet water for the benefit of its inhabitants. Artists, musicians, and poets resided there. The centerpiece of the city, the Nauras Mahal set within its nine-sided enclosure, was, in essence, a visual metaphor of the word *nauras.* Moreover, the courtyard of the Nauras Mahal must have provided the perfect setting for the celebrations surrounding the Id-i Nauras, with the spacious garden surrounding the large tank allowing plenty of room for musicians to play while Ibrahim and his court watched from the open, two-storied darbar hall. If a space is defined by the actions that take place there as much as by its architecture, then the Nauras Mahal was the centerpiece of the city not only because it was the physical focal point but also because it provided the perfect stage upon which to enact the culture of nauras.

Although most of Nauraspur's architecture has been lost, the surviving evidence supplies traces of the ideology behind the city's construction. Practical, political, and personal motivations all played a part in the founding of Nauraspur as a dual capital with Bijapur. The swiftly growing population of Bijapur required expansion, and building a new city at Torveh answered this need while providing Ibrahim Adil Shah II with an opportunity to express his power and vision. Ultimately, however, the capital's import lay in its role as an embodiment of, and space in which to enact and reaffirm, the courtly culture and identity that prevailed among the

Adil Shahi royal family, Bijapuri courtiers, poets, painters, and musicians. Perhaps nothing expresses this better than the Nauras Mahal, the palace-cum-visual-metaphor and centerpiece of the city.

The founding of Nauraspur, portraits of Ibrahim Adil Shah II, the yogini paintings, the *Pem Nem*—all express an intimate relationship between poetry and art. These artworks not only reflect the themes of contemporary poetry but also serve as visual metaphors for poetic concepts. The *Pem Nem*'s illustrations and the images of yoginis visually express mystical ideas in novel, layered ways and convey the importance of Sufism to Bijapur as well as the extent of religious and cultural interaction in Bijapur's conception of Sufism. The paintings, with their emphasis on love and longing, also reveal the importance of rasa, the emotional essence or juice of the work, and of the rasika, the connoisseur or knowledgeable viewer, to Bijapuri courtly aesthetic practices. The centrality of rasa appears again in the new capital, Nauraspur, which along with portraits of Ibrahim demonstrates the profound impact of courtly poetry on painting and architecture. Both the act of founding the city and details of the portraits of Ibrahim exhibit a recognition of larger Islamicate conceptions of kingship and rule, while materializing a specifically Bijapuri embodiment of power, one resting, in large part, on the "power of words." The examples of Bijapuri art examined in this chapter can be read as experiments, refinements, and monumental embodiments of visual metaphors that helped shape the collective identity of the Adil Shahi court.

4
Meaning in Ornament

While many Bijapuri artworks created during the late sixteenth and early seventeenth centuries, such as the illustrations in the *Pem Nem* or single-page *yogini* paintings, contain experiments with visual metaphors, in some cases the same subject matter being revisited and refined by court artists over several decades, select works from the first half of the seventeenth century display fully developed visual programs into which metaphorical elements have been completely integrated. If the earlier artistic examples embody different facets of the court's emerging identity and reveal the central role of the visual arts in shaping and reinforcing that identity, then the ensuing artworks exhibit a fully formed visual identity for the Adil Shahi court. In these later examples, metaphors and motifs relating to kingship, prosperity, poetry, and mysticism that were being developed since 1565 are now ingeniously expressed through refined ornamental forms. As parts of elaborate but efficient designs, the various types of ornament featured in these works not only lend beauty and visual distinction to the monuments and paintings they adorn but they also embody meaning.

The Ibrahim Rauza complex and several other seventeenth-century monuments, for example, display a new architectural style emphasizing exuberant carved-stone ornamentation. The style seems to have developed during the late sixteenth or early seventeenth century and reached its apex with the completion of the Ibrahim Rauza in 1633. This tomb complex in which Ibrahim Adil Shah II is buried embodies what today we consider to be the quintessential "Bijapuri style," revealing the seventeenth-century carved-stone style's continued effectiveness in conveying a specifically

Adil Shahi visual identity.[1] Some of the most distinctive Bijapuri paintings are four marbled, or *abri,* drawings of emaciated horses datable between 1620 and 1635. The works integrate the ornamental technique of marbling with striking images of starving horses, sometimes paired with equally thin riders. The creation of these artworks, both the abri drawings and the architecture, corresponds with the latter part of Ibrahim Adil Shah II's reign as well as the first few years of Muhammad Adil Shah's rule, the period just before significant political events shifted the Deccan's visual climate.

When Ibrahim II died in 1627, power transferred to his son, Muhammad (r. 1627–56). During the first eight years of Muhammad's rule, events remained largely on the course that they had been following during the previous decades. Muhammad, a Sunni Muslim, adopted his father's practice of favoring Deccani, rather than Afaqi, bureaucrats at court, and art continued to flourish in the same manner as it had been. Soon, however, the threat posed by the Mughal Empire to the north, strong during his father's reign, overwhelmed Muhammad and his kingdom. In 1635, the armies of the Mughal emperor Shah Jahan marched against Bijapur. Shah Jahan forced Muhammad Adil Shah to sign a deed of submission; however, a secret earlier alliance between the two rulers kept Bijapur from having to pay tribute as did their neighbor, the Qutb Shah dynasty of Golconda. While the defeat dealt a serious blow to Bijapur, the Adil Shahis still possessed a strong kingdom.[2] Bijapuri art continued to prosper during the remainder of Muhammad's reign; however, due to the increased contact with north India, a new Mughal influence is visible in artworks created after 1635.[3]

Thus the pre-1635 examples of Bijapuri art, such as the Ibrahim Rauza or the abri drawings of emaciated horses, can be considered the fully formed expressions of a visual identity for the sultanate just before that identity shifted. The increasing Mughal presence in the Deccan forced the Adil Shahis to reassess their self-view as well as the dynastic image they presented to others. Works of art created in Bijapur from the 1640s onward seem to embody meanings more overtly than the earlier works, indicating that their significance was directed at a wide audience. In contrast, the works created during the first part of the seventeenth century appear to have been made primarily for a local audience. Indeed, the Ibrahim Rauza and abri horse drawings, both highly refined and multilayered artworks, relied on the intimacy of a completely developed, shared visual language for their potency.

The Ibrahim Rauza

Of all the buildings gracing Bijapur, the Adil Shahi monument most celebrated by scholars and travelers alike is the Ibrahim Rauza, a royal tomb constructed between 1626 and 1633 (pl. 25). Henry Cousens, for example, labeled it "the *magnum opus* of the Adil Shahis."[4] Close examination of the tomb's decoration as well as that of similar Bijapuri structures demonstrates that the Ibrahim Rauza was the climax of a new ornamental style that signaled the codification of a visual identity for the Adil Shahi court. Not only did the ornament furnish the visual focus of the new architecture; it also provided the vehicle by which the structure's meaning was conveyed. Those involved in the construction of the Ibrahim Rauza tailored its exuberant design specifically to communicate to its audience the exalted status of the patron, who was Taj Sultana, the wife of Ibrahim Adil Shah II, not Ibrahim himself, as is often assumed.

Comparing the Ibrahim Rauza to two other prominent Adil Shahi structures, Bijapur's *jami masjid* built as part of the 1565–68 building campaign of Bijapur city (fig. 2.5) and the Gul Gumbad, Muhammad Adil Shah's tomb dateable to 1656, highlights the tomb's distinctiveness. The earlier jami masjid and the later Gul Gumbad both express their monumentality through their size. Bijapur's congregational mosque, with its thirty-six bay prayer chamber and open courtyard, remains the largest mosque in the whole of the Deccan. The Gul Gumbad boasts a dome so immense, roughly 44 meters or 144 feet in external diameter, that many accounts claim it is second in size only to the dome of St. Peter's Basilica in Rome.[5] The Ibrahim Rauza, on the other hand, is moderate in size but achieves its monumentality through its ornament. Whereas the two earlier and later monuments feature only limited plaster ornamentation, the Ibrahim Rauza boasts a profusion of carved stonework, from geometric designs framing wall bases to lacy fringe parapets dancing along the top of façades.

The royal tomb complex was part of a short-lived but important shift in Bijapuri monuments during the first part of the seventeenth century, from large-scale plaster-and-rubble buildings to more intimately scaled but highly ornamental stoned-carved ones. The principal features of the new style are bulbous domes with prominent lotus petal bases, slender minarets and finials for ornamental use only, projecting cornices supported by elaborately carved brackets, engineering feats such as flat stone-slab ceilings, and an overwhelming sense of rich ornamentation.[6] The architectural decoration of the Ibrahim Rauza highlights the significance of the stylistic shift: first, how the ornament articulates the message of the Ibrahim Rauza and similar structures, and second, how it participates in the codification of an Adil Shahi visual identity.

The Ibrahim Rauza, located just outside the walls of Bijapur city, sits on the main road from Nauraspur, which intersects the Mecca Darwaza and runs near the subterranean channel built as part of the 1565–68 building campaign to carry water from Torveh to Bijapur. The complex con-

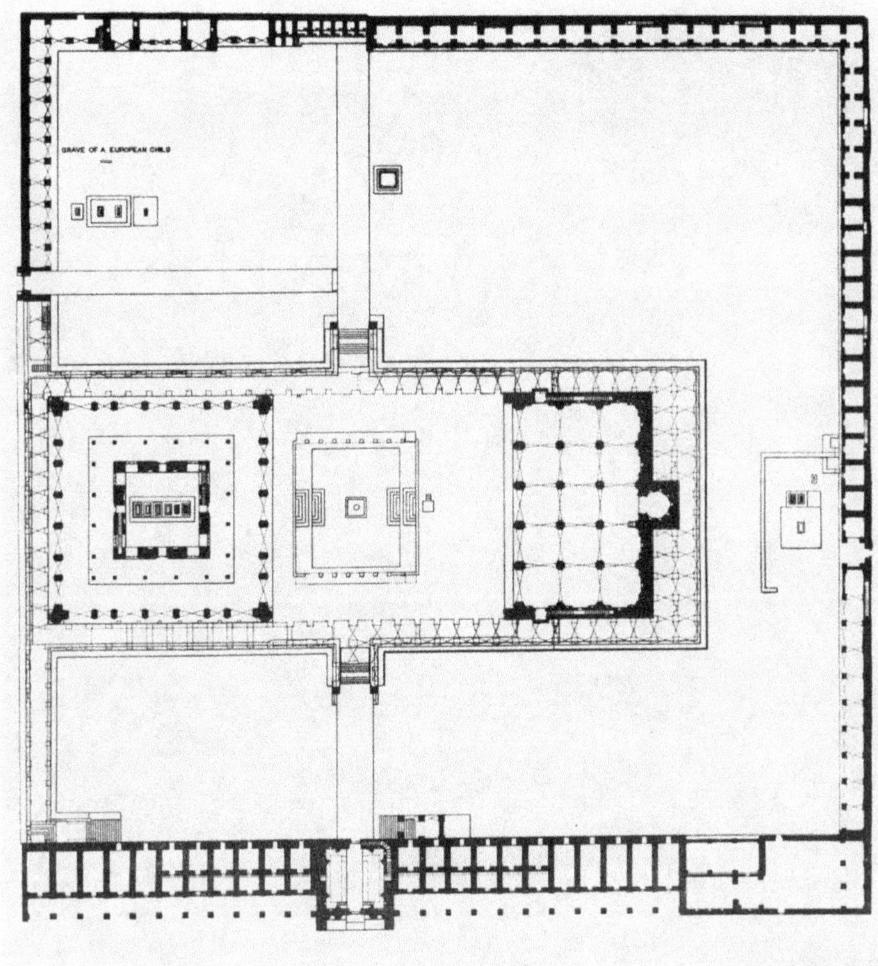

Figure 4.1. Ibrahim Rauza complex, 1626–33, Bijapur. Plan from Henry Cousens, *Bijapur and Its Architectural Remains: With an Historical Outline of the Adil Shahi Dynasty.* Archaeological Survey of India, New Imperial Series 37 (1916; reprint, Delhi: Bharatiya Publication House, 1976). Reproduced by kind permission of the Archeological Survey of India.

sists of a gateway leading to a mosque and tomb built on a single plinth, with facing entrances and a water tank between them (fig. 4.1, pl. 26). A walled garden surrounds three sides of the plinth.[7] Even from afar, the slim minarets, multiple finials, and domes with lotus petal bases provide the complex with a distinct, highly decorative skyline. Up close, the ornament lends opulence to the architecture.

The five-arch, fifteen-bay mosque (pl. 27), located on the right side of the plinth as the visitor passes through the gateway, has a wide cornice supported by brackets and topped with a pierced parapet punctuated by

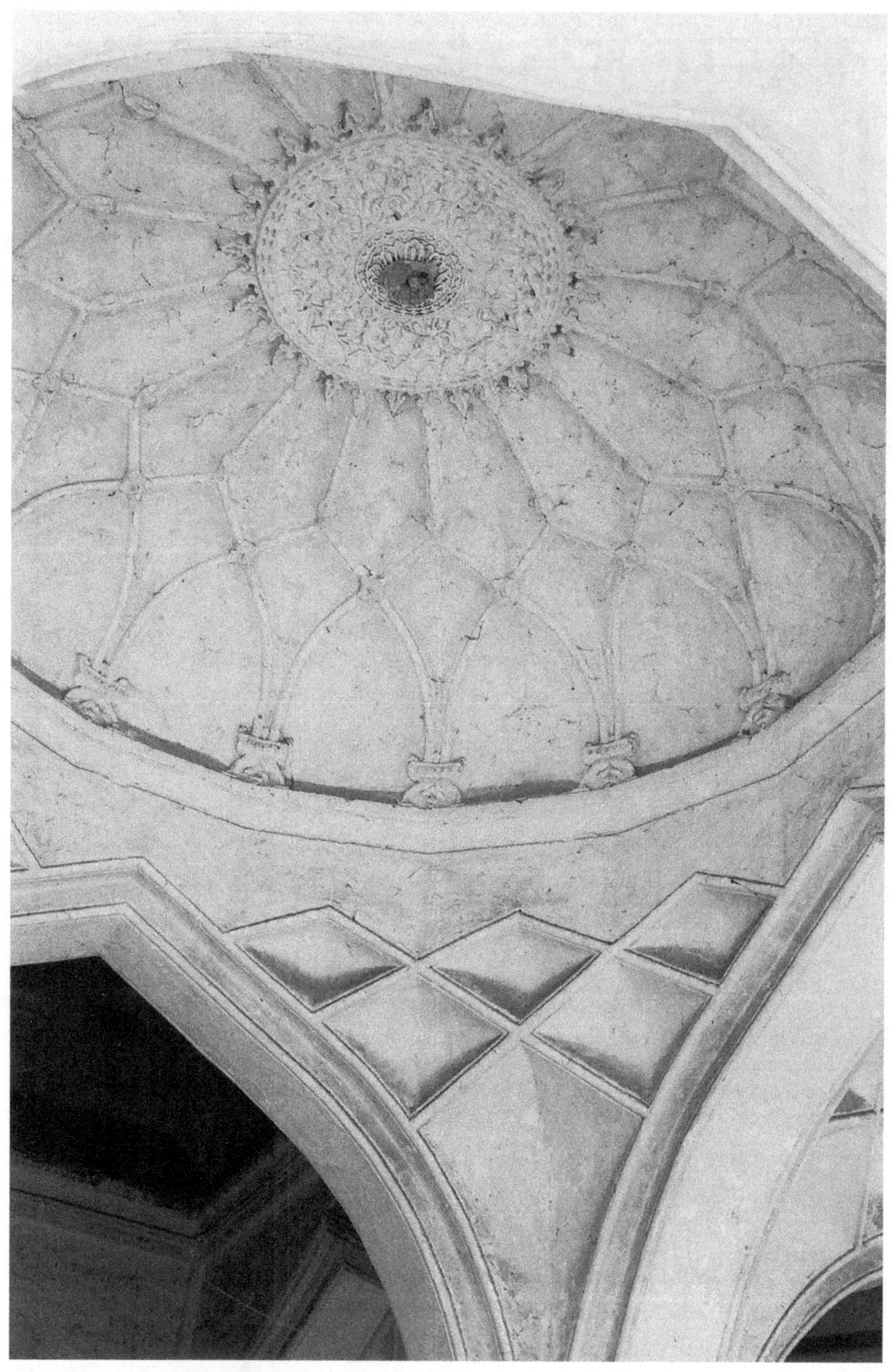

Figure 4.2. Detail of lotus burst on interior ceiling of the Ibrahim Rauza mosque, 1626–33, Bijapur. Photograph by author.

domed finials on square bases. Plaster roundels flank each archway, further adorning the façade. Projecting carved-stone window frames embellish the sides. Traces of paint on the interior suggest that at some point the arches demarcating the bays were highlighted with painted floral borders. Finally, a plaster lotus is centered on the shallow domed ceiling of each bay (fig. 4.2). The lotus, whether in bloom or in bud, is a recurrent motif in the mosque's ornamental program.

Double arcades surrounding a thirteen-meter-square chamber form the facing tomb (pl. 29, fig. 4.3), in a plan elaborating that of Ali Adil Shah I's late sixteenth-century tomb (fig. 2.7). A doorway and two windows pierce each side of the central space, which contains six cenotaphs: that of Ibrahim Adil Shah II, his wife Taj Sultana, and four other members of the royal family, two female and two male.[8] The ceilings of the interior chamber and the inner arcade are flat, made of stone slabs, each carved with differing geometric and lotus flower patterns and held together with mortar.[9] As in its companion mosque, in addition to the stone carving, traces of paint and plaster remain. For example, faint but detectable painted geometric designs cover portions of the arcade walls, and paintings of hanging lamps (pl. 30), urns filled with fruit, and vases adorn the back walls of niches placed periodically along the walls.[10] Also like the mosque, the tomb's façade features a wide, overhanging cornice, brackets, parapet, and finials. In contrast to the mosque, however, the tomb's dominant decorative element is calligraphy. The arcade walls, borders, window screens, and even the teak doors all are carved with elegant calligraphic inscriptions (figs. 4.4 and 4.5). In fact, there is more writing on this building than on any other surviving structure from Bijapur. Most of the inscriptions are excerpts from the Koran relating to paradise, as is appropriate for a tomb, but several are Persian verses composed specifically for the structure and conveying information on its construction and patronage.[11]

Although the Ibrahim Rauza is one of the best known Adil Shahi monuments, exactly who sponsored and designed the structure remains uncertain. For the last century and a half, the complex has been known as the tomb (*rauza*) of Ibrahim Adil Shah II.[12] As a result of the structure's current name, as well as the paramount role assigned to Ibrahim in Bijapur's history, popular belief commonly attributes the complex to the sultan's patronage.[13] The Persian inscriptions adorning the tomb, however, suggest that the complex was built by Ibrahim's wife Taj Sultana as her tomb, but functioned as a family mausoleum as well, with Ibrahim and four other family members buried there. The most significant of these inscriptions, located on the south side of the tomb under the pediment, not far from another Persian verse recording Taj Sultana's death, implies that Taj Sultana was both the principal figure being memorialized and the patron of the structure.

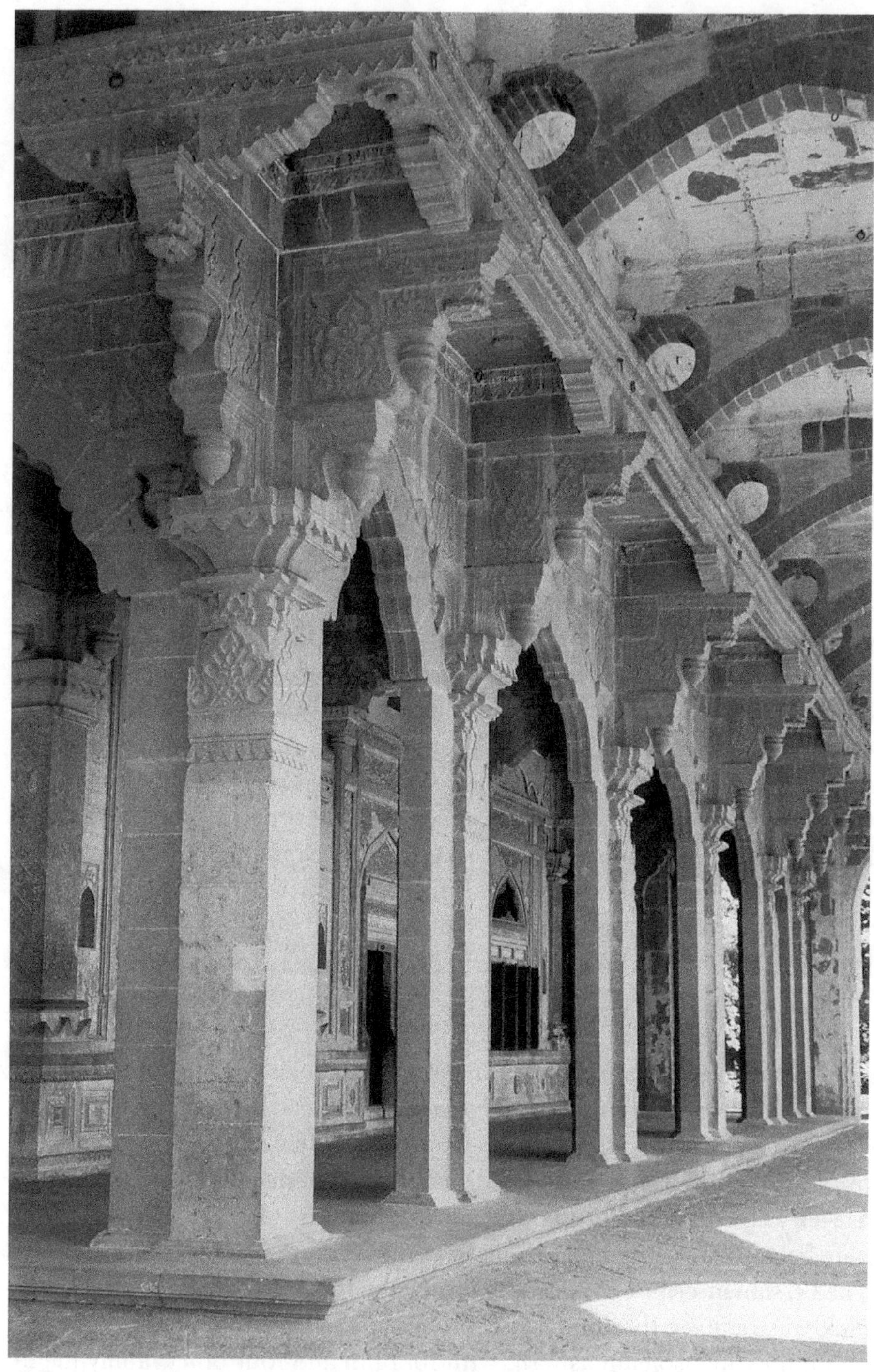

Figure 4.3. Double arcade of the Ibrahim Rauza, 1626–33, Bijapur. Photograph by author.

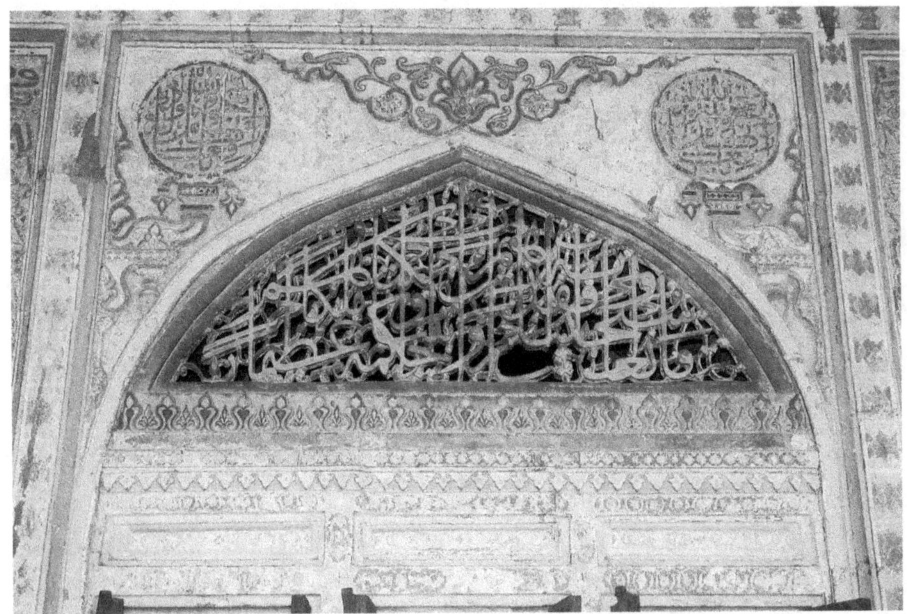

Figure 4.4. Detail of window from the Ibrahim Rauza, 1626–33, Bijapur. Photograph by author.

Taj Sultana constructed this tomb
(Such that) Paradise is wonderstruck at its beauties.
She spent on it one and a half *lakh huns,*
But nine hundred more were added thereto.
By good efforts, the work of this tomb
Was completed by Malik Sandal.[14]

As the translation demonstrates, the verse also records the large amount of money spent on the tomb's construction and the name of a noble, Malik Sandal, involved in "the work." It is sometimes assumed that Malik Sandal was the rauza's architect, but the verse includes none of the Persian terms for architect or builder.[15] Based on several historical references to Malik Sandal, which suggest he was a prominent military and political personage, as well as what we know of Bijapuri building practices, Sandal more likely acted as an intermediary figure overseeing the project's construction on behalf of the patron, Taj Sultana, rather than as the architect.[16] Sandal, an Abyssinian eunuch and high-ranking member at court who had recently arrived at Bijapur from the kingdom's northern neighbor Ahmadnagar, was probably the *sar-i kar,* supervisor of construction, for the monument, just as Ali Adil Shah I's vizier, Qishur Khan, acted as the sar-i kar for several aspects of the 1565–68 building campaign of Bijapur and Ibrahim Adil Shah II's private secretary, Shah Nawaz Khan, oversaw the founding of Nauraspur. Perhaps the peculiar wording

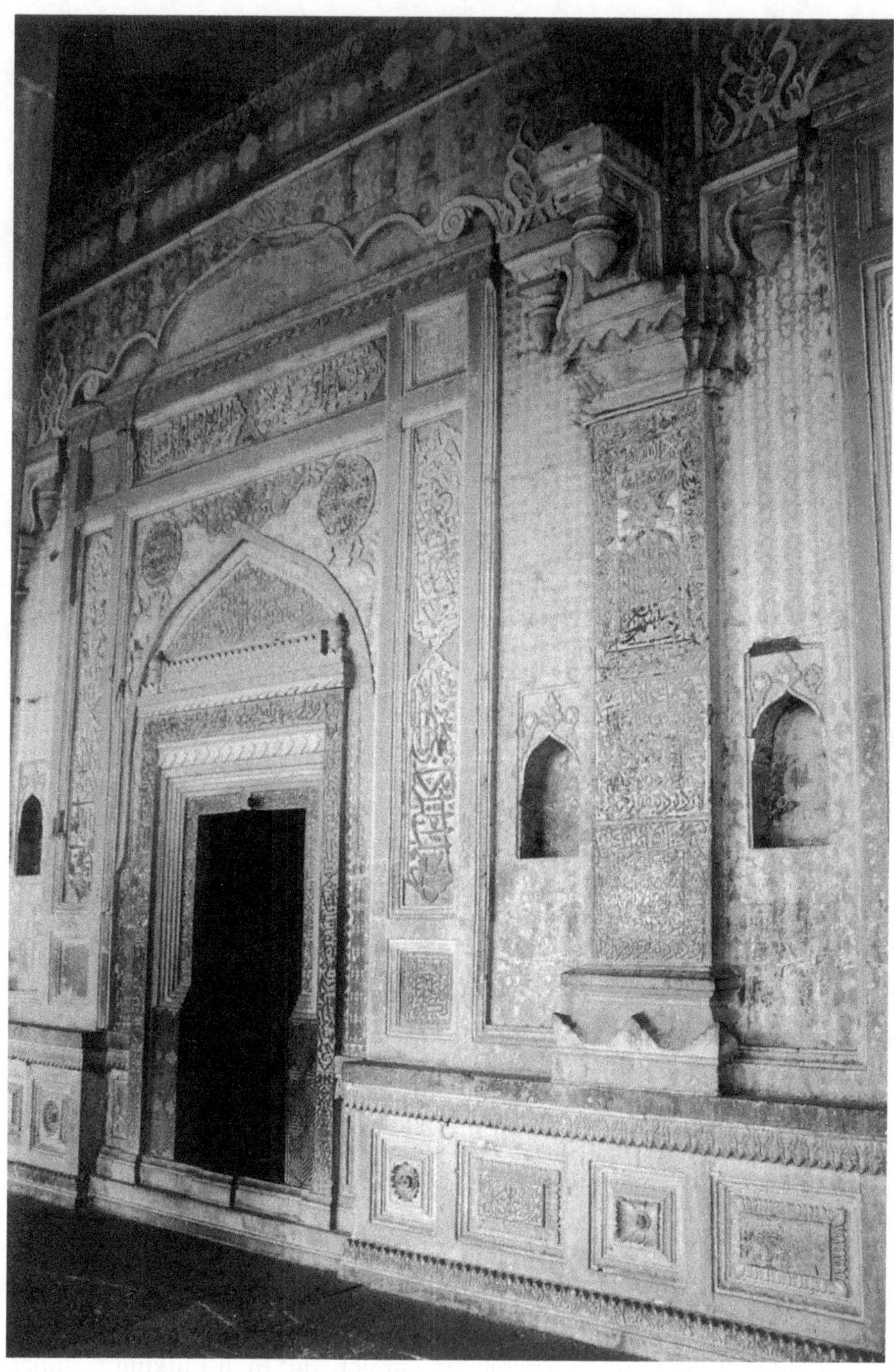

Figure 4.5. Exterior wall and doorway of the Ibrahim Rauza, 1626–33, Bijapur. Photograph by author.

of the two lines regarding the building cost, "She spent on it one and a half lakh huns, but nine hundred more were added thereto," indicates that Malik Sandal finished the project only after her death and with the addition of nine hundred huns of his own funds.[17]

Certainly the Persian verses are ambiguous. They cannot confirm Taj Sultana and Malik Sandal's exact roles, but they do remind us that the monument was more than just a reflection of the greatness of Ibrahim Adil Shah II. The design most likely evolved out of continuous negotiations between the patron, sar-i kar, master stone-carver or other senior artisan, and the various levels of craftsmen participating in the project. Thus the Persian verses are significant to our understanding of the structure because by recognizing the network of individuals involved in its construction, we link it more broadly to the Adil Shahi court, and in doing so, we are able to perceive more readily its relationship to the formation of a courtly visual identity.

The verses adorning the Ibrahim Rauza are noteworthy not only for the information they provide but also for the contribution that the calligraphy makes to the monument's design program. Oleg Grabar has theorized that two impulses propelled the development and use of calligraphy in Islamic culture: to transmit a message and to decorate an object. Both seem operative in the Ibrahim Rauza's calligraphy. The inscriptions relate information about the monument's construction, commemorate the royal family members buried there, and reference paradise through Koranic passages. The paradisiacal references emphasize the funerary function of the complex while linking its beauty, to which the calligraphy largely contributes, to the beauty of the paradise awaiting the faithful. Indeed, the calligraphy lends visual distinction to the structure in a variety of ways. The delicate, perforated screens, many of them, sadly, now broken, above the windows (fig. 4.4) and the inscriptions carved in shallow relief around the doorways (fig. 4.5) are exceptional in their elegance, while the sheer amount of calligraphy singles out the tomb from other similar structures. This building boasts more calligraphy than any other Adil Shahi monument, certainly a deliberate design choice, as calligraphy was a marker of high status and good taste in Islamic culture.[18]

In the essay "How Buildings Mean," Nelson Goodman reasons that we must consider *how* an architectural work conveys its meaning before we can address *what* it means. The primary bearer of meaning for the Ibrahim Rauza is its ornament. Other aspects of the complex, such as its layout and basic architectural components, relate to its function and general cultural context; it is the ornament that gives the complex its monumentality and singularity and can therefore be considered the most crucial mediator of meaning. To use Goodman's terms, the ornament conveys meaning through *denotation,* that is, the calligraphy provides information about the structure's construction and people entombed, while also referencing paradise, as discussed above. It also conveys meaning through *exemplification,* that is, the ornament draws attention to certain aspects of the complex such as its exuberant, elegant nature and distinctive skyline, thus giving the monument its visual notability.[19] This second manner of mediation, *exemplification,* is achieved not only through the calligraphy but through other aspects of the stone ornament as well. These include the decorative elements elaborating the rooflines of the mosque, tomb, and gateway: the perforated parapets, domed finials, brackets, and overhanging cornices, as well as the pencil-thin minarets and bud-shaped domes, common architectural blocks functioning here as ornament.

The Ibrahim Rauza is not the only Bijapuri structure to feature such ornamentation. Intimately scaled, highly ornamental, carved-stone structures that survive include a royal pavilion, a cenotaph on a plinth, and five mosques. The so-called Jal Mandir (fig. 4.7), a small pavilion located in front of the Sat Manzil, a seven-storied palace in the royal citadel area, is the only surviving secular building in the new style.[20] Just behind the tomb of Ali Adil Shah I, in the southwest portion of the city, an unidentified dark green stone cenotaph supported by a larger gray stone platform featuring sinuous brackets provides a small-scale funerary example (figs. 4.12 and 4.13). The Bukhara mosque and gateway complex (fig. 4.14), north of the royal citadel and also in the new architectural style, makes use in its main doorway of the same dark green stone as the grave platform, leading to speculation that one patron was responsible for both the mosque and the cenotaph.[21] Other mosques featuring the new carved-stone style include the Malika Jahan mosque (fig. 4.6 and pl. 31), the two-story Anda mosque, built in 1608 by the noble Itibar Khan (figs. 4.10 and 4.11), the Mihtar-i Mahal gateway and mosque, featuring a distinctive stone not local to Bijapur called laminar limestone or "Kurnool limestone" (figs. 4.15–4.17), and the Kali mosque (figs. 4.8 and 4.9), sponsored in 1617 by Ankusa Khan, the Bijapur governor of Lakshmeswar.[22]

Like the Ibrahim Rauza, the patronage of many of these structures is uncertain. In fact, only two of the monuments, the Kali mosque and the Anda mosque, bear inscriptions clearly recording their patrons: the noblemen Ankusa Khan and Itibar Khan, respectively. Based on circumstantial evidence, art historians have attributed the Malika Jahan mosque, as it is called today, to the patronage of either Ibrahim Adil Shah II or his wife Malika Jahan Begum.[23] Similarly, it is assumed the Jal Mandir pavilion was constructed at the order of Ibrahim, as it is a part of the royal palace area, but this is speculation. Some sources have linked the early seventeenth-century so-called Bukhara mosque as well as the unidentified green stone cenotaph to Ibrahim's aunt and Ali Adil Shah I's wife, Chand Bibi, but no surviving contemporary evidence supports this or any other attribution.[24] The patron of the Mihtar-i Mahal mosque complex is also unknown. We, however, can

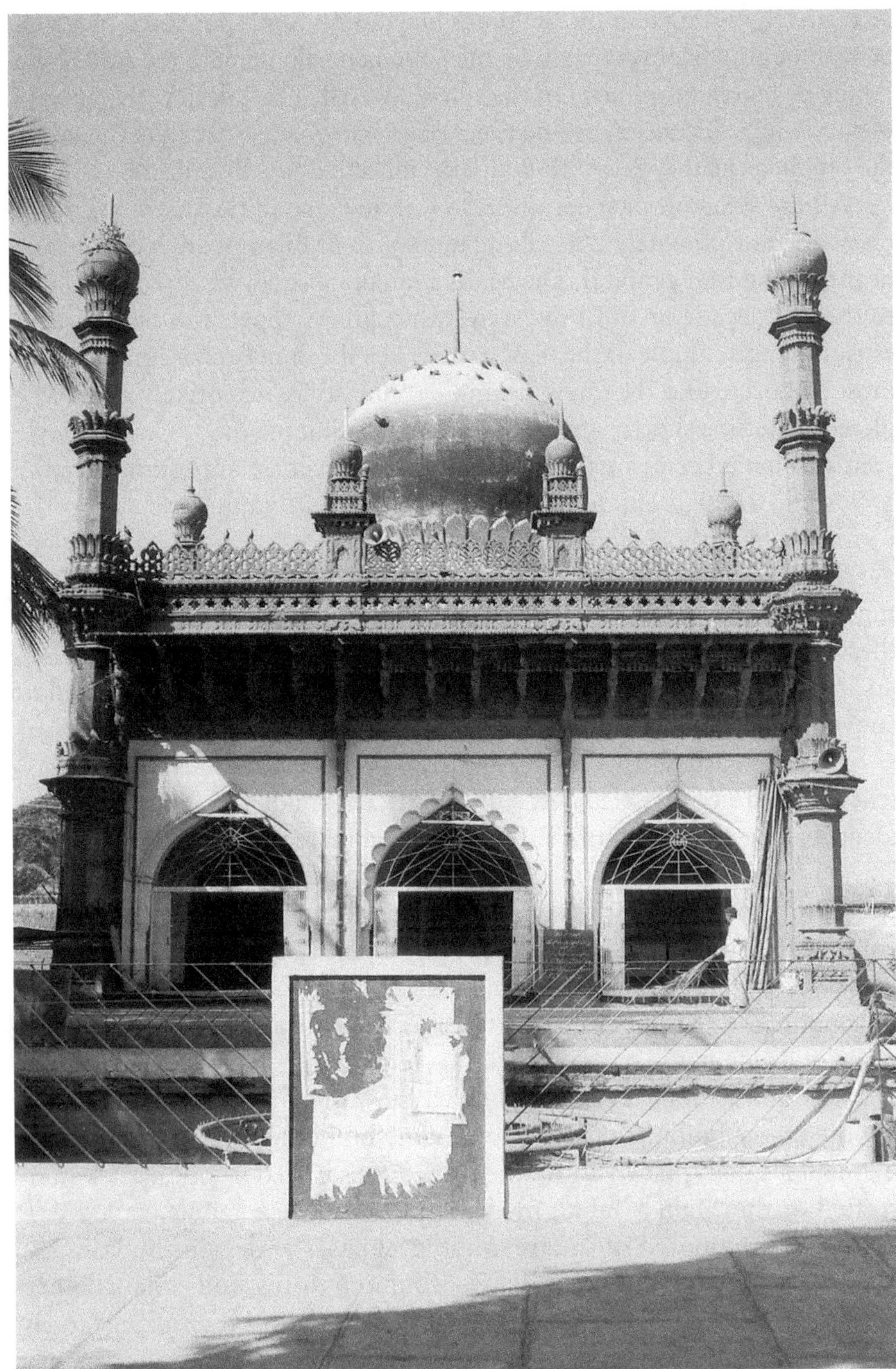

Figure 4.6. Malika Jahan mosque, ca. 1590, Bijapur. Photograph by author.

be relatively certain that the buildings in question were sponsored by members of the Adil Shahi court: noblemen, women belonging to the Adil Shahi family by marriage or birth, or the sultan himself. Thus, despite the paucity of surviving evidence regarding their exact patronage, we can still analyze the buildings as they relate to Bijapur's collective courtly culture.

All the structures except one, the Kali mosque in the town of Lakshmeswar, approximately 200 kilometers south of Bijapur, are located in or near the kingdom's capital. The Malika Jahan mosque, which can be dated to the last decade or so of the sixteenth century, appears to be the earliest surviving example of the new style.[25] The Ibrahim Rauza complex, the most elaborate and the latest example of the style, most likely was completed sometime shortly after 1633, when Taj Sultana died. Thus the style seems to have been in use for roughly four decades, approximately the 1590s and 1630s, centered on the capital city of Bijapur, and supported by members of the Adil Shahi court.

Why did this new ornamental style develop? What was its semiotic function? Or, to return to Goodman's phrasing, if the ornament is *how* these buildings conveyed their meaning to their seventeenth-century viewers, precisely *what* was it that the ornament conveyed or was intended to convey? Moreover, why was carved-stone ornament the mediator of choice?

From its earliest appearance the style is marked by a striking consistency in the decorative elements employed. Each building exhibits an almost identical repertoire of motifs, such as slender minarets rising from the plinth. These minarets, found on the mosque, tomb, and gateway of the Ibrahim Rauza (pl. 25) as well as the Malika Jahan mosque (fig. 4.6), are actually corner-colonnettes integrated with the body of the structure; they cannot be used for the call to prayer, nor do they provide structural support for the building. Their only function is as ornament, thus confirming the primacy of ornament in the new style.

Small lotus buds and petals crown these decorative minarets, echoing the larger bulbous domes capping the buildings and in turn echoed by smaller finials placed above the piers of the arched façades, as demonstrated in the Malika Jahan mosque (pl. 31). These finials, called *guldastas,* are composed of square, multilevel bases with lotus bud domes, the latter sometimes surrounded by four tiny lotus bud finials. When deconstructed thus, the profuse ornament reveals itself as consisting largely of the repetition and reconfiguration of a limited number of elements. For example, the guldastas described above are essentially miniature versions of the Jal Mandir (fig. 4.7).[26] The square, domed pavilion, dubbed the Jal Mandir at some late point in Bijapur's history, is centered in a small tank that originally would have been filled with water. On all four sides are tripartite windows and two wide cornices, one supporting the dome and one below the windows. Like the other buildings in the new style, the Jal Mandir features the lotus motif in a variety of permutations: bud-shaped domes (with one central dome and four small corner finials), petals adorning the domes' bases, and floral blooms under cornices and windows.

Other standard elements of the carved-stone architectural style, commonly found on the monuments discussed here, include perforated parapets and broad cornices supported by brackets. The brackets can be S-shaped or stepped, with lotus buds adorning each step. These elements contribute a three-dimensional quality to the new style that distinguishes it from more "typical" Islamicate architectural decoration, such as the plaster, tile, and stone inlay designs covering many Islamicate monuments. This decoration, as Lisa Golombek describes, resembles "'membrane' or fabric encasing the body of the architecture" rather than appendages adorning and articulating the structure's roofline, as the Adil Shahi parapets, cornices, finials, and slender minarets do.[27]

Augmenting this three-dimensionality at the Ibrahim Rauza mosque is a single stone medallion hanging from a chain between two stepped brackets (pl. 28). The medallion seems to be in the shape of a lotus bud or perhaps an inverted religious or royal standard. On the wall behind it is carved a two-dimensional niche framing a matching chain and medallion in relief. Originally, the whole cornice as well as the minarets of the Ibrahim Rauza mosque would have been decorated with free-hanging three-dimensional medallions and chains, each carved from a single block of stone.[28] Late nineteenth- and early twentieth-century drawings and photographs of the Kali mosque record similar chains and medallions hanging from its minarets (figs. 4.8 and 4.9). Such chains would have added dramatically to the delicate skylines of many of the other structures as well.[29]

Most chains and medallions have broken off, but many shallow-relief carved versions survive. For example, the Jal Mandir has a relief carved row of chains holding medallions running around the square base of its dome, and each petal of the dome displays a medallion hanging from its center. The unidentified stone cenotaph features shallow-relief carved niches adorned with medallions hanging from chains along the sides of its platform (fig. 4.13), while the *mihrab,* or prayer niche, of the 1608 Anda mosque (fig. 4.10) displays the motif in the same manner that hanging lamps often adorned mihrabs. This last example hints that the chain with medallion may have alluded to light just as an image of a lamp in a niche would have done. For example, the Ibrahim Rauza, which originally would have been adorned with free-hanging medallions and chains just like its companion mosque, bears a painting of precisely such a lamp in a niche (pl. 30). The lamp hangs from a chain rendered in the same manner as the relief-carved and free-hanging stone chains.[30]

At the same time that the monuments share the set menu of motifs

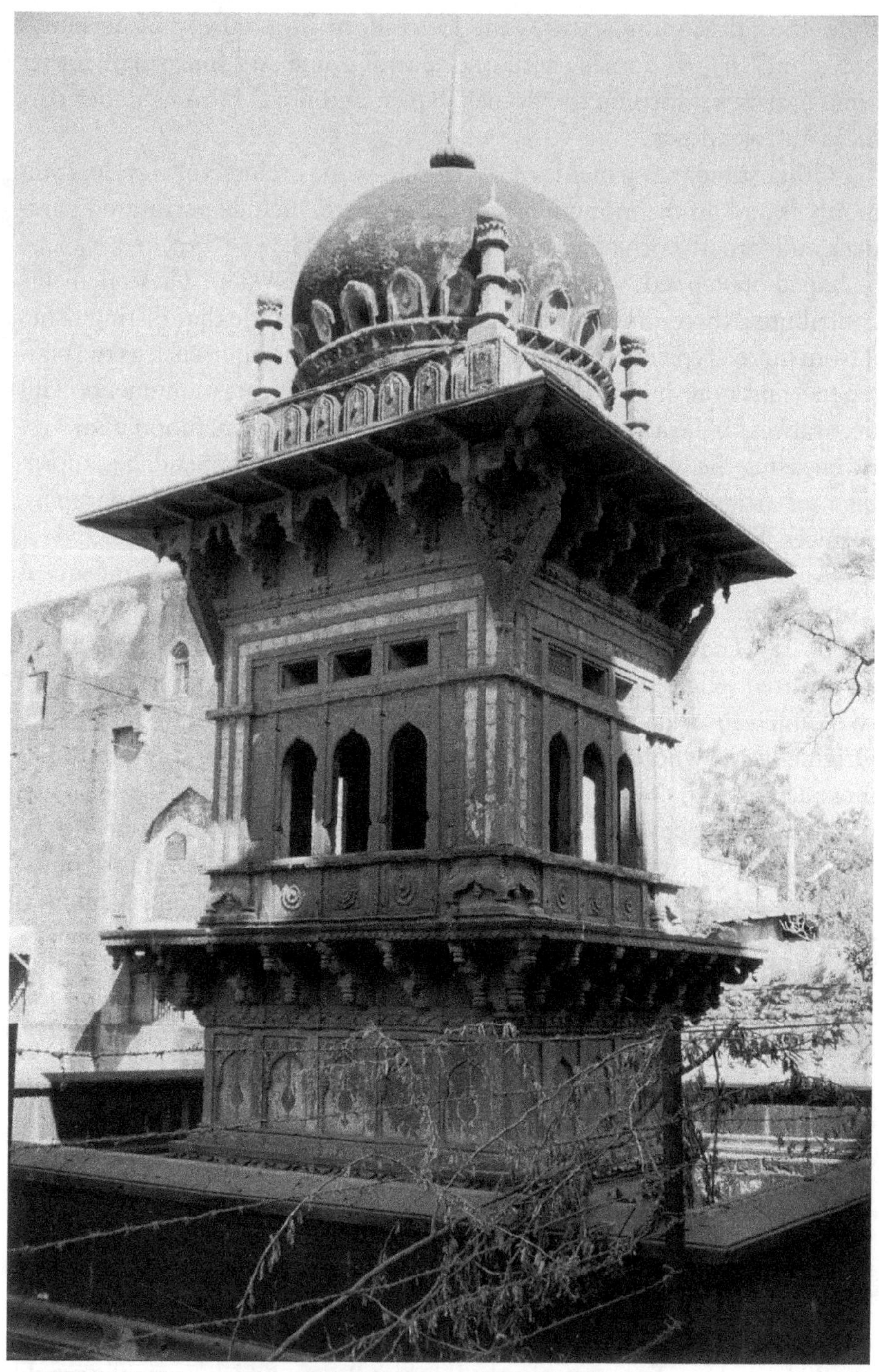

Figure 4.7. Jal Mandir, seventeenth century, Bijapur. Photograph by author.

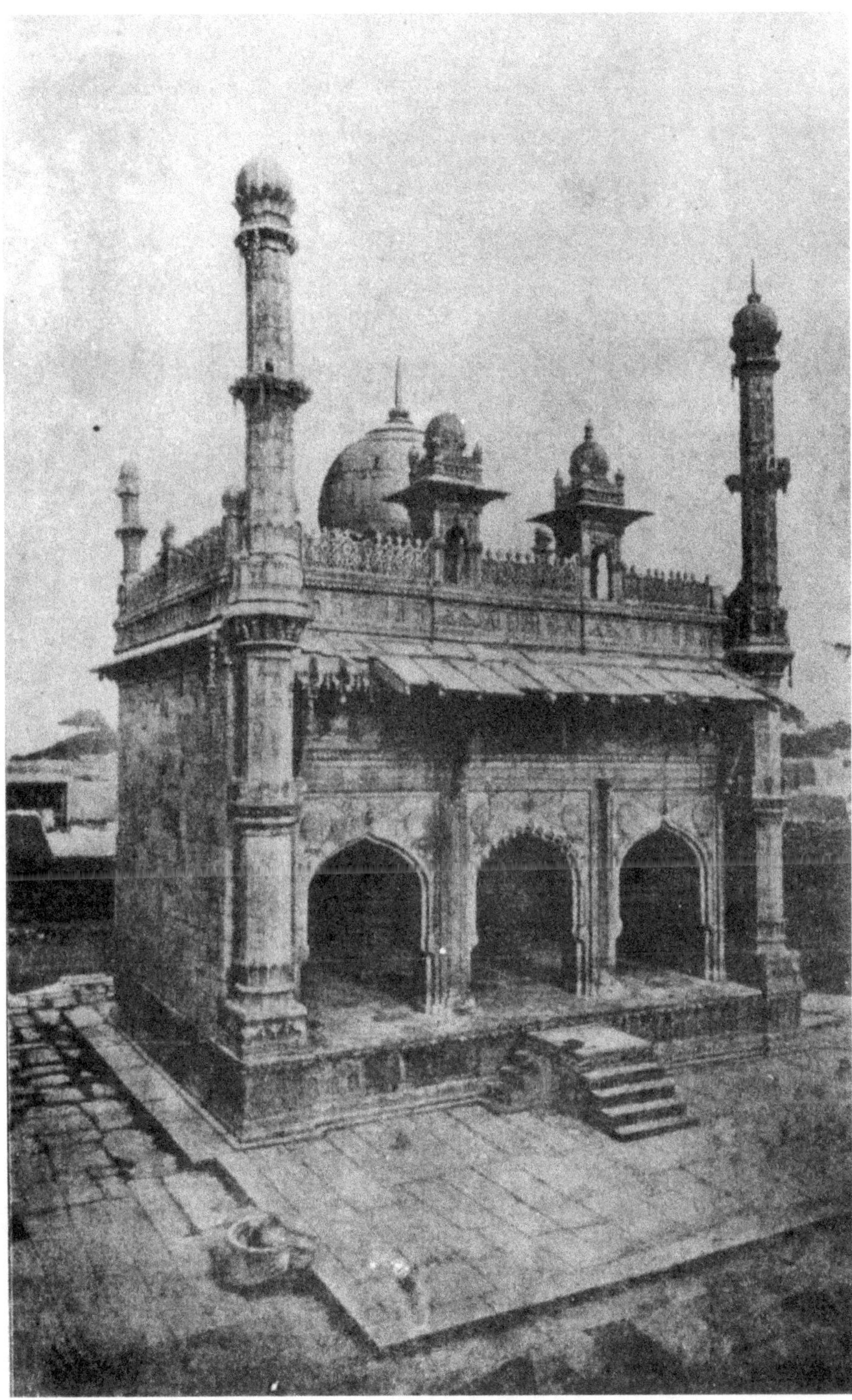

Figure 4.8. Kali mosque, 1617, Lakshmeswar. Photograph from Henry Cousens, *Bijapur and Its Architectural Remains: With an Historical Outline of the Adil Shahi Dynasty.* Archaeological Survey of India, New Imperial Series 37 (1916; reprint, Delhi: Bharatiya Publication House, 1976). Reproduced by kind permission of the Archeological Survey of India.

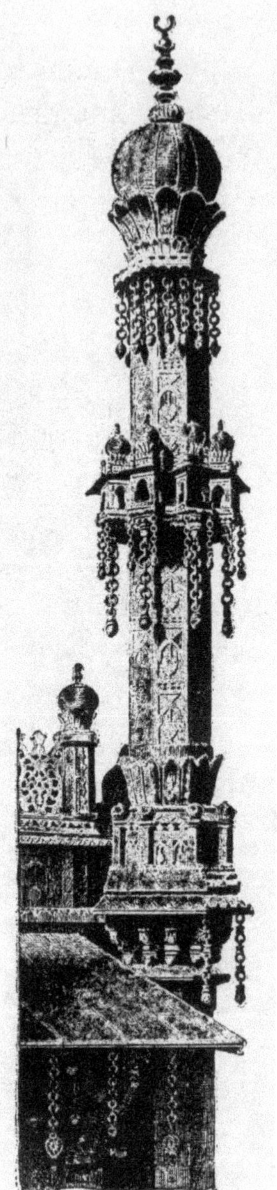

Figure 4.9. Minaret of Kali mosque, 1617, Lakshmeswar. Architectural rendering from Henry Cousens, *Bijapur and Its Architectural Remains: With an Historical Outline of the Adil Shahi Dynasty.* Archaeological Survey of India, New Imperial Series 37 (1916; reprint, Delhi: Bharatiya Publication House, 1976). Reproduced by kind permission of the Archeological Survey of India.

just described, each has at least one distinguishing feature. The Ibrahim Rauza is notable for its calligraphy. The Anda mosque is unusual for its two-story height, with the mosque proper located on the second floor (fig. 4.11).[31] A ribbed dome adds further visual distinction to the monument. The small, unidentified, but elaborately carved grave behind Ali Adil Shah I's tomb and the Bukhara mosque are both made exceptional by the dark green stone they employ in portions of the structures (figs. 4.12–4.14). The early seventeenth-century Mihtar-i Mahal mosque is famous for its palatial gateway with projecting balconies supported by intricate brackets, made possible by the fine grain and hard texture of the imported gray stone that further singles out the complex (figs. 4.15–4.17).

The Mihtar-i Mahal's stone brackets, carved with lions mounted on elephants, as well as flowers, geese, and parrots, were made to imitate woodwork. This is evident from the manner in which they have begun to crack. Their design was conceived to take advantage of tensile strength, a property of wood but absent in stone. Though few survive, corresponding wooden balconies would have adorned many of the earlier rubble-and-plaster palaces, such as the seven-storied Sat Manzil built by Ibrahim Adil Shah II

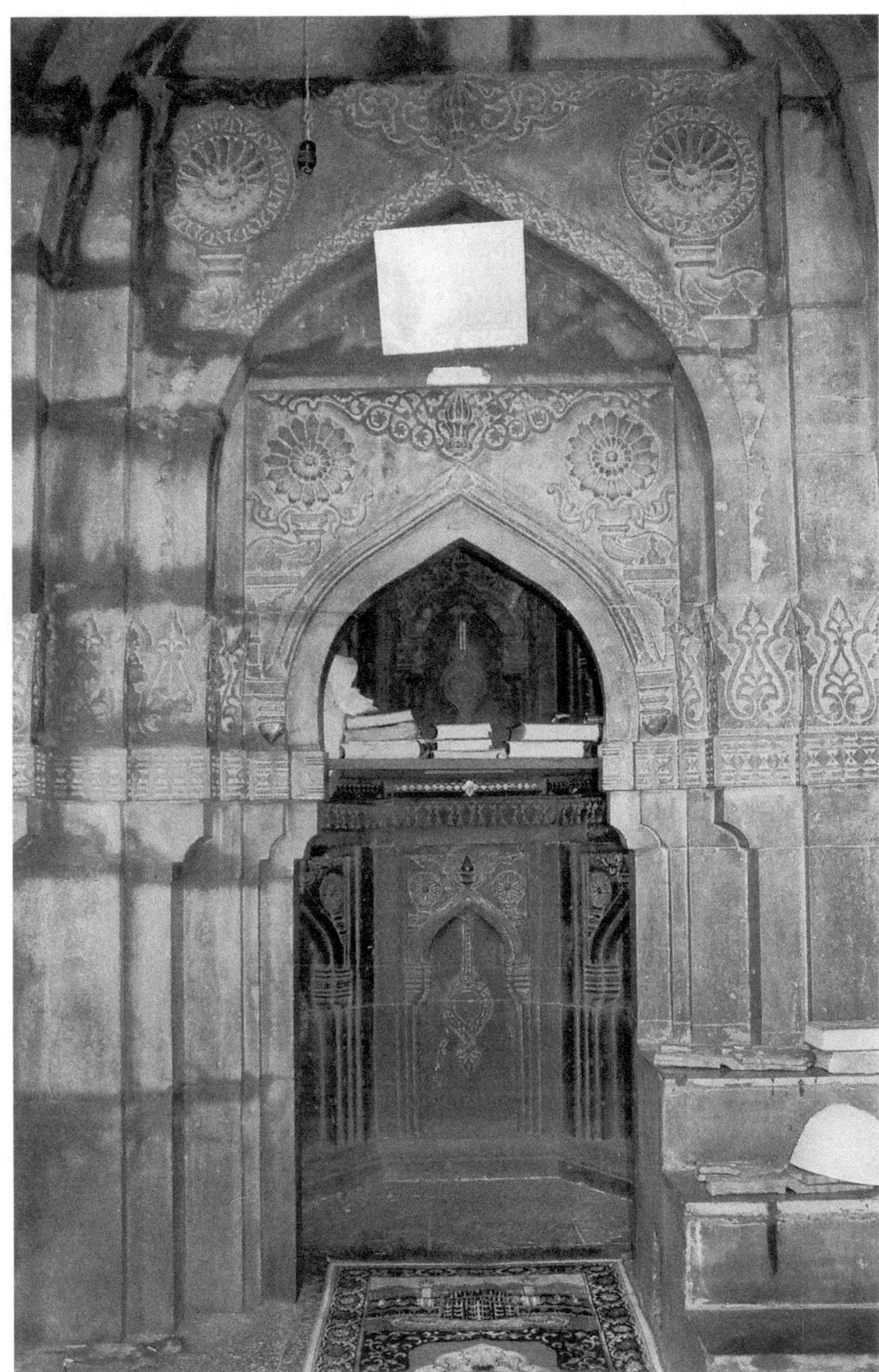

Figure 4.10. Mihrab of Anda mosque, 1608, Bijapur. Photograph by author.

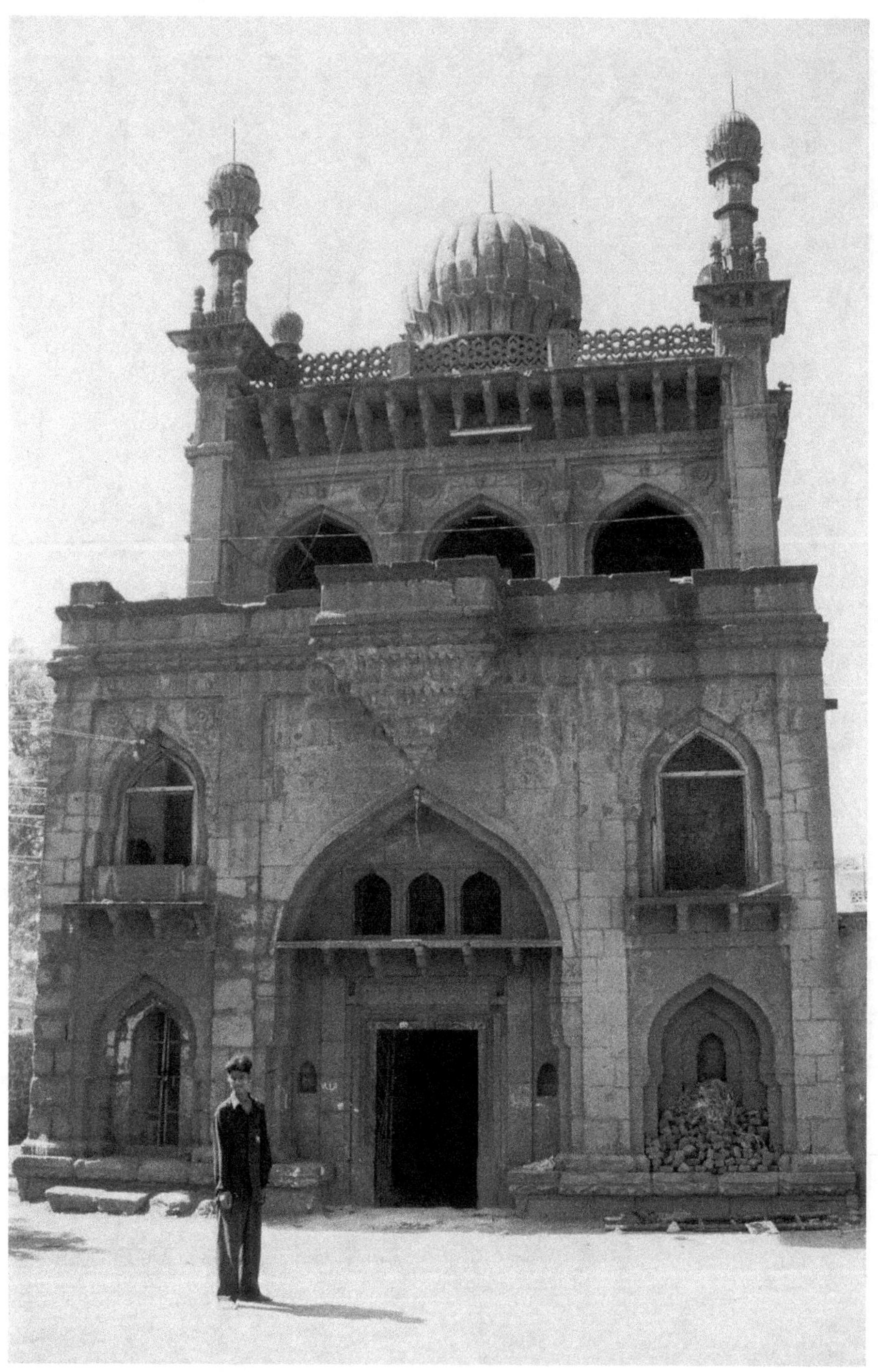

Figure 4.11. Anda mosque, 1608, Bijapur. Photograph by author.

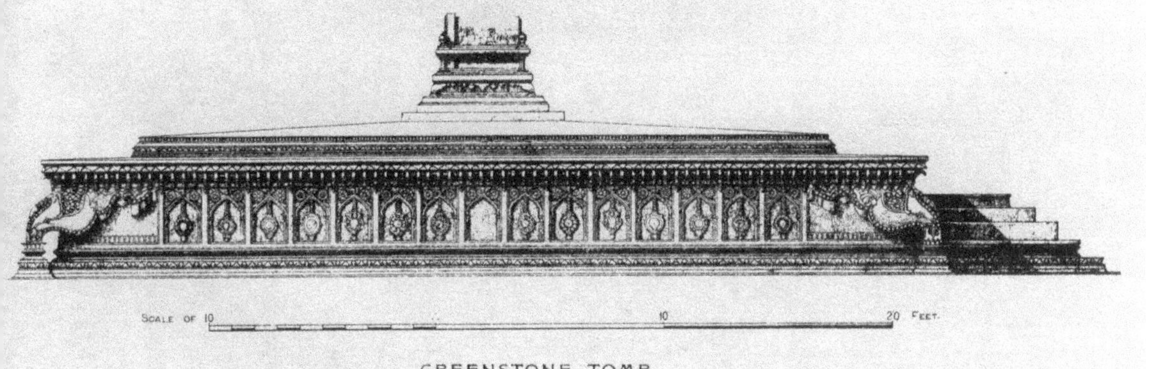

Figure 4.12. Unidentified green stone cenotaph, seventeenth century, Bijapur. Architectural rendering from Henry Cousens, *Bijapur and Its Architectural Remains: With an Historical Outline of the Adil Shahi Dynasty.* Archaeological Survey of India, New Imperial Series 37 (1916; reprint, Delhi: Bharatiya Publication House, 1976). Reproduced by kind permission of the Archeological Survey of India.

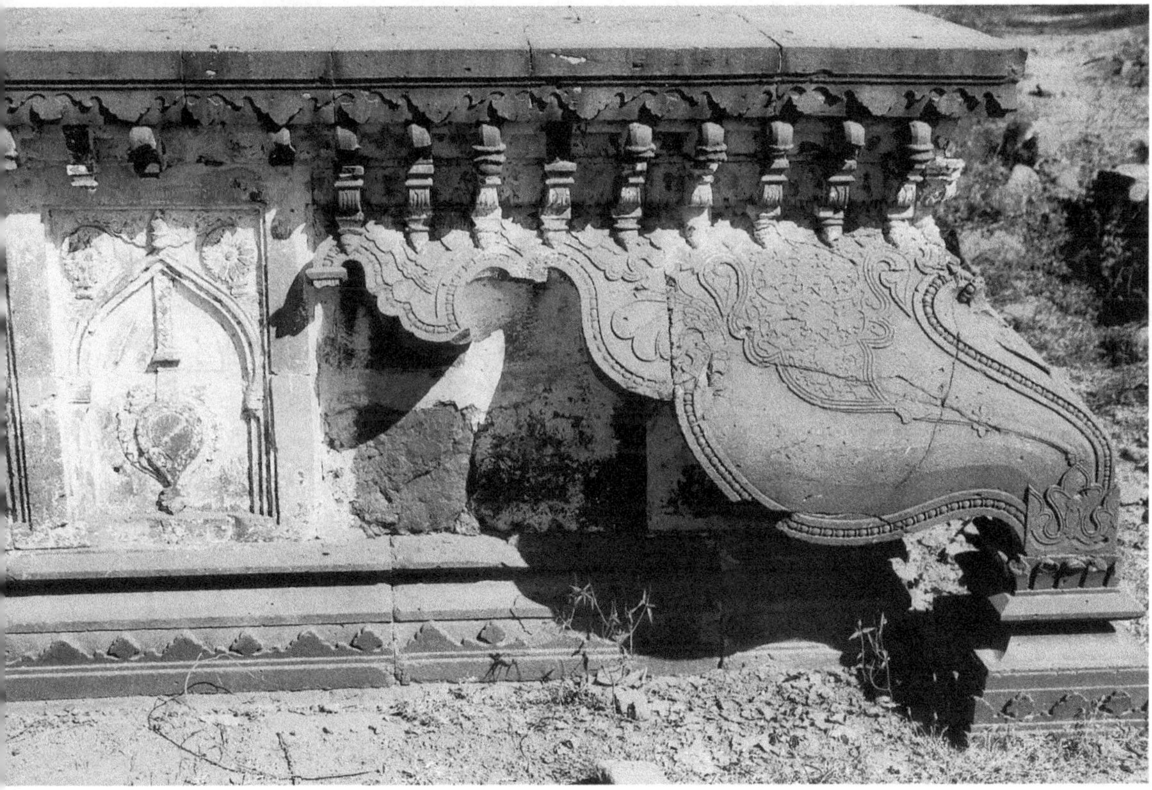

Figure 4.13. Detail of the stone-carved platform from the unidentified cenotaph, seventeenth century, Bijapur. Photograph by author.

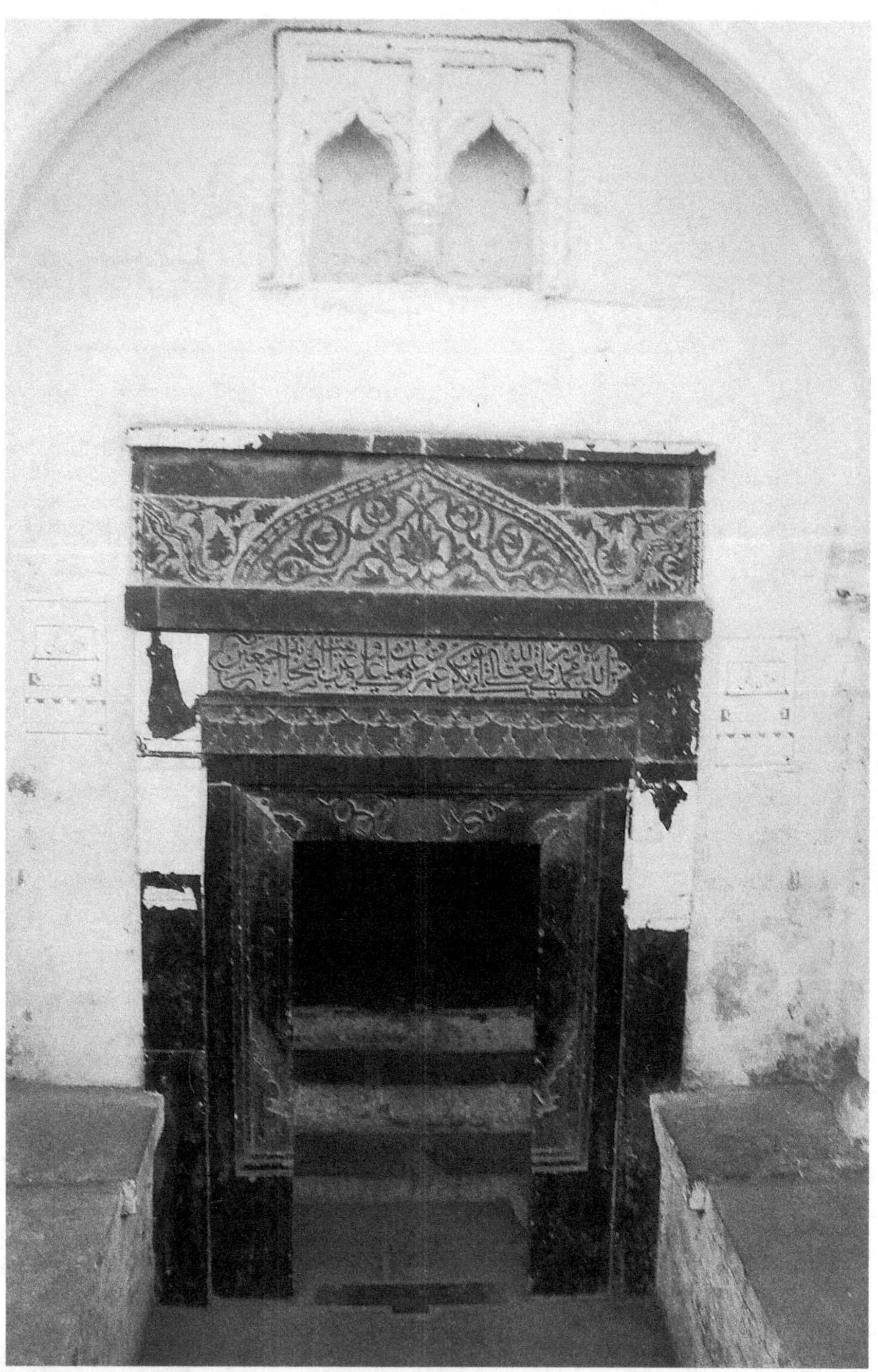

Figure 4.14. Detail of green stone doorway to the Bukhara mosque complex, seventeenth century, Bijapur. Photograph by author.

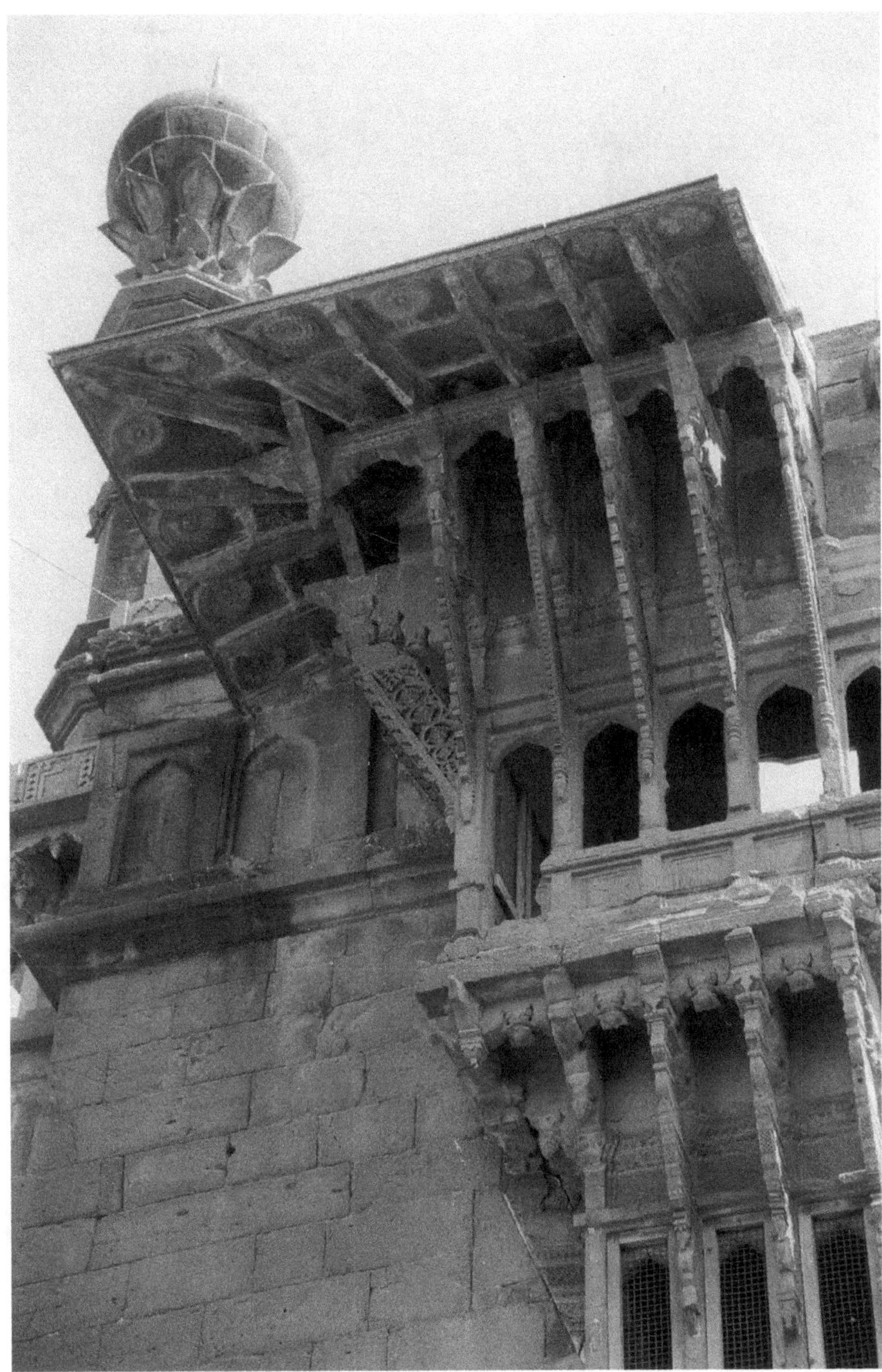

Figure 4.15. Mihtar-i Mahal gateway, seventeenth century, Bijapur. Photograph by author.

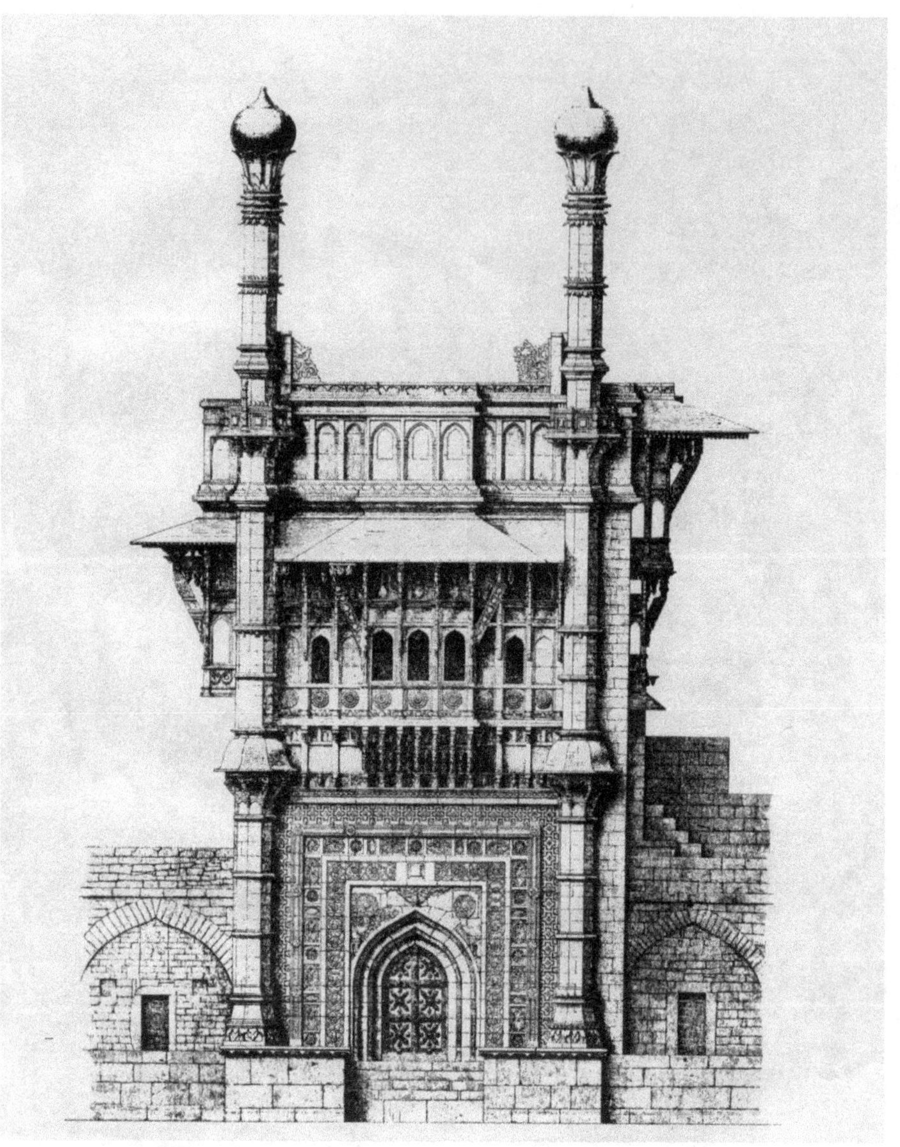

Figure 4.16. Mihtar-i Mahal gateway, seventeenth century, Bijapur. Architectural rendering from Henry Cousens, *Bijapur and Its Architectural Remains: With an Historical Outline of the Adil Shahi Dynasty.* Archaeological Survey of India, New Imperial Series 37 (1916; reprint, Delhi: Bharatiya Publication House, 1976). Reproduced by kind permission of the Archeological Survey of India.

in 1589. This suggests that by the mid-1590s when the new style emerged, some of its featured motifs may already have been current.

In fact, if the individual elements of the new style are traced, it quickly becomes apparent that they were not new. Many motifs, such as the roundels flanking façade archways, were carried over from the architec-

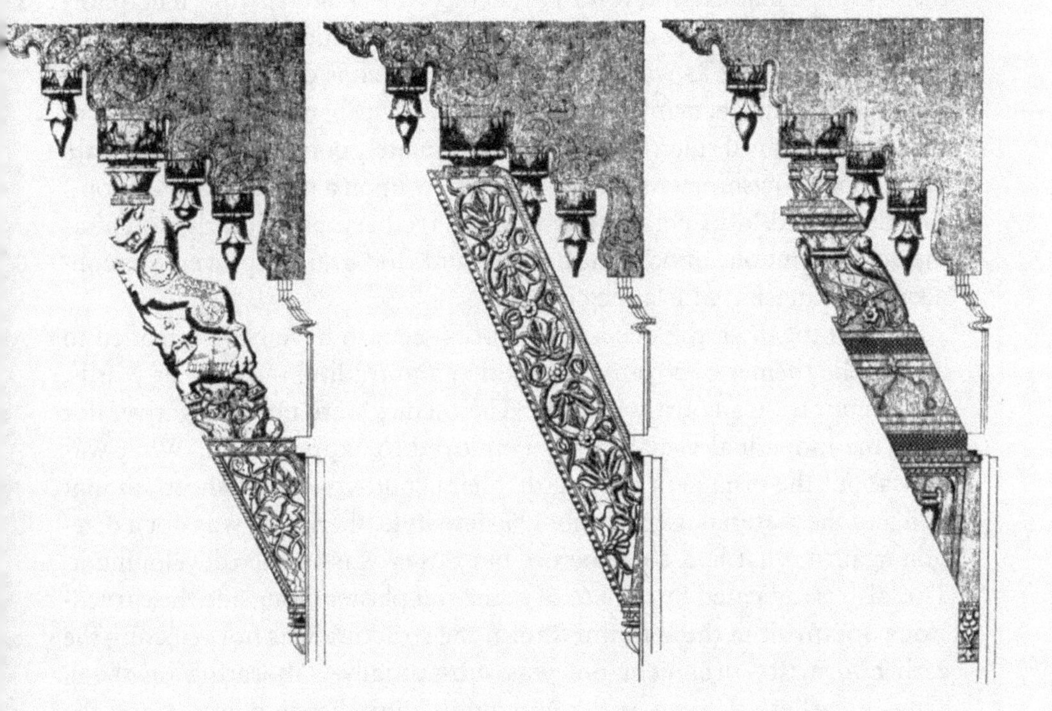

Figure 4.17. Carved brackets from Mihtar-i Mahal gateway, seventeenth century, Bijapur. Architectural rendering from Henry Cousens, *Bijapur and Its Architectural Remains: With an Historical Outline of the Adil Shahi Dynasty.* Archaeological Survey of India, New Imperial Series 37 (1916; reprint, Delhi: Bharatiya Publication House, 1976). Reproduced by kind permission of the Archeological Survey of India.

ture of the Bahmani dynasty, the earlier Deccan Islamic kingdom from which Bijapur sprang in 1490 and inherited many traditions. Other elements, such as the engaged corner-colonnettes as well as the deep cornices, called *chajjas,* and brackets supporting them, are derived from local Hindu temple architecture. The distinctive flat stone slab ceiling found at the Ibrahim Rauza, as well as in the Mihtar-i Mahal's gateway, likewise, came from Hindu temple design.[32] Moreover, not even the intermixing of various traditions was new, for intercultural exchange had been one of the central features of Bijapuri art from its inception.

And what about the most ubiquitous element, the lotus, found in various permutations throughout the ornament? The most conspicuous permutation of it, the dome resting on a ring of lotus petals, was neither new nor exclusive to Bijapur but was employed throughout the Islamicate Deccan. The *Nujum al-Ulum* reveals why this particular form may have been so popular, at least within Adil Shahi courtly circles. The visual climax of the 348-page manuscript, folio 191, depicts the *chakravartin*'s metaphorical seven-storied throne (pl. 6). The lotus, which functions as the chakravartin's seat as well as canopy, and which is depicted again at the center of the image, symbolized the prosperity ushered in by the reign of the ideal, universal ruler. The lotus was intimately connected to Adil Shahi ideas about kingship, which themselves drew upon a number of traditions. The dome and lotus petal motif would have been particularly potent as the dome, symbolic of both the heavens and God-granted power, was connected to kingship in Islamic culture.

Taken together, the decorative motifs seem to have been intended to invoke the themes of royalty, prosperity, and tradition—in other words, to communicate a courtly identity. The themes were not innovative, nor were the individual visual motifs employed to express them. What was new about the ornament in the Adil Shahi context was the sheer amount of it and the material used, stone. The new style, therefore, was not a reaction against what had come before but rather was further developing it. This also is indicated by the use of paint and plaster alongside the carved-stone ornament in the Ibrahim Rauza: the structure was not rejecting the earlier forms of ornament but was substantially elaborating on them. Thus, if earlier art, such as the *Nujum al-Ulum* throne painting and the post-1565 building campaign, explored ways to effectively assert an Adil Shahi identity based on effective rule and prosperity drawn from a variety of cultural traditions, then the monuments of the 1590s through the 1630s were codifying that visual identity. A repertoire of very distinctive, easily recognizable elements was assembled and then transferred into a costly and permanent material. Or to phrase it another way, with these monuments, a Bijapuri visual identity was, literally and metaphorically, being carved in stone. Further evidence that the buildings were meant to convey courtly identity is the fact that many of the motifs are concentrated on the rooflines and gateways of the buildings. This emphasis created distinctive skylines that would have been visible from afar and thus recognizable to a large number of people, even those who would not have been allowed within the walls of the various complexes.

Moreover, the meanings of the buildings seem to have been directed at local viewers. The intimate scale of the monuments cultivated a familiar, local aesthetic, while the significance of the ornamental program depended on the viewers' preexisting familiarity with the individual elements. Each structure contains precisely the same elements with one or two unique features to differentiate it. This suggests that by commissioning a building in this new style, the patron was demonstrating an affiliation to the Adil Shahi court while distinguishing him- or herself within it, a practice directed at a local audience who could recognize both the style and its variations.

Essentially, the monuments were intended to communicate to the other members of the nobility and to the local Bijapur populace that the patrons, and others closely involved in the construction process, not only belonged to and were conversant in Bijapuri courtly culture but, moreover, were themselves helping to shape it.

Such demonstration of concurrent affiliation and distinctiveness was critical to the members of the Bijapur nobility who were often culturally, religiously, and linguistically distinct from one another and who frequently shifted alliances from one Deccan state to the next. Malik Sandal, as an Abyssinian eunuch who fought for Ahmadnagar before aligning himself with the Adil Shahis, is an excellent example of this. High-ranking royal consorts, such as Taj Sultana, often came from neighboring states as well. For such persons, in order to advance in rank within the court, it was vital both to demonstrate affiliation to Bijapur and to distinguish oneself.

The visual success of these monuments directly resulted from a clearly articulated design program centered on a set group of localized, highly developed ornamental motifs while admitting distinctive, differentiating features. The high degree of uniformity over the series of monuments bespeaks the strength of the collaborative process—and thus the need to recognize it in analyses of the buildings. Rather than a single vision, it was fully developed, shared visions that shaped the architectural works. At the same time, the distinctive aspects of each building buttress the view that these buildings were meant to be associated with individuals and were perceived as expressing their aspirations. Finally, the costly use of elaborately carved stone as the mediator of choice confirms that those involved in the construction were sure of both the message they were communicating and the effectiveness of the visual language chosen.

Recognizing the architectural style's role as a codifier of an Adil Shahi courtly identity explains the timing of its flourishing. Elizabeth Merklinger has observed that since carved stone commonly decorates Indo-Islamicate architecture, "the puzzle is not that this [new carved-stone style] developed, but rather why the Adil Shahi Sultans did not use it earlier."[33] Certainly, after the 1565 military victory and the subsequent building campaign, it was not a question of adequate financial resources, available artisans, or artistic creativity. Rather, as a style that depended on a set program of highly developed ornamental motifs acting as mediators of meaning as well as beautifying elements in compact and efficient, yet aesthetically luxurious, designs, it had to be a product of a fully formed visual language, one that was confidently shared by patrons, artisans, and audience. Such a visual identity can only be effectively operative after a period of experimentation and development, thereby explaining the emergence of the style in the first part of the seventeenth century.

Yet if this new ornamental style so effectively expressed a Bijapuri courtly identity while allowing its producers to distinguish themselves and evolved only after decades of artistic development, why did it fall out of favor after the construction of the Ibrahim Rauza? Perhaps one answer is that the very sense of identity being expressed had become threatened. In 1635, just two years after Taj Sultana was entombed in the Ibrahim Rauza, a formidable Mughal army marched against Bijapur, and the Adil Shahis were forced to sign a deed of submission (although they were allowed to continuing ruling for another fifty years).[34] Conceivably, with the Mughals looming large over the kingdom as well as the Adil Shah's sense of power and identity, continuing to build in the intimate, localized language of ornament seemed a less effective response than turning to the universal language of "bigness," exemplified by the huge dome of the circa 1656 Gul Gumbad.

Returning now to the Ibrahim Rauza and reading it through the lens of courtly identity—specifically Taj Sultana's courtly identity—the accentuation of the skyline through the recognizable repertoire of elements would have visually linked the complex, and thus those involved in its construction, to Adil Shahi Bijapur. Simultaneously, the sheer amount of ornament, particularly the calligraphy on the tomb, would have distinguished the complex from its contemporaries, indicating the importance of it, its patron, and the family members entombed there. The calligraphy denoted Taj Sultana's participation and status and also linked her and the monument to the perfections of paradise. Each element of the complex, including the fact that her husband, the sultan, was buried there, was carefully conceived to position Taj Sultana as the highest-ranking female at the Adil Shahi court, a perception that undoubtedly benefited all participants, whether patron, sar-i kar, or artisan. The Ibrahim Rauza can be understood as the high point of an ornamental development, which itself was the culmination and codification of an Adil Shahi visual identity. With its construction, an elegant and exuberant vision of Bijapuri courtly architecture was carved into stone.

Abri Drawings of Emaciated Horses

Four abri, or marbled, drawings of horses, datable to the first half of the seventeenth century, provide some of the most unusual examples of Bijapuri painting. Their distinctiveness emerges from the otherworldly quality conveyed by the images, a direct result of marbling technique innovatively integrated with line drawings of emaciated horses. The marbling, however, not only participates in creating the visual character of the images; it also adds layers to their meaning. Indeed, in a manner similar to the Ibrahim Rauza and the other buildings in the new carved-stone architectural style, the paintings employ ornament as a mediator of meaning. While the architectural decoration communicates themes such as kingship and prosperity, the paintings' import relates to Sufism and poetic metaphors, the other main facets of Adil Shahi Bijapur's courtly identity. To fully understand the images' meanings and modes of conveyance, we need to explore the marbling technique, the emaciated horse subject matter, and how the two elements interact on the page.

The combination of abri and line drawings of gaunt horses is what makes the four abri horse drawings unique. Abri, or "marbling," itself is a widespread ornamental motif, found in the art of many cultures and periods, although it seems to have originated somewhere in the Islamic world.[35] The technique has had various uses in Islamicate culture: as a decoration for manuscript end pages, as a background for calligraphy, or as a border for album pages. At the end of the sixteenth century, examples of the ornamental technique arrived in Europe from Turkey. Europeans first called it "Turkish paper," until it became more commonly referred to as marbled, or marbleized, paper.[36] "Marbling" continues to be the term by which we know the technique today. The terminology, though seemingly straightforward, is a construction, one that relates to a specifically western interpretation of the patterning. In contrast, the original painters, patrons, and viewers of the Bijapuri marbled drawings would have referred to the technique as abri, a Persian term meaning "cloudlike."[37] In the Persian-speaking world, the technique was not viewed as an imitation of stone but rather as a representation of clouds, a distinction crucial to understanding abri's metaphorical role in the Bijapuri paintings.

Bijapur's "cloudlike" images of emaciated horses complicate the basic abri process by integrating the ornamental technique with areas of line drawing.[38] The abri drawing of an emaciated horse in the Museum of Fine Arts, Boston (fig. 4.18), and that of a horse harassed by birds in the Sackler Museum, Harvard University, Cambridge (pl. 32), are similar images: a solitary abri horse on a blank background. In the Sackler Museum image, the horse faces right rather than left as in the MFA work, and two birds, one flying above him and the other resting on his back, torment the poor creature. In both paintings, gold accentuates the horse's ribs, but in the Sackler work, the artists also used color pigment to depict other details. Particularly striking when the image is viewed in person are red drops of blood that drip down from an open sore at which one bird picks.

Rider on a Nag in the Metropolitan Museum of Art, New York (pl. 33), combines the emaciated horse imagery with an equally thin rider. While the artists filled the horse with abri, they rendered the rider in ink. The bearded man holds a small riding crop and is dressed only in a loincloth. His minimal dress, unkempt hair and beard, and his near-starving appearance indicate his status as an ascetic. The drawing accentuates his gaunt ribs, and his feet have been hooked around the belly of the horse, to empha-

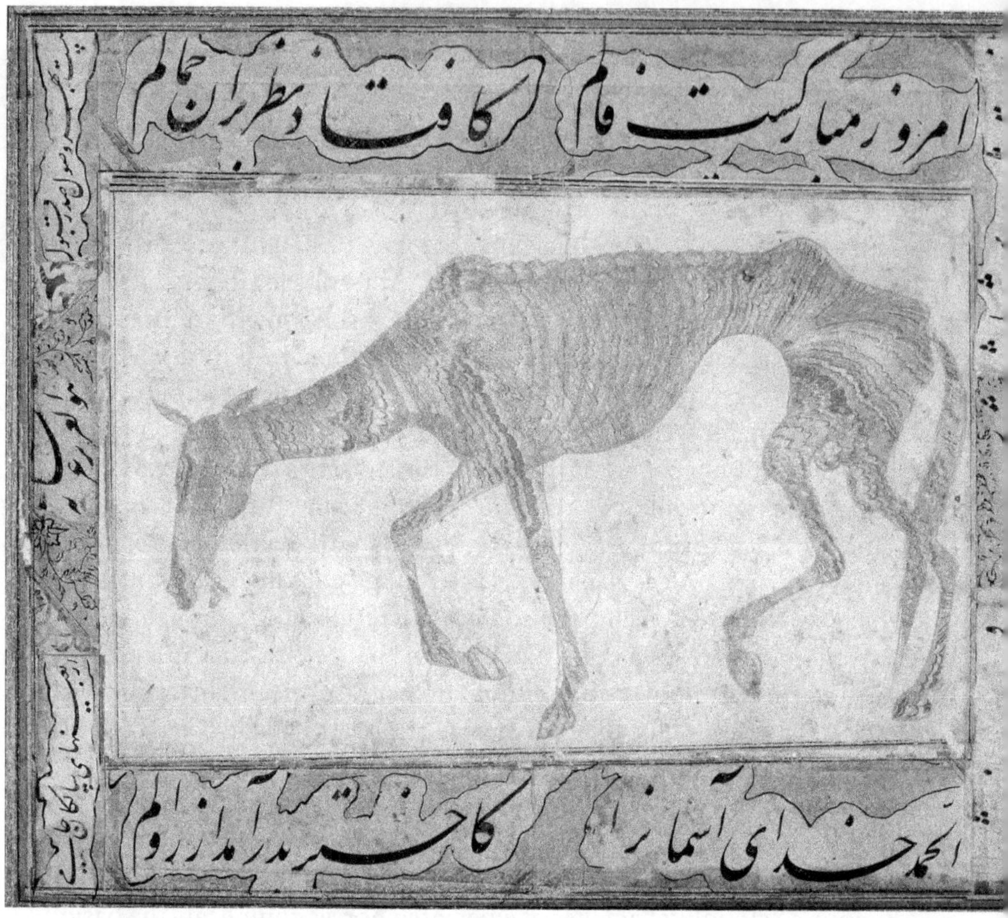

Figure 4.18. A starving horse, ca. 1620–35, Bijapur. 14.8 × 10.0 cm. Museum of Fine Arts, Boston, Francis Bartlett Donation and Picture Fund, 14.695. Photograph copyright 2006 Museum of Fine Arts, Boston.

size the extreme meagerness of his mount. At some point, the image was cut down, cropping the edge of the horse's tail and the top of the ascetic's head. The image of an ascetic riding a nag in the Pierpont Morgan Library, New York (pl. 34), is almost identical to the Met's image; however, now the artists placed the emaciated horse and rider, both drawn, on a vivid abri background, heightening the otherworldly quality of the image.

The four abri horse drawings function as a distinct subset within a larger group of abri drawings attributed to seventeenth-century Bijapur. The exact number of extant works in this category is difficult to establish, as many remain unpublished, but they seem to number somewhere in the twenties.[39] The subject matter of the drawings includes dervishes, Indian ladies, European figures, animals, and hunting scenes. For example, the Salar Jung Museum, Hyderabad, houses an abri drawing of a dervish with his pet cat, and the Jagdish and Kamla Mittal Museum of Indian Art contains an image of a *begum,* an Indian lady, wearing an abri garment and hat while holding a sprig of abri flowers. All the images combine abri areas with areas of drawings, and they can be divided into three distinct groups based on type of abri patterning, subject matter, and level of refinement. The first category, in which the abri is of a very fine pattern and the drawing is finely done as well, includes the four emaciated horse drawings being examined here, two dervish images, and the drawing of the begum in the Mittal Museum. The second identifiable group displays a distinctive striped abri pattern in the background of each image, seems to be less refined than the first group, and comprises subject matters ranging from a European bishop to a cow and her calf. The third abri drawing group includes several hunting scenes in which the artists used three or four abri patterns, usually to help distinguish the assorted animals or figures in the pictures. The quality of abri and drawing varies in this last group.

Unfortunately, the images bear no inscriptional evidence regarding their place and date of production. The clothing worn by some of the figures, stylistic details of the faces, and the similarity of the abri patterns to those found on the end pages of Bijapuri manuscripts, however, allow us to attribute the works to early seventeenth-century Bijapur.[40] I further estimate the abri horse drawings' dates as circa 1620–35 because of their correlation with changes that seem to have taken place in Bijapuri paintings during that period. Specifically, as noted in the discussions of the yogini paintings and portraits of Ibrahim Adil Shah II, in the second and third decades of the seventeenth century there seems to have been a trend toward a precise style of painting, one in which line drawing became prominent. Many of the images from this period, such as the yogini painting in the Islamisches Museum, Berlin (fig. 3.6), or the image of Ibrahim presenting a necklace to his lover in the Victoria and Albert Museum, London (fig. 3.9), are tinted drawings. These are images in which line drawing is combined with pigment, just as the abri drawings combine pigment and ink techniques. Additionally, the tinted drawings are as precise and detailed as the best abri drawings. Finally, many of the album pages from this period contain elegantly abri-patterned borders. For example, two rectangles of abri paper in patterning similar to that found on the abri horse drawings frame the Berlin yogini, and the LACMA yogini is adorned by a thick, exquisitely patterned abri border (pl. 18).

The similarities of the four emaciated horse images go beyond the subject matter and the use of abri. The drawings of the horses, each of which weakly raises one front leg and one back leg and whose tail slumps between the back legs, are almost identical. Moreover, the riders in the last two images match, right down to details such as the shape of the ascetic's beard and the small crop he holds, suggesting that they were based on the same model or models. The Israel Museum houses an ink drawing of an emaciated horse and rider on transparent deerskin that provides one possible model (fig. 4.19). The work is a *charba,* a pounce or artist's aid for tracing and reproducing images, and it appears to duplicate the two abri emaciated horse and rider drawings.[41] Other artworks featuring the emaciated horse or horse and rider combination and attributable to the first half of the seventeenth-century Bijapur survive. These images, like the abri ones, seem to follow the same model or models, but now are painted or drawn. Examples include an emaciated horse drawing housed in the Victoria and Albert Museum, London, and a painting of a young ascetic on a starving horse in the collection of the Israel Museum, Jerusalem (along with the charba).[42] Clearly the motif was a popular one in Bijapur. In fact, like abri paper, the image of the emaciated horse was common throughout the Islamic world and seems to have been especially popular during the sixteenth and seventeenth centuries.[43] It is the combination of the two elements—the starving nag and marbling—that makes the Bijapuri images so striking.

Using the references to emaciated horses found in the well-known Sufi didactic piece, the *Mathlawi-yi Mathnawi* of Jalal al-Din Rumi, and other works such as the *Kashf al-Mahjub,* al-Hujwiri's treatise on Sufism, Annemarie Schimmel has identified the pitiful creature as a representation of nafs. *Nafs* translates as "soul," but not the "soul" in the western spiritual sense of the word. Nafs is the totality of the body's base instincts that cause sin. Followers of the Sufic path must fight against their nafs in order to suppress all worldly desire. Nafs as a concept can be found as far back as the Koran, and over the centuries, mystical poets developed various types of imagery for the concept. Schimmel lists some common forms, including a black dog begging for food, a fox or mouse springing from the poet's throat, a disobedient camel, as well as a disobedient woman. She states, however, "The recurrent image is that of the restive horse or mule that has to be kept hungry and has to undergo constant mortification and training so that eventually it serves the purpose of bringing the rider to his goal."[44] This interpretation correlates with the abri horse drawings from Bijapur and explains the popularity of the emaciated horse imagery in Adil Shahi Bijapur, attuned as it was to Sufism. In fact, the Met and Pierpont Morgan images, each featuring a rider prodding his starving nag toward some unseen goal, appear to illustrate the Sufic concept literally. And what is this unseen goal toward which the ascetic urges his horse? In Sufic ideology, it is the ultimate goal, the union with the Beloved, God, which a Sufi reaches only after he has given up all desires and himself completely.[45]

The Persian border inscription on the abri emaciated horse image in Boston's MFA (fig. 4.18) reinforces the connection of the starving horse

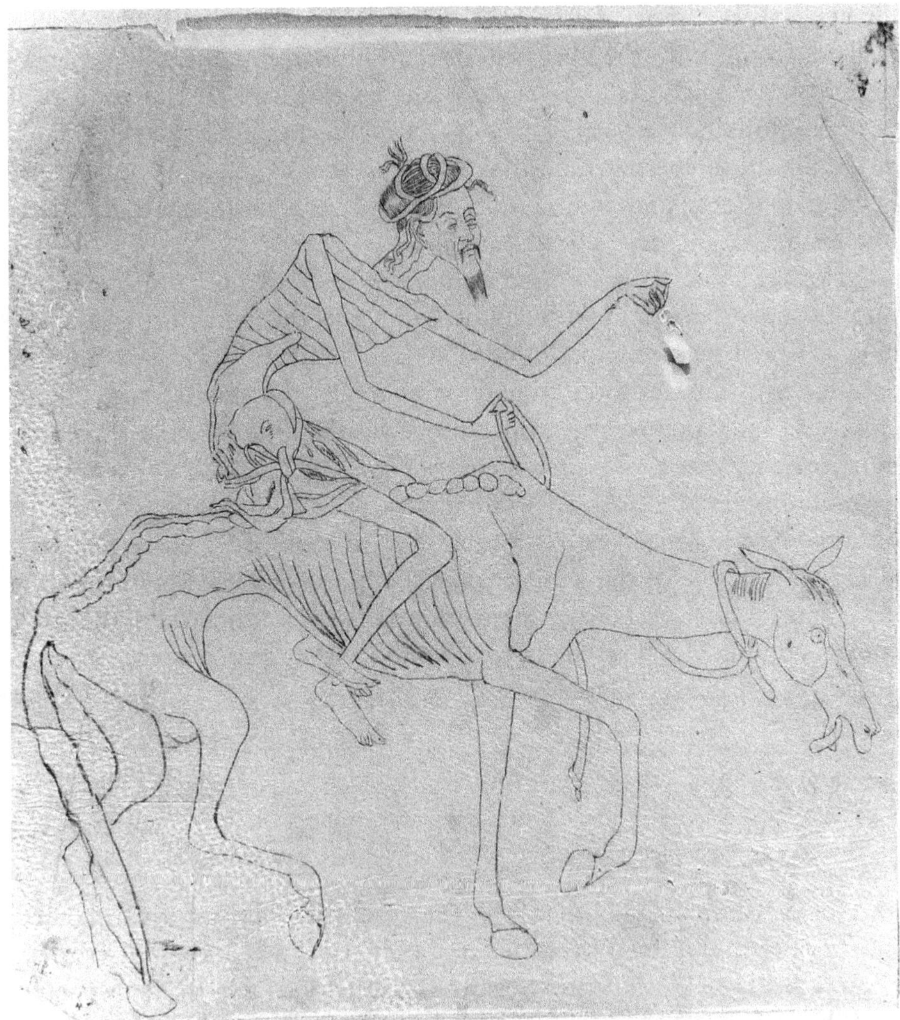

Figure 4.19. Charba of an ascetic on emaciated horse, ca. 1620–35, Bijapur. Collection, Israel Museum, Jerusalem, O.S.4070.10.77. Photograph copyright The Israel Museum, Jerusalem / Nahum Slapak.

imagery to Sufic ideas. The short mystical poem written in *nastaliq* calligraphy on a border affixed around the central image discusses how the poet's fate was decided the day that his gaze fell upon the beauty of God in the sky.[46] As discussed, the weary horse symbolizes nafs, which the mystic must constantly struggle against if he is to follow the *tariqa,* the Sufic path. This struggle is the fate of every Sufi, the same fate described in verses surrounding the image, thus linking the motif to Sufism. The poem also provides the first connection of the abri pattern to the emaciated horse. Just like the God on whose beauty the poet's gaze fell and which in turn led him to the Sufic path, clouds are of the sky. Clouds are a symbol of the heavens, the spiritual world that is sometimes thought of as the home of God. In this way, the abri pattern can be interpreted as a representation of the mystic's goal, the place where he and God are united. Moreover, the cloudlike patterning bestows an ephemeral quality to the figures, as if they sit perched at the divide between this world and the next, of material existence and annihilation, further connecting them to the goals of Sufism.

Clouds, however, have another more precise meaning in Islamic culture. Clouds, specifically rain clouds, symbolize the mercy of God, a significance befitting a religion founded in the desert. Moreover, South Asian culture, with its monsoon climate, strengthens the significance of rain clouds. In Indic poetry, the rainy season was the time when love became more intense, when lovers felt stronger pains in separation. These ideas were traditionally expressed in *baramasa* poems describing the twelve months (*bara masa* literally meaning twelve months).[47] Amir Khosrau (1253–1325), one of the greatest poets of Indo-Islamicate culture, writing in North India, picked up on the traditionally Hindu motif of the rainy season, combined it with the Islamic significance of rain clouds, and produced verses, such as the following example:

> The cloud weeps, and I become separated from my friend—
> How can I separate my heart from my heart's friend on such a day?
> The cloud weeping—and I and the friend standing, bidding farewell—
> I weeping separately, the cloud separately, the friend separately.[48]

Mirza Ashdullah Ghalib (1797–1869), another of the most acclaimed Indian poets, who lived five centuries after Amir Khosrau and wrote in Urdu rather than Persian, also frequently used cloud imagery in his poetry. Ghalib even entitled his *masnavi* "The Jeweled Cloud."[49]

Poetry, such as the verse below, further confirms that, at least to some viewers, the abri technique was not just a meaningless ornamental pattern but rather was recognized specifically as cloud imagery and thereby conveying with it the associations of love, longing, and mercy.[50] The following is an undated *ghazal,* attributed to the Indian poet Danesh:

> Let's write the pains of our heart on cloud-like paper.
> For it might, like the rain cloud, bring the news of our crying eyes.[51]

Taking into account the poetic associations of clouds, if the nag represents what the Sufi must struggle against to follow the tariqa, then the abri pattern can be understood as the mercy God bestows upon the struggling Sufi. It also could represent, with the incorporation of the Indic motif of the rainy season, the intense longing of the lover, the Sufi, for the Beloved, God. With the addition of the rider on the horse in the Met and Pierpont Morgan works, the symbolism of the Sufi struggling to control his worldly desires becomes more literal. In the latter image, when the abri pattern surrounds the horse and rider instead of being contained inside the nag, it appears as if the rider has reached his goal. It is the moment when the Sufi is engulfed by the mercy of God and is united with God.

The connection of these drawings to Sufic poetry does not end with the subject matter or with the symbolic correspondence. The processes through which the two forms of expression, the drawings and poetry, would have been "read" and understood in their original context are also parallel. For a Sufi, reading mystical poetry is like lifting veils. With each veil that is lifted, the Beloved can be seen more clearly. A poem has an outer meaning, one that relies on the literal meaning of the words. Many of the words, however, also function as metaphors. When the metaphorical, or "inner," meanings of the individual words are incorporated into the overall meaning of the poem, the message of the poem appears on various levels. Each step taken toward a deeper level of meaning correlates with the lifting of another veil.

Correspondingly, when observing an abri drawing of an emaciated horse, the viewer first sees a pattern incorporated within a drawing of a starving horse, the literal meaning of the work. Yet, just by taking in the aesthetic appearance of the work, knowing neither the meaning of the horse nor the pattern, the viewer discerns that the work is doing more than just reflecting reality. The first veil has been lifted. If the viewer understands the meaning of the emaciated horse as it relates to nafs, he or she now sees that the drawing is related to Sufism and the follower's struggle along the path. Another veil is gone. If the viewer is looking at the abri horse image complemented with poetry (fig. 4.18), considering the inscription provides another level of understanding. Then, when the viewer realizes that the pattern is an abri pattern, he makes yet another connection. The viewer may associate the cloud motif specifically with the mercy of God or with the heightened longing felt during the rainy season, or both, depending on his familiarity with the Islamicate and Indic poetic meanings associated with clouds. Once again, the work can be read on a deeper level. Thus, as the viewer studies the paintings, he moves from the outer, worldly appearance, or the *zahir,* to the inner essences, or the *batin,* simulating his movement along the Sufic path. In this way, the abri horse drawings compare to the *Pem Nem.* In that manuscript, through the spatial setting of the individual paintings, the illustrations also move the viewer from the zahir to the batin as he follows the hero of the tale on his journey to union with his beloved. In the case of the abri horse drawings, however, this movement happens within a single image rather than over a series of images as it does in the *Pem Nem.* Moreover, because the drawings do not function as illustrations connected to a narrative, they require the viewer to bring more of the associations and knowledge to experience than the

Pem Nem illustrations do. In this way the abri images recall the yogini paintings.

In fact, the abri drawings are similar in a number of respects to the yogini images. The emaciated horse motif, with or without a rider, was, like the yogini figures, a repeated subject matter intended to convey specific mystical concepts to the viewer. The yoginis embody the longing of the lover for the beloved, while the emaciated horse and rider convey the hardship that the follower must endure along the Sufic path. In both cases the images refer to poetry and poetic concepts without necessarily being directly connected to them (although occasionally poetic verses frame the images). The abri technique adds layers of meaning to the emaciated horse drawings, one that can be interpreted on a number of levels, and in the same vein, the ambiguity of the yoginis' status (were they meant to represent yoginis or noble women disguised as yoginis?) allows the yogini paintings to convey varied associations to different people, creating an intimacy between the individual viewer and the work. But in all cases, the artists, the patrons, and the intended audience must have been conversant in the metaphors and intricacies of Sufism.

Like the *Pem Nem*'s illustrations and those of the *Nujum al-Ulum,* the abri drawings convey, or were intended to convey, concepts and emotions not usually experienced visually. In each of these cases, the artists strove to communicate something beyond visual, earthly reality. In the *Nujum al-Ulum* the artists accomplished it through diagrammatic renderings and allegorical images. In the *Pem Nem,* the artists gave poetic metaphors novel visual forms, such as the face of the beloved drawn on the heart of the prince. In the four abri drawings examined here, the artists conveyed mystical concepts through the use of the cloudlike ornament applied to certain areas of the page. The integration of the abri patterns within the drawings functioned as a visual metaphor for clouds while also imbuing the images with an immediately recognizable otherworldly quality, alluding to their mystical significance and bestowing them with visual distinctiveness.

What makes the abri drawings distinct is that the artists employed a specific ornamental technique to achieve the results. The artists appropriated a common form of ornament, found a distinctive way to integrate it with line drawing, and created something new. This new technique could be employed for a variety of subjects, not all of which necessarily related to Sufism, such as the images of a bishop or cow and calf, but it had the potential, and was often used, to effectively communicate Sufic ideas.

It was neither the Sufic ideas nor the creation of visual metaphors that was new to Bijapuri art. Rather, it was the use of the specific ornamental technique to express them that made the abri drawings innovative. The appropriation of ornament to express specific ideas and concepts already current in Bijapuri culture links these drawings to the Ibrahim Rauza and the other examples of the new carved-stone architectural style. In the new architectural style, a repertoire of ornamental motifs, such as lotus buds, petals, brackets, and delicate minarets, was assembled and carved into stone, signaling the codification of an Adil Shahi visual identity. The abri emaciated horse drawings can likewise be understood as codifying the sultanate's visual identity, specifically the role of Sufism in it.

If we define "refinement" as the better expression of a particular set of ideas as well as the mastery of specific artistic techniques, it appears that the first three decades of the seventeenth century witnessed a "refinement" of Bijapuri art. Both of the examples examined in this chapter relate to themes that have been seen from the 1565–68 building campaign of Bijapur city onward. The abri drawings of emaciated horses are linked to Sufism, poetry, and the desire to express something pictorially that is not usually experienced visually, while the new carved-stone architectural ornament relates to metaphors of kingship and prosperity, all themes central to the visual identity fostered by the Adil Shahi court. These last two examples, however, express the themes in new, refined ways that resulted from, among other things, an availability of skilled artisans, a fully formed visual language, and the appropriation of a specific artistic technique. Most of all, both examples feature ornament, whether architectural or abri, often employed solely to add beauty or richness to a work of art, but here, meaning imbues the ornament, creating luxurious yet remarkably efficient and intimate artworks.

5
Conclusion

Hybridity, internationalism, multiculturalism—these are conditions that we typically associate with our own increasingly global culture. Yet these terms could be employed to define aspects of Bijapur's courtly arts as well. Whether viewing the elegantly carved stonework adorning early seventeenth-century monuments in Bijapur, the single-page paintings of *yogini* from the same period, or the images illustrating the 1570–71 *Nujum al-Ulum,* for example, one cannot help but recognize the diversity of influences and multiplicity of meanings embedded in the works. A close reading of these richly textured visual statements not only reveals the sophistication with which Bijapuri artists employed motifs and styles; it also calls into question modern art historical categories such as "Indian" and "Islamic," making the study of Bijapuri art both important and rewarding.

Of course, any investigation into the art of Adil Shahi Bijapur, including this one, must be considered an ongoing project. As more historical, poetic, and scientific works are translated, as more previously unidentified paintings come to light, and as more studies of the Deccan sultanates are completed, our view of Bijapuri art undoubtedly will shift in ways that also deepen it. By considering a select number of works, both paintings and architecture, and analyzing them individually and then as a whole, this study has constructed a picture of Bijapur's artistic development. The picture presented is neither complete nor absolute (even within the nine case studies examined here, questions remain awaiting further evidence), but it nevertheless speaks powerfully to the ways in which the visual arts contributed to the formation of an identity for the sultanate and its court.

As the 1565–68 building campaign and two royal tombs demonstrate, that identity was closely linked with, and in some cases mapped onto, the physical shape of the city of Bijapur. Symbols and motifs relating to good governance, prosperity, and kingship, as exemplified in works such as the *Nujum al-Ulum,* played integral roles as well. Sufism and poetry, one or both pervading all the artworks examined here, round out the heart of Bijapur's courtly identity. Drawing on Sufism, poetry, and kingly traditions, patrons and artists developed unique visual metaphors that served to increase the power and appeal of the specific Adil Shahi courtly culture being formed. At the height of Bijapur's artistic development, in works such as the Ibrahim Rauza and *abri* drawings of emaciated horses created during the first half of the seventeenth century, the artists were able to transform the visual metaphors into pleasing yet potent ornamental forms.

The use of metaphors augmented the intimacy of the visual language, suggesting that much of Bijapuri art was intended for, and its significance directed at, a highly localized, select audience. To properly create or appreciate the art, the artist, patron, or viewer required a specific body of knowledge. That knowledge centered on mysticism, poetry, and good leadership, and above all else reflected "the power of words" in Bijapur. Because religious mysticism, poetry, language, and conceptions of rule were sites of intercultural exchange in the Islamicate Deccan, the knowledge base included a variety of traditions, Hindu and Muslim, Indic and Persian, as well as others, making Bijapur's courtly culture inclusive as well as exclusive. The yogini paintings are excellent examples of this dual inclusive/exclusiveness. The young women, dressed as ascetic followers of the Hindu god Shiva, symbolize the lover and beloved as conceptualized in Islamic mysticism, thus bringing together religious traditions. Yet, because the single-page paintings refer to ideas expressed in Sufic literature without directly illustrating texts, they also required the producers and viewers of the works to be conversant in the literary ideas expressed. They establish a relationship between words and images that are not physically connected on a single piece of paper but rather pervade the elite cultural interests of the time.

The art provided members of Bijapur's court with opportunities to distinguish themselves while also affirming their affiliation to the sultanate. Whether artisan, supervisor, or patron, a person could elevate his or her status by creating an artwork, from a single-page album painting to a monumental tomb, admired by others. For example, Farrukh Beg established his position at court by creating two portraits of Ibrahim Adil Shah II that combined elements of Safavid and Mughal painting with aspects of

Bijapur's painting style, thereby displaying his artistic talent and pedigree. Clearly realizing the import of poetry in Bijapuri conceptions of kingship and identity, he altered his approach in a third, slightly later, portrait of the sultan, demonstrating his understanding of, and thus belonging to, the courtly culture. Likewise, by patronizing an elegant, expensive *rauza* in the new carved-stone architectural style to function as her tomb as well as a royal family mausoleum, Taj Sultana effectively exhibited her wealth, asserted her links to the Adil Shahi court, and reaffirmed her exalted position within it. By having Sultan Ibrahim buried there, she not only honored her husband but also declared her standing within the family. The building, and her role in its construction, communicated her status as Ibrahim's primary wife, mother of the heir to the throne, and thus head of the female members at court.[1] The patrons and artisans of the other monuments in the new carved-stone style, by including the recognizable repertoire of motifs with the addition of one or two unique design features, also tailored their projects to highlight their fluency in Bijapur's visual language and their ability to contribute to it.

Viewing Bijapuri art through the lens of courtly identity makes evident the participants' motivations. It also brings to the fore the Adil Shahis' sophisticated understanding and conscious employment of visual language. Written and visual evidence, when closely analyzed, makes it clear that the members of Bijapur's court understood the potential of art to create legacies, shape identities, and further specific messages through the tailoring of visual forms. For example, the historian Rafi uddin Shirazi's description of the rock-cut monuments at Ellora constructed between 600 and 1000 CE reveals that he viewed them as wholly political works marking the greatness of their legendary royal patron. Likewise, Astarabadi, in his description of the founding of Nauraspur, compares Ibrahim Adil Shah II to other Islamic rulers who had built new capitals, clearly indicating that city founding was seen as a defining act in one's rule.

The *Nujum al-Ulum,* possibly more than any other artwork examined here, reveals the conscious use of visual forms. The *Nujum*'s artists employed style and iconography in specific, often original, ways to further the message of the text. In some illustrations, the artists brought together disparate iconography to create multivalent images. The painting of Mars in anthropomorphic form, a composite of the Hindu god Shiva and the Persian hero Rustam, combines distinct imagery to portray the planet as the mighty warrior. In other paintings, the artists seem to have employed iconographic elements to show that they were aware of older traditions but were consciously creating new images to better suit their purposes. The painting of the planet Saturn in the guise of a Deccan sultan illustrates such a transformation. Typically in Islamic astrological works Saturn is shown as an old man reading, but the *Nujum*'s artists depict him as a sultan on horseback and accompanied by a royal retinue, including nobles in Persianate dress and soldiers in local south Indian dress. Yet the sultan is still a bearded old man, and he holds a book, as a nod to the traditional iconography of Saturn, thereby emphasizing the artistic transformation. Bijapur patrons and artists seem to have viewed visual traditions as tools to be used and manipulated to enhance the message of the work. The *Nujum al-Ulum* and its illustrations, as well as the other examples discussed here, make evident the cosmopolitan nature of Bijapur. More than a mere "melting pot," Bijapur's courtly culture centered on the conscious use of multiple and viable vocabularies, indicating that Adil Shahis respected and viewed these various traditions as having import and relevance.

Indeed, they seem to have consciously favored metaphors and multilayered motifs that drew on a range of traditions and meanings. The popularity of lion and lotus imagery across artistic media attests to this. Both motifs relate to the Indic ideal ruler, the *chakravartin,* as the *Nujum*'s illustration of the seven-storied throne makes clear. But both held other associations as well. The lion is a general image of kingship in many cultures, it carries a specifically Shia meaning, and when depicted with one upraised paw, it suggests links to a Deccan heritage. The lotus conveys broad associations with water, lushness, fertility, and prosperity. The motifs' multiple associations undoubtedly lay at the heart of their appeal.

Perhaps nothing illustrates the Adil Shahis' interest in establishing multivalent metaphors better than the word *nauras* and the courtly culture centered on it. For the Adil Shahis, the term *nauras* embodied a variety of meanings, depending in part on whether one read it as a Persian phrase or a Deccani Urdu one. As the poet Zuhuri explained, "The Indians call a mixture of nine juices 'nauras,' and if the Persians believe it to be the fresh fruit of the tree of his learning and perfection, it is appropriate; and in this sense also that this beloved of perfect beauty has newly appeared on the stage of existence from behind the curtain of invisibility, if it is called 'nauras' it is also right."[2] His statement reveals that in Bijapur, multiple meanings based on one's cultural and linguistic associations were not only recognized but in fact encouraged.

Frequently scholarship frames Bijapuri art and culture as becoming less "Persian" and more "Indian" over time. The common discourse suggests that as artists migrated from Vijayanagara to Bijapur, as the official state religion was switched from Shia to Sunni Islam, and as Ibrahim Adil Shah II influenced the creation of painting and architecture, Bijapuri art became increasingly Indian in character, while the Persian influence lessened. The artworks examined here, however, suggests something different. First, they establish that cultural interaction was part of Bijapuri art from its earliest development. Second, the works indicate that while the Adil Shahis recognized religious, cultural, and linguistic differences, they did not perceive them as necessarily opposing each other but rather, in many cases, as complementing each other. They seem not to have viewed the addition of diverse cultural traditions as taking away from the "pureness" or essence of the whole but rather as adding another layer to the work of art. From the Adil Shahis' point of view, the planet Mars could be fully Persianate and Shaivite, for the two were not opposing entities. When employed in the right manner, the juxtaposing of Hindu and Persian elements magnified the impression of Mars as the invincible warrior. Just as the multiple meanings of the term *nauras* only added to its appeal, the incorporation of various cultural traditions augmented the significance of the art. As the Adil Shahis might have said, adding another flavor to the mixture only makes the wine sweeter.

The centrality of visual metaphors, as found in the *Pem Nem,* portraits of Ibrahim, and even the Nauras Mahal, relates to the appeal of intercultural layering, to be sure. It also reflects the intimacy of Bijapur's visual language, intended to construct a shared identity and set of references, and it shows the "power of words" at the Adil Shahi court. It also, however, highlights one particular intention underlying much of Bijapuri art, most clearly evident with regard to painting, but discernible in architectural projects as well. Just like courtly poetry in which metaphors played a central role, Bijapuri painting was less about recording events or representing reality than about creating an ideal setting and evoking specific emotions. Moreover, beyond a disinterest in representing reality, some Bijapuri paintings seem to have been intended to express pictorially things not usually experienced visually. This includes the *Nujum al-Ulum*'s many diagrams, the *Pem Nem*'s illustrations displaying details such as the beloved's face drawn on the prince's heart, and the abri drawings of emaciated horses with their cloudlike patterning. The makers of these images seem to have intended them to communicate underlying power, emotions, or concepts, in the same way that poetry and mystical literature were about such conveyance. Taken together, Bijapuri paintings not only embody a disinterest in recording particular actions or realities of life on the Deccan plateau; they seem *deliberately* removed from the specificities of historical events. In this way, the images act as forms of escapism, providing an alternative, ideal reality, whether through diagrams, metaphors, or lyrical details.

The 1565–68 building campaign of Bijapur city and the founding of Nauraspur also were intended to create ideal spaces removed from insecurities and harsh actualities. In the case of Nauraspur, its founders conceived of the city as a place to enact the culture of nauras, one based on music, wine, and poetry, among other things. The 1565–68 building campaign provided Bijapur and its inhabitants with protective walls, plentiful water, luxurious gardens, and a monumental place for congregational prayer. The court historians called the transformed Bijapur "*shahar-i pana,*" the city of refuge. To several of these authors, having traveled from Iran to Ahmadnagar before finally arriving in Bijapur, it did indeed provide a place of security amid the fluctuating political environment in which they lived. Adil Shahi writers, furthermore, encouraged others to view Bijapur as a place where they could seek refuge. In a passage from his preface to Ibrahim Adil Shah II's *Kitab-i Nauras,* the court poet Zuhuri expressed this desire.

> This preface is an open letter by Zuhuri to the denizens . . . of the globe, that they may on every side . . . know the place of Ibrahim to be their center, and should not, through negligence, make themselves deprived . . . of his patronage. . . . In his love, leave your native land and do not remain in exile at home.[3]

Zuhuri wrote, "If they make the elixir of mirth and pleasure, they would make it from the holy dust of Bijapur," the verse which began this book and our exploration of Bijapuri art. The idea of Bijapur as an elixir of mirth and pleasure, along with the title "city of refuge," expresses the essence of the identity being created for Adil Shahi Bijapur through its visual environment: Bijapur as a refuge, an ideal place removed from the surrounding harshness of both landscape and warfare, a place filled with beauty, prosperity, and pleasure, as well as plentiful water and gardens, where poetry, mysticism, music, and learning reigned supreme and various cultural traditions came together in a flourish.

Adil Shahi patrons and artists strove to transform this identity into visual forms, and their endeavors seem to have been rewarded, at least to some degree. In his letters home, the Dutch artist Heda expressed pleasure with what he found at Nauraspur, even encouraging other artists to travel there. The Mughal ambassador Asad Beg, who visited Bijapur in 1603–1604, likewise lavished praise upon the city and its markets in the account of his stay:

> All around the gates of my residence were lofty buildings with houses and porticoes; the situation was very healthy and airy. [My residence] lies in an open space in the city. Its northern portico is to the east of a bazaar of great extent, as much as thirty yards wide and about two *kos* long. Before each shop was a beautiful green tree, and the whole bazaar was extremely clean and pure.
>
> . . . In short, the whole bazaar was filled with wine and beauty, dancers, perfumes, jewels of all sorts, palaces, and viands. In one street were a thousand bands of people drinking, and dancers, lovers, and pleasure-seekers assembled; none quarreled or disputed with another, and this state of things was perpetual. Perhaps no place in the wide world could present a more wonderful spectacle to the eye of the traveler.[4]

As an official representative of the Mughal Empire, Asad Beg would have been predisposed to prefer the capital cities of his own empire, at least in such an official account, making his glowing description of Bijapur all the more striking. He lauds Bijapur for being, among other things, healthy, airy, clean, and pure, all qualities the builders of Bijapur had worked diligently to create in the 1565–68 campaign. Asad Beg also describes "people drinking, and dancers, lovers, and pleasure-seekers assembled," presenting a "wonderful spectacle to the eye of the traveler." His tribute seems to confirm Zuhuri's commendation of Bijapur as an "elixir of mirth and pleasure." Perhaps Zuhuri's verse was more than just poetic conceit after all.

A quick review of Bijapur's history, however, reminds us that the elixir, if it existed, was constantly on the verge of being lost and often was more an illusion than reality. Ali Adil Shah and his nobles may have transformed Bijapur into a prosperous capital city through their building campaign, but the "city of refuge" did not protect Ali from being murdered by one of his servants. Qishur Khan, Ali's vizier instrumental in the creation of Bijapur as the glorious refuge, also was murdered—by other Bijapuri nobles, jealous of his success.[5] The first decade of Ibrahim Adil Shah II's reign was filled with intrigue and betrayal, leading to assassination attempts on his aunt, Chand Bibi, and to a five-year war with Ahmadnagar. The power of the Mughals pressing down upon the Deccan forced Ibrahim to give up his favorite daughter, Begam Sultana, in marriage to the Mughal prince, Daniyal. And Nauraspur, Ibrahim's beloved new city founded as the ultimate expression of an Adil Shahi courtly culture, was destroyed just twenty-five years after its inception by the invading armies of Malik Ambar.

Yet such fragility did not eclipse the Adil Shahis' identification with Bijapur as a place of refuge and an elixir of mirth and pleasure. If anything, it just increased their desire for the ideal. The Adil Shahis understood the potency of art and visual language to shape identities, forge communities, ensure status, and even fashion ideals into material forms, or at least to create an escape, however short-lived, into a poetic realm of mirth and pleasure, where even the dust was holy. Their ideal may have been an illusion, but the artistic legacy they left continues to shape our perceptions, and thus the identity, of the sultanate and its court.

Appendix A: Adil Shahi Rulers of Bijapur

Yusuf Adil Khan	r. 1490–1510
Ismail Adil Khan	r. 1510–34
Mallu Adil Khan	r. 1534–35
Ibrahim Adil Shah I	r. 1535–58
Ali Adil Shah I	r. 1558–80
Ibrahim Adil Shah II	r. 1580–1627
Muhammad Adil Shah	r. 1627–56
Ali Adil Shah II	r. 1656–72
Sikander Adil Shah	r. 1672–86

Appendix B: The Pem Nem*'s Illustrations*

The Search Scenes

Folio 46	(pl. 8)	Prince listening to yogini playing music
Folio 47		Prince sits in landscape with deer
Folio 49v		Prince sits in landscape
Folio 69		Prince stands in landscape
Folio 70v	(fig. 3.1)	Prince in landscape

Transitional Scenes

Folio 75v		Prince meets with king on carpet in landscape
Folio 80		King welcomes prince outside of palace
Folio 82v	(pl. 9)	Prince, on carpet with king, faints at sight of his beloved
Folio 87	(pl. 10)	Prince listens to court musicians in palace
Folio 89v		Prince talks with king on carpet with attendants
Folio 90v	(pl. 11)	Prince sits on rock in landscape with attendant
Folio 119	(pl. 12)	Prince and his beloved sit on throne

Harem Scenes

Folio 135		Princess with court women and pet birds
Folio 138	(pl. 13)	Princess with court women playing water games
Folio 147		Princess celebrates with court women

Palace Scenes

Folio 166		Prince faints and is caught by attendants in palace
Folio 168		Prince with men and women courtiers in palace
Folio 171		Prince kisses feet of king in landscape
Folio 172	(fig. 3.2)	Prince kisses feet of princess
Folio 176		Prince sits in front of palace
Folio 177v		Prince cries while sitting in palace
Folio 178v		Prince sits on throne in front of palace

Wedding Scenes

Folio 181v		Prince sits on throne under canopy listening to musicians
Folio 183		Prince sits on throne under canopy surrounded by women
Folio 184		Princess sits on throne under canopy with attendants
Folio 197v	(pl. 14)	Prince riding horse in wedding procession
Folio 202		Prince sits under canopy and watches court dancers
Folio 206	(fig. 3.3)	Princess puts on wedding jewelry with help of attendants
Folio 210		Prince sits on throne while women hold a curtain in front of princess
Folio 213v		Prince lifts princess into covered palanquin
Folio 215		Prince and princess sit alone on throne under canopy
Folio 219		Prince and princess sit, holding hands, alone under canopy
Folio 224v	(pl. 15)	Prince and princess washing hands together in basin
Folio 232		Princess gives prince a betel leaf

Notes

1. Introduction

1. Muhammad Zuhur bin Zuhuri, *Sehr Nathr*, in *A History of Persian Language and Literature at the Mughal Court*, 3 vols., ed. and trans. Muhammad ʿAbdul Ghani (Allahabad: Indian Press, 1930), 3:397–98.

2. For more information on the development of Hindawi literature as it relates to the spread of Sufism, see Aditya Behl and Simon Weightman, *Manjhan Madhumalati: An Indian Sufi Romance* (Oxford: Oxford University Press, 2000), i–xvii.

3. Stuart Cary Welch, *India: Art and Culture, 1300–1900* (New York: Metropolitan Museum of Art and Holt, Rinehart and Winston, 1985), 292–93.

4. Even though this study is limited to the works that I felt could be confidently if not absolutely attributed to Bijapur between 1565 and 1635, it is a possibility that some of the works may be reattributed in the future, as more studies of Deccan art are completed or more works identified, enriching and perhaps complicating our view of Bijapuri art. I present my analyses here as a way of fostering and participating in a dialogue, not as the final word.

5. The definitions of art and visual arts that I employ in this book are current ones and do not necessarily mirror the conception of art held by the Bijapuri viewers and producers of the works.

6. Unfortunately, the lack of surviving evidence and scholarship regarding decorative arts such as metalwork, woodwork, and textiles from Bijapur prohibited the inclusion of any examples, except in passing, in this study. For a general discussion of the decorative arts of the Deccan, see George Michell and Mark Zebrowski, *Architecture and Art of the Deccan Sultanates*, The New Cambridge History of India 1.7 (Cambridge: Cambridge University Press, 1999), 226–45. For metalwork in particular, see Mark Zebrowski, *Gold, Silver, and Bronze from Mughal India* (London: Alexandria Press and Laurence King, 1997).

7. Robert Skelton, "Documents for the Study of Painting at Bijapur," *Arts Asiatiques* 5, no. 2 (1958): 98.

8. For more information on the downfall of the Adil Shahi dynasty, see H. K. Sherwani and P. M. Joshi, eds., *History of Medieval Deccan, 1295–1724*, 2 vols. (Hyderabad: Government of Andhra Pradesh, 1973–74), 1:371–94.

9. For example, Henry Cousens states that Aurangzeb carried away the bulk of the royal library, but gives no evidence for this statement. Henry Cousens, *Bijapur and Its Architectural Remains: With an Historical Outline of the ʿAdil Shahi Dynasty*. Archaeological Survey of India, New Imperial Series 37 (1916; reprint, Delhi: Bharatiya Publication House, 1976), 94. Quraishi in his study of the royal Bijapur library points out that none of the surviving books from Delhi Library carries any indication of having previously belonged to the Asar Mahal. He goes on to note that, conversely, the Asar Mahal collection contains several manuscripts bearing seals indicating that they were Aurangzeb's and transferred

to the Asar Mahal. Salim al-Din Quraishi, *The Royal Library of Bijapur* (London: India Office Library, 1981), 7.

10. In the Lallgarh Palace at Bikaner is a portrait of Ibrahim Adil Shah II with an inscription in Rajasthani identifying the ruler and stating that it was taken from the Adil Shahi treasury at Adoni in 1691. This corresponds with historical records indicating that the fortress of Adoni fell to Raja Karan Singh of Bikaner at about that time. For a discussion of the painting and its inscription, see Hermann Goetz, *The Art and Architecture of Bikaner State* (Oxford: Oxford University Press, 1950), pl. VIII; and W. G. Archer, "The Problems of Bikaner Paintings," *Marg* 5, no. 1 (1951): 15–16.

11. Quraishi, 7–13, notes that of the approximately 500 surviving manuscripts in the Asar Mahal library's collection, there are no Korans, no histories, and no richly illuminated works. Yet there are copies of very obscure theological works, suggesting that the library had been looted and the most valuable books taken. Quraishi further infers that this was done after 1760 when Bijapur fell to Marathas. In 1853, after the British gained control of Bijapur, they had the remains of the Adil Shahi royal library transferred from the Asar Mahal to the India Office Library in London, where they remain housed. Descriptions of the works can be found in Otto Loth, *Catalogue of the Arabic Manuscripts in the Library of the India Office* (London: India Office Library, 1877), entries denoted with "B"; and Hermann Ethe, *Catalogue of the Persian Manuscripts in the Library of the India Office,* 2 vols. (Oxford: India Office Library, 1903–37), 2:3060–76.

12. *Gazetteer of the Bombay Presidency: Bijapur District* 23 (Bombay: Government Central Press, 1884), 592–93.

13. The author states that he compiled the history, written in Persian, eight years before the occupation of the Maratha region by the British, which would be 1811. Mirza Ibrahim Zubairi, *Basatinu's Salatin,* Persian mss. 1811; printed: Hyderabad: Saiyidi Press, 1892–93. For more information, see Sherwani and Joshi, 2:583–84.

14. English translation: Muhammad Qasim Firishta, *The History of the Rise of the Mahomedan Power in India,* ed. and trans. John Briggs, 4 vols. (London: 1829; reprint in 3 vols., Calcutta: Editions Indian, 1966). Persian text: *Tarikh-i Firishta,* ed. John Briggs and Munshi Mir Khairat Ali Khan Mushtaq (Bombay: Government of Bombay, 1831–32).

15. *Gazetteer,* 598–99 and 612.

16. Captain Philip D. Hart, *Architectural Illustrations of the Principal Mahometan Buildings of Beejapore,* ed. James Fergusson (London, 1859). The earliest British publication on Bijapur's architecture, predating the photographic studies, was probably James Bird, "The Ruined City of Bijapur," *Journal of the Bombay Branch of the Royal Asiatic Society* 1 (1843).

17. Captain Phillip Meadows Taylor and James Fergusson, *Architecture at Bijapoor, an Ancient Mahometan Capital in the Bombay Presidency* (London: Committee of Architectural Antiquities of Western India, 1866).

18. Meadows Taylor, *A Noble Queen: A Romance of Indian History* (London: C. Kegan Paul, 1878); *Tara, a Mahratta Tale* (Edinburgh: W. Blackwood, 1863).

19. Thomas Metcalf, *An Imperial Vision: Indian Architecture and Britain's Raj* (Berkeley: University of California Press, 1989), 35.

20. Fergusson divided "Indo-Sarasenic" architecture into thirteen styles, each associated with an Islamic dynasty. He considered the Mughal style the grandest, and Bijapur and Ahmedabad the best of the regional styles. He said that

Bijapur's buildings were "marked by a grandeur of conception and boldness in construction unequaled by any edifices erected in India." James Fergusson, *History of Indian and Eastern Architecture* (London: 1876, 2nd ed., 1910), 492 and 533.

21. For example, the architects William Emerson and R. F. Chisholm both erected domes in their colonial buildings based on the Bijapur method of construction. Metcalf, 42–44.

22. Ibid., 24–54.

23. Taylor's novels *Noble Queen* and *Tara,* as well as passages in *Architecture at Bijapoor,* are excellent examples of such exoticism.

24. *Gazetteer,* 599–600.

25. Henry Cousens, *Bijapur: The Old Capital of the 'Adil Shahi Kings: A Guide to Its Ruins with Historical Outline* (1889; reprint, Poona: Scottish Mission Industries Company, 1923); Cousens, *Notes on the Buildings and Other Antiquarian Remains at Bijapur,* Archaeological Survey of Western India Reports, Old Series 11a (Bombay: Bombay Government, 1890); and Cousens, *Bijapur and Its Architectural Remains.*

26. Muhammad Nazim, *Bijapur Inscriptions,* Memoirs of the Archeological Survey of India no. 49 (Delhi: Manager of Publications, 1936).

27. While the Archeological Survey of India provides for the upkeep of the most famous monuments such as the Ibrahim Rauza, the Gul Gumbad, and the Gagan Mahal, the other monuments in the city are left to ruin or have been reused. For example, the Anand Mahal is now a government office building. The Sat Manzil is in such bad condition that it has become structurally unstable and can no longer be entered.

28. For a full reconsideration of dating and names given in early scholarship, see my dissertation, Deborah Hutton, "The Elixir of Mirth and Pleasure: The Development of Bijapuri Art, 1565–1635" (University of Minnesota, 2000), 38–41.

29. See Elizabeth Merklinger, *Indian Islamic Architecture: The Deccan, 1374–1686* (Warminster: Aris and Phillips, 1981); George Michell, ed., *Islamic Heritage of the Deccan* (Bombay: Marg, 1986); and Michell and Zebrowski, *Architecture and Art of the Deccan Sultanates.*

30. N. C. Mehta, *Studies in Indian Painting* (Bombay: D. B. Taraporevala and Sons, 1926); Stella Kramrisch, *A Survey of Painting in the Deccan* (London: India Society, 1937); Basil Gray, "Portraits from Bijapur," *British Museum Quarterly* 11 (1937): 183–84; Gray, "Deccani Paintings: The School of Bijapur," *Burlington Magazine* 73 (August 1938): 74–76; Moti Chandra, "Portraits of Ibrahim Adil Shah II," *Marg* 5, no. 1 (1951): 22–28; Skelton, "Documents for the Study of Painting at Bijapur"; Karl Khandalavala, "Five Miniatures from the Collection of Sir Cowasji Jehangir," *Marg* 5, no. 2 (1952): 24–32; Douglas Barrett, *Painting of the Deccan* (London: Faber and Faber, 1958); Barrett, "Some Unpublished Deccan Miniatures," *Lalit Kala* 7 (1960): 8–13; Barrett, "Painting at Bijapur," in *Paintings from Islamic Lands,* ed. R. H. Pinder-Wilson (Oxford: Oxford University Press, 1969), 142–59; Jagdish Mittal, "Painting" in *History of Medieval Deccan, 1295–1724,* ed. H. K. Sherwani and P. M. Joshi (Hyderabad: Government of Andhra Pradesh, 1973–74), 2:201–26; Mittal, "Deccani Paintings as a Source of History," in *Aspects of Deccan History: Report of a Seminar,* ed. V. K. Bawa (Hyderabad: Institute of Asian Studies, 1975); see also *Marg* 16, no. 2 (March 1963), a special volume dedicated to Deccani painting.

31. For example, in 1958 Douglas Barrett attributed the famous yogini painting in the Chester Beatty Library to the kingdom of Golconda, circa 1605. Eleven years later, he revised his opinion based on newly studied paintings and concluded that an artist working for Bijapur produced the painting, still circa 1605. Barrett, "Painting at Bijapur," 157.

32. Most notable is Mark Zebrowski, *Deccani Painting* (Berkeley: University of California Press, 1983).

33. For an in-depth discussion of style, attribution, and dating of Bijapuri painting, see Hutton, "Elixir," 34–38, or Mark Zebrowski, "Indian Subcontinent: S VI, 4 (vi)(b): Deccani Painting Styles, 16th Century–1947: Bijapur," in *The Dictionary of Art,* ed. Jane Turner (New York: Grove's Dictionaries, 1995), 15:638–40.

34. Robert Sewell, *A Forgotten Empire* (1900; reprint, New Delhi: National Book Trust, 1970).

35. See, for example, Ghulam Yazdani, *Bidar, Its History, and Monuments* (Oxford: Oxford University Press, 1947); P. M. Joshi, "Ali ʿAdil Shah I of Bijapur (1558–1580) and His Royal Librarian: Two Ruqas," in *Sardhasatabdi Commemoration Volume* (Bombay, 1955), 97–107, and Joshi, "The Reign of Ibrahim Adil Shah of Bijapur," *Bharatiya Vidya Bhavan* 9 (1948): 284–309; H. K. Sherwani, "Cultural Synthesis in Medieval India," *Journal of India History* 41 (1963): 239–59; and Nazir Ahmad, "Farrukh Husain, the Royal Artist at the Court of Ibrahim Adil Shah II," *Islamic Culture* 30, no. 1 (1956): 31–35; and "Adilshahi Diplomatic Missions to the Court of Shah ʿAbbas," *Islamic Culture* 43, no. 2 (1969): 143–61. The motivation to reconcile Hindu-Muslim relations probably also related to the Indian nationalistic context of the mid-twentieth century and can be read as part of that history.

36. H. K. Sherwani, "Deccani Preludes to Akbar's Social and Economic Reforms," *Islamic Culture* 50, no. 1 (1976): 25–31.

37. David Gilmartin and Bruce B. Lawrence, eds., *Beyond Turk and Hindu: Rethinking Religious Identities in Islamicate South Asia* (Gainesville: University Press of Florida, 2000). Also see Cynthia Talbot, "Inscribing the Other, Inscribing the Self: Hindu-Muslim Identities in Pre-Colonial India," *Comparative Studies in Society and History* 37 (1995): 692–722.

38. Gilmartin and Lawrence, 2. I also have chosen to employ the terms *Islamicate* and *Indic* when appropriate. Therefore, when I use the terms *Muslim* and *Hindu,* I am referring to specifically religious practices. The term *Persian* refers to both linguistic and cultural practices of the larger Iranian world, and *Indian,* as employed here, refers to widely practiced cultural traditions of the Indian subcontinent, including those introduced during Muslim periods of rule.

39. Firishta, 3:22–29, states that in 908 AH/1502–1503 CE on a Friday in the month of Dhul-Hijjah the *khutba,* Friday prayer, was read in the name of the twelve imams.

40. In 1509 Yusuf sent an ambassador with gifts to seek recognition of his rule in Bijapur from Shah Ismail. Such close relationships were maintained throughout the Adil Shahis' reigns. At times the Adil Shahis even characterized themselves as *mansabdars,* or loyal underlings, of the Safavid shahs. Sadiq Naqvi, *The Iran-Deccan Relations* (Hyderabad: Bab-ul-Ilm Society, 1994), 33; Riazul Islam, *A Calendar of Documents on Indo-Persian Relations, 1500–1750* (Iran and Karachi: Iranian Cultural Foundation and Institute on Central and West Asian Studies, 1982), 130–35.

41. Daniela Bredi, "Shiism's Political Valence in Medieval Deccani Kingdoms," in *Islam and Indian Regions,* ed. A. L. Dallapiccola and S. Z. Lallement (Stuttgart: Franz Steiner, 1993), 1:137–53; D. Bredi, F. Coslovi, and B. Scarcia Amoretti, "Shiism in the Deccan: A Hypothetical Study," *Islamic Culture* 57, nos. 2–3 (1988): 97–112.

42. *Afaqis* translates as "foreigners." The makeup between these two groups was complex. For example, while the Habshis, Abyssinians, were not local, they were included with the Deccanis because they were Sunni and were not of Persian ethnicity. For a detailed discussion of the cultural makeup and political conflict between the Deccanis and Afaqis, see Richard Eaton, *Sufis of Bijapur, 1300–1700* (Princeton: Princeton University Press, 1978), 40–43. Discussion of the Habshis' role in the Deccan can be found in Andre Wink, "Islamic Society and Culture in the Deccan," in *Islam and Indian Regions,* ed. A. L. Dallapiccola and S. Z. Lallement (Stuttgart: Franz Steiner, 1993), 1:217–28, and Shanti Sadiq Ali, *The African Dispersal in the Deccan from Medieval to Modern Times* (Hyderabad: Oriental Longman, 1996).

43. Muhammad Quli Qutb Shah founded Hyderabad in 1591. For more information on its founding and architecture, see H. K. Sherwani, *Muhammad-Quli Qutb Shah: Founder of Haidarabad* (Bombay: Asia Publishing House, 1967), 11–31; and Vasant Kumar Bawa, "The Politics of Architecture in Qutb Shahi Hyderabad: A Preliminary Analysis," in *Studies in History of the Deccan, Medieval and Modern, Professor A. R. Kulkarni Felicitation Volume,* ed. M. A. Nayeem, Aniruddha Ray, and K. S. Mathew (Delhi: Pragati, 2002), 329–41.

44. An excellent example of this viewpoint is Hermann Goetz, "The Fall of Vijayanagar and the Nationalization of Muslim Art in the Dakhan," *Journal of Indian History* 19 (1940): 249–55.

45. Phillip B. Wagoner, "'Sultan among Hindu Kings': Dress, Titles, and the Islamicization of Hindu Culture at Vijayanagara," *Journal of Asian Studies* 55, no. 4 (November 1996): 851–80; Catherine B. Asher, "Islamic Influence and the Architecture of Vijayanagara," in *Vijayanagara—City and Empire: New Currents of Research,* ed. A. L. Dallapiccola and S. Z. Lallement, 2 vols. (Wiesbaden: Franz Steiner, 1985), 1:188–95.

46. Firishta, 2:266. See also Phillip B. Wagoner, "Delhi Sultanate in the Political Imagination of Vijayanagara," in *Beyond Turk and Hindu: Rethinking Religious Identities in Islamicate South Asia,* ed. David Gilmartin and Bruce B. Lawrence (Gainesville: University Press of Florida, 2000), 315–19.

47. The term Maratha evolved between about 1400 and 1600 and referred to a specific soldier group from Maharashtra, who played a role similar to that of Rajputs in Rajasthan.

48. Stewart Gordon, *The Marathas, 1600–1818,* New Cambridge History of India 2:4 (Cambridge: Cambridge University Press, 1993), 14–19.

49. Masʿud Husain Khan, "Dakhni-Urdu," in *History of Medieval Deccan, 1295–1724,* ed. H. K. Sherwani and P. M. Joshi (Hyderabad: Government of Andhra Pradesh, 1973–74), 2:19–20. Correspondingly, the Maharashtran administrators adopted many Persian linguistic elements into Marathi. One linguistic analysis of the Persian influence on seventeenth-century Marathi found that nearly forty percent of the words used by the Marathi courtiers were Persian. Eaton, *Sufis of Bijapur,* 91–92.

50. Firishta, 3:4–5, states that Yusuf was the son of Murad II, the Ottoman sultan (r. 1421–51), and he escaped Turkey to avoid being put to death by his

older brother. This story, although often repeated, is not supported in Ottoman histories or other Adil Shahi histories. It is more likely that he came from Central Asia.

51. Firishta, 3:30–31, states that Yusuf "invited to his court many learned men and valiant officers from Persia, Turkistan, and Rum who lived happily under the shadow of his bounty."

52. Eaton, *Sufis of Bijapur,* 95–97.

53. Carl W. Ernst, *Eternal Garden: Mysticism, History, and Politics at a South Asian Sufi Center* (Albany: State University of New York Press, 1992), 20–21.

54. Glenn D. Lowry and Susan Nemazee, *A Jeweler's Eye: Islamic Arts of the Book from the Vever Collection* (Washington, D.C., and Seattle: Arthur M. Sackler Gallery and the University of Washington Press, 1988), 201.

55. John Seyller, "Indian Subcontinent, S XII, 2: Patronage: Painting," in *The Dictionary of Art,* ed. Jane Turner (New York: Grove's Dictionaries, 1995), 15:739–40.

56. For example, see Catherine Asher, "The Architecture of Raja Man Singh: A Study of Sub-Imperial Patronage," in *The Powers of Art: Patronage in Indian Culture,* ed. Barbara Stoler Miller (Delhi: Oxford University Press, 1992), 183–201, and D. Fairchild Ruggles, ed., *Women, Patronage, and Self-Representation in Islamic Societies* (Albany: State University of New York Press, 2000).

57. Rafi uddin Shirazi, *Tazkira al-Mulk,* Persian mss., circa 1608–35, Salar Jung Museum, Hyderabad, Tarikh no. 142.

58. Carl W. Ernst, "Admiring the Works of the Ancients: The Ellora Temples as Viewed by Indo-Muslim Authors," in *Beyond Turk and Hindu: Rethinking Religious Identities in Islamicate South Asia,* ed. David Gilmartin and Bruce B. Lawrence (Gainesville: University Press of Florida, 2000), 98–120. Quote from page 108.

59. Ibid., 104–105.

60. K. A. Nizami, "Sufi Movement in the Deccan," in *History of Medieval Deccan, 1295–1724,* ed. H. K. Sherwani and P. M. Joshi (Hyderabad: Government of Andhra Pradesh, 1973–74), 2:182.

61. For example, at the large and popular *dargah* of Gisudaraz in Gulbarga, Afzal Khan, a noble at the Adil Shahi court, constructed a mosque in the mid-seventeenth century. For a further discussion of this mosque and other Bijapur additions to the *dargah* of Gesudaraz, see Merklinger, 127–30.

62. Firishta, 3:22–24, claims that Yusuf declared himself Shah, but epigraphic evidence shows that Yusuf referred to himself as Khan. The earliest inscription that uses the title Shah dates to 945 AH (1538–39 CE), during the reign of Ibrahim I, and the same year that the final Bahmani shah, Kalimullah, died. Nazim, 26–27.

2. Prosperous Beginnings

1. In addition to the 1570–71 *Nujum al-Ulum* discussed in this study, the surviving works datable to the 1570s include two pages from a *Materia Medica* manuscript, one in the Freer Gallery (V34.98) and another in the Sir Howard Hodgkin Collection, London; several copies (or folios from copies) of the celebrated thirteenth-century scholar al-Qazvini's astrological work, *Ajaib al-Makhluqat,* including one complete manuscript in the British Library containing an inscription identifying the patron as Kamal al-din Husayn, an Adil Shahi

courtier; as well as the *Rasapradipa tika* in the Jaipur City Palace Museum's collection and the *Javahir al-Musiqat,* in the British Library (Or. 12857), both Bijapuri illustrated manuscripts on music and dance written in local languages.

2. Zubairi, 136.

3. The size of Ali's military force doubled that of his predecessor and was not significantly surpassed by any of his successors. Eaton, *Sufis of Bijapur,* 83–87.

4. Marshall Hodgson, *The Venture of Islam,* 3 vols. (Chicago: University of Chicago Press, 1974), 2:5.

5. Zubairi, 113, states that the project was completed in three years. Firishta and Astarabadi write that the city wall was completed in just two years, in 1567, letting us know that the work began in 1565. Therefore, I date the project primarily to 1565–68. Firishta, 3:132; Fuzuni Astarabadi, *Futuhat-i Adil Shahi,* Persian mss., 1640–43, British Library, London, Add. 27.251, 123–24v.

6. I have made use of Briggs's translation of Firishta and various scholars' translations of passages of Zubairi, Shirazi, and Astarabadi when available. When employed, these translations are credited in the footnotes. Otherwise, I consulted the original Persian texts, and any translations, interpretations, and mistakes are my own. Three manuscript copies of Rafi uddin Shirazi's *Tazkira al-Mulk* exist. One is housed in the Salar Jung Museum, Hyderabad (Tarikh no. 142), the second in the Asafiyah Library, Hyderabad (Tarikh no. 1081), and the third in the British Museum, London (Add. 23,883). For my translations, I made use of the Salar Jung's manuscript.

7. Zubairi, 111.

8. For a further description of Bijapur's geographical setting, see K. Rotzer, "Bijapur: Alimentation en eau d'une ville Musulmane du Dekkan aux XVI–XVII Siecles," *Bulletin de l'Ecole Francaise d'Extreme-Orient* 73 (1984): 133–35. Precisely when people first settled Bijapur is unclear. The remains of several Hindu temples are the earliest datable architecture. Inscriptions on them record that Bijapur, or Vijayapur, "City of Victory," as it was called, was a minor regional center for the Western Chalukya dynasty from the eleventh through thirteenth centuries. Bijapur then became one of the centers of the Yadava dynasty that fell to the forces of Ala al-Din Khalji in 1294. The city's oldest mosque, built of reused Hindu temple pillars and surrounding a Sufi shrine, dates to 1320. After 1347, when the Bahmani dynasty came to power in the Deccan, the importance of Bijapur increased. Two mosques, both inside the area of the citadel and built from reused Hindu pillars, remain from this period. This includes the Malik Karim al-Din mosque, with an inscription stating that Malik erected the upper part of the mosque in 1320 and that the architect Revoya of Salhasdage carried out the work. The second mosque, located 400 yards due north of the first, is the Khawajah Jahan mosque, constructed from old Hindu pillars during the late fifteenth century. For further discussion of Bijapur's early architecture, see Cousens, *Bijapur and Its Architectural Remains,* 40–43.

9. *Gazetteer,* 573–74; Rotzer, 135. This may have been because the depression allowed easy access to groundwater.

10. Cousens, *Bijapur and Its Architectural Remains,* 26.

11. The first mosque is called both Yusuf's old jami mosque and Asen Beg's mosque, referring to Ismail Adil Shah's full name, Asen Beg Naib Ghaibat Adil Khan. It is the earliest surviving building dated by an inscription (918 AH/1512 CE). Ibrahim's old jami masjid, as the latter mosque is called, is datable on stylistic evidence to 1550. Merklinger, 119.

12. Firishta, 3:116.

13. The water tank in front of the Gagan Mahal no longer survives, having been filled in during the nineteenth century. Gagan Mahal, meaning Sky or Heavenly Palace, was a common name given to palaces in the eighteenth and nineteenth centuries. Thus it is unclear whether or not it was the original name of the building. The contemporary histories mention that Ali built a *mahal* in 1560–61, but give no specific name.

14. The Gagan Mahal continues to be preserved as the focus of Bijapur's royal citadel, but its corresponding entranceway underwent a nineteenth-century British conversion into the All Saints Church.

15. John Correia-Afonso, "Bijapur Four Centuries Ago as Described in a Contemporary Letter," *Indica* 1 (March 1964): 84.

16. Ali Adil Shah fares markedly better than Bijapur under Rodriguez's scrutiny. He writes glowingly, "This king is well conditioned, such a gentleman and very literal and magnanimous, the most well bred prince that I have seen. He maintains a great state and courtly nobility. He goes about accompanied by many soldiers and when we go to the palace so many are the meetings with crowds of people that Lisbon's Rua Nova does not have the advantage in the matter." Correia-Afonso, 86.

17. Rodriguez describes staying in tents in the gardens of nobles while visiting Bijapur because there was not a house for them to stay in. Correia-Afonso, 86–87.

18. In fact, the earliest inscription in which Ibrahim Adil Shah used the title "Shah" rather than "Khan" is located on the citadel wall. It is dated to 945 AH. Nazim, 47–48.

19. Zubairi, 111; Astarabadi, 123v.

20. Zubairi as translated in K. K. Basu, "A Chapter in the Reign of 'Ali 'Adil Shah of Bijapur," in *A Volume of Indian and Iranian Studies,* ed. S. M. Katre and P. K. Gode (Bombay, 1939), 3–4.

21. Basu, 4, states that the west gate was named after Mecca, while the rest were named after adjacent villages.

22. *Gazetteer,* 568.

23. Zubairi, 112. This patronage system, termed *alang,* was a common approach to building fortification walls in much of the Islamicate world.

24. Nazim, 49–50.

25. Zubairi, 112; Astarabadi, 124.

26. Zubairi states that nobles built houses near the three gardens after their completion. Basu, "A Chapter in the Reign of 'Ali 'Adil Shah," 4.

27. Zubairi, 112, uses the term *qariz,* not *qanat,* to refer to the underground canals.

28. *Gazetteer,* 579–80. Remnants of the second branch of the canal no longer exist.

29. Rotzer, 194; Zubairi, 112–13; Astarabadi, 124v.

30. Heinz Gaube, *Iranian Cities* (New York: New York University Press, 1979), 6.

31. Cousens, *Bijapur and Its Architectural Remains,* 121; Merklinger, 122.

32. Firishta, 3:143; Astarabadi, 124v. Additionally, in 1579 either Sultan Ali or his wife, Chand Bibi, had a large step well built inside the city, near the Shahpur Darwaza. This section of the city housed many of the lower classes, and the large tank, called the Chand Bauri, provided the local population with fresh water for their daily use. Cousens, *Bijapur and Its Architectural Remains,* 124.

33. Zubairi, 113. Shahpur also seems to have functioned as a production center for export goods. Eaton, *Sufis of Bijapur,* 87, states that artisans working on textiles for export were living in Shahpur during this period.

34. Zubairi, 113. The names given to the gardens can be read in two ways: one that stresses their Shia significance and another that does not. On the one hand, we can interpret "Ali" as referring to the Shia Imam Ali, "Alawi" as referring to descendants of the Imam Ali, and "Dwazdah Imam" as referring to the twelve imams. On the other hand, the name "Bagh-i Ali" could refer simply to Sultan Ali, Alawi means "sublime," and as mentioned, the last garden, the Dwazdah Imam, also was called the Bagh-i Darwaza, referring to its location.

35. Zubairi, 113; Astarabadi, 124v.

36. Cousens, *Bijapur and Its Architectural Remains,* 58–59, gives the construction date of the jami masjid as 1576, based on an unnamed source, and most subsequent studies of Bijapuri architecture repeat this date. Nazim, 17, for unspecified reasons gives a beginning construction date of 1537. The Persian historians, however, include the mosque as part of the 1565–68 building campaign and by doing so suggest it was begun by 1568, hence my dating of the structure. In any case, it clearly was an ongoing, long-term project. In 1636 Malik Yaqub, a member of Muhammad Adil Shah's nobility, patronized the elaborate *mihrab* that exists today, and the Mughal emperor Aurangzeb, after conquering Bijapur, built the eastern gateway and extended the courtyard ninety-five feet. Despite such attention, the last of the three arcades surrounding the courtyard was never finished, the two minarets intended to flank the façade of the prayer chamber were never built, and the parapet meant to crown the walls remains incomplete.

37. Merklinger, 119.

38. Cousens, *Bijapur and Its Architectural Remains,* 57, states that the mosque was "a permanent memorial of the great victory of Islam over the vast infidel kingdom of the south."

39. Merklinger, 32.

40. Zubairi, 113.

41. Firishta, 3:116.

42. Gaube, 11.

43. Sheila Blair, "Islamic Art: S II, 10 (ii): Urban Development: Eastern Islamic Lands," in *The Dictionary of Art,* ed. Jane Turner (New York: Grove's Dictionaries, 1995), 16:264–65.

44. Numerous inscriptions on the city walls record these improvements. See Nazim, 50–57.

45. Even Henry Cousens, who diligently recorded every Adil Shahi structure, large or small, said of the tomb, "There is very little about the building that calls for remark save its severe plainness." Cousens, *Bijapur and Its Architectural Remains,* 54.

46. Firishta, 3:143, mentions the tomb in his discussion of Ali's reign, and stylistically the tomb relates to structures built between 1570 and 1590. Most secondary sources date the tomb to circa 1580 and attribute it to Ali's patronage. See, for example, Cousens, *Bijapur and Its Architectural Remains,* 53–54; Merklinger, 121; Z. A. Desai, "Architecture," in *History of Medieval Deccan, 1295–1724,* ed. H. K. Sherwani and P. M. Joshi (Hyderabad: Government of Andhra Pradesh, 1973–74), 2:284.

47. Without contemporary written confirmation, determining whether painted ornamentation is original or a later addition proves difficult. In this case

I feel confident that the painting is original in large part because the painted ornamentation does not appear to have been touched up or restored in any way. In fact, in person it is extremely difficult to see the inscriptions and decoration. I employed photographic filters and computer enhancement to bring out the remnants.

48. For example, see Merklinger, 121. There are other theories as well. Cousens suggests that Ali devoted all his resources to the building up of Bijapur and had none left for his tomb. The authors of the *Gazetteer of the Bombay Presidency: Bijapur District* saw its humble appearance as evidence that the tomb was built after Ali's death by a later Sunni relative who did not want to honor a heretical Shia ancestor but felt compelled to build something. Cousens, *Bijapur and Its Architectural Remains,* 53–54; *Gazetteer,* 613.

49. For example, the tomb of Shaykh Muhammad Ghauth at Gwalior (d. 1563) consists of an inner chamber surrounded by an arcade, as does the tomb of Shaykh Salim Chishti (1580–81) at Fatehpur Sikri. The plan was particularly popular in Gujarati architecture, as exemplified by the tomb of Shah Alam at Ahmedabad (1531–32).

50. Merklinger, 121, in her comprehensive survey of the Islamic monuments in the Deccan, confirms that Ali's tomb was the first in the region to employ this plan.

51. The site continued to be built up during Ali's reign. For example, Fatima Sultan built a mosque there. *Hyderabad: A Guide to Art and Architecture* (Hyderabad: Publications Division, Ministry of Information and Broadcasting, Government of India, 1951), 44.

52. Merklinger, 121.

53. One source lists that during the Adil Shah dynasty, ninety-six Sufis were buried within the city walls. Saiyid Muhyi al-Din bin Mahmud Qadiri, *Sahifat-i Ahl-i Huda,* ed. and trans. M. Akbaruddin Siddiqi (Hyderabad: National Fine Printing Press, 1966), 12–16.

54. The local inhabitants with whom I spoke said that this section of the city was traditionally where Sufis were buried, but that the tombs were not kept up as well as the tombs in other areas.

55. For example, the mosque and tomb of a popular local saint from the Adil Shahi period, Hazrat Ali Shahid Pir, is not far from Ali's tomb. Some secondary sources believe that Sultan Ali, who was a supporter of the saint, sponsored the construction of the mosque during the latter half of the sixteenth century. See Merklinger, 120, and Cousens, *Bijapur and Its Architectural Remains,* 62–63. Immediately across from Ali's tomb exists an unidentified mosque and tomb that provides another possible link. The mosque, dating roughly to the sixteenth or seventeenth century, is well kept up and frequently whitewashed, but the adjacent tomb has been left to ruin. Local Bijapuri inhabitants today associated the mosque and tomb with a local Sufi, although I received conflicting reports regarding the Sufi's identity.

56. See Cousens, *Bijapur and Its Architectural Remains,* 80, for further discussion of the building and its dating. The well, named Gumat Bauri, contains an inscription stating that "Sitti Fatimah Salmansitti" constructed it. Part of the inscription reads as follows: "This Bauri was the way of Allah by Fatima Sultan Bibi, the queen of the world, may she [enjoy] exalted ranks in both the worlds! [in] Shahur Sana 962, on the 25th of the month of Dhul-Hijjah, 970. The water of this Bauri is a *waqf.*" Nazim, 65, points out that the inscription gives two dates,

corresponding with May 25, 1561, and August 15, 1563, although the reason for this is unclear.

57. B. D. Verma, "'Adil Shahi Epigraphy in the Deccan (Miraj and Kolhapur)," *Journal of the University of Bombay* 8 (1939): 14. Sherwani and Joshi, 1:396, claim that Ali called himself Adil Shah Sufi.

58. Sherwani and Joshi, 1:282.

59. George Michell and Richard Eaton, *Firuzabad, Palace City of the Deccan,* Oxford Studies in Islamic Art 8 (Oxford: Oxford University Press, 1992), 14–15.

60. Moojan Momen, *An Introduction to Shii Islam: The History and Doctrines of Twelver Shiism* (London: G. Ronald, 1985), 208–209; J. Spencer Trimingham, *The Sufi Orders in Islam* (Oxford: Oxford University Press, 1971), 133–37.

61. The Safavid dynasty began as a Sufi order, the Safaviyyah. However, once they declared themselves Shia, in 1501–1502, just a year before the Adil Shahis did, an increasing hostility developed between the court and Sufis. The Safavid shah's power relied in large part on the belief that he was the living embodiment of the perfect man, so he could not afford to recognize another leader as a perfect man. This included Sufi saints. For further discussion, see Kathryn Babayan, "Sufis, Dervishes, and Mullas: The Controversy over Spiritual and Temporal Dominion in Seventeenth-Century Iran," in *Safavid Persia,* ed. Charles Melville (London: I. B. Tauris, 1996), 117–38. For discussion of the impact of Safavid persecution on Bijapur's Sufi emigration, see Eaton, *Sufis of Bijapur,* 66.

62. For example, Eaton, *Sufis of Bijapur,* 62–70, accounts for the disparity between the large number of Sufis, 27, documented to have migrated to Bijapur during Ibrahim Adil Shah II's reign and the one sole immigrant Sufi documented during Ali's reign as a result of the two rulers' religious views. However, as the authors Bredi, Coslovi and Scarcia Amoretti point out, the development of Shiism in the Deccan has yet to be studied thoroughly. Therefore, many assumptions made about Shia rulers such as Ali Adil Shah may need reconsideration. A painting attributed to Bijapur, circa 1610–20, seems to further this viewpoint. *Dervish receiving a visitor* (Bodleian Library, Oxford, Ms. Douce Or. b.2(1), fol. 1a) depicts, as its title suggests, a Sufi receiving visitors at his *dargah* (shrine). The painting shows the dervish sitting cross-legged on a stone platform, visitors paying homage to him in the foreground, and an oversized, white parrot perched on a bush that grows from the stone. Notably four metal standards sit to the left of the platform. These standards are *alams,* copies of the standards carried by the Shia martyr Husayn and unmistakable symbols of the Shia faith. Thus we have another example, this time painting rather than architecture, in which links to both Shiism and Sufism are expressed at the same time and without any apparent contradiction. For a more detailed discussion of the painting, see Zebrowski, *Deccani Painting,* 78–81.

63. Some accounts list the *Nujum al-Ulum*'s illustrations as approximately four hundred in number, rather than nearly eight hundred, the difference resulting from whether or not certain images are counted in groups. Additionally, at some point the manuscript was rebound, resulting in a few folios being lost and others put back in the wrong order.

64. The inscriptions are found on folios 171, 334, and 348v.

65. The *Nujum al-Ulum* was one of the first examples of Deccani painting identified by modern scholars. Yet, despite frequent mention in various studies

of Indo-Islamic painting, Linda Leach's 1995 discussion of the *Nujum al-Ulum* was the first in-depth consideration of the manuscript. Crucially, Leach's study fully explores the text/image relationship through a careful reading of each, and my analysis draws on her groundwork. Linda Leach, *Mughal and Other Indian Paintings from the Chester Beatty Library* (London: Scorpion Cavedish, 1995), 819–89.

66. As quoted in Zebrowski, *Deccani Painting,* 61.

67. Joshi, "'Ali 'Adil Shah I of Bijapur (1558–1580) and His Royal Librarian: Two Ruqas," 97–107.

68. For a discussion of the copy in the Chester Beatty Library, see Leach, 891–903. For information on the Wellcome Library's copy, see Sergei Tourkin, "Astrological Images in Two Persian Manuscripts," in *Pearls of the Orient: Asian Treasures from the Wellcome Library,* ed. Nigel Allen (London and Chicago: Serindia Publications and the Wellcome Trust, 2003), 73–85. Tourkin does not identify the manuscript (Persian MS 373) as a copy of the *Nujum,* but based on the illustrations, particularly those of the Sun, Mars, and Venus, it clearly is one. I would like to thank Catherine Asher for bringing this manuscript to my attention.

69. Leach, 819–20.

70. Ibid., 830. In the *Kitab al-Burhan,* a fourteenth-century Arabic astrological manuscript, similar illustrations of simple scenes depict the activities associated with each planet. Stefano Carboni, *Il Kitab al-bulhan di Oxford* (Torino: Editrice Tirrenia Stampatori, 1988), Tav. 13. The paintings of the degrees in the *Nujum al-Ulum* may have functioned in a similar manner.

71. The text on the horses is concerned chiefly with listing their colors, yet in the majority of the miniatures, the horses were painted the wrong colors. The artists painted horses described as being blue and amber in the text as dark and light gray. Leach, 885.

72. The clothes worn by the figures often provide the only Indian elements in these paintings as they tend to be a mixture of Indic and Persian types.

73. For discussion of the 1547 translation, see Sherwani and Joshi, 1:396. Two illustrated folios from a manuscript of al-Qazvini's *Ajaib al-Makhluqat,* Bijapur, circa 1570, are in the Los Angeles County Museum of Art (M.73.5.585 and M.88.213.8). The San Diego Museum of Art houses another two folios from perhaps the same manuscript. See Pratapaditya Pal, *Indian Painting: A Catalogue of the Los Angeles County Museum of Art Collection* (New York and Los Angeles: Harry N. Abrams and the Los Angeles County Museum of Art, 1993), 317–18; and Edwin Binney, *Indian Miniature Painting from the Collection of Edwin Binney 3rd: The Mughal and Deccani Schools* (Portland, Ore.: Portland Art Museum, 1973), 152.

74. An inscription in Mecca describes Kamal ad-Din Husayn as a collector of books. He served as a courtier at Golconda until 1565, when he moved to Bijapur. Pal, *Indian Painting,* 318.

75. Eva R. Hoffman, "Islamic Art, S III, 4(ii)(a): Painted Book Illustration: Subject-Matter: Scientific and Technical Works," in *The Dictionary of Art,* ed. Jane Turner (New York: Grove's Dictionaries, 1995), 16:297–99.

76. For further discussion of the *Javahir al-Musiqat* and reproductions of its illustrations, see Zebrowski, *Deccani Painting,* 63–66.

77. Leach, 846.

78. There are not very many surviving works describing these spells. A

nineteenth-century work on conjuration also was written in Bijapur. For more information, see J. Sharif, *Islam in India,* trans. G. A. Herklots (Oxford: Oxford University Press, 1921), 219. As Leach, 846–47, explains, the author of the *Nujum al-Ulum* does cite an older source, the Imam Mumammad Siraj al-Din Sakaki, a contemporary of al-Qazvini, for the information provided in this section; however, the attribution is probably more traditional than accurate.

79. Francis J. Steingass, *A Comprehensive Persian-English Dictionary, Including the Arabic Words and Phrases to Be Met within Persian Literature* (Beirut: Librarie du Liban, 1970), 1325. My sincere thanks to James Hoover for his enlightening discussion on the meaning and possible etymologies of the term.

80. Leach, 852–53. It should be noted that the Persian term *charkh,* meaning circle, is very close to the Sanskrit term *chakra.* Because of its complexity and richness, the *Nujum al-Ulum*'s text deserves close study by a linguistic expert. Such an analysis surely would shed light on the textual subtleties and the meanings of some of the more esoteric practices and diagrams.

81. The early Hindu monarch, Samudragupta, was called a *chakravartin,* and the Jains believed that each age would see twelve chakravartins rule. H. Zimmer, *Philosophies of India* (Princeton: Princeton University Press, 1951), 129–36.

82. In his study of Tantrism, H. C. Das explains that originally the movement was believed to have been concentrated in four centers, each of which had a goddess associated with it. Over time the goddesses and places of pilgrimage grew in number. One of the original four places is Tuljapur (also referred to as Tulja Bhabani and Purnagiri in various texts), located near Bijapur. The goddess of this shrine is called Bhavani, the feminine counterpart of Bhava, one of the eight forms of the god Rudra. The *Nujum al-Ulum* includes Bhavani as the forty-sixth *ruhani.* Despite her local significance, the author does not indicate that she had any special significance for Bijapur, although it may explain why these goddesses were popular in the Bijapur region and included in the manuscript. H. C. Das, *Tantricism: A Study of the Yogini Cult* (New Delhi: Sterling, 1981), 5–6; also see D. C. Sicar, "The Saktapithas," *Journal of the Royal Asiatic Society of Bengal* 14 (1948): 17–21.

83. Das, 1.

84. Leach, 862.

85. Carboni, Tav. 19–26.

86. Leach, 862.

87. Unfortunately, the author does not mention the specific source or sources on which the information is based; however, the specificity of this section contrasts with other portions of the text in which the theories presented are sometimes vague. This suggests the author had a direct source for the ruhani information. Leach, 862.

88. Leach, 824; Goetz, "The Fall of Vijayanagar and the Nationalization of Muslim Art in the Dakhan."

89. Nora Titley, *Persian Miniature Painting and Its Influence on the Art of Turkey and India* (Austin: University of Texas Press, 1983), 80, 239, 241, 244, 246.

90. In his study of dress at Vijayanagara, Phillip Wagoner concludes that courtly dress incorporated many Islamicate elements as part of the larger process of Islamicization of Hindu culture at the court. He identifies the tall, conical caps found in the Jupiter image as well as in Vijayanagaran wall paintings as *kullayi,* and points out that a ceiling painting in the Virabhadra Temple at Lepak-

shi, dating to the 1530s, depicts a group of courtiers dressed in the same fashion as the lead figures in the Jupiter painting. Wagoner, "Sultan among Hindu Kings," 856–57.

91. The *Tarif-i Husain Shahi,* an illustrated manuscript produced in Ahmadnagar in 1565–69, provides a useful comparison to the Jupiter image. The manuscript, today housed in the Bharata Itihasa Samshodhaka Mandala, Pune, glorifies the Nizam Shah ruler Husayn and his wife, Khanzada Humayun, including recounting the Deccan sultanates' joint victory over Vijayanagara in 1565. The paintings depict the sultans with attendants and soldiers, as well as the Vijayanagara ruler, Ramraj, with his attendants and soldiers. For further discussion of the *Tarif-i Husain Shahi,* see Zebrowski, *Deccani Painting,* 17–19.

92. Another illustration, on folio 179, provides a diagrammatic rendering of the seven-storied throne. Each of the seven levels consists of squares containing Persian inscriptions. The meaning of the inscriptions as they relate to the pictorial representation of the seven-storied throne still needs to be fully probed; nonetheless, the centrality of the seven-storied throne is clear.

93. J. Irwin, "Asokan Pillars: A Reassessment of the Evidence," *Burlington Magazine* 115 (November 1973): 706–20; "Part II, Structure," 116 (December 1974): 712–15; "Part III, Capitals," 117 (October 1975): 631–43; "Part IV, Symbolism," 118 (November 1976): 734–53.

94. Zebrowski, *Gold, Silver, and Bronze,* 95–107. George Michell has shown that the *yali* was a popular motif in Vijayanagaran architecture. George Michell, *Architecture and Art of Southern India: Vijayanagara and the Successor States,* New Cambridge History of India 1.6 (Cambridge: Cambridge University Press, 1995), 273–75.

95. Leach, 857. The manuscript's makers also included a diagrammatic rendering of the eight-petal lotus immediately preceding the throne painting, further indicating its importance.

96. In early bronze and iron statues from the Deccan, depictions of *yalis* frequently show them swallowing or trampling on tiny elephants. In later examples, rather than being trampled, the elephants seem to be supporting the lion, just as in the *Nujum*'s throne painting. The exact significance of this motif is unclear, but it does seem to have been widespread in Bijapur. Zebrowski, *Gold, Silver, and Bronze,* 104–107.

97. The object, datable to the sixteenth or seventeenth century, is #442 in the museum. Another example is a large metal fountain recently acquired by the Metropolitan Museum of Art (1997.150). The fountain, attributed to the early seventeenth-century Deccan, probably Bijapur, consists of a bell-shaped double lotus body with a lion mask (*kirtimukha*) spout.

98. Correia-Afonso, 84; Firishta, 3:132.

99. Leach, 820.

3. Developing Visual Metaphors

1. Chandra, 24. Some sources also refer to the work, consisting of fifty-nine songs, as the *Nauras Nama.* The date and authorship of the work is ambiguous, but generally scholars believe it to have been composed between 1590 and 1600 by the sultan. Ibrahim Adil Shah II, *Kitab-i Nauras,* ed. and trans. Nazir Ahmad (New Delhi: Bharatiya Kala Kendra, 1956).

2. Shirazi, 101.

3. For example, the poet Zuhuri composed several panegyric works about Ibrahim II and life at court, including the *Gulzar-i Ibrahim,* the *Khan-i Khalil,* and the *Nauras,* a Persian introduction to Ibrahim's *Kitab-i Nauras.* Zuhuri's three works often are grouped together as a trilogy entitled *Sehr Nathr* (*The Three Essays*). For a complete translation of Zuhuri's *Sehr Nathr,* see Muhammad 'Abdul Ghani, ed. and trans., *A History of Persian Language and Literature at the Mughal Court* (Allahabad: Indian Press, 1930), vol. 3, appendixes A–C, 323–467.

4. There are several stories regarding Ali's murder. See Sherwani and Joshi, 1:335–36.

5. For more details on the intrigues of this period, see ibid., 1:337–46.

6. Eaton, *Sufis of Bijapur,* 90.

7. Sherwani and Joshi, 1:346–48.

8. The Mughal ambassador, Asad Beg, went to Bijapur to expedite the marriage arrangements. He records this visit and the arrangements in his account, *Wikaya-i Asad Beg.* See P. M. Joshi, "Asad Beg's Mission to Bijapur, 1603–1604," in *Prof. D. V. Potdar 61st Birthday Commemoration Volume,* ed. S. Sen (Poona, 1950), 181–96.

9. Zuhuri left the Safavid court of Shah Abbas in 1580–81 and worked at Ahmadnagar until 1601, when he fled to the more stable environment of Bijapur. Similarly the historian Muhammad Qasim Firishta traveled from Persia to Bijapur via Ahmadnagar in 1591. It seems likely that, although undocumented, artists also migrated from Ahmadnagar to Bijapur as the situation at the Nizam Shah court deteriorated. A discernable increase in the refinement of Bijapuri painting during the beginning of the seventeenth century corroborates this hypothesis.

10. Islam, 131–35; Nazir Ahmad, "Adil Shahi Diplomatic Mission to the Court of Shah 'Abbas," *Islamic Culture* (1969): 143–61.

11. For more information on the rise of Malik Ambar and Ibrahim II's difficulties with him, see Sherwani and Joshi, 1:345–50.

12. The three exceptions are folios 177v, 178v, and 184. Additionally, J. F. Blumhardt concluded that the manuscript originally contained three more illustrations, which would have increased the total to thirty-seven. J. F. Blumhardt, *Catalogue of the Hindi, Panjabi, and Hindustani Manuscripts in the Library of the British Museum* (London: British Museum, 1932), 57.

13. A production date in the 1590s through early 1600s is upheld when the paintings in the *Pem Nem* are compared with other Bijapuri paintings from the same period. For example, images of the prince from the *Pem Nem* are strikingly similar to a circa 1600 single-page painting housed in the Victoria and Albert Museum, London (IS 2–1969). The work features a young Persianate prince holding flowers and seated on a throne in the countryside. For other interpretations of the manuscript's date, see Blumhardt, 57; Barrett, "Painting at Bijapur," 143–45; Zebrowski, *Deccani Painting,* 103; Jeremy Losty, *The Art of the Book in India* (London: British Library, 1982), 73.

14. The manuscript is also sometimes referred to as *Ratan Sen* after the name of the main character.

15. For further discussion of composite nature of the *Prem Marg* type, see Behl and Weightman, xiii–xvii. The genre seems to have been popular in the sixteenth- and seventeenth-century Deccan, as illustrated by the composition of not only the *Pem Nem* but also a love *masnavi* entitled *Qutb Mushtari.* Mulla Wajhi,

a poet at Bijapur's neighboring kingdom, Golconda, wrote the work in Deccani Urdu in 1609, just a decade or so after the *Pem Nem*'s production. Although the *Qutb Mushtari*'s main character is the Golcondan ruler Muhammad Quli Qutb Shah (r. 1580–1611), the story is purely fictional, and the plot is similar to that of the *Pem Nem.* One night the young prince dreams of the princess of Bengal. He falls madly in love and sets out to find her. After many obstacles, he eventually meets the princess and they are married. Khan, "Dakhni-Urdu," 2:24.

16. David Gordon White, *The Alchemical Body: Siddha Traditions in Medieval India* (Chicago: University of Chicago Press, 1996), 238. For a translation of Jayasi's *Padmavati,* see Lakshmi Dhar, *Padmavati* (London: Luzac, 1949).

17. He is already heartsick, as is evident by the face of his beloved drawn on his heart. It may be that he has fallen in love with the yogini playing the *veena,* for one common twist in later Sufic love stories is that the heroine disguises herself as a yogini and goes out into the countryside. When the faces of the princess and the yogini completed by the same artist ("Hand A") are compared, there are similarities suggesting that they represent the same person; however, any conclusions remain speculative until the manuscript is fully translated.

18. For a more complete discussion of dress, colors, and style in Bijapuri paintings, see Hutton, "Elixir," 36.

19. Barrett, "Painting at Bijapur," 146–58, was the first to take up this issue. He assigns eighteen paintings to Hand A (folios 46, 47, 49v, 69, 75v, 80, 82v, 89v, 119, 138, 181v, 183, 197v, 210, 213v, 215, 219, and 232), fourteen paintings to Hand B (folios 90v, 135, 147, 166, 171, 172, 176, 177v, 178v, 184, 202, 206, and 224v), and two paintings to Hand C (folios 70v and 87). Losty, *Art of the Book in India,* 73, identifies fourteen paintings by Hand A (folios 46, 49v, 69, 75v, 82v, 119, 181v, 183, 197v, 210, 213v, 215, 219, and 232), fifteen by Hand B (folios 80, 90v, 135, 147, 166, 168, 171, 172, 176, 177v, 178v, 184, 202, 206, and 224v), and five by Hand C (folios 47, 70v, 87, 89v, and 138). I agree with all of Losty's attributions except for folio 47, which I believe was done by Hand A rather than Hand C.

20. Scholarship often refers to Hand A as "the Dublin painter" because of the yogini painting he is believed to have painted that is now housed in the Chester Beatty Library. For further discussion of this painter, see Zebrowski, *Deccani Painting,* 103–12.

21. Unfortunately, because the text has not been fully translated, we cannot yet connect the image to the direct poetic metaphor used in the *Pem Nem,* although the image certainly fits the type of metaphors used in Sufic love poems. For example, in one verse of Jayasi's *Padmavati,* Ratan Sen says to Padmavati, "O lady, this heart is so attached to thee (that) both during the day and throughout the night it is by thy side." Dhar, 168.

22. For a discussion of the conventions used in Persianate painting, see Oleg Grabar, *Mostly Miniatures: An Introduction to Persian Painting* (Princeton: Princeton University Press, 1999), 127–37.

23. Behl and Weightman, xvi.

24. Annemarie Schimmel, "Inner and Outer Space in Islam," in *Concepts of Space Ancient and Modern,* ed. Kapila Vatsyayan (New Delhi: Indira Gandhi Centre for the Arts, 1991), 177.

25. The exception is folio 171 depicting the prince kissing the feet of the king. This scene takes place in the countryside, and the two men sit on a carpet in the middle, with their royal retinues, including flag-bearers, behind them.

26. The two exceptions are folio 197v depicting the prince in the wedding procession and folio 213v illustrating the prince putting the princess into a covered palanquin. The artists probably did not depict the scenes in a confined space because their large compositions could not have fit.

27. Peter Gaeffke, "The Garden of Light and the Forest of Darkness in Dakkini Sufi Literature and Painting," *Artibus Asiae* 48, nos. 3–4 (1987): 223–46.

28. Behl and Weightman, xv.

29. For example, see Ali Akbar Husain, *Scent in the Islamic Garden: A Study of Deccani Urdu Literary Sources* (Delhi: Oxford University Press, 2000), 174.

30. Ehsan Yarshater, "Some Common Characteristics of Persian Poetry and Art," *Studia Islamica* 16 (1962): 62–63.

31. Ibid., 66–67.

32. David Kinsley, *Tantric Visions of the Divine Feminine: The Ten Mahavidyas* (Berkeley: University of California Press, 1997), 287.

33. Later seventeenth- and eighteenth-century yogini paintings from the Deccan include *Yogini Holding a Peacock Feather Fan, Yogini with Royal Visitors, Yogini Holding a Chauri, Yogini Holding a Peacock Feather Fan and Trident,* and *Yogini Being Greeted by a Lion,* all in the Salar Jung Museum, Hyderabad. The Pierpont Morgan Library, New York, also contains a late seventeenth-century Deccan yogini painting (M.1074.3). Outside of the Deccan, the only other images of yoginis that I have uncovered are a few paintings produced in Lucknow in the eighteenth century. These include *Yoginis in a Landscape,* later Mughal, eighteenth century, private collection, reproduced in Pratapaditya Pal, *Court Paintings of India: 16th–19th Centuries* (New York: Navin Kumar, 1983), 167; and *Yogini in a Landscape,* Lucknow, eighteenth century, Brooklyn Museum, Brooklyn (40.358), reproduced in Amy Poster, *Realms of Heroism: Indian Paintings at the Brooklyn Museum* (New York: Hudson Hills Press and Brooklyn Museum, 1994), 94–95.

34. Based on stylistic analysis, the earliest examples, dating through the mid-seventeenth century, appear exclusive to the Deccan, if not to Bijapur more specifically, providing more evidence of the particularity of the visual identity cultivated by Adil Shahi artists and patrons.

35. The six paintings discussed here are not an exhaustive account of such images from Bijapur. A few others have been identified. For example, another yogini painting in the Jagdish and Kamla Mittal Museum of Indian Art (76.406) may also be from Bijapur and datable to the mid-1590s. In this image, the yogini holds a trident and stands in a worshipping pose. The Islamishes Museum, Berlin, houses an image of a yogini visiting a male ascetic, also possibly from seventeenth-century Bijapur (T. 4596, fol. 4a). See Zebrowski, *Deccani Painting,* 111–12.

36. The Victoria and Albert Museum identifies the painting as in the hand of the artist Farrukh Beg, who seems to have worked at the Adil Shahi court circa 1596–1615, or that of one of his students; hence the dating of the work to circa 1605–40.

37. Welch, *India: Art and Culture, 1300–1900,* 296, discusses the verses surrounding the Chester Beatty image, and Pal, *Indian Painting,* 321, analyzes the LACMA painting's verses. The Chester Beatty verses seem to relate directly to the image; however, because they are on separate pieces of paper from the main image, it is impossible to determine whether or not they are original. The LACMA verses, aside from being written in the same calligraphic hand, are not related to each other, and seem to have been added chiefly for decorative effect.

38. Rachel Milstein hypothesizes that at some point several mystically oriented Bijapuri paintings belonged to the same album, based on the identical marble mounts framing the images. These include the Islamisches Museum yogini and the painting of a *dervish* in the Israel Museum, Jerusalem, along with a painting of a holy man sitting under a tree also housed in the Israel Museum (536.69) and another painting of a mystic under a tree, housed in the Victoria and Albert Museum, London (10.1925). The Israel Museum painting of a holy man under a tree has a page of mystical text mounted on the reverse side, suggesting that the album contained both paintings and selections of text, all of a mystical nature. Rachel Milstein, *Islamic Painting in the Israel Museum* (Jerusalem: Israel Museum, 1984), 176–77.

39. David James, "The 'Millennial' Album of Muhammad Quli Qutb Shah," *Islamic Art* 2 (1987): 243–54.

40. Muhammad Quli's poems, all written in a form called *vaslis,* are religious works with a Shiite emphasis, and therefore seem to bear no direct relationship to the yogini image except as a compilation of treasured works. The style of the painting as well as the artistic connection between this work and the *Pem Nem* manuscript discussed in the previous section securely connect its creation with Bijapur rather than Golconda. Golcondan painting from the same period is quite distinct. For further discussions of the Chester Beatty yogini at its Bijapuri attribution, see Zebrowski, *Deccani Painting,* 103–104; Welch, *India: Art and Culture, 1300–1900,* 292–96; James, 248; and Barrett, "Painting at Bijapur," 157.

41. Some of the figure's attributes, such as the horn he carries, also can be traced to Hindu mysticism. White, 280–81, describes one of the markings of a member of Nath Siddha, a sect of Hindu ascetics, as the *singnad,* a piece of gazelle horn into which the ascetics blow to produce the *nada,* the silent sound believed to stop the mind from wavering.

42. For a discussion of the various theories surrounding the yogini images, see M. L. Nigam, "The 'Yoginis' of the Deccani Miniatures," *Lalit Kala,* no. 23 (1988): 35–41.

43. Welch, *India: Art and Culture,* 296, describes the verses around the Chester Beatty yogini as follows: "One of these *ghazals* coos that the beloved's curly black hair, disheveled by the morning breeze, is like hyacinths that perfume the air while, because tangled, it lends confusion. The dreamy vision of the beloved's name, his mouth is fragrant as a rosebud; and remembering her, his heart is radiant as the morning. The second four couplets further elaborate the image: those with spiritual insight dream of drinking from the fountain of the beloved's lips; and the ailing heart of the lover is never without the letters *alif* and *dal,* because the beloved's stature is straight as the former, her tresses curved as the latter."

44. D. C. Verma, *Social, Economic, and Cultural History of Bijapur* (Delhi: Idarah-i Adabiyat-i Delli, 1990), 142.

45. Rajendra Sarup Bhatnagar, *Mysticism in Urdu Poetry* (New Delhi: Jamia Hamdard, 1995), 20–21.

46. Khan, "Dakhni Urdu," 2:22.

47. Schimmel explains that in Arabic culture, the beloved and the lover were sometimes female, but as Sufism spread to the Perso-Turkish world, the young male figure replaced the female; however, when Sufism spread to India, women again emerged as symbols of the beloved and the lover. Annemarie Schimmel, "The Influence of Sufism on Indo-Muslim Poetry," in *Anagogic Qualities of Lit-*

erature, ed. Joseph Strelka (University Park: Pennsylvania State University Press, 1971), 197–99. Also see Khan, "Dakhni-Urdu," 2:21–22.

48. *Bhakti* began in Tamil Nadu and seems to have developed in Maharashtra in the early fourteenth century or perhaps earlier. For a discussion of *bhakti*'s development in the Bijapur region, see Eaton, *Sufis of Bijapur,* 9–10. Shah Miranji, the Sufi author of *Khabushnama,* is known for propagating bhakti. Verma, *Social, Economic, and Cultural History of Bijapur,* 142.

49. Carla Petievich, "Making 'Manly' Poetry: The Construction of Urdu's 'Golden Age,'" paper presented at the annual South Asian Conference, Madison, Wisc., October 1997.

50. Nigam, 39.

51. Pal, *Indian Painting,* 321.

52. Parrots often were associated with mysticism. According to Schimmel, in medieval Indo-Islamic lore, the parrot was "connected with paradise because of its lovely green colour and excelling by virtue of its ability to speak, often appears to convey mystical or religious instruction." Annemarie Schimmel, "Islamic Literatures of India," in *A History of Indian Literature,* ed. Jan Gonda (Wiesbaden: Otto Harrassowitz, 1973), 8/1: 20.

53. Nigam, 35–39.

54. Evelyn Underhill, *Mysticism* (New York: Doubleday, 1990), 126.

55. Mir Hasan, *The Nusr-i-benazeer,* trans. Major Henry Court (Simla: J. Elston, 1871), 74.

56. It is worth noting that the only other yogini paintings produced outside of the Deccan that I have come across were produced in eighteenth-century Lucknow, the same time and place that the *Sihr al-Bayan* was written.

57. For further discussion of the role of Sufism in Bijapur's social and political context during the sixteenth and seventeenth centuries, see Eaton, *Sufis of Bijapur,* 83–174.

58. For example, figure 38, which depicts a youthful-looking sultan has been dated variously to 1580 or 1590 depending on whether one estimates his age as nine or nineteen (Ibrahim was born in 1571). Soustiel and David estimate the date of the painting to circa 1580 because they thought Ibrahim to be prepubescent in the image, while Zebrowski estimates Ibrahim's age in the painting as nineteen and thus dated the painting to circa 1590. J. Soustiel and M. C. David, *Miniatures Orientales de l'Inde: Les ecoles et leurs styles* (Paris, 1974), no. 25; Zebrowski, *Deccani Painting,* 73.

59. Joshi, "Asad Beg's Mission to Bijapur, 1603–1604," 193.

60. B. G. Gayani, "Kitab-i Nauras," *Islamic Culture* 19, no. 2 (1945): 152. Several different *Kitab-i Nauras* manuscripts exist (none of which are illustrated) with various dates ascribed to them. Therefore, it is not known exactly when the work was written. Most likely, the songs were composed over time.

61. Gayani, 145, notes that in the Salar Jung copy of the *Kitab-i Nauras,* the work begins with an invocation to Ganapati, the god of wisdom and intellect, instead of to the goddess Sarasvati.

62. The Sanskritized title "Jagatguru" also was inscribed on gold coins minted during his reign. Mohammad Abdul Wali Khan, "Copper Coins of Adil Shahi Dynasty of Bijapur," *Numismatic Bulletin* 1 (Hyderabad: Birla Archaeological and Cultural Research Institute, 1980), 8.

63. Ibrahim himself spoke Deccani Urdu and perhaps Marathi as well, not learning Persian until he was in his twenties. The Mughal ambassador to Bijapur,

Asad Beg, said of Ibrahim's language abilities, "He understood Persian very well, but could not speak it and if at all, broken." He went on to explain that "when Ibrahim got annoyed and excited the conversation between him and his adviser, Antu Pandit, lapsed into Marathi." P. M. Joshi, "Asad Beg's Mission to Bijapur, 1603–1604," 191.

64. I selected the eight paintings discussed here because I felt they were the most concretely identifiable portraits of Ibrahim created in Bijapur before circa 1635, but of course there are more possible portraits of Ibrahim. Some of these include: *Ibrahim Rides the Elephant Atish Khan,* private collection, circa 1600, reproduced in Zebrowski, *Deccani Painting,* 97, and John Seyller, "Farrukh Beg in the Deccan," *Artibus Asiae* 55, nos. 3–4 (1995): 323; *Ruler watching musicians,* a folio in a *Nimat nama* manuscript, c. 1600–10, State Museum, Hyderabad; *Ibrahim with elephant in the background,* c. 1610–20, Edwin Binney 3rd Collection, San Diego; *Sultan Ibrahim,* c. 1610–20, City Palace Museum, Jaipur, A.G. 753.

65. For reproductions of these paintings, see Zebrowski, *Deccani Painting,* 74–75.

66. See, for example, *Stout Courtier,* circa 1610–20, British Museum, London (1937 4-1003), reproduced in Zebrowski, *Deccani Painting,* 80.

67. Soustiel and David, no. 25.

68. Zuhuri, 425.

69. Zebrowski, *Deccani Painting,* 73. The passage is from Zuhuri, 335.

70. This painting, like the previous one, recalls Zuhuri's manner of praising Ibrahim, in this case, Zuhuri's singling out of the six most esteemed nobles who graced his court. Zuhuri, 455–67.

71. Ibid., 425–67.

72. John Seyller's recent observation is, in fact, the most recent chapter of a long scholarly debate regarding Farrukh Beg and Bijapur. For a more complete account of the debate, see Hutton, "Elixir," 133–34.

73. The book bears an inscription that, unfortunately, is illegible in the available reproduction of the painting. The painting is reproduced in color in Badri Atabay, *Catalogue of Illustrated Persian Manuscripts in the Golestan Library of Tehran* (Tehran: Golestan Library, 1974), opposite 350. (The book's title is translated from Persian.)

74. Seyller, "Farrukh Beg in the Deccan," 338. Other Bijapuri paintings attributed to the Farrukh Beg include *Ibrahim Rides the Elephant Atish Khan,* private collection; *Bull Elephant,* formerly in the collection of Sita Ram Sahu, now lost, and *Horse and Groom,* in the Victoria and Albert Museum, London (IS 88-1965).

75. Zebrowski, *Deccani Painting,* 95.

76. Mughal histories mention Farrukh Beg, and his inscription appears on paintings at the Mughal court consistently except for a gap between 1596 and 1615. Robert Skelton, "The Mughal Artist Farrokh Beg," *Ars Orientalis* 2 (1957): 393–411.

77. Seyller, "Farrukh Beg in the Deccan," 320.

78. Ibid., 340, observes that Farrukh Beg "displayed an admirable professional astuteness in deliberately accentuating that which was most exotic in each of his respective ateliers." This astuteness seems to have served him well in Bijapur, judging from Zuhuri praise of the artist.

79. Zuhuri, 462–67.

80. For further discussion of this issue, see Seyller, "Farrukh Beg in the Dec-

can," 319–41. The later inscription written on the border of *Ibrahim playing the tambur* indicates that the painting was acquired by Jahangir and pasted into a Mughal album. The inscription reads, "Glory to God. Portrait of Ibrahim Adil Khan Deccani, Governor of Bijapur, who in the knowledge of Deccani music made himself master of those who profess the art. And it is the work of Farrukh Beg in the auspicious reign, corresponding to the *hijri* 1019 (1610–11). Written by the lowest slave Muhammad Husain Zarin Qalam Jahangir Shahi." Barrett, "Painting at Bijapur," 158.

81. Ibrahim Adil Shah II, *Kitab-i Nauras,* 146. Notably, Ibrahim refers to Bijapur as Vidyapur (City of Learning).

82. Zebrowski, *Deccani Painting,* 70.

83. Ibid., 81. While describing a group of figural sculptures at Ellora that he interprets as princes and nobles, Shirazi writes, "There are some watchmen holding swords with handkerchiefs in their hands, in the Deccan fashion." Ernst, "Admiring the Works of the Ancients," 105.

84. In addition to the stylistic changes already noted, sometime in the 1620s, there seems to have been a change in turban style. In images from this period or later, including the two portraits of Ibrahim examined here, the sash becomes less prominent and the turban gains a slight bill or drape at the base of the neck when compared to the turbans featured in earlier paintings.

85. A second inscription on the painting reads "Drawn by the 'house-born' (servant) Ali Reza." Robert Skelton, ed., *The Indian Heritage: Court Life and Arts under Mughal Rule* (London: Victoria and Albert Museum, 1982), 42. Another painting attributed to Bijapur, circa 1610–35, and housed in the Victoria and Albert Museum, London (D 398–85), features a figure, perhaps Ibrahim Adil Shah II, on an elephant and also bears the signature of Ali Reza.

86. In *Sultan Abdullah Qutb Shah* (r. 1626–72) *watching a dance performance* from a *Diwan* of Hafiz, housed in the British Museum, London (1974 6–17 1–5), the Golcondan ruler is sitting on a gold throne under a canopy surrounded by courtiers. In *Darbar of Abdullah,* also housed in the British Museum, London (1937 4–10 01), he is sitting on a golden throne in an arched architectural backdrop, again surrounded by courtiers. See Zebrowski, *Deccani Painting,* 178–81. The *Tarif-i Husain Shahi,* 1565, Ahmadnagar, is housed in the Bharata Itihasa Samshodhaka Mandala, Poona, and discussed in Zebrowski, *Deccani Painting,* 17–20. For discussions of portraits of the Mughal emperors Akbar and Jahangir, see Geeti Sen, *Paintings from the Akbar Nama: A Visual Chronicle of Mughal India* (Varanasi, 1984); Milo Cleveland Beach, *The Imperial Image: Paintings for the Mughal Court, 1600–1660* (Washington, D.C.: Freer Gallery of Art, 1981); or Amina Okada, *Indian Miniatures of the Mughal Court,* trans. Deke Dusinberre (New York: Harry Abrams, 1992).

87. Shirazi, 101.

88. Cousens, *Bijapur and Its Architectural Remains,* 83, estimated this by measuring the remains of the city wall and using that information to compute the total area.

89. Some sources suggest that the Adil Shahis abandoned Nauraspur only a few years after construction begun and long before Ambar's attack because the site was believed to be inauspicious. For example, see Husain, 57.

90. Cousens, *Bijapur and Its Architectural Remains,* 82–84.

91. Unfortunately, Firishta's history does not mention Nauraspur. His chapter on Ibrahim's reign stops abruptly in 1596.

92. Cousens, *Notes on the Buildings and Other Antiquarian Remains at Bijapur,* 6–7; Nazim, 20; Rotzer, 135.

93. Shirazi, 101; Zubairi, 278; Astarabadi, 214v.

94. Zubairi, 278.

95. Notably, Hyderabad also functioned as a dual capital with the older city of Golconda until the Qutb Shahi dynasty fell to the Mughals, at which time Hyderabad became the exclusive capital.

96. Astarabadi, 214v.

97. Shirazi writes that "for a long time [Sultan Firuz] lived in that city in enjoyment and the gratification of his desires." Shirzai, 11v; Firishta, 2:227–28. Notably, both the historians' accounts of Firuzabad and the city of Nauraspur emphasize the number nine.

98. Zubairi, 278.

99. Shirazi, 102. Zubairi, 279.

100. Nazir Ahmad, *Zuhuri, Life and Works* (Allahabad: Khayaban, 1953), 142.

101. Zuhuri, 340.

102. Ahmad, *Zuhuri, Life and Works,* 142.

103. Ibid. These are also listed in Zubairi, 249–50, and Shirazi, 102.

104. Zubairi, 280. The scholar Dehlavi, writing in 1915, further described the Id-i Nauras as being celebrated by all the nobles and courtiers with music and drink. As many as four thousand musicians, along with dancers and storytellers, would assemble at court, and food was prepared for all, including the poor. Bashiruddin Ahmed Dehlavi, *Waqiat-i Mamlikat-i Bijapur* (Agra: Mufid-i An Press, 1915), 210.

105. The nine virtues that Zuhuri describes are divine knowledge; submission to the teachings of Muhammad and lifting the banner of affection for Ali; pomp and glory; justice; bravery; munificence; comely form and countenance; good nature and manners; and acquiring excellence and perfection. Zuhuri, 365–82.

106. At some point in the nineteenth or twentieth century, the Nauras Mahal had square brick piers added to help support the broad arch of the façade and a large brick platform added to the back of the building.

107. Cousens, *Bijapur and Its Architectural Remains,* 54–55.

108. The building also housed the Adil Shahi royal library and served as a theological school. Quraishi, 5.

109. Zubairi, 278.

110. Zuhuri, 455.

111. Dehlavi, 207–10.

112. Zubairi, 278.

113. Cousens, *Bijapur and Its Architectural Remains,* 55.

114. For further discussion of the woodwork, see M. S. Mate, "Deccan Woodwork," *Deccan College Building Centenary and Silver Jubilee Series* 49 (Poona: 1967), 19–24.

115. Cousens, *Bijapur and Its Architectural Remains,* 125.

116. For further discussion of the Asar Mahal's paintings, see Cousens, *Bijapur and Its Architectural Remains,* 89–95.

117. These letters also reveal how Heda came to reside in Bijapur. Heda, born in Haarlem, trained with Cornelius Cornelisz, a Haarlem Mannerist master, but eventually left the Netherlands in search of work. For a while he was employed

at the court of Rudolph II in Prague. Then he accepted an offer to work for Shah Abbas in Safavid Iran; however, on the voyage to Persia, his ship got caught in a storm and landed at Goa, the Portuguese colony bordering the kingdom of Bijapur. The Portuguese, who at the time were fighting the Dutch, took Heda captive. Somehow the painter managed to escape and flee to the kingdom of Bijapur, where he found residence in the new city of Nauraspur. What happened to him after that remains unclear. H. Gerson, *Ausbreitung und Nachwirkung der Hollandischen Malerei des 17. Jahrhunderts* (1942; reprint, Amsterdam: B. M. Israel, 1983), 541; Otto Kurz, "Kunstlerische Beziehungen zwischen Prag und Persien zur Zeit Kaiser Rudolfs II und Beitrage zur Geschichte seiner Sammlungen," in *The Decorative Arts of Europe and the Islamic East,* ed. Otto Kurz (London: Dorian Press, 1977), 5–6.

118. Asad Beg, "Wikaya-i Asad Beg," trans. B. W. Chapman, in *The History of India as Told by Its Own Historians: The Muhammadan Period,* 2nd ed., ed. Sir H. M. Elliot and John Dowson (Calcutta: Susil Gupta, 1953), 6:163.

119. Asad Beg, 165–66, recorded presenting tobacco brought back from Bijapur to the emperor Akbar for the first time.

120. Zuhuri, 444; F. N. Delvoye, "Indo-Persian Literature on Art-Music: Some Historical and Technical Aspects," in *Confluence of Cultures: French Contributions to Indo-Persian Studies,* ed. F. N. Delvoye (New Delhi: Manohar, Centre for Human Sciences, 1995), 115.

121. Nauraspur's lack of completed walls after twenty-five years, in contrast to Bijapur's massive walls that were built in less than three years, further supports Nauraspur as primarily a cultural rather than political and military capital. If the political aspect of the city had been key, then workmen, conceivably, would have completed the walls much more quickly. It is possible that the walls were not even part of the original plan, for the Qutb Shah's new city of Hyderabad, also conceived of as a twin city with the older capital, was initially left unwalled (Hyderabad's walls were added in 1740, to help defend the city against attacks from the Marathas). With the security of one well-fortified capital, the builders probably did not see walls as an essential element of the second city, which then could be left open for easy expansion and plentiful greenery. For further discussion of Hyderabad's walls, see S. P. Shorey, "Hyderabad: Garden to a City," in *Islamic Heritage of the Deccan,* ed. George Michell (Bombay: Marg, 1986), 20.

122. For a description of the founding of Hyderabad and its monuments, see Sherwani, *Muhammad-Quli Qutb Shah,* 11–31.

123. Bawa, 329–41.

4. Meaning in Ornament

1. For example, see Perween Hasan, "The Indian Subcontinent," in *The Mosque,* ed. Martin Frishman and Hassan-Uddin Khan (London: Thames and Hudson, 1994), 179.

2. In fact, on one level, the treaty with the Mughals brought security to Bijapur and allowed the kingdom to focus on other issues. In a series of campaigns, Muhammad expanded the kingdom southward, gaining fertile land that once belonged to the Vijayanagara kingdom. For more information on the political developments of this period, see Sherwani and Joshi, 1:352–66.

3. For a discussion of painting during the reign of Muhammad Adil Shah, see Zebrowski, *Deccani Painting,* 122–34.

4. Cousens, *Bijapur and Its Architectural Remains,* 70.

5. Although difficult to verify, this assertion is repeated in a variety of sources. For one such example, see Merklinger, 126. St. Peter's dome, constructed in the sixteenth century after a design by Michelangelo, has a diameter of 138 feet and a rise of 400 feet. Presumably the cited comparison is based on total volume encompassed by the dome rather than just diameter, as St. Peter's dome diameter is approximately six feet less than that of the Gul Gumbad's. In any case, with the development of late twentieth-century construction techniques, any number of sports stadiums, such as the Skydome in Toronto or the Georgia Superdome in Atlanta, have domes far outsizing that of either St. Peter's Basilica or the Gul Gumbad.

6. Z. A. Desai, "Deccan Architecture," *Salar Jung Museum Research Journal* 17 (1982): 32.

7. Today grass fills this area within which several small graves are located, including one labeled in Henry Cousens's plan of the complex as a grave of a European child (fig. 4.1).

8. According to Cousens, *Bijapur and Its Architectural Remains,* 71, the cenotaphs from east to west belong to Haji Badi Sahiba, Ibrahim's mother; Taj Sultana; Sultan Ibrahim; Zuhrah Sultana, Ibrahim's daughter; Burhan Shah, Ibrahim's youngest son; and one unidentified son.

9. Cousens, *Bijapur and Its Architectural Remains,* 74, explains that hanging appearance of the rectangular and square stone slabs was accomplished by the use of exceptionally strong mortar. This mortar must not have held throughout the building's history because the ceilings of both the tomb and the inner arcade were repaired extensively in the nineteenth century at the same time that the buttresses on the outer arcade were added to help support the structure and the outer cornices were repaired.

10. Most likely, these paintings, like many of the Koranic inscriptions on the tomb, relate to paradise. For example, urns overflowing with fruit typically suggest the abundance awaiting the faithful in paradise. Captain Sykes, a visitor to Bijapur in 1818, described the carved-stone calligraphy as gilt and its background as painted azure blue. Such expensive pigments must have further added to the feelings of opulence and bounty conveyed by the tomb's ornament. Captain Sykes, *Transactions of the Literary Society of Bombay* 3, no. 58 (London: Longman, Hurst, Rees, Orme, and Brown, 1821).

11. Henry Cousens, *Bijapur and Its Architectural Remains,* 73, asserts that the entire Koran is inscribed on the windows and the walls on the tomb.

12. It is clear that this was not the original name of the structure. It seems to have come into common usage early in the nineteenth century. Cousens, *Bijapur and Its Architectural Remains,* 71, claimed that previously the monument had been known as the Zuhrah Rauza, after Ibrahim's daughter, who also is buried there, and that "the adjacent suburb was and still is, called Zuhrahpur."

13. Even Muhammad Nazim, who translated the tomb's inscriptions, when writing about Adil Shahi architecture gave Ibrahim the credit for "raising the elaborate pile of the Ibrahim Rauza." Nazim, 17.

14. Ibid., 35. The ambiguities inherent in medieval Persian, however, must be taken into consideration. I deliberately stated that the verse *suggests* Taj Sultana was the patron, rather than categorically establishes the fact, for medieval

Persian does not always clearly distinguish between the active and passive voices. Therefore, the first line of the verse can be translated variously as "Taj Sultana constructed this *rauza*" or "the Taj Sultana Rauza was constructed." The first version implies that Taj Sultana was the patron; the second that the tomb was named the Taj Sultana Rauza. For further discussion of the patronage of the Ibrahim Rauza, as well as the Persian inscriptions, see Deborah Hutton, "Carved in Stone: The Codification of a Visual Identity for the Indo-Islamic Sultanate of Bijapur," *Archives of Asian Art* 55 (Spring 2005): 65–78.

15. For example, see Merklinger, 126; Cousens, *Bijapur and Its Architectural Remains,* 75–76. The last line of the verse reads: "Malik Sandal rasanide bapayan."

16. For a more complete discussion of the historical evidence regarding Malik Sandal, see Hutton, "Carved in Stone," 69.

17. The exact construction dates of the Ibrahim Rauza are unclear. The date recorded in the inscription around the north door, 1626, frequently is interpreted as the completion date of the construction. For example, see Michell and Zebrowksi, *Architecture and Art of the Deccan Sultanates,* 90. However, based on the number of inscriptions carved into the structure that date later than 1626, I would argue that the complex could not have been completed by then. It seems more likely that the 1626 date marks the beginning of construction, or at least the first recorded construction date, and the latest inscribed date on the tomb, that of Taj Sultana's death in 1633, marks the end date, or an approximate end date of construction. It may not have been completed even by that date.

18. Oleg Grabar, *The Mediation of Ornament* (Washington, D.C.: National Gallery of Art; Princeton: Princeton University Press, 1992), 64, 98–101.

19. Nelson Goodman and Catherine Z. Elgin, *Reconceptions in Philosophy and Other Arts and Sciences* (Indianapolis: Hackett, 1988), 31–48.

20. Cousens, *Notes on the Buildings and Other Antiquarian Remains at Bijapur,* 30, states that it became called the Jal Mandir because people later thought it was a Hindu *ratha* with its wheels buried in the ground. Extensive restoration makes it difficult to date the structure with precision, thus the loose dating of circa 1610–40 given here.

21. Popular belief often links the two structures with Chand Bibi, the powerful Ahmadnagar princess, Ali Adil Shah's wife, and Ibrahim's aunt; however, the connections cannot be confirmed. The British converted the mosque into a post office in the nineteenth century, badly damaging it, and restoration is still ongoing. The dark green stone of the doorway contains an inscription reading "Allah, Muhammad! May Allah, who be exalted, be pleased with Abu Bakr, Umar, and Uthman and Ali, and with all the rest of the companions (of the Prophet)." Cousens, *Bijapur and Its Architectural Remains,* 70.

22. The Anda mosque's inscription runs along the sides of the doorway and reads, in part, "The founder of this paradise-like mosque is His Excellency Itibar Khan. No one has seen a mosque of this style, this style is heart-ravishing." Nazim, 27–28. None of the mosques' names can be confirmed as original and were most likely later appellations. For discussion of the names and possible meanings, see Cousens, *Bijapur and Its Architectural Remains,* 70–77 and Cousens, *Notes on the Buildings,* 33–34.

23. See Hutton, "Elixir," 40–41.

24. Cousens, *Bijapur and Its Architectural Remains,* 70.

25. The Anda mosque, the Kali mosque, and the Ibrahim Rauza are dated

by inscription. The dating of the rest is based on stylistic analysis. For further discussion of the monuments' dating, see Hutton, "Elixir," 40–41, 176–79.

26. The flip side of this analogy is to conceive of the Jal Mandir as an enlarged *guldasta*.

27. Lisa Golombek, "The Function of Decoration in Islamic Architecture," in *Theories and Principles of Design in the Architecture of Islamic Societies*, ed. Margaret Bentley Sevcenko (Cambridge, Mass.: Aga Khan Program for Islamic Architecture, 1988), 39.

28. Merklinger, 124, states that some of the globular pendants were carved as a perforated hollow ball with a smaller ball inside. The remaining medallion on the Ibrahim Rauza mosque, however, appears flat.

29. Free-hanging stone chains with medallions adorn the seventeenth-century Adil Shahi mosque of Afzal Khan in the *dargah* of Gesudaraz in Gulbarga. See Merklinger, 127, for a further discussion of this building.

30. The brilliantly painted *mihrab* added in 1636 to Bijapur's *jami masjid* also displays the motif. A particularly large medallion, the interior of which is filled with gilded calligraphy, hanging from a golden chain adorns the top of the mihrab. A color reproduction of it can be found in Michell and Zebrowski, *Architecture and Art of the Deccan Sultanates*, plate 16. Clearly the medallion hanging in a niche motif, whatever the exact significance might have been, was a key Adil Shahi visual marker.

31. Since the ground floor has no mihrab, Merklinger, 123, suggests that it functioned as a rest house, with the mosque proper above. Cousens, *Bijapur and Its Architectural Remains*, 77–78, believes that the mosque was intended for women because there is no *minbar* and because, by being located on the second floor, it would have ensured privacy.

32. In general, Cousens compares this new architectural style to Chalukayan temples. Cousens, *Bijapur and Its Architectural Remains*, 72.

33. Merklinger, 99.

34. Sherwani and Joshi, 1:352–59.

35. Scholars still debate where, whether Turkey, Persia, or India, and when "marbling" originated, but by the mid-sixteenth century it was popular throughout the Islamic world, including Islamicate South Asia, as illustrated by a Mughal treatise on marbling written during the reign of the emperor Akbar and devoted to discussing the best methods, dyes, and paper to be employed. The Khuda Bakhsh Library in Patna preserves a portion of the manuscript. For more information on the manuscript, see Yves Porter, "Marbled Paper," *India Magazine* (August 1988): 20. The basic process has remained comparatively unchanged over the centuries, aside from a few chemical additions. For an in-depth discussion of the technique, particularly as practiced in South Asia, see Christopher Weimann, "Techniques of Marbling in Early Indian Paintings," *Fine Print* (October 1983): 135–37.

36. Porter, 20.

37. For example, *abri* is the term used in the Mughal treatise in the Khuda Bakhsh Library, Patna. *Abri* comes from the Persian word *abr*, or cloud, and *abri* thus literally means "of, or pertaining to clouds."

38. For example, in the abri drawing of an emaciated horse in the Museum of Fine Arts, Boston (fig. 4.18), the artist or artists who worked on the image most likely began by drawing the horse. Next, they applied starch or gum on the portion of the painting to remain white, in this case the background, which was then probably covered with additional paper. The artists then placed the entire

page on the prepared dense water to pick up the pigments that they had carefully "combed" to form the desired pattern. The abri horse drawings bear particularly finely combed patterns. In this image, there is only one abri pattern, but in pages featuring multiple abri designs, the artists would have had to repeat the entire process, with the original abri areas, along with the white areas, covered. Sometimes an image would have up to four abri patterns, as in *Stalling Elephant with Two Riders,* Brooklyn Museum of Art (TL1986.371.4) reproduced and discussed in Poster, 105–106. When the abri was complete, the artists washed and separated the paper. Finally, they added the details of the drawing, using gold pigment as emphasis. In the Boston MFA abri horse image, they applied gold to highlight the horse's protruding ribs and depict other details such as his eyes.

39. Porter, 26, states that Jagdish Mittal has documented twenty-four abri drawings.

40. The earliest discussions of the images attributed them to Ottoman Turkey, but since then scholars have deduced that they were produced in the Deccan and, more specifically, in early to mid-seventeenth-century Bijapur. A few of the drawings do in fact bear an inscription: *amal-i Shafi,* the work of Shafi. With whom and when Shafi worked, however, has not been established. Porter, 26; Zebrowski, *Deccani Painting,* 137–38.

41. Rachel Milstein, 179, states that the Victoria and Albert Museum, London, contains a painting (IM 149–1949) from about 1780 that is identical in appearance and size to the *charba* drawing and was perhaps made from it.

42. *Fakir Riding an emaciated horse,* Bijapur, mid-seventeenth century, Israel Museum, Jerusalem (78.27.107), reproduced and discussed in Milstein, 178; *Emaciated horse,* first half of the seventeenth century, Victoria and Albert Museum, London (692:15–1876).

43. F. R. Martin suggested that the starving horse imagery came from European engravings symbolizing death, while Stuart Cary Welch has hypothesized that the motif came to the Islamic world during the Mongol conquests, based on its similarity to Chinese works from the Yuan dynasty. No visual representations of emaciated horses survive from such an early date; however, early literary examples do exist, such as the references to emaciated horses found in the famous Sufic work, the *Mathlawi-yi Mathnawi* of Jalal al-Din Rumi. Zebrowski, *Deccani Painting,* 137–38; Stuart Cary Welch, "Early Mughal Miniature Paintings," *Ars Orientalis* 3 (1959): 141; Annemarie Schimmel, "Nur ein storrisches Pferd," *Ex Orbe Religionum Festschrift George Widengren* (Leiden: E. J. Brill, 1972), 104.

44. Annemarie Schimmel, *Mystical Dimensions of Islam* (Chapel Hill: University of North Carolina Press, 1975), 112–13, 191. "Soul" in the western sense of the word is the loftiest of the parts that make up the totality of a person. In Sufic ideology, on the other hand, it is the lowest, with *qalb,* or heart, above it and *ruh,* or spirit, at the top of this tripartition.

45. The illustration of *nafs* is not, however, the only usage of the emaciated horse. Annemarie Schimmel, *A Two-Colored Brocade* (Chapel Hill: University of North Carolina Press, 1992), 194, and Ahmed Ali, *The Golden Tradition: An Anthology of Urdu Poetry* (New York: Columbia University Press, 1973), 118, list some of the other uses. For example, a common way to employ the nag is as a satirical figure. The poet may describe it as a gift he was given but would like to exchange for something better. Other times, the poet uses the wearied horse in a satirical tale about the pitiful prevailing conditions of the times. The latter usage reached its peak in the Urdu poem, variously entitled "Incongruity of the

Age," "Satire on a Miser's Horse," and "The Laughingstock of the Time," by the Mughal poet Mirza Mohammad Rafi Sauda (1713–80).

46. Because the poetic verses are on separate sheets of paper than the central image, it is impossible to determine with certainty whether or not the poetry was original to the work. The inscription does indicate that the drawing was connected with Sufic thought at some point. Coomaraswamy translates the larger sections of Persian *nastaliq* verse on the top and the bottom of the drawing as follows: "Aujourd'hui mon sort est bini puisque mon regard est tombe sur cette beaute, louange au Dieu du Ciel, puisque cette etoile est passee dans mon Horoscope." A. K. Coomaraswamy, "Les Miniatures Orientales de la Collection Guloubeu au Museum of Fine Arts de Boston," *Ars Asiatica* (1929): 66.

47. Schimmel, *A Two-Colored Brocade,* 202–203.

48. Schimmel, "Islamic Literature of India," 16.

49. The title of the poem also can be translated as "The Pearl-Bearing Cloud." Schimmel, "The Influence of Sufism on Indo-Muslim Poetry," 202.

50. A Safavid image in the Fogg Museum, Harvard University, Cambridge (1950.135), further corroborates the idea that the abri technique was connected to Sufic imagery. The work, attributed to Isfahan in the mid-seventeenth century, about the same time as Bijapur's abri horse drawings were created, consists of a white and light blue abri pattern applied to the whole of the paper, with ink drawings added on top of the abri. The drawings, which follow the swirls of the abri patterning, are of Sufis and dervishes as well as a variety of animals, such as birds, fish, leopards, elephants, and even fantastic beasts. Anthony Welch has described this painting as "a visionary's journey, a visual rendering of profound spiritual experience," and compared it to a mystical work, the *Conference of the Birds* by Farid al-Din Attar. Recognizing abri as "cloudlike" imagery, rather than merely ornament, strengthens Welch's interpretation. Anthony Welch, *Shah Abbas and the Arts of Isfahan* (New York: Asia Society, 1973), 92–93.

51. As quoted by Porter, 26.

5. Conclusion

1. In *Women, Patronage, and Self-Representation in Islamic Societies,* 7–8, Ruggles discusses six categories of empowerment for royal women through artistic patronage: financial independence, sons, natal family, celibacy, education, and voice. By patronizing the *rauza,* Taj Sultana was expressing her financial independence, her status as the mother of the heir, her education in the courtly culture, and finally her voice as a leader in that courtly culture.

2. Zuhuri, 340.

3. Ibid., 465–66.

4. Asad Beg, 163–64.

5. For a full account of Qishur Khan's death and the events leading up to it, see Sherwani and Joshi, 1:337–38. See also K. K. Basu, "A Chapter in the Reign of ʿAli ʿAdil Shah of Bijapur," 8. Basu, translating Zubairi, gives a slightly different account of events than Sherwani and Joshi.

Bibliography

Adil Shah, Ibrahim II. *Kitab-i Nauras.* Ed. and trans. Nazir Ahmad. New Delhi: Bharatiya Kala Kendra, 1956.

Ahmad, Aziz. *An Intellectual History of Islam in India.* Edinburgh: Edinburgh University Press, 1969.

Ahmad, Nazir. "'Adilshahi Diplomatic Missions to the Court of Shah 'Abbas." *Islamic Culture* 43, no. 2 (1969): 143–61.

———. "Farrukh Husain, the Royal Artist at the Court of Ibrahim Adil Shah II." *Islamic Culture* 30, no. 1 (1956): 31–35.

———. "Jahangir's Album of Art—*Muraqqa-i-Gulshan* and Its Two Adilshahi Paintings." *Indo-Iranica* 30, no. 1 (1977): 26–43.

———. "The Mughal Artist Farrokh Beg." *Islamic Culture* 35, no. 2 (1961): 115–29.

———. *Zuhuri, Life and Works.* Allahabad: Khayaban, 1953.

Ali, Ahmed. *The Golden Tradition: An Anthology of Urdu Poetry.* New York: Columbia University Press, 1973.

Ali, Shanti Sadiq. *The African Dispersal in the Deccan from Medieval to Modern Times.* Hyderabad: Oriental Longman, 1996.

Annigeri, A. M. *The Glory of Bijapur.* Dharwad: Bhavani Prakashana, 1981.

Archer. W. G. "The Problems of Bikaner Paintings." *Marg* 5, no. 1 (1951): 15–16.

Arnold, Sir T. W., and J. V. S. Wilkinson. *The Library of A. Chester Beatty: A Catalogue of the Indian Miniatures.* Oxford: Oxford University Press, 1936.

Asad Beg. "Wikaya-i Asad Beg." Trans. B. W. Chapman. In *The History of India, as Told by Its Own Historians: The Muhammadan Period,* 6:150–74. Edited from the posthumous papers of the late Sir H. M. Elliot, by John Dowson. 8 vols. 2nd ed. Calcutta: Susil Gupta, 1953.

Asher, Catherine. "The Architecture of Raja Man Singh: A Study of Sub-Imperial Patronage." In *The Powers of Art: Patronage in Indian Culture,* ed. Barbara Stoler Miller, 183–201. Delhi: Oxford University Press, 1992.

———. "Islamic Influence and the Architecture of Vijayanagara." In *Vijayanagara—City and Empire: New Currents of Research,* ed. A. L. Dallapiccola and S. Z. Lallement, 2 vols., 1:188–95. Wiesbaden: Franz Steiner, 1985.

Astarabadi, Fuzuni. *Futuhat-i Adil Shahi.* Persian mss., 1640–43, British Library, London, Add. 27.251.

Atabay, Badri. *Catalogue of Illustrated Persian Manuscripts in the Golestan Library of Tehran.* Tehran: Golestan Library, 1974.

Babayan, Kathryn. "Sufis, Dervishes, and Mullas: The Controversy over Spiritual and Temporal Dominion in Seventeenth-Century Iran." In *Safavid Persia,* ed. Charles Melville, 117–38. London: I. B. Tauris, 1996.

Bailey, T. G. *A History of Urdu Literature.* London: Oxford University Press, 1932.

Barrett, Douglas. "Painting at Bijapur." In *Paintings from Islamic Lands,* ed. R. H. Pinder-Wilson, 142–59. Oxford: Oxford University Press, 1969.

———. *Painting of the Deccan.* London: Faber and Faber, 1958.

———. "Some Unpublished Deccan Miniatures." *Lalit Kala* 7 (1960): 8–13.

Basu, K. K. "A Chapter in the Reign of ʿAli ʿAdil Shah of Bijapur." In *A Volume of Indian and Iranian Studies,* ed. S. M. Katre and P. K. Gode, 1–13. Bombay, 1939.

———. "History of Ibrahim Adil Shah of Bijapur." *Journal of the Bihar and Orissa Research Society* 14, no. 4 (1938): 189–204.

Bawa, Vasant Kumar. "The Politics of Architecture in Qutb Shahi Hyderabad: A Preliminary Analysis." In *Studies in History of the Deccan, Medieval and Modern: Professor A. R. Kulkarni Felicitation Volume,* ed. M. A. Nayeem, Aniruddha Ray, and K. S. Mathew, 329–41. Delhi: Pragati, 2002.

Beach, Milo Cleveland. *The Imperial Image: Paintings for the Mughal Court, 1600–1660.* Washington, D.C.: Freer Gallery of Art, 1981.

———. *Mughal and Rajput Painting.* The New Cambridge History of India 1.3. Cambridge: Cambridge University Press, 1992.

Behl, Aditya, and Simon Weightman, *Manjhan Madhumalati: An Indian Sufi Romance.* Oxford: Oxford University Press, 2000.

Bhatnagar, Rajendra Sarup. *Mysticism in Urdu Poetry.* New Delhi: Jamia Hamdard, 1995.

Binney, Edwin. *Indian Miniature Painting from the Collection of Edwin Binney 3rd: The Mughal and Deccani Schools.* Portland, Ore.: Portland Art Museum, 1973.

Bird, James. "The Ruined City of Bijapur." *Journal of the Bombay Branch of the Royal Asiatic Society* 1 (1843).

Blair, Sheila. "Islamic Art, S II, 10 (ii): Urban Development: Eastern Islamic Lands." In *The Dictionary of Art,* ed. Jane Turner, 16:264–65. New York: Grove's Dictionaries, 1995.

Blumhardt, J. F. *Catalogue of the Hindi, Panjabi, and Hindustani Manuscripts in the Library of the British Museum.* London: British Museum, 1932.

Bredi, Daniela. "Shiism's Political Valence in Medieval Deccani Kingdoms." In *Islam and Indian Regions,* ed. A. L. Dallapiccola and S. Z. Lallement, 137–53. Stuttgart: Franz Steiner, 1993.

Bredi, D., F. Coslovi, and B. Scarcia Amoretti. "Shiism in the Deccan: A Hypothetical Study." *Islamic Culture* 57, nos. 2–3 (1988): 97–112.

Bunce, Frederick. *A Dictionary of Buddhist and Hindu Iconography.* New Delhi: D. K. Printworld, 1995.

Carboni, Stefano. *Il Kitab al-bulhan di Oxford.* Torino: Editrice Tirrenia Stampatori, 1988.

Chandra, Moti. "Portraits of Ibrahim Adil Shah II." *Marg* 5, no. 1 (1951): 22–28.

Coomaraswamy, A. K. "Les Miniatures Orientales de la Collection Goloubeu au Museum of Fine Arts de Boston." *Ars Asiatica* 13 (1929).

Correia-Afonso, John. "Bijapur Four Centuries Ago as Described in a Contemporary Letter." *Indica* 1 (March 1964): 81–88.

Cousens, Henry. *Bijapur and Its Architectural Remains: With an Historical Outline of the ʿAdil Shahi Dynasty.* Archaeological Survey of India, New Imperial Series 37. 1916; reprint, Delhi: Bharatiya Publication House, 1976.

———. *Bijapur: The Old Capital of the ʿAdil Shahi Kings: A Guide to Its Ruins with Historical Outline.* 1889; reprint, Poona: Scottish Mission Industries Company, 1923.

———. *Notes on the Buildings and Other Antiquarian Remains at Bijapur,* Archaeological Survey of Western India Reports, Old Series 11a. Bombay: Bombay Government, 1890.

Dallapiccola, A. L., and S. Z. Lallement, eds. *Islam and Indian Regions.* Stuttgart: Franz Steiner, 1995.

Das, H. C. *Tantricism: A Study of the Yogini Cult.* New Delhi: Sterling, 1981.

Deccani Painting. Marg 16, no. 2 (1963). Special issue on Deccani painting.

Dehlavi, Bashiruddin Ahmed. *Waqiat-i Mamlikat-i Bijapur.* Agra: Mufid-i An Press, 1915.

Delvoye, F. N. "Indo-Persian Literature in Art-Music: Some Historical and Technical Aspects." In *Confluence of Cultures: French Contributions to Indo-Persian Studies,* ed. F. N. Delvoye. New Delhi: Manohar, Centre for Human Sciences, 1995.

Desai, V. N. *Life at Court: Art for India's Rulers, 16th–19th Centuries.* Boston: Museum of Fine Arts, 1985.

Desai, Z. A. "Architecture." In *History of Medieval Deccan, 1295–1724,* ed. H. K. Sherwani and P. M. Joshi, 2:277–300. Hyderabad: Government of Andhra Pradesh, 1973–74.

———. "Deccan Architecture." *Salar Jung Research Journal* 17 (1982).

Dhar, Lakshmi. *Padmavati.* London: Luzac, 1949.

Eaton, Richard, ed. *India's Islamic Traditions, 711–1750: Themes in Indian History, Oxford in India Readings.* New Delhi: Oxford University Press, 2003.

———. *Sufis of Bijapur, 1300–1700.* Princeton: Princeton University Press, 1978.

Ernst, Carl. "Admiring the Works of the Ancients: The Ellora Temples as Viewed by Indo-Muslim Authors." In *Beyond Turk and Hindu: Rethinking Religious Identities in Islamicate South Asia,* ed. David Gilmartin and Bruce B. Lawrence, 98–120. Gainesville: University Press of Florida, 2000.

———. *Eternal Garden: Mysticism, History, and Politics at a South Asian Sufi Center.* Albany: State University of New York Press, 1992.

Ethe, Hermann. *Catalogue of the Persian Manuscripts in the Library of the India Office.* 2 vols. Oxford: Indian Office Library. 1903–37.

Fergusson, James. *History of Indian and Eastern Architecture.* 2nd ed. London, 1910.

Firishta, Muhammad Qasim. *The History of the Rise of the Mahomedan Power in India.* Ed. and trans. John Briggs. 4 vols. London, 1829; reprint in 3 vols., Calcutta: Editions Indian, 1966. Persian text: *Tarikh-i Firishta.* Ed. John Briggs and Munshi Mir Khairat Ali Khan Mushtaq. Bombay: Government of Bombay, 1831–32.

Gaeffke, Peter. "The Garden of Light and the Forest of Darkness in Dakkini Sufi Literature and Painting." *Artibus Asiae* 48, no. 3–4 (1987): 223–46.

Galdieri, Eugenio. "Isfahan, S 3 (vii): Chihil Sutun Palace." In *The Dictionary of Art,* ed. Jane Turner, 16:79–80. New York: Grove's Dictionaries, 1995.

Gaube, Heinz. *Iranian Cities.* New York: New York University Press, 1979.

Gayani, B. G. "Kitab-i-Nauras." *Islamic Culture* 19, no. 2 (1945): 140–52.

Gazetteer of the Bombay Presidency: Bijapur District 23. Bombay: Government Central Press, 1884.

Gerson, H. *Ausbreitung und Nachwirkung der Hollandischen Malerei des 17.Jahrhunderts.* 1942; reprint, Amsterdam: B. M. Israel, 1983.

Ghani, Muhammad 'Abdul, ed. and trans. *A History of Persian Language and Literature at the Mughal Court.* Allahabad: Indian Press, 1930.

Ghauri, Iftikhar Ahmad. "Kingship in the Sultanates of Bijapur and Golconda." *Islamic Culture* 46, no. 1 (1972): 39–52.

Gilmartin, David, and Bruce B. Lawrence, eds. *Beyond Turk and Hindu: Rethink-*

ing Religious Identities in Islamicate South Asia. Gainesville: University Press of Florida, 2000.

Goetz, Hermann. *The Art and Architecture of Bikaner State.* Oxford: Oxford University Press, 1950.

———. "The Fall of Vijayanagar and the Nationalization of Muslim Art in the Dakhan." *Journal of Indian History* 19 (1940): 249–55.

———. "La peinture indienne: les ecoles du Dekkan." *Gazette des Beaux-Arts* 13 (1935): 275–88.

Golombek, Lisa. "The Function of Decoration in Islamic Architecture." In *Theories and Principles of Design in the Architecture of Islamic Societies,* ed. Margaret Bentley Sevcenko. Cambridge, Mass.: Aga Khan Program for Islamic Architecture, 1988.

Goodman, Nelson, and Catherine Z. Elgin. *Reconceptions in Philosophy and Other Arts and Sciences.* Indianapolis: Hackett, 1988.

Gordon, Stewart. *The Marathas, 1600–1818.* New Cambridge History of India 2.4. Cambridge: Cambridge University Press, 1993.

Grabar, Oleg. *The Mediation of Ornament.* Washington, D.C.: National Gallery of Art; Princeton: Princeton University Press, 1992.

———. *Mostly Miniatures: An Introduction to Persian Painting.* Princeton: Princeton University Press, 1999.

Gray, Basil, ed. *The Arts of India.* Ithaca, N.Y.: Cornell University Press and Phaidon Press, 1981.

———. "Deccani Paintings: The School of Bijapur." *Burlington Magazine* 73 (August 1938): 74–76.

———. "Portraits from Bijapur." *British Museum Quarterly* 11 (1937): 183–84.

Guy, John, and Deborah Swallow, eds. *Arts of India, 1550–1900.* London: Victoria and Albert Museum, 1990.

Hart, Captain Philip D. *Architectural Illustrations of the Principal Mahometan Buildings of Beejapore.* Ed. James Fergusson. London, 1859.

Hasan, Mir. *The Nusr-i-benazeer.* Trans. Major Henry Court. Simla: J. Elston, 1871.

Hasan, Perween. "The Indian Subcontinent." In *The Mosque,* ed. Martin Frishman and Hassan-Uddin Khan, 159–80. London: Thames and Hudson, 1994.

Hodgson, Marshall. *The Venture of Islam.* 3 vols. Chicago: University of Chicago Press, 1974.

Hoffman, Eva R. "Islamic Art, S III, 4 (ii) (a): Painted Book Illustration: Subject-Matter: Scientific and Technical Works." In *The Dictionary of Art,* ed. Jane Turner, 16: 297–99. New York: Grove's Dictionaries, 1995.

Husain, Ali Akbar. *Scent in the Islamic Garden: A Study of Deccani Urdu Literary Sources.* Delhi: Oxford University Press, 2000.

Hutton, Deborah. "Carved in Stone: The Codification of a Visual Identity for the Indo-Islamic Sultanate of Bijapur." *Archives of Asian Art* 55 (Spring 2005): 65–78.

———. "The Elixir of Mirth and Pleasure: The Development of Bijapuri Art, 1565–1635." Ph.D. diss., University of Minnesota, 2000.

Hyderabad: A Guide to Art and Architecture. Hyderabad: Publications Division, Ministry of Information and Broadcasting, Government of India, 1951.

Irwin, J. "Asokan Pillars: A Reassessment of the Evidence." *Burlington Magazine* 115 (November 1973): 706–20; 116 (December 1974): 712–15; 117 (October 1975): 631–43; 118 (November 1976): 734–53.

Islam, Riazul. *A Calendar of Documents on Indo-Persian Relations, 1500–1750.*

Iran and Karachi: Iranian Cultural Foundation and Institute on Central and West Asian Studies, 1982.

James, David. "The 'Millennial' Album of Muhammad Quli Qutb Shah." *Islamic Art* 2 (1987): 243–54.

Joshi, P. M. "'Ali 'Adil Shah I of Bijapur (1558–1580) and His Royal Librarian: Two Ruqas." In *Sardhasatabdi Commemoration Volume,* 97–107. Bombay, 1955.

———. "Asad Beg's Mission to Bijapur, 1603–1604." In *Prof. D. V. Potdar 61st Birthday Commemoration Volume,* ed. S. Sen, 181–96. Poona, 1950.

———. "The Reign of Ibrahim Adil Shah of Bijapur." *Bharatiya Vidya Bhavan* 9 (1948): 284–309.

Joshi, P. M., and M. A. Nayeem. "Fuzuni Astarbadi's *Futuhat-i 'Adil Shahi*—an Unpublished Persian Ms. in the British Museum—Some Extracts." *Islamic Culture* 53, no. 3 (1979): 163–77.

Khan, Mas'ud Husain. "Dakhni-Urdu." In *History of Medieval Deccan, 1295–1724,* ed. H. K. Sherwani and P. M. Joshi, 2:17–35. Hyderabad: Government of Andhra Pradesh, 1973–74.

Khan, Mohammad Abdul Wali. "Copper Coins of Adil Shahi Dynasty of Bijapur." *Numismatic Bulletin* 1. Hyderabad: Birla Archaeological and Culture Research Institute, 1980.

Khandalavala, Karl. "Deccani Painting: A Consideration of Mark Zebrowski." *Lalit Kala* 21 (1985): 35–52.

———. "Farrukh Beg the Artist and the Deccani Problem." In *Rupanjali: In Memory of O. C. Gangoly* 70, ed. Kalyan Kumar Ganguli and S. S. Biswas, 163–73. Calcutta: O. C. Gangoly Memorial Society, 1986.

———. "Five Miniatures from the Collection of Sir Cowasji Jehangir." *Marg* 5, no. 2 (1952): 24–32.

Kinsley, David. *Tantric Visions of the Divine Feminine: The Ten Mahavidyas.* Berkeley: University of California Press, 1997.

Knizkova, Hana. "Notes on the Portrait of Ibrahim 'Adil Shah II of Bijapur in the Naprstek Museum, Prague." In *Facets of Indian Art: A Symposium Held at the Victoria and Albert Museum,* ed. Robert Skelton et al., 116–23. London: Victoria and Albert Museum, 1986.

Kramrisch, Stella. *A Survey of Painting in the Deccan.* London: India Society, 1937.

Kurz, Otto. "Kunstlerlische Beziehungen zwischen Prag und Persien zur Zeit Kaiser Rudolfs II und Beitrage zur Geschichte seiner Sammlungen." In *The Decorative Arts of Europe and the Islamic East,* ed. Otto Kurz, 1–22. London: Dorian Press, 1977.

Leach, Linda. *Mughal and Other Indian Paintings from the Chester Beatty Library.* London: Scorpion Cavendish, 1995.

Losty, Jeremy. *The Art of the Book in India.* London: British Library, 1982.

———. "The Development of the Golconda Style." In *Indian Art and Connoisseurship: Essays in Honour of Douglas Barrett,* ed. John Guy, 297–319. New Delhi: Indira Gandhi National Centre for the Arts, 1995.

———. "An Early Bijapuri Musical Manuscript." In *An Age of Splendour: Islamic Art in India,* ed. Karl Khandalavala, 128–31. Bombay: Marg, 1983.

———. *Indian Paintings in the British Library.* Bombay: Lalit Kala Akademi, 1986.

Loth, Otto. *Catalogue of the Arabic Manuscripts in the Library of the India Office.* London: Indian Office Library, 1877.

Lowry, Glenn D., and Susan Nemazee. *A Jeweler's Eye: Islamic Arts of the Book from the Vever Collection.* Washington, D.C., and Seattle: Arthur M. Sackler Gallery and the University of Washington Press, 1988.

Martin, F. R. *The Miniature Painting and Painters of Persia, India, and Turkey.* London: B. Quaritch, 1912.

Mate, M. S. *Deccan Woodwork.* Deccan College Building Centenary and Silver Jubilee series 49. Poona, 1967.

Mehta, N. C. *Studies in Indian Painting.* Bombay: D. B. Taraporevala and Sons, 1926

Merklinger, Elizabeth. *Indian Islamic Architecture: The Deccan, 1374–1686.* Warminster: Aris and Phillips, 1981.

Metcalf, Thomas. *An Imperial Vision: Indian Architecture and Britain's Raj.* Berkeley: University of California Press, 1989.

Michell, George. *Architecture and Art of Southern India: Vijayanagara and the Successor States.* New Cambridge History of India 1.6. Cambridge: Cambridge University Press, 1995.

———. "Bijapur." In *The Dictionary of Art,* ed. Jane Turner, 4:51–52. New York: Grove's Dictionaries, 1995.

———. "Indian Subcontinent, S III, 7 (ii) (a): 16th–19th-Century Regional Architecture: Deccan." In *The Dictionary of Art,* ed. Jane Turner, 15:381–85. New York: Grove's Dictionaries, 1995.

———, ed. *Islamic Heritage of the Deccan.* Bombay: Marg, 1986.

Michell, George, and Richard Eaton. *Firuzabad, Palace City of the Deccan.* Oxford Studies in Islamic Art 8. Oxford: Oxford University Press, 1992.

Michell, George, and Mark Zebrowski. *Architecture and Art of the Deccan Sultanates.* New Cambridge History of India 1.7. Cambridge: Cambridge University Press, 1999.

Miller, Barbara Stoler, ed. *The Powers of Art: Patronage in Indian Culture.* Delhi: Oxford University Press, 1992.

Milstein, Rachel. *Islamic Painting in the Israel Museum.* Jerusalem: Israel Museum, 1984.

Mittal, Jagdish. "Deccani Paintings as a Source of History." In *Aspects of Deccan History: Report of a Seminar,* ed. V. K. Bawa, 196–207. Hyderabad: Institute of Asian Studies, 1975.

———. "Painting." In *History of Medieval Deccan, 1295–1724,* ed. H. K. Sherwani and P. M. Joshi, 2:201–26. Hyderabad: Government of Andhra Pradesh, 1973–74.

Momen, Moojan. *An Introduction to Shiʿi Islam: The History and Doctrines of Twelver Shiʿism.* London: G. Ronald, 1985.

Naqvi, Sadiq. *The Iran-Deccan Relations.* Hyderabad: Bab-ul-Ilm Society, 1994.

Nazim, Muhammad. *Bijapur Inscriptions.* Memoirs of the Archeological Survey of India no. 49. Delhi: Manager of Publications, 1936.

Nigam, M. L. "The 'Yoginis' of the Deccani Miniatures." *Lalit Kala* 23 (1988): 35–41.

Nizami, K. A. "Sufi Movement in the Deccan." In *History of Medieval Deccan, 1295–1724,* ed. H. K. Sherwani and P. M. Joshi, 2:173–200. Hyderabad: Government of Andhra Pradesh, 1973–74.

Okada, Amina. *Indian Miniatures of the Mughal Court.* Trans. Deke Dusinberre. New York: Harry Abrams, 1992.

Pal, Pratapaditya. *Court Paintings of India, 16th–19th Centuries.* New York: Navin Kumar, 1983.

———. *Indian Painting: A Catalogue of the Los Angeles County Museum of Art Collection.* New York and Los Angeles: Harry N. Abrams and the Los Angeles County Museum of Art, 1993.

Petievich, Carla. "Making 'Manly' Poetry: The Construction of Urdu's 'Golden Age.'" Paper presented at the South Asian Conference, Madison, Wisc., October 1997.

Porter, Yves. "Marbled Paper." *India Magazine,* August 1988, 20–26.

Poster, Amy. *Realms of Heroism: Indian Paintings at the Brooklyn Museum.* New York: Hudson Hills Press and Brooklyn Museum, 1994.

Qadiri, Saiyid Muhyi al-Din bin Mahmud. *Sahifat-i Ahl-i Huda.* Ed. and trans. M. Akbaruddin al-Din Siddiqi. Hyderabad: National Fine Printing Press, 1966.

Quraishi, Salim al-Din. *The Royal Library of Bijapur.* London: India Office Library, 1981.

Rotzer, Klaus. "Bijapur: Alimentation en eau d'une ville Musulmane du Dekkan aux XVI–XVII Siecles." *Bulletin de l'Ecole Francaise d'Extreme-Orient* 73 (1984): 125–95.

Ruggles, D. Fairchild, ed. *Women, Patronage, and Self-Representation in Islamic Societies.* Albany: State University of New York Press, 2000.

Schimmel, Annemarie. *Classical Urdu Literature from the Beginning to Iqbal.* Vol. 8, fasc. 3 of *A History of Indian Literature,* ed. Jan Gonda, 123–261. Wiesbaden: Otto Harrassowitz, 1975.

———. "The Influence of Sufism on Indo-Muslim Poetry." In *Anagogic Qualities of Literature,* ed. Joseph Strelka, 181–210. University Park: Pennsylvania State University Press, 1971.

———. "Inner and Outer Space in Islam." In *Concepts of Space Ancient and Modern,* ed. Kapila Vatsyayan, 175–79. New Delhi: Indira Gandhi Centre for the Arts, 1991.

———. *Islam in the Indian Subcontinent.* Leiden: E. J. Brill, 1980.

———. *Islamic Literatures of India.* Vol. 8, fasc. 1 of *A History of Indian Literature,* ed. Jan Gonda, 1–60. Wiesbaden: Otto Harrassowitz, 1973.

———. *Mystical Dimensions of Islam.* Chapel Hill: University of North Carolina Press, 1975.

———. "Nur ein storrisches Pferd." In *Ex Orbe Religionum Festschrift George Widengren,* 98–107. Leiden: E. J. Brill, 1972.

———. *A Two-Colored Brocade.* Chapel Hill: University of North Carolina Press, 1992.

Schmitz, Barbara. *Islamic and Indian Manuscripts and Paintings in the Pierpont Morgan Library.* New York: Pierpont Morgan Library, 1997.

Sen, Geeti. *Paintings from the Akbar Nama: A Visual Chronicle of Mughal India.* Varanasi: Lustre Press, 1984.

Sewell, Robert. *A Forgotten Empire.* 1900; reprint, New Delhi: National Book Trust, 1970.

Seyller, John. "Farrukh Beg in the Deccan." *Artibus Asiae* 55, no. 3–4 (1995): 319–41.

———. "Indian Subcontinent, S XII, 2: Patronage: Painting." In *The Dictionary of Art,* ed. Jane Turner, 15:739–40. New York: Grove's Dictionaries, 1995.

Sharif, J. *Islam in India.* Trans. G. A. Herklots. Oxford: Oxford University Press, 1921.

Sherwani, H. K. "Cultural Synthesis in Medieval India." *Journal of Indian History* 41 (1963): 239–59.

———. "Deccani Preludes to Akbar's Social and Economic Reforms." *Islamic Culture* 50, no. 1 (1976): 25–31.

———. *History of the Qutb Shahi Dynasty.* New Delhi: Munshiram Manoharlal, 1974.

———. *Muhammad-Quli Qutb Shah: Founder of Haidarabad.* Bombay: Asia Publishing House, 1967.

Sherwani, H. K., and P. M. Joshi, eds. *History of Medieval Deccan, 1295–1724.* 2 vols. Hyderabad: Government of Andhra Pradesh, 1973–74.

Shirazi, Rafi uddin. *Tazkira al-Mulk.* Persian mss., circa 1608–35, Salar Jung Museum, Hyderabad, Tarikh no. 142.

Shorey, S. P. "Hyderabad: Garden to a City." In *Islamic Heritage of the Deccan,* ed. George Michell. Bombay: Marg, 1986.

Sicar, D. C. "The Saktapithas." *Journal of the Royal Asiatic Society of Bengal* 14 (1948): 17–21.

Skelton, Robert. "Documents for the Study of Painting at Bijapur." *Arts Asiatiques* 5, no. 2 (1958): 97–125.

———. "The Mughal Artist Farrokh Beg." *Ars Orientalis* 2 (1957): 393–411.

———, ed. *The Indian Heritage: Court Life and Arts under Mughal Rule.* London: Victoria and Albert Museum, 1982.

Soustiel, J., and M. C. David. *Miniatures Orientales de l'Inde: Les ecoles et leur styles.* Paris, 1974.

Steingass, Francis J. *A Comprehensive Persian-English Dictionary, Including the Arabic Words and Phrases to Be Met within Persian Literature.* Beirut: Librarie du Liban, 1970.

Sykes, Captain. *Transactions of the Literary Society of Bombay* 3, no. 58. London: Longman, Hurst, Rees, Orme, and Brown, 1821.

Talbot, Cynthia. "Inscribing the Other, Inscribing the Self: Hindu-Muslim Identities in Pre-Colonial India." *Comparative Studies in Society and History* 37 (1995): 692–722.

Taylor, Meadows. *A Noble Queen: A Romance of Indian History.* London: C. Kegan Paul, 1878.

———. *Tara, a Mahratta Tale.* Edinburgh: W. Blackwood. 1863.

Taylor, Captain Phillip Meadows, and James Fergusson. *Architecture at Bijapoor, an Ancient Mahometan Capital in the Bombay Presidency.* London: Committee of Architectural Antiquities of Western India, 1866.

Titley, Nora. *Persian Miniature Painting and Its Influence on the Art of Turkey and India.* Austin: University of Texas Press, 1983.

Tourkin, Sergei. "Astrological Images in Two Persian Manuscripts." In *Pearls of the Orient: Asian Treasures from the Wellcome Library,* ed. Nigel Allen, 73–85. London and Chicago: Serindia Publications and the Wellcome Trust, 2003.

Trimingham, J. Spencer. *The Sufi Orders in Islam.* Oxford: Oxford University Press, 1971.

Underhill, Evelyn. *Mysticism.* New York: Doubleday, 1990.

Vasantha, R., and M. A. Mannan Basha. *Islamic Architecture of the Deccan (with Special Emphasis on Rayalaseema Region).* Delhi: Sharada, 2004.

Verma, B. D. "'Adil Shahi Epigraphy in the Deccan (Miraj and Kolhapur)." *Journal of the University of Bombay* 8 (1939): 13–51.

Verma, D. C. *History of Bijapur.* New Delhi: Kumar Brothers, 1974.

———. *Social, Economic, and Cultural History of Bijapur.* Delhi: Idarah-i Adabiyat-i Delli, 1990.

Wagoner, Phillip. "Delhi Sultanate in the Political Imagination of Vijayanagara." In *Beyond Turk and Hindu: Rethinking Religious Identities in Islamicate South Asia,* ed. David Gilmartin and Bruce B. Lawrence, 315–19. Gainesville: University Press of Florida, 2000.

———. "'Sultan among Hindu Kings': Dress, Titles, and Islamicization of Hindu Culture at Vijayanagara." *Journal of Asian Studies* 55, no. 4 (1996): 851–80.

Weimann, Christopher. "Techniques of Marbling in Early Indian Paintings." *Fine Print,* October 1983, 135–37.

Welch, Anthony. *Shah Abbas and the Arts of Isfahan.* New York: Asia Society, 1973.

Welch, Stuart Cary. "Early Mughal Miniature Paintings." *Ars Orientalis* 3 (1959): 133–46.

———. *India: Art and Culture, 1300–1900.* New York: Metropolitan Museum of Art and Holt, Rinehart and Winston, 1985.

———. *Indian Drawings and Painted Sketches.* New York: Asia Society, 1976.

White, David Gordon. *The Alchemical Body: Siddha Traditions in Medieval India.* Chicago: University of Chicago Press, 1996.

Wink, Andre. "Islamic Society and Culture in the Deccan." In *Islam and Indian Regions,* ed. A. L. Dallapiccola and S. Z. Lallement, 1:217–28. Stuttgart: Franz Steiner, 1993.

Yarshater, Ehsan. "Some Common Characteristics of Persian Poetry and Art." *Studia Islamica* 16 (1962): 61–71.

Yazdani, Ghulam. *Bidar, Its History and Monuments.* Oxford: Oxford University Press, 1947.

———. "Two Miniatures from Bijapur." *Islamic Culture* 9, no. 2 (1935): 211–17.

Zebrowski, Mark. *Deccani Painting.* Berkeley: University of California Press, 1983.

———. *Gold, Silver, and Bronze from Mughal India.* London: Alexandria Press and Laurence King, 1997.

———. "Indian Subcontinent, S VI, 4 (vi) (b): Deccani Painting Styles, 16th Century–1947: Bijapur." In *The Dictionary of Art,* ed. Jane Turner, 15:638–40. New York: Grove's Dictionaries, 1995.

———. "Transformations in Seventeenth-Century Deccani Painting at Bijapur." In *Chhavi 2: Rai Krishnadasa Felicitation Volume,* 170–81. Varanasi: Bharat Kala Bhavan, 1981.

Zimmer, H. *Philosophies of India.* Princeton: Princeton University Press, 1951.

Zubairi, Mirza Ibrahim. *Basatinu's Salatin.* Persian mss. 1811. Hyderabad: Saiyidi Press, 1892–93.

Zuhuri, Muhammad Zuhur bin. *Sehr Nathr.* In *A History of Persian Language and Literature at the Mughal Court,* ed. and trans. Muhammad ʿAbdul Ghani, vol. 3, appendixes A–C: 323–467. Allahabad: Indian Press, 1930.

Index

Contemporary Indian Studies

Published in association with the American Institute of Indian Studies

Edward Cameron Dimock Jr. Prize in the Indian Humanities

Temple to Love: Architecture and Devotion in Seventeenth-Century Bengal

Pika Ghosh

Art of the Court of Bijapur

Deborah Hutton

Joseph W. Elder Prize in the Indian Social Sciences

The Regional Roots of Developmental Politics in India: A Divided Leviathan

Aseema Sinha

DEBORAH HUTTON is Assistant Professor of Art History at The College of New Jersey.

www.ingramcontent.com/pod-product-compliance
Lightning Source LLC
LaVergne TN
LVHW082002060826
844660LV00006B/275

* 9 7 8 0 2 5 3 3 4 7 8 4 8 *